FIGHTING WITH THE SOVIETS

FIGHTING WITH THE SOVIETS

The Failure
of Operation FRANTIC
1944–1945

Mark J. Conversino

University Press of Kansas

TO MY FAMILY
MARY, ALEX, EMILY,
AND NICHOLAS

© 1997 by the University Press of Kansas
All rights reserved

Published by the University Press of Kansas (Lawrence, Kansas 66049),
which was organized by the Kansas Board of Regents and is operated and
funded by Emporia State University, Fort Hays State University, Kansas State
University, Pittsburg State University, the University of Kansas, and
Wichita State University

Library of Congress Cataloging-in-Publication Data

Conversino, Mark J.
Fighting with the soviets : the failure of operation FRANTIC,
1944–1945 / Mark J. Conversino.
p.   cm. — (Modern war studies)
Includes bibliographical references.
ISBN 0-7006-0808-7 (alk. paper)
1. World War,   1939–1945—Aerial operations, American.   2. World
War, 1939–1945—Aerial operations, Russian.   3. United States—
Relations—Soviet Union.   4. Soviet Union—Relations—United
States.   I. Title.   II. Series.
D790.C657   1996
940.54′4973—dc20   96-32956

British Library Cataloguing in Publication Data is available.

Printed in the United States of America

10 9 8 7 6 5 4 3 2 1

The paper used in this publication meets the minimum requirements
of the American National Standard for Permanence of Paper for
Printed Library Materials Z39.48-1984.

CONTENTS

PREFACE

Volumes have been written on the great Allied air campaign against Nazi Germany and on the monumental clash between the German *Ostheer* and the Soviet Red Army. By comparison, relatively little exists to document a joint Soviet-American undertaking that brought these two aspects of the Allied war effort together: Operation FRANTIC. Born of American frustration in the daylight bombing campaign against German targets, FRANTIC also represented an effort by the United States to forge closer ties with Soviet Russia and gain access to Siberian bases for use by American heavy bombers in the air war against Japan. While FRANTIC failed to live up to American expectations as either a military operation or as a political ploy, it represented the most significant example of direct Soviet-American military cooperation in history.

This study is intended to provide the casual observer as well as the serious student of World War II with the political, diplomatic, and operational details surrounding FRANTIC. My primary intention here, however, is to focus on the experiences of American soldiers and airmen, from general officers to privates, who were charged with making FRANTIC "work." I also endeavor to study the role that the U.S. Eastern Command played in the politically charged final mission of FRANTIC to drop supplies to non-communist rebels in Warsaw. Included in this study are several chapters devoted to the work of Eastern Command following FRANTIC's last mission in September 1944. These activities included the recovery of downed American aircraft and air crews and, later, the repatriation of liberated American prisoners of war. It was during these final months that Soviet-American relations frayed to the breaking point, yet very little has appeared to document this remarkable period. Indeed, even American servicemen left behind in the Soviet Union during the winter of 1944–45 and the final months of the war felt forgotten and neglected by their own countrymen and adopted "Forgotten Bastards of the Ukraine" as the unit's moniker.

This study, then, is intended to serve the memory of the "Forgotten Bastards." They served not only as soldiers but as ambassadors, vital members of an organization designed to serve higher political purposes, more than immediate military ends. The reader will find a discussion of the higher elements of strategic planning that led to FRANTIC as well as details of the various missions of the operation. Central to the purpose of this work, however, is an effort to chronicle the human side of one of World War II's lesser known episodes and a grand, if ultimately unsuccessful, attempt at drawing the United States and Soviet Union closer together as Allies in the war against the Axis powers and beyond.

ACKNOWLEDGMENTS

I owe a great debt of gratitude to a number of people who made this study possible. My thanks go to the staffs of the Air Force Historical Research Agency, Maxwell Air Force Base, Alabama, and the Military Records Division of the National Archives, Washington, D.C. I am also grateful to Mr. Duane Reed, head of the Special Collections Section of the U.S. Air Force Academy Library for his assistance in locating manuscript collections and photographs that I might otherwise have overlooked. The inspiration for this work came from the men of the 390th Bomb Group who graciously spent many hours talking with me about their experiences in Operation FRANTIC.

I also wish to thank a number of fine scholars and historians for their advice and guidance during the preparation of this manuscript. Robert F. Byrnes, George Juergens, and John Lovell all provided me with a great deal of support and contributed immensely toward improving the quality of this monograph. D'Ann Campbell's enthusiasm, incisive review of my writing, and constant encouragement kept me going when I might have otherwise preferred to have gone on to something less demanding. Above all, the late John E. Wilz provided firm and steady advice and guidance that greatly improved both my writing and my analysis of the events chronicled herein. Many of my colleagues and fellow officers at the U.S. Air Force Academy provided me with valuable feedback during the course of my research and writing, particularly Captain Mike Grumelli and Navy Lieutenant Doug Foster.

I also wish to thank Colonel Carl Reddel and the Air Force Academy's Department of History for giving me the freedom in the spring of 1992 to pursue this endeavor. I am indebted to Colonel Phil Meilinger and Lieutenant Colonels Mark Clodfelter and Bill Williams for their constant advice and support throughout the preparation of this manuscript.

Three people earned a very special place in my heart for the tolerance, patience, and cheerfulness they maintained during the many stress-filled months required to complete my work. I can hardly find the proper words to thank my wife Mary, son Alex, and daughter Emily for letting me do what I knew I had to do. The credit is all theirs for my success in completing this study but, of course, I assume full responsibility for any flaws contained in the following chapters.

ILLUSTRATIONS

ONE

THE GENESIS
OF FRANTIC

In the late spring of 1944, Nazi Germany would face the next round of Allied offensives with a fair measure of confidence. German troops remained entrenched on Soviet soil. Army Group Center held the region around the city of Vitebsk, 290 miles west of Moscow. At the closest point, the Red Army was 550 miles from Berlin. Despite the Anglo-American bombing offensive, German industrial production was on the upswing and Germany's supreme warlord, Adolf Hitler, was confident in the German Army's ability to throw any Allied forces that undertook an amphibious landing in northern France back into the English Channel. Notwithstanding enormous losses in men and equipment suffered in the East and the Mediterranean, the German war machine remained powerful and full of fight.[1]

The Soviets, too, looked to the future with confidence. The Red Army had succeeded in sweeping the German invaders from much of the territory of the Soviet Union. Still, Soviet leaders knew a great deal of hard fighting lay ahead. They believed that their nation had borne the brunt of the war against Germany, while the Western Allies—Britain, the United States, and Canada—repeatedly delayed the opening of a "second front" in France that would cause the Germans to withdraw substantial numbers of divisions from the East.[2]

Though Moscow often deprecated the efforts of the Western Allies, Anglo-American forces had done much to bring about German defeat. Allied units were waging a bitter struggle on the Italian peninsula against stiff German opposition. The city of Rome lay just beyond the grasp of American and Commonwealth troops. In the south of England, a massive Allied buildup for OVERLORD, the cross-Channel invasion, was nearing completion. Meanwhile, waves of Allied bombers ranged deep into the heart of Germany, the Americans by day, the British by night. Both Allied and German leaders knew that the war was reaching a critical turning point in the spring of 1944.[3]

The spring of 1944 also witnessed the arrival of ground units of the U.S. Army Air Forces on Soviet soil. These American units were to help prepare and operate three air bases from which heavy bombers of the United States Eighth and Fifteenth Army Air Forces would operate against targets in eastern Europe. Code-named FRANTIC, the scheme to use Soviet bases to conduct "shuttle-bombing" from bases in Britain and Italy represented perhaps the most significant example of joint Soviet-American military operations in World War II. The two nations would work jointly through Lend-Lease, the partitioning of Iran into zones of occupation, and in ferrying American-built aircraft between Alaska and Siberia. Yet, U.S. soldiers and airmen were destined to serve inside the USSR itself for more than a year, living and working side by side with the Soviets. American planners hoped that such direct contact would foster warmer relations between the two countries that, in turn, would lead to further examples of Soviet-American co-operation.

The circumstances that led to the direct exposure of U.S. personnel to the Soviet Union, its military, government, and people, were diverse and rooted in several circumstances and perceptions: the American doctrine of strategic bombardment, the Western Allies' desires for closer collaboration with Moscow, and Washington's hope that the USSR would become a belligerent in the war against Japan.

The underpinnings of American strategic bombing doctrine in the 1920s and 1930s were derived largely from the opinions of an international brotherhood of airmen, in particular, the writings of Italian Air Marshal Guilio Douhet and the U.S. Air Service's own Brigadier General William "Billy" Mitchell. Airmen in the United States readily embraced Douhet's and Mitchell's theories of strategic air power, which claimed that the bomber was in itself a war-winning weapon. Moreover, air enthusiasts believed that bombardment aircraft, fitted with the proper defensive armament, would be virtually unstoppable and therefore would require no escort by pursuit planes.[4]

Mitchell wrote in the 1920s that future wars would be fought by armies of aircraft flown by a "special class" of flyers who would be akin to the armored knights of the Middle Ages. By attacking a nation's war industries, "vital centers" Mitchell called them, air forces could bring an enemy to its knees without the grueling land battles of attrition like those waged throughout the World War I. To appeal to America's isolationist attitudes, Mitchell claimed that long-range aircraft could also defend the nation's shores from attack by hostile navies. In independent air missions such as the foregoing, airmen saw an opportunity to gain greater autonomy, if not outright independence, for the Army's air arm, as, in fact, the Royal Air Force had achieved by 1918.[5]

Throughout the decade of the thirties, the faculty at the Air Corps Tactical School (ACTS) at Maxwell Field, Alabama, distilled further the doctrine of strategic bombardment that would guide the thinking of American airmen when the United States entered World War II. By 1939, a group of young and enthusiastic air officers had formulated the "industrial web" concept from the ideas of Mitchell and from observations made by American airmen at the end of World War I. The men who adhered to this idea believed that the machinery of a modern, industrial state would cease to function if certain vital elements within a nation's economy were destroyed. Flying in well-planned formations, so the industrial web theory went, bombardment aircraft could execute pinpoint precision bombing in daylight from high altitudes. Once such strikes had been successfully carried out, airmen believed, an enemy, regardless of the strength of his forces in the field, would lack the means and perhaps the will to support continued military action.[6]

The development of aircraft for the U.S. Army Air Corps both reflected and guided the ACTS' doctrine of strategic bombing. By the mid-1930s, the Boeing B-17, the aircraft destined to take part in the air war against Germany and the shuttle-raids to the Soviet Union, had appeared in prototype. When it first appeared, the B-17 appeared to outclass existing fighters. By 1943, the "G" model of the B-17 appeared in large numbers (more than 8,600 B-17Gs were built during the war). This final variant of the "Flying Fortress" embodied the ideal of a battle plane that could claw its way through enemy fighter defenses unescorted. The aircraft bristled with thirteen machine guns positioned to cover virtually every conceivable angle of attack by hostile fighters. With a ten-man crew, the B-17G could fly a maximum distance of 3,400 miles at a cruising speed in excess of 200 miles per hour. The typical mission load of approximately 4,000 pounds of bombs reduced the B-17's range to 1,100 miles. The plane was capable of carrying up to nearly eight tons of explosives over shorter distances.[7]

Flying singly or in loose formations, even heavily armed bombardment aircraft would still be easy prey for modern fighters. Contrary to what many believe, Mitchell recognized the necessity of "pursuit" escorts; Douhet considered them irrelevant. In the absence of a suitable long-range escort fighter, the Army Air Forces (so named after June 1941) devised the tactic of formation flying for its bomber units. As tactics evolved, B-17s and other heavy bombers, notably the B-24 "Liberator," would fly in tight, box-like formations where the defensive weaponry aboard each aircraft would be integrated with that of other airplanes into interlocking fields of fire, deadly to attacking fighters. After reaching the target, the plane's Norden bombsight, the most accurate instrument of its kind in use during the Second World War, would allow these huge formations to obliterate enemy industries with pinpoint accuracy. Or so the airmen believed.[8]

The Army Air Forces thus entered 1941 with the best available technology to support its doctrine. Still lacking was a coherent plan directed at a specific enemy. President Franklin D. Roosevelt gave the airmen, supremely confident in air power's war-winning potential, an opportunity to lay the foundation for America's approach to the air war in Europe.

As the possibility of being drawn into World War II loomed large over the United States, the president tasked the War Department on July 9, 1941, with formulating the requirements of a war with the Axis powers. American and British military staffs had already agreed in March 1941 that the air forces of the two nations would mount a sustained air offensive against Germany when and if the United States became a belligerent in the European war. Within the broad framework of this agreement, known as ABC-1, Army Air Forces commanding general Henry H. Arnold's infant air staff set to work to formulate the requirements for the air arm. The chief of the newly established Air War Plans Division (AWPD) of the Air Staff, Lieutenant Colonel Harold L. George, oversaw the work of a group of young officers as they put together a plan for the air war over Germany.[9]

The requirements plan developed by AWPD, called simply AWPD-1, established the strategy that was later to be used in the Combined Bomber Offensive of 1943. Released in August 1941, AWPD-1 reflected American air doctrine. After some discussion, the air staff planners decided that the Army Air Forces' overall objective should be to "attempt to defeat Germany, then Japan, through air power alone." Failing that, the Air Force should prepare the way for a land invasion of the European continent (then Japan). Beyond that statement, the airmen reflected Mitchell's approach to aerial warfare by selecting 154 "vital targets" that, if eliminated, would fatally cripple Germany's war machine. These targets were largely elements of three critical industries: electric power, transportation, and oil. Almost as an afterthought, AWPD members added to the list of objectives the "overriding intermediate" goal of neutralizing the *Luftwaffe*.[10] Though the Air Staff would revise its plans following America's entry in the war, the basic ideas concerning the role and use of strategic air power remained essentially unchanged from AWPD-1's publication until autumn of 1943.

The British, too, had independently developed a doctrine of strategic bombing. As chief of the Air Staff between 1919 and 1929, General Hugh Trenchard put his own stamp on British military policy by declaring the bomber offensive as the United Kingdom's primary means of *defense*.

Trenchard and other Royal Air Force officers predicted that strategic bombing of an enemy's cities would produce a moral paralysis, leading to internal collapse. This idea appealed to a nation haunted by memories of the appalling casualties suffered by the British Army during World War I.[11]

Events in 1939 and 1940 undermined British hopes of victory through air power. The Royal Air Force learned early in the conflict how expensive its prewar doctrine truly was. The RAF found in the fall of 1939 that the cost of unescorted daylight precision bombing raids was prohibitively high and soon thereafter adopted a policy of night bombing. By the spring of 1942, RAF Bomber Command accepted the inaccuracy of night raids and dropped all pretense of precision bombing. Under the leadership of Air Marshal Arthur "Bomber" Harris, Bomber Command turned to area bombing, or "city busting." The RAF aimed to break German morale and Harris rationalized that area bombing also had an impact on industrial production by destroying workers' homes and killing their families thereby causing absenteeism to rise and production to sag. Harris also claimed that saturation raids were bound to destroy factories and transportation facilities if only by happenstance.[12]

Unfortunately, the Army Air Forces paid scant attention to Bomber Command's early disappointments with daylight bombing. On September 9, 1942, American air planners under the direction of Brigadier General Haywood Hansell released their updated policies in a document known as AWPD-42. AWPD-42 continued to stress the need to strike at key German industries, and like its predecessor, AWPD-1, assumed a great degree of accuracy on the part of the bombers and continued to minimize the need for fighter escorts. AWPD-42 differed from earlier plans in that it envisioned a combined aerial offensive, the RAF bombing by night, the AAF by day. Though only a forecast of the production requirements AAF leaders deemed necessary to wage war on the Axis, AWPD-42 would form the United States' basis for the Combined Bomber Offensive.[13]

British airmen tried to warn their American counterparts of the dangers inherent in daylight bombing. The German Blitz against Britain in 1940–41 had shown that well-organized antiaircraft defenses combined with good fighter interception could inflict heavy casualties on daylight bombers. The RAF had attempted its own daylight campaign and received a drubbing at the hands of an increasingly powerful and efficient German air defense network. Early AAF raids carried out in late 1942 and early 1943, however, were all within range of existing escort fighters and resulted in tolerable American losses. Major General Ira C. Eaker, commander of the first operational United States bombardment units to penetrate western Europe in

1942, downplayed the role of the fighter escorts in keeping losses among the bombardment units relatively light. Eaker saw the Army Air Forces' faith in massed bomber formations operating in daylight vindicated by the apparent success of these early raids.[14]

Indeed, Eaker and other AAF leaders viewed mass as the key to successful daylight bomber operations. At the beginning of 1943, Army Air Forces' leaders worried that their assets in men and aircraft would be dispersed among the various theaters, preventing them from amassing in Britain the forces called for by both AWPD-1 and AWPD-42 and robbing the airmen of a chance to flex their muscles before a major land invasion of western Europe took place. The idea contained in AWPD-42 of an Anglo-American Combined Bomber Offensive (CBO) from the United Kingdom presented a solid means of applying the doctrine of concentration of force, without which the air forces would be ineffective.[15]

With the support of U.S. Chief of Staff General George C. Marshall as well as President Roosevelt and British Prime Minister Winston S. Churchill, American airmen won a secure place in Allied strategy in January 1943 during the Casablanca Conference. The Casablanca Directive called for a sustained air offensive with the stated purpose of bringing about the progressive destruction of the German military, industrial, and economic systems. The directive also borrowed a page from Douhet's book when it tasked the air campaign with undermining German morale "to a point where the capacity for armed resistance is fatally weakened."[16]

In response to the Casablanca Directive, the Army Air Forces developed plans for POINTBLANK, the AAF conception of the Combined Bomber Offensive called for in AWPD-42. Major General Eaker presented the outline of POINTBLANK to the Joint Chiefs of Staff on April 29, 1943. The new plan clung to the tenets of the "industrial web" theories evident in AWPD-1 and the ACTS doctrine of deep penetration and unescorted daylight bombing. Like AWPD-42, POINTBLANK also called on the RAF to continue to bomb Germany at night. Round-the-clock attacks, the airmen believed, would wear down the German defenders and erode civilian morale, through sheer exhaustion, if nothing else. The Anglo-American Combined Chiefs of Staff approved the plan at the Trident Conference in Washington, D.C., on May 18, 1943. The CCS added a single sentence to POINTBLANK's general objective. The Combined Chiefs left the previous Casablanca directive intact but added that the fatal weakening of Germany's capacity for armed resistance was to be "construed as meaning so weakened as to permit initiation of final combined operations on the Continent."[17]

POINTBLANK retained the destruction of the German air force as an intermediate objective that still had to be fulfilled before the remainder of the operation's military and industrial objectives could be effectively destroyed. Once these targets had been neutralized, Germany would be ripe for conquest. POINTBLANK and the Combined Bomber Offensive began late in May 1943. Before the end of the year, Allied airmen would have to pause and reconsider their plans, tactics, and expectations in the face of fierce German resistance.

The bombing campaign had already acquired a special niche in Anglo-American policy long before the opening of the Combined Bomber Offensive. By the middle of 1941, the Germans had evicted the British from the continent three times in just over a year—from Norway in April 1940, from France in May 1940, and from Greece in May 1941. Struggling to hold together an imperial defense network spanning much of the globe with military forces that had not begun to prepare for war until 1938, Great Britain viewed Bomber Command as its sole means of striking directly at Germany following the debacles of 1940 and 1941.[18]

Germany's invasion of its erstwhile Soviet ally in June 1941 prompted the British to attach greater importance to the bomber offensive. On July 18, two days after German tanks rolled into Smolensk on the road to Moscow, the Soviet dictator Joseph Stalin asked the British to open a "second front" in France or Norway to draw German forces from the Eastern Front. This would not be the last such plea from Stalin. Throughout the summer and autumn of 1941, as German troops closed on Moscow, the Soviet government made repeated demands for a British amphibious landing in western Europe. Indeed, on September 13, 1941, Stalin suggested that Britain send twenty-five to thirty divisions to the Eastern Front via Murmansk to shore up Soviet defenses against the onrushing Germans! Churchill responded to Stalin's calls for a second front by explaining to the Soviet leader that the British Army had not recovered sufficiently from its own defeats to stage a landing in France while simultaneously defending such links in the imperial defense network as Egypt. Offering to send supplies and aircraft, Churchill promised to aid the Soviets in every way possible.[19]

Paradoxically, with the U.S.'s entry into World War II in December 1941, pressure grew on the British to cooperate with the Americans in making a major landing of amphibious forces in northwest Europe as early as 1942. Popular sentiment in both the United States and Great Britain favored a second front. As Roger Beaumont wrote, "What was popular, however, was not feasible." With most American resources going to the Pacific in the early months of 1942, the British were able to persuade their new ally that a landing in France in 1942 would be both premature and disastrous.[20]

Arguing that a second front in France in 1942 was improbable, Churchill offered up the bomber offensive as a substitute. "Bombing," Churchill stated in March 1942, was "not decisive, but better than nothing." When the chiefs of the Royal Navy and the British Army asked for an inquiry into the diversion of resources to Bomber Command, the admirals and generals were hard pressed to refute the counterclaim of Sir Archibald Sinclair, British Secretary of State for Air, that "The United Nations have two instruments for hammering Germany in 1942—the Red Army and the Royal Air Force."[21]

As the possibility of a second front in France receded further into the future following the Anglo-American landings in North Africa in autumn of 1942, Soviet sniping at and carping over the Allied war effort increased. At the end of 1942, Stalin expressed only slight satisfaction with the Allied landing in northwest Africa and continued to press his version of a second front, *i.e.*, in France. Stung by Stalin's brusque dismissal of Allied efforts, Churchill began to routinely cable the results of Bomber Command's raids to the Soviet dictator. This was Churchill's way of showing Stalin that Britain was striking the German homeland itself while the Red Army grappled with the bulk of the *Wehrmacht*.[22]

The Soviets remained unimpressed by Allied bombing or by Anglo-American operations in the Mediterranean that led to the invasion of Sicily and the collapse of Mussolini's Fascist Italy in the summer of 1943. At that time, the Soviets began to routinely charge their allies with bad faith for failing to follow through on plans for a second front in France. The Soviet press paid scant attention to the battle for Sicily in July and August 1943, a mere skirmish in the Kremlin's eyes compared with the titanic armored struggle simultaneously under way on the Kursk sector of the Eastern Front.[23]

Stalin began to hint darkly by late summer 1943 that, in the absence of a second front in France, the Soviet Union might not be able to sustain its resistance against Nazi Germany. According to historian Adam Ulam, Stalin was a "fast learner" when it came to the weaknesses of foreigners. He realized the fear with which the Anglo-American Allies viewed the prospect of a separate Nazi-Soviet peace and began to use the threat of such a move to spur the opening of a second front in France.[24] As early as January 1943, American diplomats in Switzerland had begun to report that contacts with "reliable sources" indicated that a Soviet-German armistice might be in the offing. By August, similar reports emerged from Helsinki and Stockholm. Quite possibly the work of Stalin's own agents, rumors of a separate peace between Moscow and Berlin persuaded the Western Allies of the need to show the Soviets that the Anglo-Americans were fighting with all the means at their disposal.[25]

The Soviets apparently employed means other than rumors of a separate peace to influence their allies. The American ambassador in Moscow, Admiral William H. Standley, opined in a message to Secretary of State Cordell Hull on September 7, 1943, that Soviet carping and propaganda were creating an "inferiority complex" among the peoples and leadership of the Western Allies. The Soviet Union's great string of battlefield victories in the summer of 1943, he went on, had overshadowed the narrow triumph gained by Anglo-American forces at Salerno, Italy.[26] The Belgian Ambassador told Standley that by playing on Western sympathies for the sufferings of the Soviet people, the Kremlin could bring great psychological pressure to bear on its allies to make them tailor their plans to those favored by the Red Army, namely an immediate landing in France.

The "second front in the air" had certainly failed, in Soviet eyes, to relieve much pressure being exerted by the Germans on the Eastern Front. While Churchill reported the tonnage of ordnance dropped on this or that German city, Stalin replied with statistics concerning the number of German divisions and tanks his army was engaging.

Most Allied airmen likewise realized that the Combined Bomber Offensive was in trouble by early autumn 1943. The CBO's "intermediate objective" of neutralizing the German Air Force had not been achieved. The *Luftwaffe* had shown an amazing resiliency against both British night bombers and American day raiders. As Eaker had pointed out in his presentation of POINTBLANK to the JCS in April 1943, a failure to defeat the German Air Force would make the rest of the operation and subsequent amphibious landings by the Western Allies on the continent impossible. During ensuing operations, American planners nonetheless had failed to concentrate the air assault against the *Luftwaffe* and its supporting infrastructure. Instead, the AAF had dispatched its bombers against a vast array of targets, including submarine pens, aircraft factories, and other industries. The resultant dispersion of effort had meant that any meaningful damage caused by a single raid was usually not followed up by subsequent strikes that would have rendered German repair and recovery operations more difficult and costly.[27]

In addition to the foregoing dispersion of effort, German defenses inflicted crippling losses on the Allied bomber streams throughout the latter half of 1943. Though new bombing radar technology assisted British bomber crews in improving their accuracy, German night-fighters and flak knocked the RAF attackers from the skies in alarming numbers. For example, Bomber Command listed 764 heavy bombers available for operations in January 1943. By the end of the year, the RAF had written off more than 2,700 of the four-engine machines. Harris's attempt to win the war by leveling Berlin from November 1943 to March 1944 had cost his units 1,128 aircraft, nearly all four-engine bombers. His other efforts at "city-busting" were equally expensive to Bomber Command. On the last night of March 1944, Bomber Command lost 108 bombers over Nuremberg, Germany, nearly 20 percent of the force dispatched. Together with losses suffered over Berlin and Essen, the RAF lost 190 bombers in a single week. No air force could sustain such losses for long.[28]

While Bomber Command's nightly attacks grew ever more costly, Eaker's earlier confidence in the B-17's ability to penetrate German defenses in daylight evaporated in the skies over the Third Reich in the late summer and fall of 1943. The death knell for the AAF's prewar doctrine of unescorted bombing raids sounded in October 1943. In a three-day period spanning October 8–10, the Eighth Air Force lost eighty-eight bombers in raids on Bremen, Danzig, and Munster, a loss rate of 18.4 percent of available crews. On the 14th, the Eighth staged a deep penetration raid against the ball-bearing works at Schweinfurt. German fighters and flak shot down sixty bombers and inflicted various degrees of damage to another 138 aircraft. The loss rate for the Schweinfurt raid stood at 20.7 percent and the damage rate at 47.4 percent. In a week's time, the AAF lost 148 bombers in deep penetration strikes against Germany. Even by American standards, that represented unacceptable attrition.[29]

American airmen were forced by the attrition suffered in the skies over Germany to re-evaluate the tactic of daylight precision bombing. Even General Arnold recognized the need for long-range fighter escorts that could remain with the bombers all the way to a target and back. With drop tanks, P-47s could cover most of western Germany by August 1943, though this did not include Schweinfurt. In November, P-38 twin-engine fighters could reach Berlin but these aircraft were inferior to German day fighters. By March 1944, the superb P-51 Mustang, equipped with drop tanks, could actually operate east of Berlin. But the appearance of the latter aircraft was still many months off in autumn of 1943. While the search for a suitable long-range escort plane progressed, American bombers struck targets in western Europe that lay within range of existing escorts. In the meantime, Arnold revived an old idea that he hoped would help revitalize the bomber offensive.[30]

Since the early days of the war, according to the Army Air Forces' official history, AAF leaders had taken interest in the idea that shuttle-bombing among widely dispersed bases might pay huge dividends. Aircraft departing bases in Britain would strike targets deep inside Axis-dominated Europe and land at airfields in North Africa or, possibly, the USSR. From these landing sites, aircraft could mount further operations before returning to their original bases. The first raid on Schweinfurt in August 1943, which also included a strike on an aircraft factory in Regensburg, was itself a shuttle raid from bases in England to landing fields in North Africa. Though losses were heavy on this mission as well, the Army Air Forces perceived that air attacks from multiple directions could confuse, divide, and disperse German defenses, thereby helping the AAF to achieve POINT-BLANK's goal of neutralizing the *Luftwaffe*. The establishment of the Fifteenth Air Force on bases in newly liberated southern Italy in the fall of 1943 was the result, in part, of an AAF desire to carry out shuttle raids.[31]

His bombers suffering crippling losses over Germany, Arnold in October 1943 secured the approval of the Allied Combined Chiefs of Staff for inclusion of a proposal for the use of Soviet bases for shuttle-bombing as one of the objectives of a U.S. Military Mission about to be established in Moscow under Major General John R. Deane. The objective of the mission was to promote the closest coordination possible between the military efforts of the United States and the Soviet Union. The mission contained an Army Division under Brigadier General William E. Crist, a Navy Division under Rear Admiral Clarence E. Olsen, and a Supply (Lend-Lease) Division under Major General Sidney P. Spalding. An Air Division under Major General Robert L. Walsh would be added in June 1944 when the shuttle mission commenced.[32]

The use of Soviet bases, Arnold concluded, would force the German Air Force to disperse its fighter units throughout Europe to guard against American air attacks from three directions. Bombers landing at Soviet airfields instead of returning to Britain would fly shorter total distances and could strike at targets normally outside the range of U. K.-based aircraft. All of Nazi-occupied Europe would be vulnerable to aerial assault. To provide a 360-degree defense of the Reich, the *Luftwaffe* would have to withdraw fighter units from the West. Such a dispersal of German fighters would, in turn, ease the task of bomber units attacking from Britain. Moreover, every German fighter drawn toward the Soviet front would be one less German fighter that the Anglo-American air forces would have to face over the proposed invasion beaches in Normandy. The RAF politely declined to partake of shuttle-bombing; Harris regarded such bombing as a mere publicity stunt, related to the second front issue.[33]

The call for shuttle-bombing was one example of the AAF's efforts to bring maximum pressure to bear on Germany from the air. With two numbered strategic air forces—the Eighth and Fifteenth—in operation by the end of 1943, the Army Air Forces also recognized a need for centralized direction of the POINTBLANK campaign to ensure that the physical separation of bomber units did not lead to a dispersal of strength. On January 1, 1944, Lieutenant General Carl A. Spaatz assumed command of the U.S. Strategic Air Forces in Europe (USSTAF). Major General James H. Doolittle took over the Eighth Air Force while Eaker was assigned to the post of head of the newly formed Mediterranean Allied Air Forces (MAAF). USSTAF would oversee the operations of the Eighth and Fifteenth air forces only. The RAF would retain its own chain of command. To better employ the Anglo-American tactical air forces for the impending invasion of France, code-named OVERLORD, the Combined Chiefs of Staff formed the Allied Expeditionary Air Force, directly under Supreme Headquarters, Allied Expeditionary Forces (SHAEF) and its head, Supreme Allied Commander U.S. General Dwight D. Eisenhower.[34]

As Anglo-American air leaders worked to overcome problems of command and control brought about through the international composition of the forces at their disposal, the idea of basing Allied air forces in the Soviet Union was not new in autumn of 1943. Army Air Forces planners wrote in AWPD-1 that the force of more than three thousand heavy bombers necessary to carry out a full-fledged air war against Germany would require 117 airfields in the United Kingdom, the Middle East (for the new B-29s), Iceland, and Soviet Russia. AWPD-1 was written just a few weeks after Hitler's invasion of the USSR in June 1941. In the months before Pearl Harbor, the plan's authors, however, were apparently unsure of the relationship that would exist among the wartime Allies in the event the United States became a belligerent in the European war. The Air Staff could not plan with certainty on the availability of Soviet bases, and AWPD-1 contained a vague warning that "use of Russian bases will depend on future situations that cannot be predicted." Whether this phrase referred to American doubts about the survivability of Stalin's regime in the bleak summer of 1941 or perceptions of Soviet xenophobia and uncooperativeness was not made clear in the text of the plan.[35]

With America's entry in the war in December 1941, the Anglo-American Allies sought direct military means through which they could aid the hard-pressed Soviet Union. The Red Army had managed to hold the Germans before Moscow and to launch a stunning counterattack that drove the exhausted and half-frozen German units westward, in some places more than 100 miles. Nevertheless, the *Wehrmacht* remained unbeaten, and was still deep inside Stalin's empire. In addition to material aid, including Lend-Lease assistance sanctioned by President Roosevelt in autumn of 1941, and a "second front" in the air over Hitler's Reich, the Allies tried to find other ways of cooperating with the Soviets. As the historian Richard C. Lukas has written, the "most feasible form of military collaboration between the United States and the Soviet Union involved air forces."[36]

The British took steps in the early days of the German invasion of the Soviet Union in the summer of 1941, to establish ties with the Red Air Force. The first British convoy carrying war materials to the USSR set sail in August 1941. The Germans had concentrated powerful naval and air units in occupied Norway to raid Allied shipping. Because British fleet and air units were tied down in other theaters, London requested aerial protection by the Soviets. When the Red Air Force (*Voyenno-vozdushnyye sily* or VVS) replied that it was too hard pressed on the main front to divert significant numbers of aircraft to the far north, the RAF sent its own aircraft aboard cargo ships as well as the aircraft carrier *HMS Argus,* which sailed for Murmansk in September 1941. These fighters formed the nucleus of No. 151 Wing, tasked to defend the port of Murmansk and convoy traffic passing to the north of Norway from German air attack from bases near that northern port city.[37]

The British unit at Murmansk operated successfully from Soviet soil until autumn of 1942. By then, supply routes to the Soviet Union through Iran, over which much of the equipment provided through Lend-Lease traveled, were well established. The northern convoy route thus became less important than before. The availability of additional British aircraft carriers in late 1942, the neutralization of German surface units by RAF Coastal Command bombers, and the deployment of additional VVS units in the Soviet Arctic region also obviated the need for continued British operations from Murmansk.[38]

While Hurricanes flying from bases north of the Arctic Circle in the summer of 1942 helped protect British convoys to Murmansk, the Germans prepared to launch their second great summer offensive in the East against the southern portion of the front. Anxious to assist the beleaguered Soviets, President Roosevelt suggested in May 1942 that U.S. air units might help protect the oil fields of the Caucasus region.[39]

As the Air Staff studied the president's proposal, the U.S. War Department in June 1942 opened negotiations with the Soviets for the use of airfields on Soviet soil on which a task force of fewer than two dozen AAF B-24 "Liberators" might land following a raid on the oil fields at Ploesti, Romania, from bases in the Middle East. Approval by the Soviets for the use of their territory as landing sites for the task force materialized at the end of June 1942 but came too late for the Americans. The B-24s had already struck Ploesti on June 12. By then, Axis forces were deep inside Egypt threatening to seize the Suez Canal, Britain's link with its Asian empire. The AAF subsequently concentrated what units it had available in the Middle East, and plans for Soviet bases went on hold until the crisis in North Africa abated.[40]

In August 1942, Churchill traveled to Moscow to inform Stalin that the second front in the West was about to be opened in northwest Africa and not France, as the Kremlin desired. He was alarmed by the Soviet dictator's negative reaction when told of Anglo-American plans for a Mediterranean strategy. While in Moscow with Churchill, the chief of the Imperial General Staff, Field Marshal Sir Alan Brooke, proposed direct air force aid to the Soviets. Churchill seized the idea of aerial assistance as the quickest and best way to prove Allied good faith.[41]

From this desire to assist the Soviets on the Eastern Front grew Operation VELVET. By highlighting Allied comradeship-in-arms, Churchill believed that Anglo-American air units operating in direct support with the Red Army in defense of the Caucasus would have an enormous effect on German morale. At first, Marshall opposed the idea. The American chief of staff urged direct action in the form of offensive operations in the West to aid the Soviets. He argued that Lend-Lease obviated the need for further "moral" and "political" gestures, and he was concerned that dispersing AAF units around the periphery of Europe would complicate supply and maintenance operations. Nevertheless, the Anglo-American decision in the late summer of 1942 to suspend the Murmansk convoys because of catastrophic losses and Stalin's growing irritation over the lack of a second front in France prompted Roosevelt to approve the idea of joint air operations in the Caucasus, Operation VELVET.[42]

VELVET thus served to fill the gap between Soviet expectations and Allied abilities in autumn of 1942. In October, with German troops fighting their way into the city of Stalingrad on the Volga and the foothills of the Caucasus Mountains, Churchill notified Stalin that he and Roosevelt were anxious to deploy an Anglo-American air force on the southern flank of the Eastern Front. This force would operate under the strategic control of the Soviet High Command and consist of nine RAF fighter squadrons and five bomber groups. The AAF would contribute one heavy bombardment group and one transport group. The Anglo-American air units would provide air support to the Red Army, protect the Caucasus oil fields from German aerial attacks, and strike at targets designated by the Soviets. In the same message, Churchill also notified Stalin of the formal decision to suspend convoys to Murmansk but promised that shipments would resume in January 1943.[43]

Stalin expressed an interest in VELVET in October 1942 but his ardor for the project would not last long. On November 8, the battle of Stalingrad was nearing its climax and the Soviet dictator called for the "speedy despatch" to the Caucasus of the Anglo-American air force. American Brigadier General Elmer Adler and British Air Marshal Sir R. M. Drummond arrived in Moscow on November 21, 1942, to open discussions on VELVET. In October, Stalin had apparently thought the Allies were ready to send the aircraft immediately; by the third week in November, the Soviet counteroffensive at Stalingrad was well under way. The German Sixth Army was trapped in the city by the 23rd and the Axis line in the south was in disarray. When the crisis passed in the south, Stalin lost all interest in VELVET. Adler and Drummond sat through a succession of frustrating and unproductive meetings. The Soviets requested aircraft without Anglo-American crews; the Western Allies refused on the basis that Lend-Lease already provided such aid. With each side accusing the other of delaying, negotiations broke down quickly, and in early December the Soviets requested that Adler and Drummond leave Moscow.[44]

Roosevelt was not yet ready to let VELVET die. On December 16, in a message to Stalin, he repeated his willingness to send AAF units to the Caucasus region. Two days later, Stalin politely declined the offer. What the Red Air Force needed more than anything, he informed Roosevelt, was aircraft, particularly fighters, but without Anglo-American crews. "A feature of the Soviet Air Force," Stalin wrote, "is that we have more than enough pilots but suffer from a shortage of machines."[45] The scheme to place Anglo-American air units inside the Soviet Union thus collapsed when Stalin no longer saw it as necessary to successful defensive operations against the Germans. Churchill concluded that if the Soviets could survive the winter, they could reject the presence of Western personnel, which they considered an infectious contact and as a blow to their national and martial prestige. Both Adler and Drummond believed that Soviet xenophobia was a major factor in the Kremlin's ultimate refusal to accept VELVET after the German threat to the Caucasus had passed.[46]

In truth, the Americans had far greater interest in deploying air units in a part of the Soviet Union thousands of miles from the Caucasus. From the earliest days of United States' belligerency in the war, American military leaders, particularly those of the AAF, expressed an interest in gaining access to the Soviet Maritime Provinces in Siberia. The Joint Chiefs considered a Japanese attack on the USSR a very real possibility throughout 1942. General Arnold believed that if such an assault materialized, Moscow should allow the U.S. Army Air Forces access to Siberian bases from which heavy bombers could strike at the Japanese homeland. With Imperial Japanese forces sweeping all opposition before them in Southeast Asia and the Western Pacific in the spring of 1942, Siberia remained the only real estate in friendly—albeit neutral—hands that had airfields from which American bombers could reach Japan.[47]

In June 1942, Roosevelt pledged American support to the Soviet Union in the event of a Japanese attack on the USSR. The president tried to make a United States presence in Siberia as attractive to the Soviets as possible even if the Japanese did not strike Soviet territory. He understood Soviet fears that overt cooperation with the Americans in the Far East might provoke the Japanese, who had signed a neutrality pact with the Soviets in the spring of 1941. Roosevelt requested that Moscow permit AAF survey teams into Siberia to help set up airfields that would provide landing sites for Lend-Lease aircraft ferried from Alaska. Americans thought a Siberian route would be faster and safer than one requiring airplanes to fly across Africa, over the Middle East, and then into the southern Soviet Union via Iran. Such a route would also provide the AAF with an opportunity to lay the foundation for gaining Siberian air bases for combat operations against Japan.[48]

In July 1942, Roosevelt notified Stalin that the United States was sending a mission headed by Major General Follett Bradley to oversee preparations and arrangements aimed at opening the Alaska-Siberia (ALSIB) aircraft ferry route. Negotiations went reasonably well at first. The Soviets resisted a proposal that American pilots fly the aircraft into Siberia, and Bradley agreed to allow Soviet crews to fly to Alaska to pick up aircraft at Fairbanks. When Bradley and a small team of American officers were allowed to survey existing airfields in Siberia, the general remarked that when American combat units operated from Siberian bases, they would have to construct suitable airfields from scratch.[49]

On September 21, the Soviets suddenly reversed their stance on ALSIB. They apparently did not believe American claims that the United States was unable to provide as many transport aircraft as the Red Air Force requested. The Soviets were obviously attempting to use American interest in Siberia as leverage for increased aircraft deliveries. Moscow now claimed that the ALSIB route to the Soviet Union was unsuitable for ferrying aircraft. Tired of Soviet indecision, the War Department on October 4 ordered ALSIB closed. Their bluff called, the Soviets protested immediately, Stalin himself requesting to see Bradley. The Soviet dictator told Bradley that the Red Air Force was quite anxious to use ALSIB and that Moscow had canceled the program only because the AAF had not yet brought Lend-Lease planes to Alaska. Citing the presence of a group of A-20 twin-engine light bombers at Fairbanks awaiting shipment, Bradley denied Stalin's allegations. In the face of this second Soviet reversal, the War Department agreed to keep ALSIB open.[50]

Before returning to the United States, Bradley specifically raised the issue of Siberian bases for operations against Japan. The Soviets simply ignored his queries and refused to provide any further information on airfields in the Soviet Far East. Nevertheless, Bradley's after-action report sparked in Washington a Siberian base project, code-named BAZAAR, and led Roosevelt to make further offers of assistance to Stalin. On December 30, 1942, the American President, apparently hoping to win Soviet support for BAZAAR, offered 100 four-engine bombers should the Japanese move against the Soviet Union. He asked that Bradley be allowed to make a full and comprehensive survey of potential airfields in the Maritime Provinces. On January 5, 1943, Stalin brought BAZAAR to a speedy end. In a response to Roosevelt's offer of aircraft, Stalin insisted that the Red Air Force indeed required aircraft but "not in the Far East, where the U.S.S.R. is not fighting, but on . . . the Soviet-German front."[51]

Stalin obviously did not want to run even the slightest risk of embroiling his country in a two-front war while the Germans remained such a formidable and dangerous foe. Despite Stalin's repeated refusals to allow American officers into Siberia to survey airfields, the AAF and the Joint Chiefs of Staff remained convinced of the necessity of gaining access to Siberian airfields for the air war against Japan. In their studies for future operations in the Pacific, both the JCS and the Anglo-American Combined Chiefs of Staff repeatedly called for U.S. air bases in Siberia, despite Soviet neutrality in the Anglo-American-Chinese struggle with the Japanese Empire.[52]

Thus, Anglo-American attempts to introduce air force units onto Soviet soil were derived from a number of motives. Both Churchill and Roosevelt wanted to demonstrate to Stalin that the Western Allies were waging war on the Germans with every means at their disposal. Air units fighting alongside the VVS could emphasize Allied solidarity while Anglo-American forces gathered their strength for the opening of a second front in either northwest Africa or France. The Americans also imagined that their display of eagerness to assist the Soviet Union would be repaid by a Soviet sanction of the use of bases in the Soviet Far East from which Arnold's airmen could participate in an "independent" strategic air mission in the Pacific, namely,

the bombing of the Japanese home islands. Early attempts at direct cooperation with the Soviets through VELVET and BAZAAR failed when the Kremlin did not foresee that gains would be commensurate with the efforts and
possible risks entailed in allowing large numbers of foreign airmen and
their aircraft to operate from Soviet soil.

By the dawn of 1943, the United States had already gained experience in
China in establishing and operating air bases in relatively remote and alien
areas. China held a special place in the minds of many American leaders.
America's unwillingness to acquiesce in Japan's conquest of China was
the root cause of the war in the Pacific. The Roosevelt Administration
viewed the Nationalist regime of Generalissimo Chiang Kai-shek as a valuable if unsteady ally whose collapse would release dozens of the Imperial
Japanese Army's best divisions for combat elsewhere. Throughout the war,
the United States spent billions of dollars and sent many of its finest men in
a vain effort to make China a major contributor in the Far Eastern-Pacific
War.[53]

Unlike the Soviet Union, which could largely fend for itself by 1942,
Chinese leaders were clearly aware of their nation's relative military weak-
ness and dependence on others. Since before Pearl Harbor, China had
received weapons and equipment under American Lend-Lease. A U.S. Military Mission had operated in Chiang's capital, Chungking, and an American Volunteer Group (AVG), the celebrated Flying Tigers, provided air support to the Chinese Army. Colonel Claire Lee Chennault, official air adviser
to Chiang and retired Army Air Corps officer, helped recruit fliers for the
volunteer group. By the summer of 1941, the AVG was composed of American aviators and technicians who technically worked for the Central Aircraft Manufacturing Company (CAMCO), thus avoiding embarrassing legal questions concerning U.S. citizens fighting for a foreign power.[54]

In July 1942, the AVG was dissolved and replaced by the China Air Task
Force (CATF), remaining under the command of newly promoted Brigadier
General Chennault, recently recalled to active service in the AAF. The
CATF was subordinate to the U.S. Tenth Army Air Force headquartered in
India. To regain operational freedom, Chennault played Chiang off against
other Americans, including Major General Joseph W. Stilwell, who had arrived in Chungking in February 1942 to serve as Chiang's chief of staff and
commander of all American troops in the China-Burma-India (CBI) theater.
Chiang hinted darkly of imminent collapse if supply tonnage, now flown
from India to China over "the Hump" of the Himalayas following the Allied collapse in Burma, was not increased and a larger air force put in place
on Chinese soil. Persistent Chinese demands for air and material support,

together with Chennault's machinations, resulted in the activation of the
Fourteenth Air Force on March 10, 1943.[55]

Many American military leaders doubted the wisdom of establishing a
full-fledged air force in an area that was dependent on supply by air. Chiang
Kai-shek was pleased with the move: China gained a U.S. commitment for
increased tonnage via "the Hump," aircraft for Chinese pilots, and an air
force commanded by Chennault, a general whose interests were focused on
China. The AAF viewed the activation of the Fourteenth Air Force as more
of a political expedient designed to encourage continued Chinese resistance
in the war against Japan than a sound military move. In truth, the Fourteenth represented little more than a nuisance to the Japanese throughout
much of 1943. By the end of October 1943, the same month in which the
Americans initially approached the Soviets on the probability of shuttle-
bombing operations, the Fourteenth mustered 209 aircraft, of which thirty-
two were B-24 heavy bombers. Supply problems prohibited a significant increase in strength. Nevertheless, the presence of American bomber aircraft
deployed in China that were capable of reaching Japan alarmed Tokyo. Orders from the Japanese Imperial General Headquarters tasked the China
Expeditionary Army to "frustrate the [American] plan to raid the Homeland from bases in China."[56]

Deprived of bases in Siberia for use in operations against Japan's home
islands, the AAF turned to China. Considering that an American air force
was already operating on Chinese soil, the idea of basing new B-29 very
long-range bombers near Ch'eng-tu in the mountainous Szechuan province
of southeast China proved attractive to the AAF. Huge quantities of precious supplies were diverted from the Fourteenth Air Force as well as the
Chinese Army to provide bases for the B-29 "Superfortresses." The massive
logistic preparations for B-29 operations included laying new railroads and
building roads, bridges, and fuel pipelines, as well as constructing sprawling
airfields capable of handling the huge bombers. "Hump" aircrews strained
to bring in the requisite supplies, as the AAF estimated that a stockpile of
some 60,000 tons of fuel, bombs, and spare parts was necessary for sustained B-29 operations from China. Hump tonnage in March 1944 was
stuck at 11,000 tons a month; at least 20,000 a month was necessary to
build up the required stores at the air base complex near Ch'eng-tu.[57]

Washington hoped that B-29 operations from China, code-named
MATTERHORN, would both boost Chinese morale and expose Japan's "Inner
Zone," which included the home islands, to large-scale air attack. The
B-29s mounted their first raid from China in June 1944 against Bangkok,
Thailand. But the operational rationale for maintaining bases in China, at

great expense and with enormous difficulty, was undermined when, in June 1944, American amphibious forces opened a successful assault on the Mariana Islands in the Central Pacific. Bases on the islands of Guam, Tinian, and Saipan would place B-29s within range of Japan and would be far easier to supply and operate than the base at Ch'eng-tu. Meanwhile, major B-29 operations from China faded by the end of 1944 when the Chinese Army crumbled before a Japanese offensive. Without strong forces on the ground to guarantee the safety of B-29 bases, the AAF had to admit that further heavy bomber operations from China were too risky. Fearful of the big American bombers operating against their homeland, the Japanese overran several American bases in China, and threatened Ch'eng-tu as well. China at this point teetered on the brink of total defeat, despite American air and logistical support. Only Japanese exhaustion and desperate Allied efforts to reinforce the Chinese saved Chiang's regime from collapse.[58]

In any event, Chennault and Chiang looked askance at the vast supply demands of the B-29s, and neither man did anything to persuade the AAF to leave the bombers in China. The "Superfortresses" moved to India in January 1945. By that point, B-29 bases on the Marianas had been in operation for several months.[59]

Thus, when General Arnold made his request for Soviet bases to support American shuttle-bombing efforts in the European theater, he did so with the experience the AAF had gained in constructing and maintaining bases in a remote theater of war. The Americans would not have to fear a collapse of the Red Army that would endanger the safety of air bases on Soviet soil. Unlike China, the Soviet Union was a powerful ally in its own right. By autumn of 1943, Stalin was confident in victory over the Germans whereas Chiang realized that his future would be determined largely by continued American assistance and goodwill. Moscow controlled a first-rate military juggernaut; Chungking could barely ensure its own survival. The relative security of air operations on the Soviet-German front appealed to the AAF. American airmen considered Soviet territory, as it did Chinese, a staging area from which the Army Air Forces could carry out independent operations.

Apart from distracting German fighter defenses in an effort to help the flagging POINTBLANK operation, what did AAF and U.S. political leaders hope to gain from shuttle-bombing operations? The AAF, the Military Mission in Moscow, and the United States Embassy in Moscow had approximately six identifiable objectives for the operation, which varied only in precedence. The Army Air Forces originally viewed the shuttle-bombing operation in the following manner:

1. Strategic bombing on the Eastern Front.
2. Shuttle-bombing on a cross-continental scale.
3. Air support for tactical operations on the Eastern Front.
4. Stimulation of Soviet support for American operations in the Far East.
5. Improvement in Soviet-American communications.
6. Development of Soviet-American relationships generally.[60]

While staging operations from Soviet bases, the AAF planned to strike German targets normally out of range for Britain or Italy-based bombers, such as oil refineries and industrial plants. Such objectives would be selected by the Soviets from a list prepared by American air planners. Strategic operations from the East would be carried out to fulfill both Soviet and POINTBLANK objectives.[61]

In addition to operations mounted from Soviet bases, AAF planners hoped to use Soviet bases to mount shuttle raids, which could extend the range of bomber aircraft by allowing them to land at Soviet airfields, a shorter distance than if they had to return to bases in Britain. Such bombing operations, truly "shuttle raids," would strike targets en route to the USSR. After landing, rearming, and refueling at Soviet bases, the American bombers would return to Britain or Italy, hitting another target on the way.[62]

To make the shuttle operation more attractive to the Soviets, AAF planners envisioned American air units also flying missions in support of the Red Army. In this case, officers of the VVS could request that American aircraft strike targets selected by the Red Air Force. Such missions might typically involve bombing transportation facilities or Axis airfields and troop concentrations.[63]

While Arnold and other AAF leaders viewed shuttle operations as an important addition to the air war against Germany, they also sought other results as well. By impressing the Soviets with the power of strategic bombing, the AAF hoped to gain Soviet support for similar strikes against the Japanese home islands from bases in Siberia. Arnold also reasoned that experience gained through joint Soviet-American operations in Europe would prove valuable when and if Moscow granted the AAF use of Siberian airfields.[64]

In terms of the fifth of the foregoing goals, the AAF believed that the presence of American units on Soviet soil would naturally lead to an expansion in radio and wire communications. The Americans hoped for a greater exchange of weather and intelligence information between the Red Air

Force and the AAF as a result of shuttle operations. The Americans saw this as particularly valuable in that weather data provided by the Soviets would assist USSTAF in planning raids on targets in eastern Europe. Intelligence on the size and composition of the German Air Force on the Eastern Front would also assist the Americans in assessing the true strength of the *Luft-waffe*.[65]

The AAF viewed the strengthening of Soviet-American relations in general as the last of its objectives for shuttle operations. Certainly, American airmen wished to work more closely with the Soviets but only insofar as such collaboration led to the achievement of other goals associated with the shuttle-bombing plan, namely, those previously discussed that would directly affect the air war in both Europe and in the Pacific.[66]

The AAF's priority for accomplishing the aforementioned objectives would change with time so that by mid-summer 1944, USSTAF viewed the establishment of a precedence for the operation of American forces from Soviet soil and the experience of joint Soviet-American operations with an eye toward gaining access to Siberian airfields as the two most important objectives of the shuttle-bombing venture. At the same time, assisting the Soviets fell to last among the AAF's priorities.[67]

Deane's Military Mission, on the other hand, was interested in long range goals from the beginning. This organization viewed the stimulation of Soviet support for Far Eastern operations as the shuttle-bombing scheme's first priority, the improvement in Soviet-American communications as second, and the development of general Soviet-American relationships third. The last three objectives, in the Military Mission's order of priority, were shuttle-bombing, strategic bombing on the Soviet front, and tactical support for the Red Army.[68]

The U.S. Embassy in Moscow viewed the operation in much the same fashion as the Military Mission. Newly installed American Ambassador W. Averell Harriman simply considered the development of Soviet-American relationships in general as the first objective of the shuttle-bombing scheme. The other objectives remained in the same order of priority as that of the Military Mission.[69]

In its efforts to impress the Soviets with strategic bombing, the AAF was disinclined to provide the Soviets with four-engine heavy bombers in mid-1943 as part of Lend-Lease. American leaders, including Secretary of War Henry L. Stimson, preferred that AAF units be brought up to strength before any heavy bombers went to the VVS. The Air Staff also believed that the Soviets, who lacked their own strategic air force (at least by American standards), would "misuse" heavy bombers by employing them in battle-field support roles.[70]

The AAF was not averse to trying to impress the Soviets with a first-hand demonstration of strategic bombardment, something that could be achieved, or so Arnold believed, through shuttle-bombing operations to and from Soviet soil. Once the Red Air Force saw firsthand the effectiveness of America's heavy bombers, the AAF believed, the Kremlin would be more amenable to allowing the United States access to Siberian airfields. The objective of gaining the use of Soviet Far Eastern airfields remained constant throughout the planning and execution of the shuttle-bombing operation and led the AAF to persist in the shuttle scheme long after the operational rationale for doing so had all but disappeared.[71]

Thus, the shuttle-bombing operation, destined to be named FRANTIC, was to achieve a number of objectives. Militarily, the AAF hoped to expose all of German-held Europe to aerial attack and force the dispersal of German fighter defenses prior to the Normandy landings to meet the new American threat from the East. FRANTIC task forces would bomb targets en route to the Soviet Union as well as on the return flight to either Britain or Italy. Additional operations involving American aircraft mounted from Soviet bases could also aid the Red Army directly by striking targets designated by Moscow. Through shuttle-bombing, the Americans also hoped to show the Soviets that, in the absence of a second front, they were fighting the Germans by every means possible. This, in turn, would strengthen Allied relations and perhaps reduce some of Moscow's obvious irritation over the lack of a second front in France.[72]

Because of the varied military and nonmilitary goals of the shuttle-bombing operation, the men and units that would participate in FRANTIC would serve not simply as soldiers and airmen but as "ambassadors" as well. Their behavior could either help or hurt Soviet-American relations and thus, the attainment of diverse objectives far removed from the prosecution of the air war against Germany. All that remained now was to persuade the Soviets of the merits of strategic bombing in general and shuttle-bombing in particular.

The Red Air Force placed little faith in strategic bombing. The Soviets had flirted briefly with Douhet's ideas in the late 1920s. Moscow's central direction of the economy resulted in the rise of a large, if somewhat backward, aircraft industry in the first decade of communist rule. In 1931, state aircraft industries began production of a four-engine bomber, the Tupolev TB-3. This mammoth aircraft had a wingspan of more than 132 feet, a top speed of 179 miles per hour, and a range of nearly 2,000 miles. Armed with six machine guns, the TB-3 could carry up to two and a half tons of bombs. For its time, the TB-3 was quite an achievement of design and engineering. As Soviet doctrine moved toward an emphasis on ground support, or tactical, aviation, interest within the Red Air Force in four-engine bombers waned. Production of the TB-3 ceased at little more than 800 aircraft. Still in service at the time of the German invasion, the TB-3 was by 1941 obsolete as a bomber and performed in the role of air transport until withdrawn from service in 1944.[73]

Furthermore, Soviet experience in combined air-ground operations gained in the Spanish Civil War had convinced Stalin by 1938 of the need for largely tactical air forces. General and theorist Alexander Lapchinskiy concluded that, based on the lessons of the Spanish conflict, strategic bombing would not by itself impair civilian morale. He reasoned further that strategic bombing would only be possible after the enemy's military resistance had been broken because until then all available air units would be required at the front.[74] Thus, unlike many of their counterparts in the United States and Britain, Soviet airmen did not speak longingly of winning wars from the air by destroying an enemy's industrial infrastructure or will to resist.

Stunned by the rapid German victory in France in the summer of 1940, the Soviets recognized the inevitability of war with Hitler's Reich. Stalin attempted to buy time through diplomatic posturing. The Red Army adopted a posture of strategic defense, though, as David Glantz and Jonathan House have written, its operational concepts remained offensive in nature. Suffering from obsolescence and the lingering effects of Stalin's purge of his military leadership, the VVS remained the largest air force in the world with 9,576 aircraft. On the eve of the German onslaught, the basic task of the Red Air Force was to assist the ground forces in combat operations and to ensure control of the air.[75]

The fury of the German assault on June 22, 1941, caught the Red Air Force flatfooted. *Luftwaffe* pilots were delighted to find Soviet airfields packed with aircraft often lined up wing tip to wing tip as if on display. By the end of the first day, the German tally of Soviet aircraft reached more than 1,800, of which 1,489 were destroyed on the ground. By the end of the first week, Soviet losses exceeded 4,000 planes. German losses stood at 150 aircraft. Indoctrinated in the art of the offense, the VVS found itself thrown onto the defensive. Reeling under the blows of the German attack, the Red Air Force abolished its Strategic Long-Range Aviation command temporarily. Even if the Red Air Force had believed in strategic bombardment, it would have been in no position to undertake such operations in the wake of this catastrophe.[76]

In the face of a seemingly unstoppable German invasion, the Soviets threw everything into the struggle to halt the *Wehrmacht* on the ground. As the Red Air Force attempted to regain its balance in the early months of the war, Soviet long-range aviation paradoxically carried out what the Germans referred to as "quasi-strategic" raids against Berlin. In August 1941, with German tanks less than 200 miles from Moscow, a handful of Soviet twin-engine bombers struck the German capital in a series of small night raids that were largely symbolic only of the Soviet Union's determination to resist. Losses among the unescorted Soviet formations were high and damage to Berlin slight. Soviet bombers would not reappear over German cities for years to come as the front receded deep inside the territory of the USSR.[77]

In March 1942, General A. A. Novikov took command of the Red Air Force. His mandate from the High Command was to reorganize the Soviet air arm and make it an instrument for the destruction of the German *Luft-waffe* in the East and for assisting the Red Army in its quest to drive the invaders out of the Soviet Union. One of his innovations was the formation in the spring of 1942 of "air armies." Air armies were assigned to the Soviet equivalents of army groups known as "fronts." The air units operated in conjunction with and at the direction of the front commander, though the High Command could shift air armies across the front as the changing strategic situation required.[78]

The first air armies were typically composed of eight to ten fighter regiments, one bomber regiment, two ground attack regiments, and training and reconnaissance units. The 1st Air Army, formed in May 1942, possessed slightly more than 200 aircraft. By 1943, as Soviet aircraft production and Lend-Lease deliveries acquired momentum, air armies often numbered between 1,500 and 2,000 aircraft. An elaborate command and control network allowed the air armies to provide overwhelming firepower on demand to front commanders.[79]

Novikov also reorganized the Soviet bomber command, forming a new long-range bombardment arm in March 1942. But the great distance from most Soviet airfields to many worthwhile industrial targets in German-occupied Europe precluded sizeable strategic operations throughout much of the war. The new bomber arm flew most of its sorties in direct support of the army and its equipment reflected this. The Soviets' fleet of four-engine bombers was minuscule compared with that of the Anglo-American air forces. Soviet industry produced a successor to the TB-3, the four-engine PE-8, only in very small quantities, the total manufactured numbering fewer than ninety machines. The most numerous Soviet bomber was the twin-engine PE-2, of which more than 11,000 were produced from 1940 to the end of the war. The PE-2 had a range of 746 miles and carried a bomb load of 1,323 pounds. Other twin-engine short- and medium-range bombers rolled off Soviet production lines in large numbers. Given their range and relatively small bomb load, these aircraft were most usefully employed close to the front.[80]

By 1943, the Soviets had gained the upper hand in the air along the Eastern Front. German losses mounted in the face of intense Soviet air operations. The Soviet air armies now greatly outnumbered their foes, and the quality of aircraft at the disposal of Soviet pilots was comparable to that of the Germans. The *Wehrmacht* employed its air units as mobile "fire brigades" on the Eastern Front in a desperate effort to provide firepower to the ground units and compensate for the German Army's losses in tanks and artillery pieces. Unprepared for a multifront war of attrition, the *Luftwaffe* found itself locked in a life-or-death struggle with the Soviet air force at a time when the tempo of Allied air attacks on Germany was accelerating.[81]

In its efforts to help destroy the German *Wehrmacht* on Soviet soil, the Red Air Force was indeed successful. Soviet air doctrine was tailored to the realities of the war on the Eastern Front. Soviet industry did not have the luxury of diverting significant resources away from those instruments designed to save the Soviet Union and then destroy the German Army—the ground forces and tactical air—to wage a strategic bombing campaign against Germany. Like the Red Army, the Soviet air force overwhelmed the enemy *at the front,* chewing up one German unit after another. At the same time, the Soviets pragmatically avoided duplicating the Allied strategic air campaign.

On the other hand, the Germans knew they had little to fear from long-range Soviet aviation in 1943. German military planners dismissed a Soviet strategic threat because of the lack of suitable long-range bombardment aircraft in the VVS, existing Soviet doctrine, and prevailing Soviet tactics. Though the Soviet bomber arm gained in strength and efficiency despite the low priority assigned it by the High Command, it posed little threat to German or German-held targets far behind the battlefront in eastern Europe.[82]

Recognizing the lack of a strategic air threat to Germany from the East, General Arnold wanted to fill this void with shuttle-bombing. The AAF faced a very skeptical ally. The Red Air Force was quite pleased with its efforts at the front, and most Soviet airmen doubted the effectiveness of strategic bombardment. Before shuttle-bombing from the USSR could take place, then, the Americans would have to overcome traditional Soviet mistrust of foreigners as well as the doubts of Stalin's military men that assisting the AAF in strategic bombardment was worth the effort.

Then, late in the afternoon of October 18, 1943, an American C-54 transport plane landed on the runway at an airdrome west of Moscow. Among those aboard the aircraft were the new U.S. ambassador to the Soviet Union, W. Averell Harriman and his daughter Kathleen, Secretary of State Cordell Hull, and Major General John R. Deane, chief of the newly established U.S. Military Mission. With Deane were the men who would head the various divisions of the Military Mission, as well as AAF Brigadier General Hoyt S. Vandenberg, a member of Arnold's staff. The JCS authorized Vandenberg to stay in Moscow for only a few months. Arnold had charged him with selling the idea of strategic bombing to the Soviets.[83]

The first task of the new American delegation was to meet with their British and Soviet counterparts in Moscow to discuss diplomatic and military matters in advance of the "Big Three" conference to be held in Tehran in November. The Moscow Conference opened with a sumptuous luncheon at 1:00 P.M. on October 19. Deane described the luncheon as "a beautiful time," punctuated by repeated toasts of vodka to Churchill, Stalin, and Roosevelt. Even the usually dour Soviet Foreign Minister Vyacheslav Molotov raised his glass in a robust and friendly manner.[84]

Following the meal, the delegates, some a bit tipsy, moved to a conference room where Molotov called the first formal meeting to order. The Soviet contingent, including Vice Commissar of Defense Klimenty Voroshilov and other officers of the Soviet High Command, had one item foremost in their minds—an Anglo-American amphibious landing in France. For the next few hours, the British and American representatives attempted to persuade their Soviet hosts of the Western Allies' determination to aid the Soviets with every means at their disposal. The British military delegate, General Sir Hastings Ismay, joined Deane in outlining Allied prerequisites and plans for a cross-Channel landing. When the Soviets pressed for an exact date of the projected invasion, the Allies could only promise that the landings would take place in the spring of 1944. Deane and Ismay were relieved and gratified when, following the Anglo-American presentations on strategy, the Soviets registered their satisfaction with the intentions of their allies.[85]

Vandenberg now took the floor in an attempt to impress the Soviets with the efficacy of strategic bombing. The general's lecture, complete with slides, dealt with a recent American air raid that had apparently destroyed the Focke-Wulf aircraft factory at Marienburg, Germany. The Soviets seemed favorably moved by Vandenberg's talk, although one Soviet airman was overheard to say that "all altitudes above fifteen feet over the tree tops are wasted."[86]

Taking advantage of the atmosphere of seemingly good feelings and mutual respect, Deane stepped forward to talk specifics. With Harriman's approval, he placed three American proposals before the Soviets: that, to effect shuttle-bombing of targets in German-held eastern Europe, the Soviets provide bases on their soil on which USAAF aircraft could be refueled, repaired, and rearmed; that the U.S. and USSR improve signal communications for a more efficient exchange of weather information; and that the two nations cooperate to improve air transport between them. The Soviet delegation sat silently for several moments. Deane realized immediately, so he later recalled, that his proposals had apparently hit Molotov and his countrymen "as a bolt from the blue." Molotov stated that the Soviets would study the American requests.[87]

Two days later, Molotov informed Deane and Vandenberg that the Soviets had agreed "in principle" to the American proposals. Believing they had scored a great diplomatic triumph just days after their arrival in the USSR, both American generals were elated. Their euphoria evaporated quickly; Deane discovered that Soviet agreement "in principle" meant little. Molotov refused to include Deane's requests in the final communique following the conference's termination. When Vandenberg met with Colonel General A. V. Nikitin, deputy commander of the VVS the following week, he was unable to make any headway concerning the matter of shuttle bases.[88]

Weeks passed with no word from the Soviets on Deane's conference proposals. In Washington, Arnold spoke with President Roosevelt about the stalled negotiations. The AAF commander stressed the importance of shuttle-bombing to defeat Germany and the valuable experience such operations would provide when the day came that American bombers could strike Japan from Siberia. Roosevelt agreed to bring the matter up with Stalin in Tehran.[89]

The Allied conference at Tehran began with informal talks among the "Big Three"—Stalin, Roosevelt, and Churchill—on the evening of November 27, 1943. During the course of the next few days, the Allied leaders and their staffs discussed plans for the defeat of the Axis and the maintenance of peace following the war. Despite the British Prime Minister's persistent and eloquent arguments against a second front in France (he put forward other options in the Aegean and Adriatic seas, for example), the leaders of the anti-Hitler coalition agreed that the long-awaited Anglo-American invasion of northern France would take place in the coming spring. Stalin, in turn, pledged that the Soviet Union would enter the war in the Pacific within months of Germany's collapse.[90]

On November 29, Roosevelt asked Stalin to support the shuttle-bombing plan Deane had put forward at the Moscow Conference. The President took care to mention to the Soviet dictator that Molotov had already agreed "in principle" to the request. Roosevelt handed Stalin a memorandum outlining the shuttle-bombing and weather information exchange proposals together with brief additional memoranda concerning American interest in the use of Soviet bases in the Far East. Harriman recalled later that Roosevelt stressed the importance of getting started on the planning for U.S. air and naval activity in the North Pacific so that operations could begin the instant the Soviets entered the war against Japan. Stalin accepted the memoranda and promised to study the documents. Unfortunately, on December 1, the Soviet leader informed the President that he had not found time to consider the American requests. He assured Roosevelt that he would take up the matter with Harriman following their return to Moscow.[91]

Once again, weeks elapsed before the Soviets reopened the issue of shuttle-bombing. Deane's initial happiness over his assignment to the Soviet Union had long since faded, and the chief of the American Military Mission was convinced that the Soviets purposely stalled and threw up verbal smoke screens to hide their true position and wear down the patience and will of their allies so that Moscow's views could prevail.[92]

Meanwhile, on December 26, nearly a month after Roosevelt raised the issue of shuttle-bombing with Stalin, Harriman finally received some welcome news from Molotov. The American ambassador cabled the president that Molotov had given him a memorandum from Stalin in reply to the Tehran request, approving the shuttle-bombing operation "in principle." Molotov assured Harriman that discussions would begin immediately regarding the coordination of the scheme with other Soviet war plans. More than two months had passed since Deane first broached the issue of using Soviet bases for shuttle-bombing at the Moscow Conference. To the Americans, it appeared that Stalin's assent to the operation had cleared the way for action at long last.[93]

In sum, the ultimate failure of the AAF's prewar doctrine of unescorted, daylight precision raids provided General Arnold with the incentive to renew the quest for bases in the Soviet Union from which his bomber fleets could open a new front in the air against Germany, thereby dispersing and weakening the German *Luftwaffe*. Shuttle operations would also extend the range of American bombers, thereby exposing all of Hitler's empire to aerial attack. In the context of the European war, shuttle-bombing was also a stop-gap measure while the AAF waited for an escort fighter with the range necessary to escort the bombers all the way to their targets and back. Only when such aircraft were available, would the losses sustained on raids over German-occupied Europe fall to acceptable levels.

Shuttle-bombing would also serve, so the Americans hoped, to draw the United States and USSR closer together, demonstrate Allied solidarity to the world, and lay the foundation for greater joint endeavors in the Far East. Collaboration with the Soviets via the use of air forces was not a new idea, and experience in China showed the AAF that it was possible to mount and support aerial operations from even the most remote and undeveloped areas.

Thus, from its inception, American shuttle-bombing to the USSR sought to fulfill diplomatic and political objectives as well as military ones. The men and units dispatched eastward would carry the weight of varied goals and expectations with them. A great experiment in direct Soviet-American military cooperation was about to begin.

AMERICA COMES TO THE UKRAINE

February–May 1944

The Americans would learn quickly that Soviet dictator Joseph Stalin's "assent" to the use of Soviet bases for shuttle raids was not the end of the negotiating process but merely the beginning. January 1944 passed with virtually no movement on any matter related to the shuttle-bombing scheme. Growing impatient, USAAF commanding general Henry H. Arnold forwarded a message to Major General John Deane in Moscow from Lieutenant General Carl A. Spaatz, which stated that the use of Soviet bases would significantly increase strategic bombing capabilities and that the Americans had an immediate need for landing facilities in the Soviet Union for photo reconnaissance aircraft. Deane forwarded this message to Major General N. V. Slavin, assistant chief of staff of the Red Army. This not so subtle maneuver must have worked; three days later, on February 2, Stalin summoned Harriman to the Kremlin for a formal meeting on the issue.[1]

That evening, at six o'clock, Harriman met the Soviet dictator in the Kremlin. Harriman opened the meeting by stating that he had wanted the appointment with Marshal Stalin to discuss the military proposals made by Roosevelt at Tehran, particularly with reference to shuttle-bombing. Stalin proceeded to ask Harriman about the number of aircraft involved in the proposed operation, fuel supplies, national composition of ground staffs, and the type of fields required for four-engine heavy bombers. Stalin expressed his confidence that the operation would cause the Germans great discomfort, then added bluntly, "We favor it." He agreed with the ambassador that the details could be settled in subsequent discussions between General Deane and representatives of the Red Army.[2]

With Stalin's unmistakable backing now out in the open, the Americans felt confident that negotiations with their Soviet counterparts could move forward quickly. Indeed, on February 6, USSTAF appointed Colonel John S. Griffith the commanding officer for the shuttle-bombing project, now dubbed BASEBALL. The Americans forged ahead with a succession of conferences and meetings in Britain aimed at setting personnel and material requirements for an operation that envisaged the use of 200 bombers per mission, four missions per month, together with sixty photo reconnaissance sorties a month by F-5s, a variant of the twin-engine P-38 fighter. By the 16th, an American staff under Colonel Griffith produced a completed plans book for BASEBALL.[3]

Even at this early date, American staff officers realized the broader potential of BASEBALL beyond its contribution to the Combined Bomber Offensive. A memo from two staff officers, one of whom, Major Albert Lepawsky, was destined to play a significant part in the future of the operation, emphasized the fact that the shuttle operation was not simply a military undertaking but had the potential to achieve broader political and diplomatic goals as well. Playing on the code-name of the operation, the memo stated that "the main objective of BASEBALL itself is to prove to the other Ballteam how well we plan and play the game, so as to convince them to let us to use their other Ball-fields. Whether they let us use their Ball-fields or not, we are going to be playing somewhere in the League, and we must profit from both our lessons and failures. . . . The other Ball Team is a unique Ally with a state of mind and system of politics few of us understand."[4] The obvious references to gaining access to Siberian airfields ("other Ball-fields") made it clear that BASEBALL was simply part of a larger policy of cooperation with the Soviets and not an end in itself.

The Americans wanted the shuttle operations in full swing prior to the impending Anglo-American landings in France to draw *Luftwaffe* fighter units away from Normandy. Thus, by early February, a distinct sense of urgency gripped those individuals charged with the planning and negotiating associated with the operation. The Americans and Soviets had to agree on sites for bases, personnel, supply, communications, and the target selection process.

The Americans, then, had to move quickly to establish their own chain of command and designate responsible officers to carry on negotiations with Moscow. Chief of Staff General George C. Marshall informed Spaatz and Deane on the 19th of February that all negotiations with the Soviets that pertained to the shuttle-bombing scheme would be conducted through the chief of the Military Mission in Moscow, Major General Deane. Deane would exercise administrative control over those elements of the U.S. strategic air forces while in the Soviet Union through an operational commanding officer, designated by Spaatz. Lieutenant General Spaatz, as commanding general, USSTAF, would direct operations, subject only to restrictions imposed by the Soviets. The Military Mission would also handle any operation requested by the Soviets by simply referring it, once again, to Spaatz.[5]

To carry out the "nuts and bolts" of preparing for the operation, the First Echelon of personnel destined for the Soviet Union departed London on February 17. This small group comprised three colonels and the crew of the B-17 that transported them to Moscow. Colonels Alfred A. Kessler and Paul T. Cullen accompanied the project's commanding officer, Colonel Griffith. All three were experienced officers, selected by General Arnold himself. Kessler had accompanied Donald M. Nelson, chairman of the War Production Board, on a three-week tour of Soviet Russia in 1943. Kessler was impressed by the Soviets and Arnold thought it wise to have an officer sympathetic to their new hosts. Cullen, an aerial reconnaissance expert, was commanding officer of the Seventh Photographic Group in Great Britain. His job was to coordinate reconnaissance efforts with the Soviets, a vital part of any air operation. Unfortunately, Kessler, who was charged with handling operational matters relating to FRANTIC, remained in Cairo for ten days because of a bout of bronchial pneumonia. Cullen and Griffith arrived in Moscow on February 25.[6]

Together with Deane, two other officers of the Military Mission, and an interpreter, Griffith and Cullen had their first meeting on February 28 with representatives of the Red Air Force. Following the introductions and other pleasantries, Griffith informed the Soviets that the B-17 in which they arrived was the same type of aircraft the Americans expected to deploy in the Soviet Union. He invited the Soviets to look over the plane, including its Norden bombsight. The ranking Soviet representative, Red Air Force Deputy Commander Colonel General A. V. Nikitin, promised to try to avoid as much "red tape" as possible in coordinating the arrangements for the shuttle operation but also warned that the Foreign Liaison Office (OVS) of his air force could not be bypassed. With that, Deane presented the first question relating directly to the operation: the location of airfields.[7]

Deane stated that the Americans preferred fields located centrally on the front so that aircraft could reach them from either Britain or Italy. The Soviets proposed fields at Poltava and Kharkov in the Ukraine, with Kursk as a possible alternate. The Americans expressed concern that these fields might be too far to the east and might lack the requisite facilities, including runways capable of handling both the weight and takeoff requirements of a fully loaded B-17 bomber. The conferees left the matter open pending inspection tours of the proposed sites by Soviet and American officers.[8]

The participants then moved to matters relating to personnel, supply, and communications. Deane indicated that nearly two dozen selected staff officers, vital to setting up the U.S. command in the Soviet Union, were ready to depart Britain as soon as the Soviets approved their visas, a matter that also still needed to be resolved by the Soviet Foreign Ministry. In answer to Nikitin's query about the overall number of personnel the Americans wanted to bring in, Griffith estimated that approximately 2,000 "bodies" would be required to support flying operations. While some historians and Air Force officers later claimed that the Soviets unnecessarily restricted the number of Americans allowed into the country, one should note that at this meeting, it was Griffith who expressed a desire to keep U.S. personnel to a minimum and to utilize as many Soviet troops as possible.[9] The remainder of the meeting dwelt on the mundane issues of supply, routes of delivery for equipment, ordnance and fuel requirements, and communication facilities.

Though the officers participating in this discussion had left much unresolved, they had come to some initial understandings and agreements that would serve as a foundation for all subsequent planning and negotiating. The atmosphere of the meeting was cordial, and the two sides displayed a willingness to work together as efficiently as possible. Though the Americans would soon learn that their Soviet counterparts often lacked the authority to agree to changes in plans while sitting at the conference table, they also came to realize that this was not deliberate obstruction but rather a feature of the highly centralized decision-making process of the Soviet military and government in Moscow.[10]

After his recovery from pneumonia, Kessler left Cairo on the first of March and arrived in Moscow, after a stopover at Stalingrad, on the sixth. He was dismayed to discover that his colleagues had conferred only once with the Soviets, but found himself two days later on a Soviet DC-3 bound for the proposed air base sites at Kharkov and Kiev. Brigadier General William C. Crist, Deane's chief of staff, accompanied Kessler, together with Cullen and other representatives of the Military Mission. Kessler was not happy with what he found. The Soviets had recovered the region just the previous fall, and the Germans had carried out an extensive "scorched earth" policy, which, combined with battle damage, had reduced the airfield facilities at both Kharkov and Poltava to ruins. The runways were too short and housing, messing, and maintenance facilities were practically nonexistent. Kessler recommended that the Military Mission secure sites farther west in the Kiev area. He also believed building the airdromes completely from scratch would be more efficient than utilizing the meager facilities available at Kharkov and Poltava.[11]

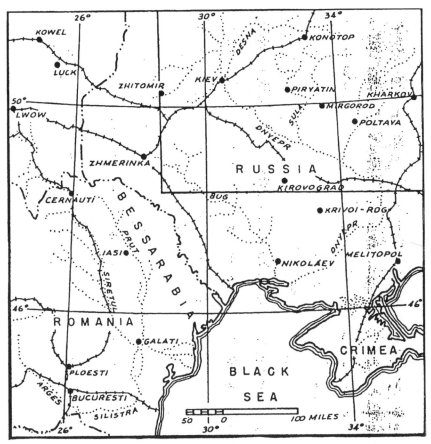

Map. Ukraine and Southeastern Europe. This AAF map was included in the planning documents for FRANTIC and shows the locations of Poltava, Mirgorod, and Piryatin relative to the rest of the area. *Courtesy U.S. Air Force.*

In a separate memo to Deane, Griffith, following a brief tour of the region conducted by the Soviets, recommended the use of two, possibly three, sites in the area of Kiev that were either already in use or could be more readily repaired than Poltava or Kharkov. These sites should have space for the construction of one 6,000-foot and two 4,500-foot runways with parking space for at least sixty bombers. Other factors Griffith deemed desirable were adequate power and water sources, access to rail facilities and hard-surface roads, and telegraph, telephone, and teletype lines. He wrote that such housing as was available would be used, but that the Americans could make do with tent camps during the summer months and that permanent housing facilities need not be considered a factor in the selection of the sites. Having said all of this, Griffith then hedged by concluding that the foregoing "outline is basic and need not be adhered to strictly as the maximum amount of improvisation and adaptation is considered essential." He probably did not realize how prophetic his last statement was.[12]

In light of these conclusions, Deane continued to press the Soviets for airfields farther west than Poltava, even if it meant entirely new construction. The Soviets, though sympathetic to American concerns, replied that all the airfields west of the Dnieper River were already congested because of the Red Army's continuing operations against German Army Group South in the western Ukraine. In a meeting with Deane on March 16, Nikitin finally proposed three bases in the area of the Ukraine between Kharkov and Kiev. He suggested Poltava as the main base, Mirgorod, fifty miles to the west of Poltava, as a second base, and Piryatin, another fifty miles farther westward as the third airdrome. All three bases were on the Kiev-Kharkov railroad and were located in an area that had only been liberated from German occupation the previous September.[13]

While these bases were hardly ideal from the American viewpoint, Nikitin agreed to provide one engineer battalion to perform the necessary preparation and construction under the supervision of American engineers. He also agreed to provide a specialist battalion of five hundred men (and women) for each airfield to carry out housekeeping, guard, and other miscellaneous duties. Armed with that information, Griffith opened preliminary discussions with the Soviets regarding American personnel levels. Still, the Americans wanted to see the prospective airdromes firsthand and did not commit themselves to final acceptance at the meeting of the 16th.[14]

Claiming that the weather was unsuitable for flying, the Soviets did not grant the Americans clearance to visit the three sites until the 31st of March. While many of the Americans commented acidly about the seemingly slow response to their request for this trip and believed weather was not a factor in the delay, the Soviets can be excused for being preoccupied with other matters at this point in the war. The Red Army had been on the offensive since breaking the Germans' third summer offensive, Operation CITADEL, the previous July. Crossing the Dnieper in autumn of 1943, the Soviets continued large-scale offensive operations throughout the early months of 1944 in an effort to expel Hitler's forces from the western Ukraine before spring thaws rendered further operations impossible. Thus, the Red Air Force and its commanders at virtually every level were understandably concerned first and foremost with providing the Red Army with maximum close air support.[15]

Nevertheless, on March 31, Colonels Griffith and Kessler headed a small American team tasked with inspecting the proposed airdromes. They were accompanied by a group of Soviet officers led by Major General Alexei Perminov, who was, as of the 29th, the Soviet project commander. He was destined to become a familiar and respected figure among the American officers serving in the Ukraine.[16]

The inspection trip simply reinforced previous American assessments of Poltava and other fields in the area. The DC-3 in which the party of officers was flying could not land at Piryatin because of the muddy condition of the sod field. They did manage to land at both Poltava and Mirgorod, each of which had concrete block runways, but found little to inspect when disembarking from the aircraft. Both fields lacked runways of the requisite length for B-17s, and neither had even the most basic facilities to support American flying operations. As Kessler predicted earlier, the airdromes were in such disrepair that they would have to be rebuilt virtually from the ground up. On the positive side, however, the flat terrain in which all the fields were situated would permit the construction of new runways. For this, the Americans were already preparing estimates as to how much pierced-steel matting would be required.[17]

Though deprived of what they might have considered "ideal" bases, the Americans knew that they were running out of time if the operation was to start prior to OVERLORD. By the first week in April, the Military Mission accepted Poltava, Mirgorod, and Piryatin. The shuttle-bombing operation, officially renamed FRANTIC in early March of 1944, had a firm footing. As Griffith pointed out to the Soviets in a meeting on March 28, no other important decisions could be reached without agreement on the bases. Now that the agreement had been reached, preparations for FRANTIC could proceed in earnest.[18]

The next major task facing the Americans was the movement of required personnel into the Soviet Union. Throughout March, personnel officers of the Eighth Air Force searched through their units for qualified individuals for FRANTIC. As noted earlier, Griffith initially estimated the required personnel strength for FRANTIC at more than 2,000. At a conference on March 18, the Soviets informed Griffith that they would provide a total of 882 aircraft maintenance technicians in addition to an aviation battalion of 472 men for housekeeping duties at each base and two engineer battalions of 339 men each for airdrome construction and maintenance. In light of these offers, the Soviets viewed American plans for more than 2,000 AAF personnel as excessive. By the end of March, the U.S. negotiators reduced their manning requirements to a minimum of 1,200. The Soviets accepted this number and, as they were to show in every other facet of the operation, once they believed they had reached an agreement, they stuck to it.[19]

Meanwhile, FRANTIC project officers were having mixed results in the selection process of men who would then move to the Soviet Union in numbered personnel "echelons." Officers chose equipment specialists and other experienced support troops. Medical personnel were chosen by specialty. Naturally, men who possessed Russian language abilities were considered as well. First Lieutenant George Fischer, himself a Soviet émigré, interviewed more than 300 Russian-speakers in Britain in late April and early May in an attempt to find a few dozen qualified interpreters. Twenty-two were selected largely for their ability to communicate in maintenance terminology or operational matters. The majority of all those destined for the Ukraine came from active Eighth Air Force units in Great Britain. The remainder were drawn from various maintenance and replacement depots, while a handful of personnel came from the Ninth Air Force. Fifteenth Air Force would send technicians and other ground personnel on a temporary basis to provide support for the large numbers of P-38s and P-51s dispatched for FRANTIC III and IV later in the summer.[20]

Because of the hurried nature of the deployments, inspectors reported that they found personnel engaged in the project to be in a "rushed and confused" state, while both the men and the processing centers at which they were arriving lacked proper equipment and clothing. Officers charged with screening those sent by their units complained that personnel records were incomplete, many of the men were physically unfit, or were simply unqualified for the specialty for which they had been chosen. Personnel officers rejected those who possessed only a few months' experience or who lacked adequate training. There were several instances of officers sending unqualified technicians simply to get rid of them. Many of the enlisted men who were rejected for FRANTIC suffered from, among other things, venereal disease, hernias, and bad teeth, while others arrived filthy and lacking proper clothing. Screening physicians diagnosed one technician as a Section VIII (mentally unfit for service) case who was transferred to the Detachment of Patients.[21]

Inspectors concluded that men sent directly from active Eighth Air Force units were chosen with care and were far superior to those sent from replacement units, where many had been on "casual status" or, despite their rank as senior noncommissioned officers, pulled "KP" for months at a time. Those who reported for deployment also complained that they had received very little warning or notice and had as little as half an hour to get packed before departing for assembly areas for the trip to the Soviet Union. Despite such problems and complaints, 153 officers and 1,068 enlisted men had been screened and selected for FRANTIC by April 8. These men possessed anywhere from one month to three years' experience with active AAF units. Screening officers grudgingly accepted those with the least amount only as a last resort; consequently, Eastern Command's ground echelons were composed largely of seasoned airmen.[22]

Regardless of their individual combat experience, very few of the Eighth Air Force personnel selected for FRANTIC had yet endured the kind of primitive and even dangerous conditions that awaited them in the Ukraine. As we shall see, both air and ground crews had grown accustomed to the relative safety, security, and comfort of Great Britain. Though the *Luftwaffe* continued to mount nuisance raids on Anglo-American airfields in the United Kingdom, many of those in the FRANTIC contingents had not been through a major enemy air attack. The handful of ground personnel and those aircrews from Fifteenth Air Force, on the other hand, had endured harsh living conditions in both North Africa and war-ravaged southern Italy. Indeed, FRANTIC-bound personnel were not yet fully informed of their destination. Thus, few of the Americans heading for Eastern Command would know fully what to expect on their arrival in the Ukraine.

The most serious personnel problem the Americans faced, however, was one that would remain entirely outside their control throughout the operation. The Soviets were particularly sensitive to the movement of foreigners across their borders. Deane pointed out that "Russian acceptance of us as partners in this project is in complete reversal [*sic*] of a traditional resistance to foreigners that is as old as is Russia itself."[23] Thus, he was not surprised that the Soviet government, regardless of its commitments to FRANTIC, wanted to maintain strict control of entry and exit procedures for personnel of the American ground and air units.

On March 22, Deane reported to Spaatz that officials in Moscow had agreed to allow U.S. ground staff into the Soviet Union without individual visas. Indeed, the Second Echelon arrived under a group visa. A week later, Kessler, who found the pace of the preparations thus far agonizingly slow, wrote in his diary that the matter of passports and visas for personnel finally had been cleared up. Headquarters, Persian Gulf Command, would certify ground staff in Tehran as necessary to FRANTIC and then submit a list of those in each echelon to the Soviet Embassy for approval and entry on a group visa. They would simultaneously radio the same information to Deane who, in turn, would transmit that information to the Soviet Foreign Office in Moscow. On arrival at the bases, the Soviet commander would use

the same personnel roster and two passport photos to prepare Soviet identification cards for each individual.[24]

Obviously, combat crews could not go through this process. After landing, the aircraft commander would submit a list of all crew members aboard
his plane to a representative of the U.S. base commander, who would then
pass it to the Soviet commander. During departure for Britain or Italy, the
crew would follow the same procedure. Most American officers who were
familiar with Soviet procedures were quick to point out to their superiors
that the use of group visas was without precedent and that they should
be pleased with this apparent breakthrough. The road to Poltava now appeared open. Unfortunately, this was not quite the case.[25]

With the location of the bases and the movement of personnel apparently resolved, what would those Americans selected for FRANTIC find when
they arrived in the Ukraine? The Soviets had begun renovating the three
bases even before the Americans had agreed to use them. Ten American
officers were to leave Moscow for Poltava on April 14 to serve as the cadre
for the newly created Eastern Command. Unfortunately, the Soviet C-47
that was to transport them and their baggage was already so overloaded
that only six of the officers could make the flight. Kessler and the other four
officers left the next day.[26]

In the meantime, Colonel Alfred Kessler assumed command of Eastern
Command on April 10, replacing Colonel Griffith. Griffith had grown increasingly irritated by Soviet delays and began to openly manifest his lack
of patience through his behavior and attitude toward his hosts. Deane also
apparently found Griffith's disposition too openly anti-Soviet, and believed
his participation with the British anti-Bolshevik expeditionary force in
1918 and 1919 might offend Soviets sensibilities. Spaatz reluctantly agreed;
Griffith left Moscow for Tehran on the 11th.[27]

Kessler, on the other hand, was a homely, genial officer with a fine combat record in the Eighth Air Force whom the Soviets quickly, though affec-
tionately, dubbed "Uncle Ugly." As commander of the 95th Bombardment
Group in the fall of 1942, a unit destined to partake in FRANTIC, Kessler
prepared that outfit for deployment to Britain and its first taste of war. His tact
and patience ensured the smoothest possible relations between the Soviets
and Americans during the two crucial months following his assumption of
command. Only the best teamwork possible could guarantee that the bases
would be ready to receive combat missions before D-day in the West.[28]

Kessler and his staff found that the Soviets had done much to improve Poltava since the inspection visit several weeks earlier, but conditions
were still primitive. His Soviet counterpart, Major General Perminov, had

already established his headquarters at the base. A keen, straightforward flyer, he routinely used his authority to cut red tape and settle on the spot the myriad problems that arose each day. He immediately concerned himself with seeing to the needs of his newly arrived and somewhat bewildered guests. The Americans also believed that the appointment of such a senior Soviet officer to the project reflected Moscow's commitment to FRANTIC. Kessler and his staff officers informed Deane that they felt uncomfortable, as colonels and majors, dealing with Soviet general officers. They suggested that USSTAF send an American general to Eastern Command as soon as possible.[29]

Poltava was the joint Soviet and American headquarters from the outset. Kessler designated the base Army Air Force Station 559. Though no Americans were deployed at the other two bases, he designated Mirgorod AAF Station 561 and Piryatin AAF Station 560. Both Poltava and Mirgorod would serve as bomber bases while any escorting fighters would use Piryatin, the westernmost of the three bases.[30]

The Soviets set up the 169th *Aviatsionyu Bazu Osobogo Naznacheniya* (ABON or Air Base Special Task Force). In addition to the construction and support personnel mentioned earlier, this Task Force assumed the responsibility of defending the American air bases. Perminov controlled a number of 85-mm and 37-mm searchlight-equipped antiaircraft batteries. To challenge any German raiders in the air the Soviets brought in fighters, primarily Yak-9s, of the 210 Fighter Interceptor Division. The Americans wanted to use pre-established air corridors through Soviet front-line air defenses, an idea the Soviets disliked intensely. Soviet intelligence reports stated that the Germans possessed a number of captured B-17s and B-24s and that they might learn the location of these corridors and use them to penetrate Soviet defenses. The Germans had, in fact, captured a handful of American bombers by early 1944, but there was no evidence to support Soviet fears that the *Luftwaffe* was using these to penetrate allied air defenses. The Soviets did admit that the state of their communications network was such that they needed at least twenty-four hours' notice for authorities in Moscow to clear flight plans and notify the front line troops and air defense units. Fearing that their operations would be hampered by lengthy notification times, the Americans were not happy with this arrangement, and they stubbornly persisted in debating the issue until after the first mission had taken place.[31]

Despite Soviet efforts to improve them throughout March and early April, Poltava and the other bases were in sad shape for Kessler's arrival. On his earlier inspection tour at the end of March, Kessler estimated that the

The only usable substantial structure at Poltava, the "U-shaped" building. Eastern Command offices were located on one wing of the building. A handful of American B-17s can be seen on the airfield in the background. *Courtesy U.S. Air Force.*

city of Poltava, which had a prewar population of 130,000, was 95 percent destroyed. Heavy fighting had occurred all around the city before it was finally liberated by the Soviets on September 22, 1943. Before retreating, the Germans attempted to destroy everything of value that they could not take with them. Judging from Kessler's observations, they were successful; he reported that not a single structure larger than a small single-story dwelling was left intact.[32]

The air base at Poltava was in similar shape; a prewar installation of the regular VVS, it once boasted many large buildings and hangars. In mid-April 1944 the only structure remaining was a partially demolished six-story building constructed in the shape of a "U" that stood at the south end of the existing north-south runway. The Soviets had managed to restore electrical power to part of the structure, but sewage and sanitation systems, rather primitive to begin with, were now virtually nonexistent as a result of battle damage.[33]

As a stopgap measure, the Soviets offered Kessler the use of several rail coaches, including three sleepers and a dining car, which could be parked on the railroad siding at Poltava and used as the American headquarters. Though a "final" agreement on this arrangement was reached on April 11, Kessler informed Perminov at the time of his arrival at Poltava on the 15th that these railcars were no longer necessary inasmuch as he and his staff could be billeted in the large "U"-shaped building. Nevertheless, the rail-cars showed up nearly three weeks late on May 4, a rather embarrassed Perminov explaining that it just was not as easy to cancel or countermand an order in the Soviet military as it apparently was in the American.[34]

The Soviets had cleaned out and redecorated one entire wing of the building. They had already provided approximately 100 beds with straw ticks, sheets, and blankets. Though only two rooms had electricity, Kessler seemed satisfied with the efforts the Soviets were making to establish habitable quarters for the Americans. The medical staff was not at all happy with the conditions they found at Poltava. Captain Robert H. Newell of the Medical Corps rated the general environmental sanitation as "very unsatisfactory." Latrine facilities were "malodorous," bathing facilities "unsanitary, inadequate, and primitive," and the water supply suspect. He described the living quarters as cold and damp, and infested with rodents and other vermin. Most of the windows lacked glass and the bed space was insufficient, in his opinion, for the proper housing of those present. Indeed, Newell recommended that the building be completely demolished, because it, together with unfilled trenches and shell holes, were breeding grounds for rodents and insects.[35]

Nevertheless, while the Soviets continued to prepare the airdrome for operations, Kessler pressed forward with his own plans. By April 17, his staff had selected camp sites for both permanent and transient personnel, designated fuel and bomb storage areas, and aircraft parking areas. The headquarters section and officers' quarters would remain in the large U-shaped building. A destroyed hangar that the Soviets had cleaned up would serve as the base supply and repair depot. To airmen who were accustomed to the relative comfort of Eighth Air Force bases in Britain, their new surroundings hardly looked inviting. It was a start, and thus far the Soviets and the small contingent of Americans were working together in a friendly and cooperative atmosphere.[36]

On April 20, Kessler and eight of his officers accompanied Perminov and his staff on an inspection of Piryatin. The field still had no facilities whatsoever except revetments and campsites near the field that Kessler considered unsatisfactory because of their distance from the proposed aircraft parking and maintenance areas. The transient campsite, for example, was located in an uncleared wooded area more than a kilometer from the field. Permanent personnel were to be housed and fed in a rebuilt girls school on the edge of the town of Piryatin, some 12 kilometers away. That facility did have electricity, water, and a working sewage system. The base headquarters, hospital, and all supplies except rations would be located on the airdrome. Ration storage would remain at the girls school. Still, given the dearth of facilities at the site, Kessler accepted this layout. The Soviets had also laid out a 2-kilometer runway, but Eastern Command's engineers had yet to approve its location.[37]

Of the three bases, Piryatin was certainly the "barest" of them all. The town of Piryatin itself was more than 7 miles from the field. Its prewar population of 10,000 had virtually disappeared, and the Germans had carried out the same kind of methodical destruction prior to their withdrawal as they had at Poltava. The town did contain a Soviet army headquarters, military hospital, and civilian medical dispensary. Otherwise, there was very little that would be of interest to American troops. This remoteness would lead to incessant problems in maintaining the morale of American troops at Piryatin once FRANTIC operations began.[38]

The following day, April 21, the group of Americans left Piryatin for Mirgorod, a fifty-five minute flight in a Soviet C-47. On arrival at Mirgorod, Kessler and his staff found the Soviets at work renovating an old field artillery school for use as a headquarters and barracks for the Americans. Located in the town of Mirgorod itself some 2 kilometers from the field, the school had potable running water, electricity, and a working sewage system. Kessler surmised that the Soviets had built an excellent barracks with both storehouses and messing facilities. The visiting group selected a tentative long runway that, as at Piryatin, would have to be approved by engineering officers following a complete survey.[39]

The area around the base was rolling steppe country, which offered little protection from the searching, Siberian winds and the scorching summer sun. Retaken from the Germans in late September 1943, Mirgorod was also largely destroyed by the fighting and German demolition squads. The roads here and throughout the region in which the bases were located were unpaved, dusty in dry weather and sticky quagmires following even a moderate summer shower. The roads concerned the medical officers most. After seeing the condition of the roads, Eastern Command's command surgeon, Lieutenant Colonel William M. Jackson, ordered the hospital site moved to the airdrome. He realized that the medical facility would be in jeopardy in the event of a raid, but believed that the roads were too rough to permit the comfortable, convenient, and efficient evacuation of casualties.[40]

Indeed, the Americans were extremely concerned about the availability of medical care for their sick and wounded in the Soviet Union. As early as March, American medical officers reported that, based on firsthand observations, the practice of medicine in many respects was fifty years behind the time. "This is in refutation of some American physicians," the medical officers reported, "who claim Soviet medicine is one of the most advanced in the world." They credited the Soviet system with providing far more medical care now than under the Czarist regime but that it remained inferior to the medical care of most other countries. American physicians cited examples of antiquated equipment, outdated treatments, severe shortages of basic medicines, and training that fell far short of Western standards as the basis of their conclusions.[41]

Given such negative impressions of the state of Soviet medicine, the American medical staff in the Soviet Union, headed by Lieutenant Colonel Jackson, was understandably anxious to avoid any reliance on the Red Army for the care of Army Air Forces personnel attached to Eastern Command. Perceiving these misgivings in their American counterparts, the Soviets agreed with Jackson and Deane that for the purposes of morale and to avoid recriminations it would be best to have the Americans assume complete responsibility for the care of their own sick and wounded.[42]

As a result of these agreements, the Americans planned for standard field hospitals at each of the three fields, though the number of American personnel was reduced because the Soviets agreed to provide help in terms of general housekeeping and maintenance. Each base would have a station surgeon in the rank of major, two to three other surgeons, a dentist, and several female nurses. Jackson, his executive officer, the chiefs of the medical and dental service for Eastern Command, a veterinarian, and the principle chief nurse were also at Poltava. Relations between the medical staffs of the two nations were warm and cordial from the beginning of the operation and would generally remain so until the very end.[43]

Kessler and his staff returned to Poltava from their inspection tour on April 22. Insofar as the work at the bases was concerned, Kessler had every reason to be pleased with the progress made by the last week in April. Still, Army Air Force leaders were growing visibly apprehensive over the apparent lack of progress toward the establishment of fully operational installations in Soviet Russia. Deane was moved to report to Spaatz and Arnold that he could not "emphasize too strongly what a good job Kessler and his staff are doing. They are living under the most difficult conditions in an area that has been completely devastated by the Germans." Given the diplomatic and political aspects of FRANTIC, Deane thought it important to report that "the whole atmosphere of the place between the Russians and Americans on the ground is one of extreme friendliness and cooperation." He reminded the Air Force generals that the "Russians have very definite ideas as to how things should be done" and any delays were not because Kessler or his men lacked initiative but that "things progress on in the tempo that they [the Soviets] set." Though a great deal of work remained to be done before the first mission could take place, by late April Eastern Command was ready to begin receiving the supplies and personnel that would get FRANTIC off the ground.[44]

Even before the bases for Eastern Command were selected, the Soviet and American staffs opened negotiations over the type of and manner in which supplies were to be brought into the Soviet Union for use in FRANTIC. The Soviets agreed to receive five cargo ships laden with heavy cargo—steel matting for airfields, high octane gasoline, and vehicles—at the port of Archangel on the Arctic coast. The ships set sail from Britain on March 20 and arrived after an uneventful voyage on April 5, though ice in the harbor entrance at Archangel forced the Soviets to send the ships to Murmansk for unloading.[45]

The Americans were not particularly happy about this route, however, because of the continuing threat of German air or submarine attacks on Murmansk-bound convoys. The Soviets somewhat reluctantly agreed to allow material and personnel destined for Eastern Command to come via the southern route through Iran that had been established previously for Lend-Lease shipments. The Soviets were understandably concerned about an interruption of the flow of Lend-Lease. Deane assured them that shipments to Eastern Command would not slow the movement of other supplies, and both sides agreed on March 28 that the U.S. Persian Gulf Command would assume responsibility for keeping Eastern Command supplied once USSTAF furnished an initial sixty-day stockpile.[46]

The U.S. Army Air Forces were responsible for virtually all the supplies and material used in FRANTIC. Steel matting, essential for constructing the runways at the three bases, high octane gasoline, special purpose vehicles, most rations, and all housekeeping supplies would come from American sources. If the Americans had to resort to Soviet stockpiles for such materials for whatever reason, they promised to replenish them from Lend-Lease shipments. The Soviets agreed to provide some vehicles, fresh meat, fruits and vegetables, bedding, and, of course, housing. They also provided 250-kilogram bombs as well as machine gun ammunition for the bombers' defensive armament. The Soviets agreed to unload all shipments at the point of entry and move them by rail or truck convoy to Eastern Command bases.[47]

To expedite construction at the bases, the Americans gave the Soviets a priority in which their dockworkers were to unload the ship-borne equipment, with 50 percent of the steel matting being first. To Deane's and Kessler's embarrassment, the steel mats had been loaded first and therefore, would be the last items taken off the ship. Nevertheless, by April 23, the Soviets off-loaded all the cargo, more than 26,000 tons, and had already begun moving the first trainloads southward from Murmansk on the 18th. The first train reached Poltava on April 28 and Soviet soldiers, including large numbers of women, began laying the steel matting on May 1. By May 12, 445 carloads out of a total of 2,100 had reached the bases. When the first U.S. bombers landed on June 2, only 75 percent of the supplies had arrived, but the hard work of the Soviet troops, together with excellent planning and coordination between Eastern Command and Perminov's staff, ensured that enough had gotten through to guarantee the success of that inaugural mission. What made this accomplishment all the more remarkable was the fact that the Soviets managed to move these trains through a rail network already strained by the massive buildup of 166 Soviet divisions opposite German Army Group Center in Belorussia prior to the start of their great summer offensive code-named BAGRATION.[48]

In the meantime, Eastern Command's engineers determined that all three fields required steel mat runways. Throughout April, Soviet construction troops rolled the grassy fields in preparation for the arrival of the steel matting. When this material eventually reached the bases, it actually caused quite a stir among the personnel of both sides. As the Soviet soldiers started placing it on the proposed runways that first day of May, Kessler wrote that, "It was quite an event, with all the Soviet rank present. They were very enthusiastic and we had some trouble getting started in teaching their men because the officers wanted to 'play' with it."[49]

The Americans on hand were greatly impressed by the fact that the Soviets transported the equipment all the way from Murmansk in such a relatively short period of time. What struck them even more, was that much of the work in laying the matting was done by women soldiers of the Red Army. The Americans were somewhat taken aback by the use of women in heavy labor and were very pleased with their stamina and dedication to the task at hand. Nevertheless, the comments and observations of many American officers betrayed traditional American attitudes and biases toward women in this role. The Mediterranean Allied Air Forces' (MAAF) offi-

Soviet female soldiers unload pierced-steel runway
matting. American personnel marveled at the strength
and stamina of these women. *Courtesy U.S. Air Force.*

cial wartime record of FRANTIC commented that when these Soviet women
heard that U.S. engineers, typically all males, laid ten yards of matting per
man per day, "these great, brawny, exuberant wenches went out and laid
[twelve]." Indeed, every American at Eastern Command knew that without the efforts of these women, FRANTIC would have been delayed possibly
until after the start of OVERLORD.[50]

The Americans expressed great, albeit somewhat condescending, admiration for the common Soviet soldier working at the bases. Kessler noted
that the "Russian after proper instruction, becomes very adept and metricu-
lous [*sic*] in erecting tents." He was pleased with the pace at which the Soviet troops set up the camp's facilities but remarked that the latrines and

washrooms being constructed by "Mongol troops invalided [*sic*] from the front" were "too elaborate and permanent but there is no use in trying to stop them, it will do no good and will only end up in delay." The MAAF history noted, however, that "almost without exception these Russian workers were efficient, energetic and quick to learn. They got on fine with the American soldiers and the heavy construction work at the three bases moved fully as fast as the flow of supplies permitted."[51]

On other matters as well, the Soviets and Americans were cooperating fully. They agreed to an exchange of intelligence data and photos and to provide each other with assistance as necessary. The Soviets were unable to provide the kind of detail the Americans were accustomed to on German fighter dispositions behind the front or the location and strength of German flak batteries. This was not an intentional slight; the VVS simply did not track that kind of information, because the vast majority of their sorties were flown at or close behind the front itself. They also tended to present information relative only to a particular mission and not to the theater as a whole. Such procedures would create a problem for Eastern Command's intelligence officers during the FRANTIC missions as the aircrews would complain bitterly about the lack of accurate data concerning German fighter and flak defenses.[52]

The Soviets also agreed to set up a weather station at Poltava and to provide their guests with full weather reports, maps, and predictions in exchange for American-supplied weather information in the United Kingdom and Italy. The American weather officer, Colonel Lewis Mundell, perhaps in an effort to flatter his hosts, claimed that the Soviets' weather facilities and forecasting abilities were the best in the world.[53]

Communications were another matter entirely. Without control of communications, the Americans believed they simply could not operate. They had to be able to communicate among the three bases, with inbound and outbound aircraft, with Fifteenth Air Force in Italy (at Caserta), with Eighth Air Force in Britain (through London), and, of course, with the Military Mission in Moscow. In his postwar memoirs, Deane wrote that AAF communications needs "horrified" the Soviets. He realized that control over communications would give the Americans a degree of autonomy by foreigners inside the Soviet Union that was unprecedented in the Soviet experience. Without direct access to and control over communication facilities, Eastern Command and other elements of the air forces could not circulate weather updates, changes in targets or plans, and other vital information in a timely fashion.[54]

As Deane wrote after the war, General Nikitin and his communications experts were fully aware of the operational necessity that the Americans control their own communication net. By mid-March, Nikitin had approved the American proposals, but their implementation was to prove time-consuming. USSTAF dispatched both men and equipment to Eastern Command to set up the long-range radio equipment, while the Soviets worked to refurbish the local communications system because the Germans had stripped the area of wire. Manual radio circuits between Poltava and London, Caserta, and Tehran were in operation by June. These circuits, alas, were soon crowded with both weather information and operational messages.[55]

Of greater concern to the Americans of Eastern Command was the state of communications inside the Soviet Union. While given total freedom to communicate with American aircraft over Soviet soil, the Americans had to rely on a rudimentary Soviet teletype service among the three bases. By June, Eastern Command had resorted to courier aircraft for interbase messages because of the technical unreliability of the teletype network. Telephone lines among the three bases simply did not exist.[56]

While these weighty issues absorbed the attention of those in command, many of the details were worked out by captains and majors of both air forces. By the end of April, American and Soviet airmen, according to Kessler, were getting along beautifully. Red Air Force and USAAF maintenance officers agreed that a Soviet assistant crew chief and two helpers would always be assigned to the same American crew chief. An American transportation officer oversaw the training of Soviet auto mechanics to work on U.S. special purpose vehicles. The Soviets were enthusiastic and, so the Americans thought, adept at making ad hoc repairs, and the Americans commented quite favorably about their abilities.[57]

By mid-May, most of the problems involved with erecting the bases had been resolved. On May 5, Kessler noted with satisfaction in his diary that the camp and field hospital sites at Poltava were complete. Transients would live in a large tent camp alongside the airdrome. The finishing touches were going on the latrines and washrooms, and the medical staff was busy setting up the hospital. Officers returning from Piryatin and Mirgorod also reported that those two bases would be totally ready well in advance of the 15th, when the largest contingent of personnel, that of the Fourth Echelon, was due to arrive at Eastern Command.[58]

Also on May 5, Soviet border patrol personnel arrived at Poltava, which the Foreign Office had designated a "border station." In a significant gesture of cooperation, the Soviets agreed to discard their standard and rather cumbersome practices and rely instead on a very simple cross-check of group visas and aircraft passenger manifests for arrivals. For departures, the Americans had only to submit their request for clearance to the border authorities in triplicate the day before leaving, and outgoing passengers would then be checked against this request on the day of their passage.[59]

Typical of the degree of cooperation reached by the two sides at this point was the discussion on May 20 between U.S. Major Albert Lepawsky, who had been in the country since mid-March, and a Soviet major named Kompaniets. Regarding living facilities, they agreed that the Soviets would provide two barbers every Wednesday, bath day would be Wednesdays from 1 P.M. to 6 P.M. or on any other day when twenty men were available for baths. Bed linens would be changed on Wednesday, while Soviet workers would collect the laundry every Thursday for return on the following Wednesday. The Americans agreed to order vodka in bulk and for cash. And to help control rats and mice, the Soviets would supply a cat. Despite this otherwise fine piece of diplomacy, Lepawsky recorded the disappointment felt by the Americans when they learned that both Deane and the Soviets would not approve the use of a Red Cross unit consisting of "8 ARC [American Red Cross] girls and two clubmobiles."[60]

Thus, by the first of June, Eastern Command was fully operational. Kessler, who had labored so long and so well with Perminov to ensure that the bases were ready on time, turned over head of Eastern Command to Major General Robert L. Walsh, who had transferred in from command of the U.S. Air Transport Command's South Atlantic Wing. Amiable and energetic, Walsh was one of Arnold's favorites. Surprised in the middle of a trip from Brazil to Washington of his selection to go to the Soviet Union, Walsh requested a few days' delay to return to his headquarters to pick up personal belongings and take care of a few personal matters. Kessler remained at Poltava as Walsh's deputy, and his replacement was in no way a reflection of his work but a recognition on the part of USSTAF that Eastern Command was sufficiently important to merit a general officer in command. Indeed, Kessler had every reason to be proud of his unit's accomplishments. He and his men had worked hand in hand with the Soviets, avoided major embarrassments, and saw to it that everything was done properly. Kessler wrote glowingly, "We have chiseled nothing from the Russians."[61]

The two sides had learned to cooperate under very trying conditions. Despite early misunderstandings, and delays, the Soviets and Americans had achieved a great deal in just two months. Indeed, probably the most remarkable incident of the past few weeks came when Soviet troops found three German 250-kilogram bombs in a barracks adjacent to the large U-shaped building at Poltava. A few days later, on April 28, they traced wires running from these bombs to a central control box located in a field. From there, other wires ran into the large U-shaped building that housed the American and Soviet headquarters and staffs. In the basement of the building, the Soviets discovered nearly ten tons of explosives that were wired to the control box. Kessler speculated that perhaps the Germans planned to detonate them from the air when the building was fully occupied and the field operational. Whatever the Germans' motives for planting the mines, no one at Poltava needed to be persuaded to evacuate the building. Several Americans spent the night in a small cottage in town while Kessler and twelve members of his staff slept in several cramped rooms in the control tower.[62]

Disregarding obvious dangers, Soviet engineers disarmed and removed the German explosives, and the Americans moved back into the building the morning of the 29th. This appalling lack of security on the part of the Soviets was even more remarkable considering the fact that the retreating Germans routinely mined and booby-trapped structures they did not destroy outright. The Soviets had occupied the airfield since September; why this discovery was not made sooner remains a mystery. If anything, the incident helped bind the two groups together, with the Americans showering praise on the Soviets for their bravery and concern for their guests' well-being. It also served to remind the Americans that not only were their surroundings different from those to which they were accustomed in Britain, but that they were seeing a very different aspect of the war.[63]

Despite the undeniable progress and the admirable efforts on the part of both Soviet and American officers to work harmoniously, several issues remained unresolved and even at this stage, threatened to undermine FRANTIC before it really got under way. The first of these problems was the earlier agreement to admit American ground staff on group visas. While the bases were under construction, American personnel began leaving the United Kingdom for the Ukraine. In effect, these groups left before the Soviets had agreed on either strength levels for the American contingent or the Americans had accepted the three sites for their bases. The Americans realized what they were doing but were so anxious to get the operation under way that they were willing to accept delays at the Soviet border rather than wait until all other decisions were final before dispatching their personnel.[64]

The Second Echelon, composed as it was of a small group of staff officers, experienced very little difficulty in entering the Soviet Union from Tehran. Indeed, these officers were duly impressed by the apparent speed and ease with which they were allowed to enter the country. The much larger Third Echelon, however, would not be so fortunate. Both of these groups made the journey from the United Kingdom by air via the ATC (Air Transport Command) Route, which took them across North Africa to Tehran. Whereas the Second Echelon departed Britain on March 15 and arrived in Moscow on the 24th, the Third departed the United Kingdom March 17 and did not even begin moving out from Tehran until April 22. The delay was the result of confusion on the part of the Soviet Consulate in the Iranian capital and, as Deane put it, "the red tape of several [Soviet] departments [was] mixed up in the question and there must be clarification to ensure orderly procedure from now on."[65]

The Headquarters of the Persian Gulf Command notified Kessler on April 9 that everything was ready at Tehran but that no Americans could move to the Soviet Union because the Soviet Embassy had not received the group visa plan. Angry over the delay caused by this bureaucratic mix-up, Deane wrote a strong letter to Nikitin.[66] The fact that the bases were actually not ready to feed and house large numbers of Americans yet did not seem to cross Deane's mind. Feeling the pressure to get things moving, he viewed any delay with great irritation.

The news of delays over visas also caused Kessler considerable concern. Throughout the month of April, Kessler noted in his diary that there was no news from Tehran about the movement of people or supplies. On April 13, he wrote in apparent disgust that "nothing has moved out of [Tehran] since 21 March except Capt. Coleman." Coleman had piloted a C-47 to Iran with the Second Echelon, but he and his crew had stayed behind because of some administrative problems regarding their clearances. Kessler knew that Deane wanted the bases operational by mid-May, and every day that "nothing moved" from Tehran complicated matters for Eastern Command. Indeed, on April 22, Deane cabled Spaatz and Arnold that he was unable to estimate a date when FRANTIC operations could begin. Much still depended on supplies arriving on time but he was hoping for a start date in late May. He retained his sense of humor, closing his message by saying that "this group visa business has driven me 'Frantic' and I can make no promises. I will give you an estimate as soon as I have been to the bases."[67]

In the meantime, the Fourth Echelon was making its way by ship, rail, and road toward the Soviet-Iranian border. The largest single American increment, this group contained sixty-seven officers, four warrant officers, and 680 enlisted men. They traveled by ship from Liverpool, England, on March 26 and disembarked at Port Said, Egypt, on April 13. From there, they entrained for Haifa, Palestine. The officers in charge were aware that elements of the previous echelon were still in Iran because of the visa snafu, but determined to press onward nevertheless.[68]

At Port Said, the Echelon broke up into two "serials" for the purpose of movement. The first serial crowded aboard an Egyptian troop train, seventy-four enlisted men to each of five third-class coaches, while thirty-four officers rode in the first-class car. The enlisted men had no idea of their destination; they knew only that they were assigned to Detachment 5, ASC USSTAF, and were part of a secret "special project." The train was not too uncomfortable until it stopped to take on a British officer and 100 Indian troops who were stranded at Kantara, Palestine. Already worn out by the long sea voyage, many of the men were completely exhausted when, on the 27th, they reached Haifa, where they were transferred to a truck convoy.[69]

This convoy then rattled along tortuous and dusty roads at minimal speeds. Stopping every night, the Americans made it to Baghdad, Iraq, on May 1, where they spent a few days resting and seeing the sights. Leaving Baghdad on May 3, the convoy arrived at Camp Park, Hamadan, Iran, on the afternoon of May 5. They spent four days there, the officers eating in a new officers' club, recently built at a cost of $45,000. The Post Exchange stocked candy and toilet articles, and allotted for sale five cans of beer to every member of the command.[70]

At this point, news reached the First Serial commander, Lieutenant Colonel Curtis P. Boas, that some fifty officers and men had to be eliminated to keep American strength at 1,200. The Soviets had agreed to the latter figure earlier and had made their own plans in good faith based on that number. After making the long, hazardous trip from Britain, fifty men had to be "weeded out." The men, actually forty-seven enlisted men and six officers, were chosen and their records updated, whereupon they were transferred to the Persian Gulf Command pending reassignment.[71]

While the Fourth Echelon had struggled forward, the men of the Third Echelon had finally made their way to Eastern Command bases aboard C-47 cargo planes. Fortunately for the Fourth Echelon, Deane and Ambassador Harriman had solved most of the visa troubles yet many of these individuals actually looked forward to stops and delays as a way to recuperate from the tortuous trip itself.[72]

After leaving Hamadan, on May 10, the American convoy stopped just south of the Soviet-occupied zone of Iran for the night. There, for the first time, an officer briefed the men on their final destination and mission. The group reached Tabriz, in Soviet-held territory, the next day and from there,

Arriving American ground personnel muster for roll call, May 1944. *Courtesy U.S. Air Force.*

traveled on a Soviet train, complete with sleeper cars and, so it was reported, "sheets and champagne for all." The second serial arrived at Poltava at five in the morning on the 16th. Except for two dozen interpreters and a handful of other specialists, Eastern Command now had its personnel, detachments going to both Piryatin and Mirgorod as well as Poltava.[73]

The other preparations were complete by the beginning of June. The arrival of the bulk of Eastern Command's personnel now made it possible, after so much anxiety, for Deane and USSTAF to plan the first operation. Lieutenant Colonel Boas, after spending nineteen months in Britain, took command of the base at Poltava. Colonel David B. Lancaster and Lieutenant Colonel James R. Irish, both experienced officers, assumed command of Piryatin and Mirgorod, respectively. Unfortunately, one issue remained unresolved in the latter half of May: target selection.

On May 3, Spaatz directed Fifteenth Air Force to prepare plans for the first FRANTIC mission. He realized that the Eighth, already heavily involved in the bombing of the German transportation network in Northwest Europe, would be committed to OVERLORD in the not-too-distant-future.

By May 15, the Fifth Wing of the Fifteenth Air Force had a preliminary plan in hand for FRANTIC.[74]

Deane was simultaneously negotiating with the Soviets in Moscow over targets. Initially, as a courtesy, Spaatz informed the Soviets, through Deane, that USSTAF suggested striking from Eastern Command bases at the Heinkel aircraft works at Riga, Latvia, or at Mielec, a town near Lwów, Poland. He stated that because the avowed purpose of FRANTIC was to bomb targets normally out of reach of bombers based in Britain and Italy, a raid on these factories would make the Germans realize that all their industrial assets were now vulnerable to attack from the air.[75]

The Soviets disagreed. On May 10, Deane cabled Spaatz that the Soviets preferred targets in the southern Balkans, including the Ploesti oil fields in Romania. Spaatz persisted, however, and bombarded Deane with a flurry of messages throughout May in which he continued to list both Riga and Mielec as well as airfields at Galatz (present-day Galati), Romania, and marshalling yards at Lwów and Brest Litovsk, Poland, and Kaunas and Vilna (Vilnius), Lithuania. He also notified Kessler and Deane on May 26 that the initial mission would "go in" with the first favorable day of weather after June first.[76]

With its tactical orientation, the VVS was clearly interested in striking targets that would aid the advance of the Red Army. Nikitin agreed that refineries and synthetic oil plants would be high priority targets because the Soviets claimed that the German *Wehrmacht* in the East did not appear to be suffering any shortage of fuel. The Soviets stated that changing combat conditions would dictate what transportation concentrations and facilities FRANTIC bombers should hit. Some AAF officers also speculated that the Soviets did not want American raids in the area of their impending offensive because they feared such activity would allow the Americans to claim some of the credit for any subsequent successes on the ground.[77]

By May 30, the Soviets had categorically refused to clear any of the targets Spaatz suggested. Deane reported that the Soviets would apparently consider hitting these targets after the first mission. He recommended adhering to their requests simply to get the operation under way, but also suggested that in the future, "we simply inform them of what targets we propose . . . without asking for specific approval."[78]

Eaker reacted harshly, suggesting that FRANTIC operations be postponed until the target controversy was put to rest. He wanted definite clearance for targets that the Americans deemed worthwhile hitting from the Soviet Union before his planes departed Italy. He did not want American aircraft sitting on Soviet bases "while we haggle for targets." If the mission did go forward, he recommended that the task force return immediately if the Soviets refused to clear Mielec or Riga for attack from Poltava and Mirgorod.[79]

The same day that Eaker sent his objections to Spaatz, Deane cabled a more complete account of the negotiations with the Soviets. He said he had stressed to the Soviets that hitting the targets Spaatz suggested would put the bases to the best possible use and that the Americans would have trouble understanding why their target lists were not approved. The discussion with the Soviet General Slavin had become heated but Deane believed the general was acting on instructions from higher authority. Deane speculated that the Soviets feared that striking targets in Poland or the Baltic states might "telegraph" to the Germans their attack plans for the summer. Realizing that the Soviets were not going to budge, Deane recommended hitting the targets the Red Air Force specified east of a bombline Bucharest-Ploesti (Romania)-Cluj-Oradea-Debrecen-Miskolc-Budapest (Hungary). He was confident that after the first mission and the opening of the Anglo-American "second front" in France, Soviet attitudes toward their allies would warm and the Americans would have greater freedom of action in choosing their targets. Spaatz agreed; he ordered an attack on the targets requested by the Soviets as soon as possible after June 1.[80]

With that, the final obstacle to FRANTIC was swept aside. After months of negotiations and often harried and rushed preparations, Eastern Command was ready to accept the first mission of this historic operation. The units in Italy were now busily preparing final plans for FRANTIC JOE, Fifteenth Air Force's inaugural "shuttle raid" that would terminate in the Soviet Union. Despite inevitable misunderstandings and problems, the Soviet and American air forces had proved that they could work together in a common undertaking.

The Soviets and Americans had accomplished a great deal in the previous three months. Together, they had managed to construct operational bases from the ruins that existed in March. The officers of both sides had cooperated to work out the massive logistical requirements for the operation. The Soviets had displayed an openness that surprised many of the Americans, and the close working relationships forged by the two staffs were instrumental in the relatively rapid progress made throughout the spring. They had agreed to share intelligence and weather data as well as food and drink. If a few issues remained open, the Soviets and Americans at Eastern Command had every reason to be pleased with their handiwork.

As the weather over southern Europe remained clear that second day of June, the crews of three bombardment groups and two fighter groups of the Fifth Combat Wing reported to their aircraft in preparation for the flight to the Ukraine. While the air war over Europe continued, Operation FRANTIC was finally about to begin.[81]

THREE

SUMMER FRENZY

June–July 1944

At the same time that preparations for FRANTIC were under way, the air war in Europe approached a critical turning point. The American disaster over Schweinfurt in October 1943 had ended, as a common practice, the tactic of unescorted daylight bombing raids. Though the Eighth Air Force continued to strike targets in northwestern Germany—all within range of operational escort fighters—the AAF reluctantly accepted the need to change both doctrine and tactics and await the appearance of an aircraft capable of protecting the bombers all the way to the target and back again. It had been this setback in the air that had prompted AAF commanding general Henry H. Arnold to request that the Military Mission in Moscow seek Soviet cooperation in the shuttle-bombing scheme.[1]

The Americans were not the only ones absorbing punishing losses in the air during autumn of 1943. German fighter squadrons had suffered heavily in their defense of the Reich. The Germans lost 560 fighters in the western theater of the European war in September and October 1943. The *Luftwaffe* had indeed won a costly and fleeting tactical victory. Thus, both Allied and German air forces had reached a point of exhaustion. The Eighth still held the strategic advantage because of the vast resources at the disposal of the American air forces, cold comfort to the survivors of Schweinfurt.[2]

The decision to await long-range escort fighters and the exhaustion of the Eighth Air Force resulted in a suspension of deep penetration raids in Europe by the USAAF over the winter of 1943–44. The lull would not last long. By February 1944, at the same time that Stalin had given his final approval of the use of bases by the Americans in the Ukraine, the Eighth Air Force was preparing to resume an all-out attack against Germany. The bomber offensive would now serve as an indirect means of facilitating the impending Anglo-American amphibious invasion of France, Operation OVERLORD. Code-named ARGUMENT, the air operation opened on February 20. Its goal, as mandated by the OVERLORD directives, was the destruction of the German air industry and air force. The Eighth now went into battle escorted by fighters carrying drop (or "belly") tanks to extend their range. Among those escort fighters were more than 300 new P-51 Mustangs, which had the range necessary to escort B-17 and B-24 bombers all the way to the German capital and back to Britain. In a sense, the bomber, seen by interwar air enthusiasts as a war-winning weapon in its own right, had become bait to lure German fighters into battle with the escorts. The tactic proved successful. The unremitting attacks against the *Luftwaffe*'s infrastructure, together with rapidly mounting losses in the air, finally broke the back of the German daylight fighter force. From January to May 1944, the Germans lost 2,262 fighter pilots in the West, a figure that represented nearly their entire strength of the previous December.[3]

The directives for OVERLORD ordered the strategic forces not only to deplete the German Air Force, but to destroy and disrupt the German transportation and communication network in northern France and the Low Countries in an effort to isolate the Normandy region, proposed site for the Anglo-American landings. USSTAF commander Lieutenant General Carl A. Spaatz also used the directives against the *Luftwaffe* as a way to justify throwing his bombers against the German oil industry. Though the results of the latter series of attacks would not begin to hamper the Germans for several months, they further strained dwindling *Luftwaffe* resources by forcing German fighters into battle. Indeed, by the end of May, the German headquarters in France reported to OKW, the German High Command, that the transportation and supply situation had become critical. In the meantime, Anglo-American air forces had crippled the *Luftwaffe* in the West. On D-day, June 6, the Allies employed 12,837 aircraft; German *Luftflotte* 3, based in northern France, mustered only 300 operational aircraft.[4]

Thus, even before the first FRANTIC mission took place, one of the prime operational considerations for the use of Soviet bases appeared to have become moot. U.S. planners had hoped that FRANTIC would disperse and dislocate German fighter units prior to OVERLORD by threatening Germany with bombardment from the east. It now appeared that ARGUMENT had effectively crippled the German fighter arm without the aid of shuttle operations. Nevertheless, one could also say that the Germans were now even more vulnerable to an air campaign mounted from three directions. Thus, FRANTIC still appeared to have an important role to play in the war. With all preparations at the bases complete, Spaatz ordered Fifteenth Air Force to launch Operation FRANTIC.

Lieutenant General Ira C. Eaker's plan for FRANTIC JOE reported that the primary aim of the operation lay in the "unique opportunity" it offered to "give immediate tactical assistance to the Russians," to strike at "remote eastern industrial targets" and thereby increase the effectiveness of the bomber offensive, and to "establish a practical working basis for extensive future operations in other theatres [*sic*] involving the use of Russian bases by USAAF." Eaker stated further that he considered this last objective the most important. "It is imperative that we gain the full confidence and respect of the Russians by starting our collaboration with an efficiently executed operation of immediate significance to them."[5]

The Fifteenth Air Force operational plan called for the deployment of four groups of B-17s from the 5th Wing together with one "fortified" group of P-51s from the 306th Wing. The total strength of FRANTIC JOE was 130 bombers and seventy fighters. This task force was only part of a much larger armada from the Fifteenth that would strike targets in eastern Romania. The FRANTIC task force would then carry out as many as three missions from bases in the Soviet Union, striking targets designated by the Red Air Force.[6]

The ultimate objective of the operation, according to the plan, was to "impress the Russians with the power and capabilities of Strategic Air Forces." Thus, the task force was to avoid facing strong opposition that might result in serious battle damage, which would be difficult to repair in the Soviet Union and create a bad impression among the Soviets. The Fifteenth wanted a successful mission en route, nonetheless, and wanted its planes to arrive in the Ukraine with an impressive array of bomb strike photography.[7]

The Fifteenth's plan contained an "Indoctrination Annex" that stressed the true importance of this first mission. "Our performance will be the yardstick by which the Russians will judge the fighting capabilities, the discipline, the morale, and the energy of the whole of the American forces, Ground, Naval, and Air." The annex instructed American airmen to "forget all preconceived prejudices" and to avoid political discussions or comparisons of the two countries' institutions. The annex warned that "the Russians do not recognize personal opinions in the armed forces," and would accept personal statements as "official opinions of the [U.S.] government."[8] In terms of personal conduct, the order explained that the Soviets were "shy on first acquaintance" and like all "fighting men" respected physical prowess. Soviet women were "quite friendly and open" but the G.I.s were warned not to mistake this as an "invitation to further intimacy." Above all, the order reminded the men that "11,000,000 FIGHTING MEN IN THE SERVICE OF OUR COUNTRY THE WORLD OVER ARE BEING JUDGED BY THE IMPRESSION YOU CREATE" (emphasis in original).[9]

The Americans reluctantly agreed to open the FRANTIC campaign by hitting Balkan targets requested by the Soviets. The target for June 2 for the FRANTIC JOE task force was the marshalling yards at Debrecen, Hungary. Five outfits, the 2nd, 97th, 99th, and 483rd Bomb Groups, together with the 325th Fighter Group, left their bases in southern Italy early on the morning of the 2nd. Forming in clear weather over the Adriatic, the task force was joined by Lieutenant General Eaker on board the "Yankee Doodle II," a B-17 assigned to the 97th. The general had flown with the 97th on August 17, 1942, as it participated in the first American heavy bomber raid on Europe. Eaker decided to fly with the task force to ensure that all went well and to underline the importance that the Americans attached to this operation. He also planned to speak to the Soviets about target selection during his stay in the USSR.[10]

Eaker chose the units of FRANTIC JOE with great care. Not only was the future of further shuttle operations on the line with this first mission, Eaker believed that the prestige and reputation of the AAF itself was at stake. The 2nd Bomb Group was one of the oldest units in the Army Air Forces. Under the command of Colonel Herbert E. Rice, the 2nd had served in North Africa under 12th Air Force before being reassigned to the Fifteenth. By the time of FRANTIC JOE, the group had already earned Distinguished Unit Citations just one day apart for its role in deep strikes within Europe in February 1944. The 2nd's arrival in the Ukraine also gave the Eastern Command medical staff its first big challenge: a Lieutenant Johnson of the 96th Bomb Squadron required an appendectomy shortly after landing. Another veteran outfit, the 97th, under Colonel Frank Allen had, as previously mentioned, opened AAF raids on occupied Europe, utilizing American-built heavies, in August 1942. Transferred to the Mediterranean in November 1942, it was the first group assigned to the 12th Air Force and transferred to the Fifteenth one year later, where it would remain until the end of the war.[11]

The 99th Bomb Group possessed a distinguished combat record as well. Led by Colonel Ford J. Lauer and a veteran unit of the Mediterranean campaign, the 99th marked its 200th mission on the June 2 shuttle mission. The 483rd, on the other hand, was the "baby" of FRANTIC JOE. Commanded by Colonel Paul L. Barton, the unit went into action only the previous April. Still, the group had so favorably impressed Eaker that he included it in this select group of battle-tested groups. The amount of battle experience held by individual crews and crew members varied but each of the aforementioned groups was led by highly respected, combat-tested officers.[12]

Escorting the bombers were the "Checkertails" of the battle-hardened

325th Fighter Group. The group commander, Lieutenant Colonel Chester L. Sluder, swore his staff to secrecy over the impending mission to the Ukraine. The unit had only recently converted from P-47s to P-51s but had maintained its operations tempo throughout the period. Sluder and his squadron commanders were all aggressive and battle-tested pilots; the commander of the 317th Fighter Squadron, Major "Herky" Green was the leading American ace in the Mediterranean at the time of FRANTIC JOE. All would participate in this vital mission to Eastern Command. Forty-two maintenance men, including three officers, flew to the Ukraine aboard B-17s to provide additional service for the fighters on their arrival at Piryatin.[13]

This first mission was generally uneventful. All groups struck the target, achieving, in the opinions of the crews, "good" results. Photo reconnaissance showed all tracks in the rail yard cut by the bombing and 200 railcars destroyed. Only one B-17 was lost when an engine fire apparently caused it to explode over the target area. Other aircraft in the formation reported seeing no parachutes. One P-51 was also missing, but the rest of the task force droned on to the Ukraine.[14]

Between 1:20 and 2:30 P.M., on the afternoon of the second, the Allied aircraft began landing at the Soviet bases. Standing in a cold drizzle at Poltava, were Ambassador W. Averell Harriman and his daughter Kathy, U.S. Generals John Deane and Robert Walsh, and Soviet Generals Alexei Perminov, and, representing General A. V. Nikitin, Lieutenant General D. D. Grendal, chief of the Red Air Force's Intelligence and Reconnaissance Branch. Deane later described the scene as one of suppressed excitement. Soviet, British, and American correspondents, he wrote, were everywhere. The only sour note of the day occurred when Soviet General N. V. Slavin, who was napping in the headquarters, awoke to the sound of approaching aircraft and ran to the airfield only to be forbidden entry by armed American soldiers who were under orders to keep "spectators" beyond a certain line. Deane tried to take the blame for the situation but Slavin instead attacked Perminov in a violent verbal outburst.[15]

As the news spread that the American bombers were approaching, American and Soviet personnel rushed to the field to watch the landings. Despite a 500-foot ceiling, the groups arrived at Poltava on schedule and, to the delight of all who were watching, in formation. The first three aircraft, flying in a V-shaped wedge, broke through the cloud cover. They were followed by another sixty-one bombers. After circling the field, Eaker's plane, "Yankee Doodle II," landed. The rest of the planes followed at one-minute intervals. The Soviet women, who had worked so long to lay the steel mat-

MAAF commander Lieutenant General Ira C. Eaker shortly after arriving at Poltava, 2 June 1944. Major General Alexei Perminov stands to the left of Eaker. Ambassador Averell Harriman, wearing a dark overcoat, stands to the right. Major General Walsh, Eastern Command's CO, stands in profile on the far right. Harriman's daughter, Kathleen, is second from the left. *Courtesy U.S. Air Force.*

ting for the runway, were visibly pleased as the aircraft landed without incident.[16]

The assembled crowd greeted Eaker warmly. He awarded Perminov the Legion of Merit for his role in preparing the bases for the operation. In return, Perminov and his staff presented Eaker with two large bouquets of flowers, but the Soviet general insisted that all credit was due Alfred Kessler. Members of Perminov's staff presented a blushing Kathy Harriman with huge bunches of roses. Perminov was so excited by the whole thing that he could scarcely contain himself; Deane reported happily that he had "just avoided the victory embrace." Reporters spoke eagerly with crew members of the B-17s, who, according to one newsman, made a "very favorable impression by their military bearing and smart appearance."[17]

This first day marked the high tide, in Deane's opinion, of Soviet-American military relations. Following the ceremonies on the airstrip, the high-ranking officers piled into jeeps and drove to Eastern Command headquarters for an immediate conference on future operations. About an hour later,

Eaker confers with Ambassador Harriman, Walsh, the
Military Mission in Moscow's chief, Major General John
R. Deane, and Eastern Command's deputy commander,
Colonel Alfred Kessler. *Courtesy U.S. Air Force.*

Eaker, accompanied by the Harrimans, Deane, Slavin, and Grendal,
boarded a Soviet DC-3 bound for Moscow. Once in the Soviet capital, Eaker
argued for greater freedom of action in the selection of targets. Deane's pre-
diction had come to pass; in light of the apparent success of FRANTIC JOE,
the Soviets granted Eaker permission to strike at Mielec, Poland, the target
he originally wanted to hit on the way from Italy.[18]

The participants agreed that Moscow should issue the first press releases
concerning FRANTIC JOE. London and Washington followed with carefully
generalized and identical statements. The Soviet state news agency *TASS* issued several favorable statements on June 3 and 4, and both *Izvestia* and

Pravda reported the mission. The reporter from *Izvestia* remarked that the American fliers "were met here with the warmest reception by the population and the Soviet fliers-brothers at arms." The *Pravda* correspondent commented on the material wealth evident at the American bases and wrote that the bomber crews, all of them anxious to visit Soviet Russia, "remarked that they will be the envy of the officers and men who remained on their former bases." The Soviet reporter concluded that "sincere and friendly relations between American and Soviet fliers strengthens with each hour."[19]

Indeed, this last point was the one that U.S. leaders wanted to emphasize. On June 2, 1944, the Joint Chiefs of Staff informed Deane that official statements and press releases should state clearly that Soviet personnel were working at the American air bases and dwell on the warm reception the Soviets gave the first American bomber crews. The Chiefs wanted propaganda releases to stress to the world, and especially to the Germans, that U.S. air power was vast and flexible and could now be brought to bear from many directions. They instructed military spokesmen to point out that, contrary to German propaganda, the United States and Soviet Union were fighting together toward a common goal—the defeat of Nazi Germany. Now that bomber operations could take place from the east, the Germans would "have no place to hide; no place to work" that American bombs could not touch.[20]

U.S. officials inside the Soviet Union also reported a distinct change in Soviet attitudes toward the Western Allies. Maxwell M. Hamilton, minister counselor of the embassy in Moscow, informed Washington that the shuttle raids, the fall of Rome to Allied ground forces on June 4, and the Normandy landings on June 6 had eliminated the "chary praise and carping criticism which [had] been a feature of Soviet press comments on [Western] Allied military operations up to this time." Now, according to Hamilton, Soviet statements and press releases expressed "admiration and appreciation for the recent military achievements of [the] Anglo-American military forces."[21]

Harriman also reported that "Soviet officials, both civilian and military, [placed] prime importance on the initiation of frantic as the first combined military operation and thereby establish a basis for lasting friendship between the two countries." He explained that the "annoying delays" over visas, aircraft clearances, and the like were not the fault of the Red Air Force, but resulted from the resistance of other departments (which ones he did not say) in breaking down "historic inhibitions." In fact, he praised the Red Air Force for its cooperation.[22]

Perminov leads high-ranking Soviet and American visitors on a tour of Poltava. *Courtesy U.S. Air Force.*

These warm feelings were apparent among all personnel at the bases of Eastern Command. From the beginning of the operation, Perminov made it clear that he was anxious that American personnel mingle with the local population. He and his staff planned entertainment for their guests such as dances, parties, and stage shows. The Soviet general did express his concern that "a soldier would be a soldier" and that "freedom without control would lead to difficulties." Nevertheless, Perminov told Kessler that he wanted the Americans, both ground staff and aircrews, to mix with the civilians, visit local points of interest, and witness the destruction wrought by the Germans so that they could better appreciate the situation of the Soviet people in this war. The people of Poltava, Perminov announced, did not know exactly why the Americans were there, but appeared to be pleased about the presence of their allies.[23]

In fact, while the officers of Eastern Command realized that they could not transplant British bases to the Soviet front, they had tried their best to bring America to the Soviet Union. In Kessler's opinion, they had succeeded. In July, Kessler told an AAF historian that "we actually have three little patches of America in the middle of the Ukraine—for the first time in the history of Russia." In accordance with Perminov's wishes, American personnel could go anywhere at any time. Kessler remarked that, "G.I.s walk around the town [Poltava] just as they walk around London." The townspeople near all three bases received the Americans warmly, waving to the ground crews as they bumped along the roads on their way to the airfields and inviting others into their homes. "They [American servicemen]," Kessler reported, "go around with a big grin on their faces, and the Russians are crazy about them. They [the Soviets] even drag those G.I.s out to dance with the Russian girls." Like virtually every other American in Eastern Command, Kessler could not help making some comment about Soviet women. "Incidentally," he said, "those girls [helped] to build most of our airdromes, and are all very strong."[24]

The degree of freedom the Americans enjoyed in the Soviet Union at the outset was a pleasant surprise to most Army Air Forces personnel. The Soviets did not attempt to censor American mail, leaving that up to U.S. postal and military authorities. The Soviets also allowed the Americans to bring copies of popular magazines and newspapers into the country, provided they were not circulated among the general population. Soviet authorities were well aware of the free flow of criticism and debate that characterized the American press and did not want articles critical of either President Franklin Roosevelt or Marshal Joseph Stalin to become available to their citizens. Eastern Command officials did all they could to respect these wishes and officers briefed all new personnel, including aircrews, that American periodicals and other literature were not to be given out to Soviet troops and civilians. Despite Eastern Command restrictions, copies of *Yank, Time,* and *Life* were in wide circulation among Soviet soldiers and local residents in a short time. Perminov himself requested that the Americans make up a set of American magazines and papers that he wanted to see for his own information and entertainment.[25]

The crews of FRANTIC JOE found three bases that had undergone radical transformation in just four months. Inevitably, some problems and deficiencies persisted. Because of the amount of work required to make the bases operationally ready, American commanders devoted little time to recreational facilities. At the beginning of June, such facilities were virtually nonexistent. At both Mirgorod and Piryatin, inspectors commented on the shortage of radios and athletic equipment. The Soviets showed movies several times a week in Mirgorod, but the movies were unpopular with the G.I.s, in part because the Americans could not understand the dialogue. In the town of Piryatin, 7 miles from the base itself, the Soviets also showed movies, on a bimonthly basis.[26] As the headquarters base, Poltava had a bit more to offer in the way of off-duty entertainment for the men. The Soviets staged folk-music concerts on a makeshift stage in the ruins of a hangar, and dances attended by Soviet women were quite common. In the holiday atmosphere that pervaded Poltava in the immediate aftermath of the first mission, the Soviets threw several parties for the Americans.[27]

Recreational facilities improved steadily through June and July of 1944, largely as a result of the efforts of Chaplain (Captain) Clarence Strippy, who voluntarily filled the post of Special Service officer in addition to his regular duties. Strippy divided his time among the three bases, spending three days showing films at each stop. Sufficient supplies of equipment—phonographs, books, radios, and athletic gear—were among the cargo arriving with the main contingent of ground staff, but the lack of an accountable officer resulted in this material becoming, as official reports noted, "scattered among individuals." In other words, American and possibly Soviet troops stole it. Strippy made repeated requests to USSTAF for new equipment, and succeeded in replacing at least some of the missing gear.[28]

By mid-July, Strippy's efforts and the arrival of a full-time Special Service officer helped establish a healthy recreational program at Eastern Command. Troops laid out baseball and softball fields, constructed day rooms equipped with radios, phonographs, and magazines, and dug horseshoe pits. The newly assigned Special Service officer, Captain Charles Heintzelman, formed interbase baseball and softball leagues, organized G.I. shows, and helped start classes in, among other things, the Russian language. Once the novelty of the FRANTIC operation wore off and the number of missions declined, such activities would prove invaluable to maintaining the morale of the American soldiers of Eastern Command.[29]

Strippy served as command chaplain. A Protestant, he also conducted Catholic and Jewish services as well. Because he could not remain at each base for more than a few days, Strippy often relied on other officers to hold religious services in his absence. At Poltava, the construction of housing, messing, and storage facilities left little in the way of labor or materials for a base chapel. Strippy used the mess tent as his chapel or, when the weather cooperated, a large warehouse that was missing its roof and was used for crew briefings. The Americans were pleasantly surprised to see large numbers of Soviet personnel show up for religious services on the base, considering communism's commitment to atheistic doctrine. In turn, Eastern Command personnel routinely ventured into town to watch Orthodox religious processions and ceremonies. Apparently, the Soviet people were taking advantage of Stalin's war-induced relaxation of religious restrictions.[30]

While spartan by the standards of the Eighth Air Force in Britain, the

A view of the American tent camp at Poltava, summer 1944. *Courtesy U.S. Air Force.*

housing was nevertheless more than adequate at the bases considering that Eastern Command was operating under field conditions. The facilities at Mirgorod were by far the best of the three bases. With the exception of the hospital staff, all personnel were housed in the old artillery school barracks, which were permanent brick structures with concrete and wood floors. The buildings were clean and well-ventilated; American inspectors commented favorably on the fine renovation work carried out by the Soviets. Though transients were also housed in similar quarters, tents were available to handle any overflow. The hospital unit occupied a small tent camp near the airfield.[31]

At Poltava, headquarters staff personnel continued to be housed in the large, partially destroyed building that medical inspectors had recommended for demolition earlier in the spring. The majority of permanent personnel and all transients were housed in pyramidal tents, with five men to a tent. The tents had wooden floors and were suitable for summer occupancy, but would be wholly inadequate should the base remain operational through the winter. Numerous visitors expressed concern that the main tent camp was too close to the airfield, and thus would expose the ground personnel to great peril in the event of an enemy attack. The tents were spaced at regular intervals and were very close together. To reduce the peril, Lieutenant Colonel Curtis Boas, Poltava's base commander, in early June, ordered some of the tents dispersed. At Piryatin, officers were initially billeted in the refurbished girls' school, and by mid-June were moved to a tent camp with the rest of the men. The camp was located about a mile and a half from the airstrip. As at Poltava, five men shared each pyramidal tent. Hospital personnel also lived in tents, four to each, while patients would be quartered in hospital tents that held sixteen patients each. Given the warm summer weather, none of the tents had heaters. The tents at all three bases had electricity, provided by Soviet sources, and were quite comfortable by Soviet standards. While inspecting the tent camp at Poltava in June, Soviet officers applauded the many improvisations of the individual that would be conducive of his comfort. They termed this "typical Americanism."[32]

The medical officers of Eastern Command were greatly concerned with the proper storage, preparation, and serving of food. Soviet women worked in the kitchens at all three bases under the supervision of a small number of American mess sergeants. From the outset of the operation, American medical and food service officers faced the considerable task of bringing existing Soviet facilities and practices up to the standards of the U.S. armed forces. The Soviets agreed to provide Eastern Command with fresh fruits, vegetables, and meat. The Americans were sensitive, however, to the fact that the Soviet population and armed forces were under a severe rationing system, and that local farms had been devastated by prolonged fighting as well as the German occupation. Therefore, they took care initially to look after the nutritional needs of their own people without making disparaging remarks about Soviet foodstuffs.

The Communist Party elite and government bureaucrats had access to special stores and restaurants that provided them with foods that were unavailable to the average Soviet citizen. The population at large appeared to subsist well on meat, bread, and potatoes. The men of the armed forces, in the rear areas, ate three large meals per day, which usually included generous portions of meat and potatoes. These soldiers only occasionally received fruits and vegetables but sugar was plentiful in both candy and desserts. At the front, Soviet soldiers actually ate better, except when on the march, and frontline units usually received American food brought in under Lend-Lease. Each Soviet officer and enlisted man received a minimum of 100 grams of vodka per day.[33]

While American observers did not find widespread malnutrition among Soviet civilians or soldiers or a shortage of foodstuffs in the Ukraine, the

AAF's primary concern was not the quantity of food that would be available to its men. What bothered Eastern Command's medical teams was the backward state of food storage and preparation in the Soviet military. As late as June 8, Lieutenant Colonel Jackson, command surgeon, reported that the supplemented rations available to U.S. personnel were "sufficient in bulk and quantity but very unappetizing to the American taste and prepared under sanitary conditions far below American standards." Of the three bases, Mirgorod had the best facilities and handling. A Soviet staff prepared food in a large, tile-floored kitchen equipped with both Soviet and American stoves and boilers. Soviet doctors examined the kitchen personnel every ten days for infectious diseases, but the effectiveness of such examinations was unknown to Jackson and his assistants.[34]

Poltava was an entirely different matter. In April, American medical inspectors found that the Soviet staff simply stored food in open containers without any protective measures being employed to protect it from insects, rodents, and dust. The kitchen had no refrigerators, and the condition of food when served was questionable. The cleanliness of the food handlers as well as dishes, silverware, and cooking utensils was clearly below American sanitary standards. The Soviets used very little soap to wash cooking implements, hence pots, pans, and dishes were often dirty and covered with a film of grease.[35]

By the middle of May, as the large contingent of personnel arrived with the Fourth Echelon, an inspection by Captain Robert H. Newell, one of the command's surgeons, found little improvement. The kitchen was located on the first floor of the U-shaped building and lacked running water and plumbing. Newell reported that the kitchen equipment was "ancient, dirty, and inadequate." The wood-fired stoves were so poorly ventilated that the kitchen itself was often permeated with smoke and fumes. "The malodorous evidence of the latrines," Newell wrote, was invariably noticed when "the wind [was] from the right direction." Kitchen personnel, mainly civilian women, were reported to be "untrained, slovenly in their work, dress and state of cleanliness," and many worked in their bare feet. A Soviet mess sergeant informed Newell that washing dishes with soap caused diarrhea and that he preferred to use a solution of baking soda, a procedure that left the dishes in the greasy condition American inspectors noted earlier.[36]

The Soviet mess sergeant also informed Newell that food was stored somewhere other than the rooms that were open for American scrutiny and not under the supervision of the sergeant in charge. During the same inspection, Captain Vernon Chadwick, Eastern Command's veterinary officer who was accompanying Newell on the inspection, found a large platter of dis-

colored, uncooked meat that was destined for the evening meal and declared it unsuitable for human consumption. He also found a large wooden
barrel in the corner of the kitchen that was filled with moldy bread. The
Soviets explained that this bread had been soaked in hot water and allowed
to ferment for forty-eight hours, after which the liquid was to be drained
and served in place of tea or fruit compote. The Soviets called this mixture
kvass and considered it a delicacy. The Americans were not immediately
interested in trying it. The Soviets had also placed two large wooden barrels
near the door that were filled with garbage. "Repugnant in appearance and
odor," they remained in place until full, at which time the Soviets hauled
the solids off to a local pig farm. They dumped the liquid waste in a shallow
trench some 200 yards from the kitchen.[37]

As a result of his inspection, Newell recommended that the Americans withdraw from the existing Soviet kitchens to more suitable facilities
that were available at the Base Mess. These latter messing facilities, however, would not be adequate for the large numbers of American troops now
deployed at Poltava. Given Soviet standards, Newell saw little hope for
change. He advised his superiors that any negative "diplomatic" effects re-
sulting from confronting the Soviets on such matters could not outweigh
the risks posed by the health hazards he had uncovered during his inspection.[38]

Problems persisted well into the summer months. Brigadier General
William C. Crist, Deane's chief of staff, noted that the Soviet women working in the kitchen needed "cleaning up." He reported with apparent alarm
that these women had only recently learned to use toilet paper. Crist
claimed that he saw only "some of the girl K. P.'s washing their hands after
doing a dirty job." Indeed, some transient aircrews, even the hungry ones,
refused to eat in the Soviet mess after seeing the conditions prevailing there.
By August, the Americans had corrected most of the foregoing deficiencies
by simply establishing messing facilities in the two tent camps at Poltava.
They now exerted direct control over food storage, preparation, and handling, and could rely on their own equipment. Soviet women continued to
work in these new mess tents and an inspecting sanitary engineer, Major
John Finney, still recommended that more U.S. mess personnel were necessary to ensure that standards did not regress.[39]

Piryatin also suffered from many of the defects found at Poltava. A
handful of American cooks supervised a large kitchen staff of Soviet
women. The women waited on the tables as the American airmen filed into
the mess hall, a small brick building on the post. The food was rich and
nourishing but the menu lacked variety. Chicken, dark bread, rice, and

ersatz coffee brewed from parched barley were regular offerings. The Soviets looked on this fare as excellent, however monotonous it seemed to the American airmen. As the number of personnel at the base increased in May 1944, the cooking facilities could not keep pace, and the Americans were soon grumbling about a diet that consisted of American corned beef hash and beans.[40]

New kitchen equipment arrived at Piryatin in May but the Americans discovered that their long-awaited field ranges required white gas; none was available at the time. By August, the Americans had adapted the ranges to operate on locally available fuels. The kitchen had already moved into a standard square mess tent. American medical personnel examined food handlers monthly, while Soviet doctors were responsible for the civilian women who were assisting in the kitchen.[41]

Jackson and his staff were generally satisfied with the storage facilities at Piryatin, but expressed some doubts about Soviet procedures for handling fresh meat. American medical officers did inspect all meat prior to use. This was necessary because the quality of the meat and sanitary conditions at the Soviet-run slaughterhouse had not been inspected for what one may describe as diplomatic reasons. Jackson, in particular, was acutely aware of Soviet sensibilities and, provided his staff could ensure that the food reaching the tables of American airmen was satisfactory, did not want to risk insulting or embarrassing the Soviets by demanding full access to all of their facilities. In his earlier reports, Jackson noted that the Soviets were quick to admit deficiencies and would become either sullen and defensive or overly generous in an effort to compensate for perceived shortcomings.[42] By late summer, despite continuous complaints from aircrews about the quality of the food at Eastern Command, Jackson and his staff believed they had brought available facilities and food-handling practices as close as possible to the standard of the rest of the U.S. Army Air Forces.

The Americans treated water at all three bases with chemicals and then boiled it before consumption. More often than not, all liquids consumed (apart from alcohol) were in the form of coffee, tea, or soup. The chemically treated and boiled liquids did not prove completely safe, unfortunately, and as late as July, more than a dozen pilots were unable to return to their bases in Italy as the result of dysentery they had contracted during their brief stay at Eastern Command.[43]

The retreating Germans had destroyed what passed for a sewage system in the area of Eastern Command's bases. When the first Americans arrived at Mirgorod, for example, they found that the Soviets emptied their sewage untreated into a nearby river. The barrack area at the artillery school contained five large, open, and full pit latrines that the Americans considered unsuitable. The Americans immediately asked the Soviets to drain the cesspools and construct new latrine facilities. Once again, American medical officers pointed out that the Soviets did not share Western standards of sanitation. Lieutenant Colonel Jackson reported that it was "extremely difficult to convince them [the Soviets] of the need for strict control and supervision."[44]

The Americans built entirely new latrine facilities for their own use at each base but complaints continued. Where American personnel had to rely on Soviet facilities, such as at the dispersal base near Zaporozh'ye, they found conditions completely unacceptable, with urine and excreta covering the seats and floors of latrines. A report from the 95th Bombardment Group, written in July, remarked that "throughout Russia the latrine situation was, to put it mildly, nauseating. Even in our own quarters, policing, de-orderizing [*sic*] and general maintenance was poor."[45]

The Soviets constructed their latrines to allow the user to simply squat over an opening in the floor, eliminating contact with a seat and thereby preventing, in their opinion, the spread of disease. The Americans found this to be the chief cause of the unsanitary conditions that characterized Soviet facilities. Once again, in the interest of "diplomacy," Eastern Command's medical officers refrained from challenging this Soviet practice. They did object to the Soviet soldiers using precious toilet paper for rolling cigarettes. Such protests had no effect and the Americans simply removed the paper from the enlisted men's latrine.[46] Despite the difference in sanitary standards between the Soviets and Americans, Eastern Command managed to construct and maintain suitable latrine facilities. Most combat crew members still complained but the previous health hazards were gone.

Fifteenth Air Force's historian for FRANTIC, Major James Parton, described bathing among the Soviet populace to be "at best a biennial event." As might be expected, he wrote, "local health standards were far below American norms. Contrary to the popular impression that all Russians are strapping giants glowing with health, the local peasants . . . exhibited signs of malnutrition, bad teeth, scabies and other unpleasant ailments."[47]

Again, the Americans had to overcome both primitive conditions and Soviet bad habits. At Poltava, for example, medical officers reported that bathing facilities were "extremely unsanitary, inadequate, and primitive." At this stage, in April 1944, the Soviets set aside three hours a week for the Americans to use the bath house. The bath house was in the cellar of the large U-shaped building. Bathers heated the water in buckets over a wood fire. The floors were filthy and slippery and an American medical officer reported that "the discerning individual would not consider a bath without wearing his [boots]." By late summer, the Americans had installed wash basins and an immersion type water heater in an ablution tent. They also set up a mobile bath unit at the nearby Vorskla River to provide warm showers for all personnel. Obviously, this arrangement would not be suitable beyond the summer months. Though most of the American personnel, both ground staff and aircrews, would have liked to bathe more often than once a week, Eastern Command had provided more than adequate facilities considering prevailing conditions in the region.[48]

Mirgorod also had bathing facilities, under canvas by summer, and a mobile bath unit at a nearby stream. Combat crews often went into Kharkov to use public showers. On one occasion, a group of men from the 95th Bombardment Group realized that their bathing activities also entertained the local female population. Marched into town by their operations officer, Colonel Joseph A. Moller, the men prompted quite a stir. As they entered the shower facility, the American airmen did not notice a row of windows near the ceiling. As they proceeded to lather up, the men became aware of dozens of Soviet women who had climbed on a ledge outside and were peering in through the windows, laughing and pointing, and generally enjoying themselves. Taken aback, the stalwart men of the 95th finished their showers.[49]

If American servicemen continued to gripe about the food, housing, and showers, conditions at Eastern Command were far superior to those found at most Soviet airfields. Many Red Air Force installations comprised little more than a grass airstrip with a few crude huts or tents. Considering the primitive state in which the Americans found the bases, the medical and engineering staffs had made great strides toward bringing all facilities up to the standards of U.S. forces operating under field conditions. Situated on the rolling steppes of the western Ukraine, basking in the warm summer sun, Eastern Command was as close to "America" as its personnel could make it.

From the beginning of the American presence in the Ukraine, relations between Americans and Ukrainians had been very good. Given the freedom to move about the region, the Americans quickly infiltrated the surrounding areas and made friends with local civilians. Despite orders from Spaatz forbidding bartering with the local populace, G.I.'s often returned to base at the end of a day on the town with chickens, eggs, or fresh vegetables.[50]

Throughout the early stages of construction and preparation at the bases, both Perminov and Kessler encouraged fraternization. Kessler's diary covering the early months of April and May contains numerous references to the cordial feelings that prevailed between his men and the Soviets. As the personnel of each echelon arrived at the bases, the Soviets treated them warmly, and the Americans were hard-pressed to repay the Soviets for the many parties they threw for their guests.

The civilians in the areas surrounding Eastern Command's bases also greeted the G.I.s openly and in a friendly manner. The townspeople were open-hearted, and many invited Americans into their homes. Americans wandered about the local bazaars, buying, among other things, caps like those worn by peasant farmers. After wearing them for a few days, the G.I.s usually mailed them home when told by their officers that they could not wear civilian caps while in uniform.[51]

A favorite trick of the G.I.s at Eastern Command was to teach the Soviet women and girls who worked in the mess halls select words and phrases of profanity and slang. When things did not go right on a given day, many of these women were heard to say "Oh my aching back," much to the amusement of the Americans within earshot. During the many inspection tours of Eastern Command facilities, these same women sought to impress visiting senior American officers by smiling broadly and saying, "How do you do, you lousy son-of-a-bitch?" or "Would you like some goddamned coffee?" Startled, many of these officers barely managed a weak smile and a polite "hello" or "No thank you" before storming off to report the matter to an American officer.[52]

Still, the tempo of preparation and the early operational missions kept most Eastern Command personnel fairly busy. Often, they had little time to do more than go into town to watch a Soviet movie or use the public showers. During the spring months, including June, members of the Soviet and American air forces appeared to get along well together. The Americans struggled to learn some Russian—fewer than three dozen interpreters were assigned to Eastern Command—while the Soviets did their best to make their allies feel at home. Kessler stated that he was "firmly convinced that they are all for us, and that they like us. I have never seen anything like the spontaneous jubilation or excitement they displayed when the first outfit . . . arrived." The real test of Soviet-American friendship at this lowest level of international relations would come after FRANTIC began its long slide into irrelevance.[53]

In the summer of 1944 aircrews looked at a mission to the Ukraine as something of an adventure. Accustomed to a relatively comfortable life in wartime Britain, many combat crew members were anxious to see this strange land. Though they griped and complained about the food, lack of bathing facilities, and the quarters, the men generally returned to Italy or Britain with a favorable view of the Soviet people.

Many combat crew members returned to Britain or Italy with pleasant memories of the Soviet people. Volmer L. Miller, a tail gunner assigned to the 569th Bomb Squadron, remarked that the Soviets were friendly and that the area around Mirgorod looked "just like home," back in the western United States. Miller also differed from most of his colleagues in his opinion of Ukrainian food. He thought it good, in fact, like "the kind my mother made at home." Raymond Strate, a pilot with the 571st Bomb Squadron, noticed that the local population consisted largely of older women and little children. He and other crew members gave candy to the children, but when he shared his rations with a Soviet guard, the group commander, Colonel Fred Ott, chewed him out. Apparently, his superiors viewed such action as a violation of Spaatz's order against bartering or giving away American supplies.[54]

Some of the combat crews saw a chance to make money while in the Ukraine. They often sold cigarettes and candy to the local populace, while personnel who were permanently stationed in Eastern Command simply gave away such items. The Soviets quickly realized what was going on and were offended that some Americans gave them things while others sold similar goods. At first, this was a minor irritant. Later in the summer, when the selling of American commodities would blossom into full-blown black-marketeering, the Soviet authorities would take action.[55]

Though more senior American flying officers had little time for mingling with Soviet civilians, they still managed to get a glimpse of life in wartime Soviet Russia. Colonel Moller recalled a trip into Mirgorod with a female interpreter, Maja. A large group of civilians was gathered around a small billboard, which served as the town's newspaper. He noticed quite a stir and figured that the people must have been agitated over some important war news. Maja dispelled that notion when she told him what was causing the commotion. Stalin, she said, had decreed that on-the-spot divorces were no longer allowed. The contending spouses would now have to register for a divorce and then remain together another three days before it was final. "That's what all the hullabaloo was about," Moller stated.[56]

The aircrews saw relatively little of their opposite numbers in the Red Air Force. The two groups would mix occasionally at local restaurants, and Soviet navigators and radio operators routinely flew on the cargo planes making the trip to and from Iran. The crews did see Soviet ground personnel. At times, the heavy bombers slid over the edge of the steel matting because of hydraulic systems failures or blown tires. A pilot of the 390th, then First Lieutenant John Warner, recalled watching in amazement as the Soviets brought out "a whole bunch of people" to pull his aircraft out of the mud and get it back on a solid surface.[57]

When members of the two air forces did work together, they often found that they could get along quite well. Second Lieutenant James Webb, a bombardier with the 568th Squadron, recalled that a Soviet navigator flew with his crew when they left for Italy on June 26. He did not know the man's name, but knew the Soviet officer had flown between 150 to 200 combat missions. He arrived at the aircraft in his dress uniform, complete with medals. Once over the Balkans, Webb believed the crew's American navigator was lost. The Soviet navigator was looking out the window at the mountainous terrain below, and tracing the flight path on his map with his finger. When he realized that his AAF counterpart was lost, he moved to the navigator's position and put his finger down on the map. After some quick calculations, the American navigator, "Gus" DiMarco, began laughing and nodding. The Soviet was right. The Americans were astonished at the man's dead reckoning skills. After landing in Italy, the Soviet major spent a few days with Webb and his crew before boarding a C-47 for the long trip home.[58]

Soviet and American airmen appeared to share a bond that did not exist to the same degree elsewhere between personnel of the two armed forces. Alexander Werth, correspondent for the London *Sunday Times,* who spent the entire war in the Soviet Union, pointed out that while the Soviets constantly complained of the "unequal sacrifices" they were making relative to the Anglo-American war effort, their airmen tended to have a higher regard for the West, in part because of the large numbers of aircraft brought into the country through Lend-Lease. Soviet airmen, according to Werth, were greatly impressed by the news of the Allied bombings of Germany.[59] The Americans would point out at every opportunity that they found their counterparts in the Red Air Force very cooperative and friendly.

The airmen singled out Soviet women, even those in uniform, for extra attention. After strafing Axis airfields in Romania, fifteen P-38s of the 82nd Fighter Group that were participating in FRANTIC III touched down at Piryatin on July 22. During the debriefing, the crews' attention was drawn to a blonde, female Soviet interpreter. The men vied with one another to see who could sit with her that evening during a movie shown in the town, supposedly to take advantage of her language skills so that the G.I.s could follow the action on the screen. They also noticed that all the other young women they saw were in uniform. As the 82nd's official narrative reported afterward, "the girls' faces were not hard to look at but the bodies were awe-inspiring—arms like the village smithy. They were good-natured and friendly. Some of the lads turned on the charm, but couldn't overcome the language barrier."[60]

The crews complained that they needed more information about the customs of the locals. Crew members believed their lack of knowledge about Ukrainian culture prevented them from mixing freely with the Soviet people or from moving about the area and seeing something of the country. Perhaps their inability to charm the local women caused several crews to suggest more language training or better language guides.[61]

The crews praised Soviet mechanics for their ability to learn as they helped repair both American fighters and bombers. One group commander reported that "the Russians showed a marked inclination to take something apart even if they couldn't put it together again." Soviet officers usually stood back, taking notes. The Americans were somewhat upset by the fact that, while Russians climbed all over the B-17s, P-38s, and P-51s, Americans were forbidden to do the same to Soviet aircraft. A frosty reception was accorded any attempt to get information on the Red Air Force. The Soviets refused American mechanics access even to aircraft built in the United States and provided through Lend-Lease. Happily, this was a minor irritant, one that would not threaten the otherwise generally good relations existent in early summer.[62]

The ground and aircrews of the AAF had not come to the Ukraine to simply socialize with the Soviet populace. In June 1944, USSTAF was anxious to make the best possible use of the shuttle-bombing bases as the Western Allies struggled to expand the Normandy bridgehead. Certainly, fostering good relations with the Soviets was a primary objective of FRANTIC. Thus, the generally friendly atmosphere between the Soviets and Americans at Eastern Command was gratifying to the AAF and the Military Mission in Moscow. But General Arnold and his staff wanted bombing missions with which they could prove the value of strategic operations to the Red Air Force.

As the aircrews of FRANTIC JOE mingled with the Soviets at Eastern Command bases, Lieutenant General Eaker had reached an agreement with the Soviets about targets for FRANTIC's bombers. As a result of Eaker's bargaining in Moscow, the Soviets finally approved an American proposal to strike the airdrome and Heinkel works at Mielec, Poland. But as luck would have it, a weather low moved in over eastern Germany and Poland, and it would be several days before the units of FRANTIC JOE could strike the target. In the meantime, Eastern Command and Fifteenth Air Force officers planned a mission for June 6 against the Axis airdrome at Galatz (present-day Galati), Romania, near the mouth of the Danube.[63]

As Anglo-American armies were wading ashore in Normandy hundreds of miles to the west, a force of 112 B-17s and forty-seven P-51s struck Galatz. Five of the fighters and five of the bombers returned early because of mechanical problems. The bombing force encountered two dozen German fighters and the flak was meager and inaccurate. First Lieutenant Cullen J. Hoffman scored the first American aerial victory on the Eastern Front when he shot down a German JU-88 twin-engine bomber. The American force lost two P-51s, but intelligence officers considered the bombing results as "good," with reconnaissance photos showing more than a dozen Axis aircraft destroyed on the field and bomb craters scattered across the runways. In all, the American force claimed eight German fighters in the air. The first American raid mounted from shuttle bases in the Ukraine had been relatively successful.[64]

As the attack force returned to its Ukrainian bases, Soviet and American personnel once again turned out to watch the aircraft land. At Poltava, the aircraft returned within two minutes of the previously announced arrival time. The big bombers put on an impressive show for the crowd, flying a few hundred feet over the field in squadron elements of six ships each. One element after another peeled off for landing, the aircraft touching down at precisely thirty-second intervals. One officer of the Fifteenth remarked that "the magnitude of the spectacle and the precision with which the landings were affected impressed everyone."[65]

The weather refused to cooperate for a strike on Mielec, however, and the group commanders prepared to return to Italy rather than wait for clearing skies. Spaatz signaled Eastern Command late in the day on June 6 and ordered the crews to remain in the Soviet Union. With the invasion of Europe under way, he thought it important to maintain an air threat to Germany from the east. Thus, the Fifth Wing dawdled for the next five days while the persistent low refused to move.[66]

The crews now found themselves with virtually nothing to do other than undergo routine equipment checks and minor equipment repairs. To fill their days, the post-mission summary reported, they "lolled in the warm sun, played softball in the thick clover, [and] ambled curiously through the ruined towns." As G.I.s inevitably did regardless of their posting, they sought out female companionship. They flirted with the handful of American nurses stationed at each base and made approaches to Soviet women, both military and civilian. The Soviets staged several concerts and the men attended dances at which they were bemused by the sight of Soviet male soldiers dancing together. The Soviets were equally astonished by the American "jitter-bug." Alexander Werth wrote that it was "strange to see in the heart of Gogol country" American G.I.s eating "vast quantities" of American food, flirting with the local women, and making such remarks that the area looked just like "back home in Indiana."[67]

With the weather still precluding operations against Mielec, Spaatz finally issued orders for the force to return to Italy. On the morning of June 11, 129 B-17s and sixty P-51s formed up in the skies over Mirgorod for the flight back to Italian bases. The target for this mission was another airfield in Romania, this time at Focsani. One P-51 crashed on takeoff while six B-17s and seven P-51s returned to Eastern Command bases because of mechanical problems. The remaining planes pushed on, encountering fifteen enemy aircraft over the target as well as accurate and heavy flak. This antiaircraft fire hit a B-17 from the 97th Bomb Group, causing it to straggle out of formation. Lurking German fighters finished it off. Still, the task force struck Focsani, with relatively poor results. The weight of the attack missed the airfield itself. The force landed in Italy without further loss due to hostile action.[68]

FRANTIC JOE was officially over. American officers termed it an "outstanding success." Losses had been light, and if the primary target, the Heinkel aircraft factory and airdrome at Mielec, escaped the task force's attention, the Germans were now fully aware that they faced yet another "front" in the air. Eaker sent a message to Major General Nathan Twining, Fifteenth Air Force commander, commending the crews of the Fifth Wing. Eaker stated that he was "particularly happy with the performance of [Twining's] personnel" while they were in the Soviet Union. "Their conduct," he continued, "was a model in every respect and did much to promote friendly relations between the American and Russian peoples. . . . " Eaker also believed that this first mission had done much to impress the Soviets with the power and efficiency of U.S. strategic forces. Overall, the Americans and Soviets had every reason to be pleased. Months of hard work and frustration in constructing Eastern Command's bases had apparently borne fruit in this first mission.[69]

With Allied forces firmly ashore in Normandy by the middle of June, Eighth Air Force units were becoming available once more for missions against objectives not directly related to the landings. On June 15, Headquarters, Eighth Air Force tasked the Third Bombardment Division to provide units for the second shuttle to Eastern Command. The VIII Fighter Command would provide escorts. The "warning" order for the mission mandated that all crew members "be thoroughly indoctrinated as to the importance of making a good impression" on the Soviets. "Every individual should consider himself a committee of one" to ensure that the Soviets retained the high opinion of American servicemen they apparently had formed during the past weeks.[70]

Once again, the AAF dispatched veteran units on FRANTIC. The Thirteenth Combat Wing included the 95th, 100th, and 390th Bomb Groups. Colonel Thomas S. Jeffrey's 100th, for example, entered combat operations in June 1943. By the time of FRANTIC II, the group had earned the nickname "Bloody Hundredth." A myth spread throughout the AAF that during the Regensburg mission of August 1943, a bomber belonging to the group had lowered its wheels as a token of surrender. When three German fighters moved in to escort the aircraft down, one or more of the gunners opened fire, destroying the Nazi aircraft. The 100th's combat losses thereafter seemed to reinforce the notion that the *Luftwaffe* now nursed a vendetta against B-17s marked with the unit's "square D" on the tail. Indeed, other units lost more aircraft than the 100th. However, as one veteran later wrote, when the group lost, "we lost big." The unit lost nine crews over Regensburg and seven over Bremen and twelve at Munster in October 1943. The group's heaviest losses came over Berlin; fifteen crews failed to return on March 6 and another nine were lost in May.[71]

The remaining groups of the Thirteenth Wing, the 95th and 390th, did not boast such spectacular reputations but each possessed fine combat records. Both units received Distinguished Unit Citations for their part in the August 1943 raid on Regensburg. Commanded in June 1944 by Colonel Frederick W. Ott, the 390th flew the Regensburg mission only five days after entering active combat operations. Both groups participated in Big Week in February. The 95th, Colonel Kessler's old unit, was now under Colonel Karl Truesdell, Jr. It received another citation for action seen over Berlin on March 4, 1944. The 390th was awarded a second citation for its part in the second Schweinfurt mission of October 1943.[72]

The Forty-fifth Combat Wing, destined to land at Poltava, contained the 96th, 388th, and 452nd Bomb Groups. The 96th and 388th had been in action since May and July 1943, respectively. The 96th, led by Lieutenant Colonel Robert J. Nolan, had already earned two Distinguished Unit Citations by June 1944. The 388th under Colonel William B. David, possessed three; it would earn a fourth for the upcoming mission to Soviet Russia. Colonel Thetus C. Odom's 452nd, blooded in combat during Big Week just a few days after its activation, had quickly proven its mettle during the spring of 1944 and earned a berth on FRANTIC II.[73]

Elements of two fighter groups, the 4th and 352nd, were picked to escort the bombers to Eastern Command. The 4th's commander, Colonel Donald J. Blakeslee, was an experienced and reliable combat leader. The 352nd had been in action since the previous September. Under Colonel Joe L. Mason, the unit came to Spaatz's attention by earning a citation for routing a numerically superior force of German fighters while escorting bombers to Brunswick, Germany, on May 8, 1944. Flown by aggressive and experienced pilots, led by able and competent officers, the P-51s of both groups were representative of the Allies' growing might in the air over Germany.[74]

The man Spaatz selected to command the second FRANTIC task force was Colonel Archie J. Old, Jr. Old earned his wings in 1932, leaving active service the following year. Returning to the Air Corps as a captain in April 1940, he rose quickly in both rank and position, becoming a lieutenant colonel in July 1942. In December 1943, he assumed command of the 45th Combat Wing and was promoted to colonel the following March. Old flew forty-three combat missions, suffering wounds during the October 1943 attack on Schweinfurt. Briefed that part of his mission was, as he later recalled, to "get along with the Russians," Old was a superb choice to lead the second shuttle. He would go on to attain the rank of brigadier general in November 1944 and emerged from the crucible of war as one of the AAF's most respected commanders.[75]

At 5:30 on the morning of June 21, 163 B-17s and seventy P-51s took off from fields in southeastern England. The target for this second FRANTIC task force was the Ruhland oil refinery south of Berlin. Because of mechanical problems, five fighters and eighteen bombers returned early. The force encountered meager flak but tangled with approximately forty-five ME-109s near the target and along the route to Eastern Command. German defenses claimed three B-17s and two fighters. Twenty-six bombers drifted off course and bombed a factory in nearby Elsterwerda. The crews still rated the results of the bombing as "good." Ruhland would be hit several more times by Eighth Air Force units that were participating in POINT-BLANK.[76]

The second FRANTIC task force attracted the attention of the *Luftwaffe* as it droned on to the Ukraine. During the flight from Berlin to the Soviet Union, an American bomber crew reported a German single-engine fighter tailing the formation. When P-51 escorts moved to challenge him, the German pilot played a game of cat-and-mouse in the clouds. Only bad weather at the Soviet-German front caused the enemy fighter to break contact.[77]

The task force began arriving at bases in the Soviet Union late in the afternoon. Despite the fact that many of their bombers were short of fuel

The main parking apron at Poltava, June 1944. Note that many of the B-17s are sporting silver paint, which causes them to stand out more clearly on the ground to aircraft passing overhead. *Courtesy U.S. Air Force.*

by this point, the crews of the 45th Combat Wing put on the usual "air show," flying over the field at Poltava in perfect formation. Within forty-five minutes, seventy aircraft had landed. The 13th Combat Wing touched down at Mirgorod. Five bombers landed in the area near Kiev, having run out of fuel. Only one suffered any damage during the forced landings.[78]

To check the identities of the crews, Soviet border guards met the aircraft as they taxied into parking areas at each of the three fields. After the usual crew interrogations and debriefings, the weary airmen sought something to eat and looked forward to getting some sleep after an eleven-hour flight. Colonel Old had a late dinner at Eastern Command headquarters with Walsh, Kessler (who had been promoted to brigadier general earlier in the month), Perminov, and several other Soviet officers.[79]

While the newly arrived crews got their first taste of the Soviet Union, a German long-range reconnaissance plane circled the American field at Poltava, taking photographs of the large numbers of B-17s, their silver paint reflecting the rays of the late afternoon sun. As the German plane returned to its base, it passed near the field at Mirgorod, where, Colonel Joe Moller asked the Soviets for permission to contact Piryatin to send up P-51s and bring the German plane down. The Soviets refused his request. German reconnaissance aircraft routinely passed over Soviet air bases without a *Luftwaffe* attack following their visits. Besides, the Soviet base commander told Moller, if the P-51s did go up, "then it would be said you had to defend yourself at Soviet bases." The German aircraft returned unmolested to the large German air base at Minsk.[80]

As Old, Walsh, and Kessler enjoyed dinner with their Soviet hosts, a large formation of German bombers passed over the front heading in the direction of Eastern Command. At approximately 11:20 P.M., the Soviets sounded the alarm at Poltava. The generals scrambled out of the building to ensure that their personnel were taking shelter and then took cover themselves. Less than an hour later, Soviet antiaircraft batteries began firing into the night sky as searchlights probed the darkness for enemy aircraft. For nearly a quarter of an hour, the Americans heard only the sound of Soviet flak batteries. Then, at 12:30 A.M., June 22, a German aircraft roared over, dropping flares to illuminate the field and aircraft below. This was no false alarm; the *Luftwaffe* was attacking Poltava.[81]

Unfortunately, the base was extremely vulnerable to attack. Because the crews were so tired, the group commanders agreed to postpone the indoctrination lecture from 9:00 P.M., on the evening of the 21st to 9:00 A.M., the next morning. This lecture would have provided the crews with information on the necessary precautions to take in the event of an air raid. Furthermore, Eastern Command had made little attempt to camouflage the installation, although the steel matting for the runway was painted green and the grass growing through the holes and gaps of the material helped to hide it. Dispersed and stored in revetments, ammunition was otherwise visible from the air. Because of a lack of underground storage capacity, nearly half a million gallons of high octane gasoline sat in stacks of 55-gallon drums around the perimeter of the field. As widely dispersed as possible, the B-17s, in their silver paint, gleamed brightly in the light of the German pathfinders' flares.[82]

Several factors had combined to lull both ground staff and aircrews at Poltava into a sense of complacency. First, the apparent strength of Soviet air defenses impressed the Americans. Though they questioned their effectiveness early on, Eastern Command's officers seemed satisfied by the sheer number of antiaircraft guns at the field and Soviet promises of both day- and night-fighter protection. Secondly, most of the Americans had grown accustomed to the relative security of their bases in Britain; few had ever undergone a major German raid. Finally, the Americans knew that their bases in southern Italy, which were much closer to the front than those of Eastern Command, had never suffered a serious attack by the *Luftwaffe*. The presence of the German reconnaissance plane earlier in the day may have rankled some of the bomb group commanders, but apparently did not concern them sufficiently to prompt them to order the dispersal of the force to other fields. Thus, when the alarm sounded, most of the task force personnel reacted in the same fashion as they would have had they been back in Britain. In Colonel Old's words, "they merely turned over and cussed because they had been awakened, however, [*sic*] when the bombs started falling they found the ditches and shelters in record time." Slit trenches dug near the tent camp could accommodate 300 people; there were over 1,100 Americans present in the camp at the time of the attack.[83]

In the confusion caused by the attack, many of the newly arrived crew members became disoriented. First Lieutenant Raymond C. Estle, a pilot with the 96th Bomb Group, slept through the alarm, only to be awakened by the sound of exploding bombs. He and his co-pilot, Flight Officer Joseph G. Lukacek, ran out of their tent but realized they had no idea where the slit trenches were located. Running aimlessly, Estle and Lukacek dove behind a loose stack of bricks. A bomb exploded less than 12 feet away. Estle felt numerous fragments tear into his body. He called to Lukacek and in the eerie glow of the flares, saw that his co-pilot was dead. Unable to move, Estle cried out for help. After several groups of men ran past without stopping, another combat crew member paused to help him. Lieutenant Colonel Jackson arrived on the scene, gave Estle some morphine, and had him moved to the hospital. Surgeons amputated Estle's mangled left leg. He died of complications a few days later.[84]

A handful of Americans were caught on the airfield itself when the German attack began. Staff Sergeant Samuel C. Perla of the 388th Bomb Group was one of a small number of combat crew members who were on guard duty that night. Actually, he was asleep in the waist of his B-17 when the raid opened. Like most of his comrades, he was not alarmed by the sound of antiaircraft fire; he later recalled that he thought "it was another 'dry run' as we were used to in England." As the bombs began to fall, Perla tumbled out of the plane. Frightened, he attempted to extinguish some of the flares by dousing them with sand. He could not find any shelter "and being out in the midst of all this inferno" he recalled later, continued his firefighting to "keep from losing my mind and to have something to do." Struck by bomb fragments, he finally decided to leave the field. A Soviet guard fired at Perla as he staggered away from the burning aircraft. When the soldier realized that Perla was a wounded American, he carried him to a truck and roared off toward the hospital. Perla doubted he would make it there alive; the Soviet soldier kept stopping to help put out fires. Reaching the hospital where a doctor gave him morphine and dressed his wounds, Perla survived—and spent the remainder of the raid in a slit trench.[85]

Fortunately, most Eastern Command personnel kept their wits about them and reacted quickly to the raid. The nurse on duty at the hospital awakened the patients and herded them into the trenches. Luckily, there were only four patients and none was in serious condition. Throughout the raid, as the bombing increased in intensity, the members of the hospital staff and several of the young Soviet girls who were attached to the medical unit shielded the patients with their own bodies in an effort to protect them from deadly bomb fragments.[86]

The German raid lasted nearly two hours. At 2:20 A.M., bright flashes from photo flash bombs illuminated the field. German reconnaissance aircraft were flying over to record the results of the strike. Though the Soviet antiaircraft batteries continued to blaze away for more than a quarter of an hour longer, the German force was gone. It left behind the smoldering wreckage of forty-three B-17s. Every other bomber on the field had also been hit. Three days later, accordingly, only nine of the original force of seventy-three were flyable. The Germans also destroyed more than 250,000 gallons of gasoline as well as hundreds of bombs and hundreds of thousands of rounds of machine gun ammunition. The German force, nearly 150 bombers of German General Rudolf Meister's Fourth Flying Corps, returned intact to its bases in Belorussia.[87]

During the raid, Soviet troops, both male and female, rushed out onto the airfield proper to fight the fires. Using shovels or their bare hands, they threw dirt onto the flames. The single fire truck and two fire trailers available were totally inadequate to a task of this nature. The Soviets' firefighting operations placed many of Red Air Force personnel in serious danger. After cratering the field with large demolition bombs, the Germans dropped incendiaries and thousands of antipersonnel mines. Dubbed "butterfly" bombs because of a set of flaps that sprung open to serve as a triggering mechanism, these antipersonnel devices claimed many of the Soviet troops who ventured onto the field.[88]

Indeed, the Americans were astounded at both the bravery and recklessness that Soviet troops displayed during the attack and the cleanup operation afterward. Few Americans were so inclined, but the Soviets refused to let those who wanted to help fight the fires on the airfield emerge from their trenches and hiding places. They seemed overly concerned for the

A glimpse of the wreckage of American aircraft following the German attack on Poltava, 22/23 June 1944. *Courtesy U.S. Air Force.*

well-being of the American airmen. For example, at 4:30 A.M., on the 22nd, as fires raged and exploding ordnance rocked the airfield, a Soviet soldier, Sergeant-Mechanic Tubisin, and a USAAF captain approached Lieutenant Colonel Jackson who was in a jeep searching for casualties. They told Jackson that an explosion had injured several soldiers in the north-central sector of the field. Jackson directed the enlisted man who was with him to take a Soviet truck back to the hospital and bring back an ambulance.[89]

A Soviet officer, Lieutenant Ivan Sivalobor, climbed aboard Jackson's jeep, giving directions and pointing out butterfly bombs. Sergeant Tubisin sat on the front of the jeep, also watching for the mines, while Mechanic Luckor Georgy walked out in front, picking up the small but deadly bombs and carefully laying them aside. He cleared away more than forty of them by the time the little group arrived at the scene of the explosion. There, Jackson administered first aid to two Soviet soldiers. One was critically injured and had a leg completely blown off, while the other had multiple wounds and a compound fracture of the right leg. Both Georgy and Tubisin assisted Jackson in keeping the wounded men warm and calm. After putting the casualties in the jeep, the two Soviet soldiers repeated their mine-clearing operation until the vehicle made it safely out of the mined area. Jackson cited both men for extraordinary bravery and recommended that they receive the appropriate Soviet decorations for their heroism.[90]

Over the course of the next several weeks, Soviet troops cleared the field of thousands of butterfly bombs. Once again, the Americans who witnessed their operation expressed amazement over the manner in which the Soviets carried out this dangerous activity. Colonel Old reported that some Soviet sappers gently picked up the bombs—each weighed slightly more than two pounds—and threw them as far as possible, then "either [fell] full flat on their face or else [ran] like hell." First Lieutenant Leo S. Haynes of the 390th Bomb Group recalled seeing "Russian troops, men and women, walking down the length of this field, not quite shoulder to shoulder . . . to recover all of these anti-personnel mines . . . Very impressive to see but not very kind to human life."[91]

The 95th's Joe Moller expressed disgust over the Soviets' apparent lack of consideration for human life. He remembered watching Soviet troops armed with rifles moving slowly down the airfield. When one spotted a butterfly bomb, he would shoot at it until it blew up. "Once in a while, a piece of the bomb would hit one of these guys and down he'd go. [The others] didn't pay any attention to him."[92]

The German strike hobbled Eastern Command. Casualties among the Americans had been light: two officers killed, six enlisted men severely wounded. The losses in aircraft, however, represented one of the costliest days of the American air war in Europe. Fortunately, the Germans had bombed with superb accuracy. The proximity of the tent camps to the airfield would have led to a slaughter of aircrews and ground personnel had the Germans not concentrated on the giant B-17s exposed on the field.[93]

Soviet losses were heavier, with approximately twenty-two Soviet personnel killed on the airfield and another dozen who were serving the antiaircraft batteries. More than sixty Soviets were wounded during the raid. These figures do not include those killed and injured while clearing the field; American reports clearly indicate that an equal number became casualties during the following weeks. The Soviets also lost a C-47 and twenty-five fighters and trainers. Despite expending more than 28,000 rounds of antiaircraft ammunition, the Soviets could claim no German aircraft. When asked about the apparent absence of Soviet night-fighters in the sky during the raid, General Perminov informed the astonished Americans that the Soviets had attacked German airfields during and after the *Luftwaffe* attack. For those combat crews who watched as the Germans destroyed their aircraft, the general's answer seemed ludicrous.[94]

The Germans struck at Mirgorod and Piryatin the next night. Having learned their lesson, the Americans had already dispersed their aircraft to other locations. The 95th and 100th Bomb Groups went to Kharkov, while the 390th moved to Zaporozh'ye on the eastern bank of the Dnieper River. The field at Mirgorod suffered heavy damage, but the Germans dropped their bombs nearly 3 miles away from Piryatin. At Poltava, nonflyable aircraft were dispersed around the field while American and Soviet work parties moved the remaining stores of fuel and ammunition. Crews stranded by the destruction of their aircraft were evacuated several days after the raid on six C-47s via the southern route through Iran. In the days that followed the strike on Poltava, the Soviets showed concern and genuine embarrassment over the loss of the American aircraft. Many American officers, on the other hand, openly questioned the Soviets' ability to protect Eastern Command and doubted that the FRANTIC operation should continue.[95]

The Americans' most immediate concern was how to report the news of the attack to the world. Berlin Radio reported on the 23rd that German aircraft had mounted a highly successful raid on American bases in the Soviet Union. Deane wanted to avoid any recriminations or finger-pointing. He hoped that the event could yield dividends in that the Soviets might become more amenable to American requests for greater cooperation, particularly in the Far East, and that the shock of the attack would make the two sides work more closely. Anxious to avoid any hint of inter-Allied problems, Deane recommended that the fifteen British and American correspondents who were present at Poltava during the raid cite examples of heroism and how the Soviets and Americans had worked together under fire. He managed to arrange simultaneous press releases from London and Moscow for the 24th.[96]

Much has been written about the German strike on Poltava and the reasons for its success. The causes of the American disaster at Poltava can be attributed to a combination of three factors: Soviet doctrine, American complacency, and German preparedness.

First, the Soviets did not view the concept of "defense" favorably. The Red Army defended something only as a prelude to launching a counterattack. Oriented toward ground support, the Red Air Force had few heavy bombers. Thus, the Soviets lacked both the equipment and the experience required to defend installations utilized by heavy bombers. They favored passive measures to safeguard their aircraft: dispersal, camouflage, and the building of phony airfields designed to draw the *Luftwaffe*'s attention. While some officers at Eastern Command suspected the success of the raid was somehow a result of Soviet duplicity or gross incompetence, the

Soviet Yak-9s assigned to defend Eastern Command bases. B-17s are visible in the background. *Courtesy U.S. Air Force.*

Soviets had, in fact, provided what they considered to be an adequate defense.[97]

Following a long talk with Nikitin, Deane reported to Arnold that he learned Soviet night-fighters did not carry airborne radar sets, by then common to both the Germans and Western Allies, but instead worked with searchlights. The Soviets also lacked complete radar coverage and continued to rely on ground observers. Nevertheless, the Red Air Force saw nothing wrong with their system. Too great an emphasis on defense went against their grain; Stalin himself called it "loafing."[98]

Second, the Americans themselves cannot be held blameless. Senior American officers reported both before and after the raid that Eastern Command had taken few precautions against a German attack. Brigadier General William C. Crist complained that tents were lined up in neat rows, too close to the airfield, as if Poltava was a stateside camp during peacetime maneuvers. The men had done little in the way of camouflaging supplies. American personnel, accustomed to the near-total security of their bases in Britain, were apparently unable to adjust mentally to the more dangerous state of affairs on the Soviet front. Eastern Command's officers may have questioned the condition of Soviet equipment, but apparently never thought to ask the Soviets how they used it. The Soviets also claimed afterward that they had tried unsuccessfully to convince the Americans to disperse their aircraft around the fringes of the field. Nikitin did warn the Americans that the Germans were quite familiar with Poltava and its environs; the headquarters of German Army Group South were located there in the summer of 1942 and the *Luftwaffe* had used the airfield well into 1943. Such factors obviously indicate that the Americans seemed to discount the possibility of a German attack. Paradoxically, an American intelligence report issued in mid-June had pointed out that Eastern Command was only 400 miles from German bases in Belorussia. Those bases held an estimated 200 long-range German bombers that were capable of reaching the American installations.[99]

Finally, the concentration of so many four-engine bombers at the Soviet airfields provided the Germans with a most lucrative target. The units the Germans used to strike at Poltava had been raised as part of a larger scheme, undertaken the previous autumn, to form a strategic bomber force capable of striking key Soviet industrial targets. This plan took shape too late, since by the spring of 1944, the Germans had been pushed out of range of the targets they wished to hit in the Urals and beyond. In the brief lull before Operation BAGRATION, the Soviet offensive of the summer of 1944, the *Luftwaffe* found itself with a considerable offensive force at its disposal and a worthwhile and relatively poorly defended target within reach at Poltava. In the aftermath of the Poltava raid, BAGRATION eliminated this German bomber force as a threat to Eastern Command by overrunning German airfields and forcing the *Luftwaffe* to throw every aircraft available into the desperate attempt to stem the Russian flood westward in the late summer of 1944.[100]

The German raid on Poltava did have an effect on the men and women of Eastern Command. Lieutenant Colonel Jackson, Chaplain Strippy, and other officers reported a noticeable drop in morale by the end of June. As the next chapter will chronicle in detail, the drop in morale was not attributed solely to the attack of June 22. Most of the men, however, remained favorably disposed toward the Soviets and were eager to continue fostering good relations with them.[101]

The American troops did feel a measure of resentment over the Soviets' apparent inability to protect them from enemy air attacks. Still, the G.I.s expressed their displeasure with the alleged failure of their own superiors to determine prior to the beginning of operations whether the Soviets could adequately protect the airdromes. Many among the American combat crews and ground staff admired Soviet soldiers, male and female, for the bravery they exhibited during the German attack. On the other hand, some of the more senior officers felt betrayed and misled by the Soviets, and suspected that they had allowed the Germans to attack the base as a signal that the American presence was no longer desirable in the perspective of the Kremlin.[102]

Though the Americans remained committed to FRANTIC, events now began to overtake the operation. On the morning of June 22, 1944, three years to the day after Hitler's troops launched Operation BARBAROSSA, more than 24,000 Soviet artillery pieces opened fire on the positions of German Army Group Center in Belorussia. The Soviet operation, BAGRATION, involved 1,254,000 troops in the first assault waves alone. By concentrating their resources against selected zones along the front, the Soviets attained a 10:1 advantage over the Germans in armor, artillery, and aircraft. With the British and Americans firmly ashore in Normandy and growing more powerful by the day, the Germans could not shift reserves from the west to the east as they had in the past. Hamstrung by Hitler's no-retreat orders, Army Group Center was cut to pieces. By the middle of July, the Soviets had all but evicted the Germans from their soil and were approaching the frontiers of East Prussia.[103]

As the Soviets rolled forward, they took possession of many of FRANTIC's potential targets in eastern Poland. With each passing day, the front moved farther from Eastern Command's bases. Undeterred by this development, the Americans pursued plans to beef up the defenses at Poltava, Mirgorod, and Piryatin so that FRANTIC missions might continue. By the second week in July, however, Deane realized that basing aircraft permanently in the Soviet Union, as well as deploying adequate defenses such as night-fighters and antiaircraft batteries, would require a force of 18,500 Americans. He revised his estimates of projected operations to accommodate two "shuttles" per month, each of which would include five to six missions from Soviet bases. Even this latter scheme would require nearly 9,000 American personnel, including one night-fighter squadron and three battalions of antiaircraft artillery.[104]

The Soviets reacted coolly toward suggestions of an expanded American air defense establishment at the Soviet bases. General Nikitin saw little cause for alarm; the Germans were now too busy fending off disaster in Belorussia to scrape together units with which to strike Eastern Command. He regretted the losses of American planes as a result of the German raid of June 22, commented that losses were unavoidable, and surmised that more could be expected in the future.[105]

For their part, the Americans were reluctant to send additional bombers to Eastern Command until they could reach a satisfactory air defense agreement with the Soviets. Thus, on June 26, the surviving bombers of the second FRANTIC mission, seventy-two B-17s escorted by fifty-seven P-51s, struck the oil refinery at Drohobycz, Poland. The force suffered no losses and attained, in the crews' poststrike analysis, "excellent" results. The aircraft went on to land in Italy. From there, the task force flew three additional missions before returning to Britain. FRANTIC II, as the mission was called, had ended without the same enthusiasm that had accompanied the conclusion of FRANTIC JOE.[106]

July would see no bomber operations at Eastern Command at all. For FRANTIC III, Fifteenth Air Force dispatched a large force of P-38s and P-51s from Italy near the end of the month. These units attacked German airfields and fighters in Romania and Poland. Three separate missions, one to the Soviet Union, one from Eastern Command bases, and another en route back to Italy, claimed 120 Axis aircraft destroyed for the loss of seven P-38s. Fine combat tallies, perhaps, but these missions had little effect on the course of the fighting in the East and nothing at all to do with FRANTIC's original operational mission to bomb Nazi-held Europe from the east.[107]

The German strike on Poltava cast a pall over FRANTIC. The Soviets sensed that the AAF was reluctant to continue with the operation. The Americans in the Ukraine were nervous and, in light of the great successes of BAGRATION and the rapid German collapse in the East, doubted the need for continuing shuttle-bombing. The suspension of bomber missions in late June following the *Luftwaffe* raid led to a greatly diminished operational role for Eastern Command.

By July, even transient aircrews who were on the ground for only a few days noticed that relations between Americans and Soviets were showing signs of tension and strain. The heady expectations and enthusiasm of the previous weeks were fading. The feverish pace of the preparation of the bases, as well as the novelty of the first two missions, had given way to relative inactivity at Eastern Command. As the war hurtled toward a decisive turning point in the summer of 1944, FRANTIC appeared less and less important to the Soviets. Though good relations had survived the shock of the German attack on Poltava, other factors were about to interfere with the Soviet-American experiment in the Ukraine. The summer opened with high hopes; it would conclude in a far different manner.

FOUR

SUMMER BREAKDOWN

July–August 1944

On the morning of July 2, 1944, Sergeant Doc Blalock of Eastern Command was enjoying the warm summer weather in one of Poltava's parks. He struck up a conversation with a civilian woman, and as the two stood there in the grass attempting to overcome the language barrier, a Soviet officer approached them, his breath smelling of vodka. Without saying a word, the officer swung his fist at the couple but missed them both. He began shouting at Blalock and his companion, but the American could not understand him. A few moments later, another Soviet officer arrived on the scene and ordered two soldiers to escort the first officer away. Not exactly sure of what had just happened, Blalock returned to the base and did not report the incident for nearly another two weeks.[1]

Despite the overall good health of Soviet-American relations thus far during FRANTIC, incidents such as the one involving Sergeant Blalock were neither unexpected nor alarming, provided they remained sporadic. Both Brigadier General Alfred A. Kessler, Eastern Command's deputy commander, and Soviet Major General Alexei Perminov expected some friction because, as the Soviet general put it, "soldiers would be soldiers." Through the spring and into the summer, the Soviets and Americans had worked harmoniously to prepare the bases and support the first missions. By early July, however, the tempo of operations had slowed dramatically, and the Americans now found themselves with far more free time to wander about the area and mingle with the populace. What Blalock had experienced was simply the first of a number of incidents that marked an irreversible downturn in relations between American airmen and local Soviets.

This initial incident involving the harassment of Soviet women in the company of an American had been a relatively mild affair in light of what was to follow. On the evening of July 7, First Lieutenant Edward A. Coutts was in the park talking with two Soviet women. A male civilian approached the trio, grabbed one of the women, and kicked her several times while shouting in Russian. He then seized the other woman and kicked her as well. Both women managed to break away from him and ran. The Soviet did not threaten Coutts, who recalled Eastern Command directives that discouraged Americans from interfering in what appeared to be purely internal Soviet matters. The lieutenant thus simply stood there, bewildered and alone.[2]

Half an hour later, Technician Fourth Grade Judson J. Sorrell was walking with a female civilian when an armed Soviet officer stopped them and began to speak with the woman. She apparently argued with the officer for a few moments before he began kicking her on the legs and backside. She fled down the street. Once again, the Soviet made no attempt to harm the American involved, but neither did he offer an explanation.[3]

Even Soviet women in uniform found themselves targets of similar abuse. In the first week in July, Technical Sergeant Ralph Mowery was walking about the park with a Soviet female lieutenant and a female private. Twice, the same group of Soviet officers stopped them and spoke only to the women. As the time had come for him to return to base, Mowery made a date with his companions for the following night. The next evening, the women failed to show up and Mowery finally found them in another part of the park. Through their gestures, the women made Mowery understand that they could not be seen with him. He asked a passing American soldier who spoke Russian to help him figure out why the women appeared so upset. They told this other soldier that they "had orders not to go out with American soldiers."[4]

Indeed, Soviet women were among those, both in and out of uniform, who confronted other Soviet women who were in the company of Americans. On July 6, Corporal Peter Nicolaef, an American interpreter born in Odessa in 1903, was sitting on a park bench with a civilian woman when a female Soviet officer confronted them. Fluent in Russian, Nicolaef understood the lieutenant to say, "You whore, why do you sit with an American soldier?" Getting no response, the officer then accused the woman of sleeping with Germans and stormed off.[5]

Moments later, several Russian males, both military and civilian, approached the couple. When Nicolaef's companion introduced him to the group as "our friend, an American," the Soviet officer in the group replied, "This evening he is our friend, but tomorrow he may be our enemy." The officer proceeded to insult the girl, again calling her a whore and threatening to kick her. When Nicolaef spoke to him in Russian, the Soviet officer, apparently surprised, immediately shook hands with the other men and the group left. As Nicolaef escorted the woman home, he asked her why one of the civilians was carrying a pistol. "NKVD," she replied. Nicolaef was apparently satisfied with her answer.[6]

As the men shared their experiences among themselves, it became clear that none had been the victim of an isolated incident. On July 9, Second Lieutenant Seymour Auerbach of the headquarters section reported to the headquarters commandant, Major Albert Lepawsky, that several of the airmen who were working for him had had embarrassing experiences in town. On July 10, Lepawsky interviewed four of the men and decided that the matter warranted further investigation. He also discovered from Mirgorod's station commander that similar incidents had occurred there. Though Mirgorod's commander had dismissed the incidents as acts of individual prejudices, Lepawsky speculated that official Red Air Force policy permitting fraternization had not been clearly expressed "down the line." He also considered the possibility that these incidents indicated that an organized Soviet effort to stifle fraternization was under way.[7]

Responding to Lepawsky's concern, Eastern Command's inspector general, Major Ralph P. Dunn, conducted his own investigation from July 11 to the 14th. He found that, whereas incidents of harassment had been few and minor in nature earlier in the year, during the two weeks following Blalock's encounter of July 2, thirteen such encounters had taken place. These encounters involved Soviet officers, soldiers, and civilians, and possibly political operatives. Dunn deemed the situation "very serious and [requiring] the utmost tact in handling." He recommended reporting the incidents to the Soviets and placing the city of Poltava off-limits to Americans if the situation remained unchanged.[8]

American officers differed as to the causes of these incidents, as well as to how the Americans should respond to them. USSTAF's director of intelligence, Brigadier General George C. McDonald, noted in an August report on FRANTIC that local jealousies had led to similar clashes in all countries where foreign troops were quartered. Still, McDonald went on, one must remember that the incidents could adversely affect FRANTIC because one of the operation's primary objectives was to foster good relations between the United States and the Soviet Union. As they continued to investigate the situation, Eastern Command officers began to conclude that this unfavorable turn of events was indeed the result of organized Soviet activity. This perception impaired relations further.[9]

The situation continued to deteriorate in July. American authorities had to take some immediate action to protect their men until they could determine the causes for the apparent decline in the state of relations between American airmen and local Soviets. Colonel Paul T. Cullen, Eastern Command's director of operations, met with Major General Perminov on the morning of July 17. After hearing Cullen's account of recent assaults on

Soviet women in the company of Americans, as well as incidents in which Soviets physically and verbally abused the G.I.s themselves, Perminov stated officially and solemnly that neither Soviet military nor civil authorities had issued any instructions limiting fraternization. He protested that such action would have been entirely contrary to the purpose for which Soviet and American personnel had been assigned to Eastern Command bases.[10]

Cullen hesitated to discount completely Perminov's disclaimers. Still, he was also reluctant to accept them at face value. The evidence, Cullen concluded, indicated that a deliberate campaign instigated by individuals outside the Red Air Force was under way to discourage fraternizing between Soviet women and American men. He predicted a further strain on relations if the trend continued. Cullen recommended that Eastern Command restrict its personnel to base after dark, and that an effort to secure evidence to either prove or disprove Perminov's assertion continue. The Soviets, in the meantime, refused to allow Eastern Command officers to question any of their personnel.[11]

Given the warm and friendly relations that had characterized FRANTIC thus far, this abrupt downturn was all the more remarkable. It is quite possible that Soviet soldiers and civilians felt some natural resentment toward foreigners dating their women so soon after the German occupation. At the same time, this deterioration in relations might have been more apparent than real. With more time available because of a dearth of operational activity, Eastern Command personnel visited the surrounding areas in larger numbers and with greater frequency. Eastern Command records alluded to two incidents involving the harassment of Soviet women who were with American airmen before July 1st. Thus, the number of such incidents may have increased simply because more Americans were on the streets of Poltava. It was the frequency with which these incidents occurred in July that reinforced the impression of Eastern Command's officers that an official Soviet policy of interference was at work.

The Soviets did offer both official and unofficial reasons for the harassment. They often claimed that they were saving American personnel from diseased women who had consorted with the Germans. They usually offered this as an explanation when an American officer protested their acts. The Americans were aware that venereal disease (V.D.) was widespread among the local population. The Soviets blamed the German Army for its spread. The American medical staff considered V.D., together with typhus, malaria, and dysentery, as the greatest threat to the health of the G.I.s. Surprisingly, Eastern Command's detailed medical reports showed that the incidence of V.D. among Eastern Command personnel was relatively low, perhaps fewer than half a dozen cases a month by late summer. Most Americans did not accept Soviet claims that they were trying to protect the G.I.s from V.D. as the motivation behind the incidents of harassment.[12]

Soviet officers also dismissed the hostile actions of those Soviets involved in incidents as having been inspired by "German agents." Indeed, their attitude often appeared to be one of nonchalant flippancy. A Soviet colonel at Mirgorod quipped that the two sides were fighting on the "petticoat front."[13]

American officers thought otherwise and viewed the whole situation quite seriously because it touched on so many other aspects of Soviet-American relations and morale of American airmen. Because the Soviets did not appear to offer any solutions to what they perceived to be a fraternization problem, Eastern Command acted unilaterally. By the end of July, accordingly, American servicemen only moved about the local area in groups of two or more. Though they were still under orders not to start trouble, the G.I.s were to help each other in case of an altercation with Soviets. The transient fighter crews of FRANTIC III reported in late July that the local populace remained friendly, but the official post-mission report noted that "the Russians appeared to have been instructed to keep their distance, and there were instances of Russian girls being beaten up for going out with Americans."[14]

Fraternization problems were responsible for only part of the friction developing between the Soviets and their American guests by high summer. As they had earlier in the year, the Soviets reminded the Americans that in their opinion the Red Army was carrying the brunt of the war against Nazi Germany. While reports favorable to the shuttle-bombing operation continued to appear in the Soviet press, Ambassador Averell Harriman warned Washington that the Soviets were beginning to question the amount of time it was taking the Allies to break out of the Normandy beachhead. Moscow also expressed resentment over articles in the Western press implying that the relatively rapid German collapse in the East was a result of the movement of *Wehrmacht* divisions to the front in France. Indeed, on July 17, the Soviets paraded 57,000 German prisoners, including a number of generals, through the streets of Moscow as a demonstration of the extent of the German debacle in Belorussia.[15]

Soviet pride in the Red Army's successes was evident at the bases as well. As the Soviet offensive rolled deeper into Poland, Soviet troops drew comparisons between the success of their forces and the stagnation of the Anglo-American drive into France. Such comparisons occasionally led to pushing and shouting matches between members of the two air forces. With

Soviet soil virtually free of the Germans by mid-August, Red Air Force troops and officers exhibited an air of cockiness and nationalistic zeal. American officers interpreted Soviet victory proclamations as a sign that Moscow wanted foreigners out of the country now that the war seemed won. By late August, this perception was so pronounced that senior American officers recommended terminating FRANTIC immediately. Major General Hugh J. Knerr, USSTAF deputy commander for administration, reported to USSTAF Commander Lieutenant General Carl A. Spaatz that "the changed war situation [had] brought about a changed attitude toward our cooperative air operations. The Devil [was] no longer sick and not interested in becoming a Monk for the defeat of Germany." He predicted that once the Soviets believed they no longer needed the Americans in the Pacific, the same situation as the one then developing at Eastern Command would arise if the AAF had gained the use of Siberian air bases once the USSR entered the war against Japan.[16]

At the same time, American personnel leaving Eastern Command committed various indiscretions that had an adverse effect on Soviet attitudes toward the operation. As aircrews returned to Britain, for example, they were often quite free with their impressions of the Soviet Union. On July 19, the New York *Daily News* ran a lurid piece by reporter Howard Whiteman entitled "Nude Welcome to Russia Shocks U.S. Bomber Pilots." The story was reprinted in major newspapers across the country. The article made much of the Russian custom of nude mixed-sex bathing. It also quoted bomber crew members as saying that Soviet officers offered to procure women for them and to take them to brothels. The personnel quoted were not identified but the story originated at a bomber station of the Eighth Air Force in Britain. The story somehow got past United States censors in Britain. The Soviets were aware of the article and how quickly it had been accepted by the American press. The damage to Soviet-American relations was done.[17]

Officers at the United States Military Mission in Moscow held a news conference in an attempt to set the record straight. The War Department issued a press release denying the story, and quoted sources both in Moscow and Poltava as saying that the Soviets treated Americans in their country with "the utmost hospitality and courtesy." Unfortunately for the Americans, few newspapers printed the denial. As late as September, Soviet publications referred to Whiteman's article as evidence that elements hostile to the Soviet Union controlled the American press.[18]

Just how seriously the Soviets viewed the appearance of the "Nude Welcome" article was difficult to determine at the time. Other pieces carried in the American press were quite sympathetic to the Soviet Union and its people. Writing for *Reader's Digest* in August, John Gunther praised the Red Army and its accomplishments. Perhaps cognizant of FRANTIC's political and diplomatic role, he also predicted hopefully that "the new U.S. strategic air base in the Ukraine [would] be used for more than shuttle bombing" and Eastern Command represented merely the first of many joint Soviet-American operations. Nevertheless, the semiofficial history of Eastern Command, written in November 1944, speculated that Whiteman's aforementioned story had further hardened Soviet attitudes toward fraternization.[19]

In an effort to ensure that stories akin to Whiteman's did not appear, Spaatz issued an order in early August that all USSTAF personnel were to refrain from making any statements, particularly to reporters, that might offend either the Soviet government or its people. He ordered tightened censorship of all mail going to or coming from Americans stationed in the Ukraine. Still, more than a month and a half later, Major General Robert L. Walsh, commanding general of Eastern Command, felt compelled to remind all those personnel returning to Britain or Italy that the Soviets had done a great deal to assist the Americans. He admonished the men to be fair and accurate in their statements about the Soviets. Above all, he ordered, the men were to "STICK TO FACTS."[20]

The content of Whiteman's article contradicted official Soviet statements regarding prostitution in the USSR. Moscow maintained that prostitution and brothels simply did not exist in the Soviet Union. Veterans of FRANTIC did not recall the existence of any houses of ill repute or the presence of streetwalkers near Eastern Command bases. Indeed, the Soviets may have moved to stifle contact between American airmen and Soviet women out of the fear that the G.I.s were buying the affections and attention of Soviet women with consumer goods and food unavailable to Red Army personnel. Soviet soldiers resented the fact that they simply could not compete for women in the face of obvious American wealth. Thus, Soviet personnel hurled insults such as "whore" or "prostitute" at women who preferred the company of Americans.[21]

American airmen probably resorted to exchanging goods for intimate contacts when they found that their expectations of Soviet women had been misplaced. McDonald reported in August that "preconceived notions of the loose morals of Russian women entertained by our personnel and [the] subsequent finding out of the opposite were factors in lowering morale." Soviet women were only too happy to socialize with American G.I.s but that did not mean they would enter into physical relations with them. Many civilian women complained that Soviet females in uniform were indeed sexually aggressive, causing Americans to think that all Soviet women lacked proper morals.[22]

Problems created by the perception of illicit sexual activity between G.I.s and Soviet women arose at a time when morale at Eastern Command was already plummeting. Certainly, most American personnel were upset over the new limitations placed on their freedom of movement and their ability to fraternize. Denied free access to civilian social contact and sources of entertainment by August, Eastern Command's men had to rely on their own resources for recreation. Captain Charles Heintzelman, the special services officer at Poltava, thought that despite his efforts and those of the chaplains to provide recreational materials and activities for the men, his facilities were still inadequate given the relative isolation and growing operational idleness of the command.[23]

Many of the men were simply not interested in participating in what activities Heintzelman did arrange. Despite a dearth of combat missions, Eastern Command was still on a seven-day work week throughout July and August. These two factors combined to undercut morale at all three bases. Inspectors reported that both officers and men complained incessantly, military courtesies such as saluting were rarely rendered, and the bases' physical appearance had deteriorated, a result of apathy and neglect. The command spent most of July in idleness, apart from supporting the fighters of FRANTIC III. Both fighter and bomber missions took place in early August, but no other operations apart from photo reconnaissance involved Eastern Command until mid-September. The men passed their days in tedious and boring camp routine.[24]

The men of Eastern Command were, in part, the victims of their own expectations. The day-by-day attitude of merely marking time that characterized mid-summer was in marked contrast to the enthusiastic anticipation and hurried activity that preceded the first two FRANTIC missions. The novelty of being in the Soviet Union had worn off and the men no longer believed they were taking part in an important part of the war. An Eastern Command report on morale noted that both officers and enlisted men expressed "remorse and self-pity at having given up more important and comfortable jobs . . . to take part in a failure and to lead a boring existence." Whatever the accomplishments of FRANTIC, these fell far short of what the men had been led to believe would take place. Furthermore, many Eastern Command personnel had volunteered for the assignment because of obviously hollow promises made by overzealous personnel officers in Britain that they would gain rapid promotion and tickets home to the United States at the end of the operation. Thus, idleness and loss of faith in the mission were probably the most significant factors contributing to Eastern Command's low morale in July and August.[25]

After the devastating German raid on Poltava, rumors circulated throughout the command that the operation would be terminated soon. As the apparent Soviet attitude toward the Americans began to sour, belief in an impending evacuation took hold throughout the command. Medical officers at Piryatin reported in late July that "morale at this base [was] at its lowest ebb—the men [were] nervous and irritable. . . . Rumors [were] always in circulation. A main subject [was] that one concerning the end of the stay in Russia." In the absence of official information regarding the end of FRANTIC, the men viewed their predicament not as temporary, but one without any end in sight.[26]

Eastern Command's officers shared the foregoing attitude and made no effort to conceal their own displeasure from the men. In a dismaying display of poor leadership, Poltava's officers vented their frustration in front of their subordinates. They exhibited an attitude of complaining discontent that was readily communicated to the enlisted men because of the close living and working quarters. The men subsequently adopted similar attitudes and believed further that their officers and commanders had little interest in performing more than their necessary routine duties.[27]

On the other hand, inspectors from USSTAF commended officers at Mirgorod and Piryatin for taking a genuine interest in the welfare of their men, thus helping to build unit cohesion. They credited this involvement with the troops for producing higher morale at those bases than at Poltava. Indeed, commanders and officers at Poltava appeared to lack both the time and inclination to attend to the needs of the men. Because Poltava was headquarters and main base for the command, its officers had more to do: the issuance of weather reports, escorting innumerable high-ranking visitors, and processing all manner of requests. They found such work boring and without any operational value.[28]

Obviously, in that sort of environment, the men were particularly sensitive to what might otherwise be considered trivial matters. In early July, for example, the Soviets opened restaurants or snack bars at each of the bases. At first, the Americans viewed these enterprises positively. Here, Soviet and American airmen could mingle and relax together in a relatively friendly atmosphere. The establishments were not open to civilians and, hence, the Americans could avoid the risk of additional confrontations involving women. The Americans also saw these eateries as a means of supplementing their diets. Eastern Command personnel were unhappy with the amount and quality of items available through the small post exchanges of the three bases. Candy sold or even issued from the exchanges was stale and discolored, and the cigarettes available were of the cheapest, most unpopular brands. Thus, the Americans found the idea of going to a restaurant or snack bar refreshing.[29]

But, as with virtually everything else they had experienced thus far, the men of Eastern Command quickly lost enthusiasm for the Soviet eating establishments. Prices for food and drinks were inordinately high, considering the dollar–ruble exchange rate. Early in the operation, FRANTIC planners decided that the men would receive only a portion of their pay while in the Ukraine, and that payment would be in the form of rubles. The exchange rate prior to July 6 was approximately seventeen rubles to the dollar. After that date, the rate dropped to five to one. The men earned only $40 a month, roughly 200 rubles. A beer at one of the restaurants cost seventeen rubles! The Americans found themselves in a situation that few of them had ever endured; lacking ready cash, they were unable to patronize the restaurants that quickly became de facto officers' clubs for the Soviets.[30]

At the same time, many Americans, bitter over their inability to fraternize freely, did not want to mingle with Soviet male personnel. Perhaps sensing the G.I.s' bitterness, Soviet officers picketed the new restaurants. Soviet officers descended on the clubs and one sat at each table, thereby, in the opinion of most Americans, forcing themselves on their guests. Americans either had to sit with a Soviet or forego a seat. The Soviets had apparently intended the restaurants to serve as a lucrative means of improving Soviet-American relations and American morale. Like FRANTIC itself, the results quickly became the opposite of those intended. As noted later in this chapter, these establishments provided the setting for some of the worst clashes of the entire Soviet-American experience.[31]

Unhappy with the relative shortage of cash, many Americans adopted an entrepreneurial attitude and sought ways to increase the number of rubles in their pockets. Aircrews often made a proverbial fast buck by selling extra candy or cigarettes while permanent personnel had in the past given away such items. Now, in July, American military men looked around them at the poverty of the war-ravaged Ukraine. The tired, shabbily clad populace still had relatively large amounts of rubles, but virtually nothing on which to spend them. The men of Eastern Command saw money-making opportunities beckoning in the ruins of the towns outside their bases.

Black market activity was nothing new to either the Soviet people or to the USAAF. In June, Spaatz issued very specific orders prohibiting the barter of American goods and supplies. At the conference of July 17 at which

Perminov and Cullen discussed problems with fraternization, the Soviet general also expressed his concern over an apparent increase in bartering for rubles; in other words, black-marketeering by Americans.

As early as July 11, the first examples of illicit economic activity involving Americans emerged in the countryside. Corporal E. R. Gentzen and Staff Sergeant C. V. Bennett had stopped in the village of Belaya Tserkov some twenty-five miles east of Mirgorod. Manning a truck that was part of a supply convoy, they had moved too far in front and were waiting for the rest of the convoy to catch up to them. An elderly female villager named Paraska Piyenkova approached the two Americans and told them that just the day before two officers from Eastern Command had stopped in the village with a jeep full of items for sale. She produced a price list that one of the Americans had written on a piece of V-mail paper. Gentzen, able to speak some Russian, talked with the woman at length. He persuaded her to let him see the list. Among the many items the American officers were apparently selling were shoes, blankets, canteens, and watches. The prices were extremely high: 600 rubles for a pair of shoes, 2,000 for a blanket, and 5,000 for a watch. She told Gentzen that the Americans were due back in the village the next day, July 12.[32]

The woman told Gentzen that the jeep used by the officers had a registration number ending in "200." After returning to Mirgorod that afternoon, Gentzen checked the motor pool record and learned that an American jeep bearing the last three digits "200" had come from Poltava on July 11, and the driver requested five gallons of gasoline. Gentzen considered that sufficient evidence to substantiate the woman's claim. Unfortunately, in the days immediately following his discovery, Gentzen accidentally shot himself in the leg while cleaning a pistol, and he was unable to make a full report of what he had learned.[33]

When Gentzen and Bennett did report the incident to officers at Mirgorod, the station commander took immediate action to investigate the matter. He notified Major Dunn, the command's inspector general, who appointed Russian-speaking First Lieutenant Elias Bacha as investigating officer. On July 26, Bacha and a Soviet captain named Klyablin went to the village of Bela Tserkovka and questioned the woman who had spoken with Gentzen. Paraska Piyenkova told the two officers that two American officers—she recognized their rank insignia—stopped along the road two weeks earlier and offered items for sale to women who were working in the area. She proudly displayed two bars of Lux toilet soap that she had purchased for 120 rubles. Though she had burned the price list she had shown Gentzen, she did direct Bacha and Klyablin to other women who had purchased goods from the two Americans. Maria Sklyar and Anna Fonenko showed Bacha a United States Army blanket that they had purchased for 700 rubles. The two women also stated that Americans frequently stopped along the road and offered items for sale. After learning of Bacha's findings, Kessler immediately recognized the seriousness of the situation, given Perminov's earlier statement of concern over black market activity. He instructed Dunn to keep the investigation as quiet as possible, but by the end of July the incident was common knowledge among both Soviet and American personnel at Mirgorod. In the meantime, Bacha discovered that the jeep in question had been signed out from the motor pool at Poltava by two captains named Smith and Hamm. The two officers had visited the intelligence section at Mirgorod on or about July 12, a fact confirmed by the base intelligence officer at Mirgorod.[34]

In the middle of the investigation, the Soviets made a discovery that would further embarrass the Americans. On July 22, while conducting a routine check of personal documents in the Poltava area, a Soviet patrol under a Captain Belych found an apparently intoxicated American soldier sleeping in the nude in the home of one citizen Pysyr. Beside the bed on which the soldier, Technician Fifth Grade Alvin Jennings, was sleeping was a large box filled with American produce and a new uniform. Suspecting black market activity, the Soviets confiscated the goods and escorted a groggy Jennings to the American duty officer at Poltava.[35]

Considering the amount of tension generated by previous allegations of American black-marketeering, Jennings' actions had simply reinforced the perception among the Soviets that such illicit activity was widespread. Recognizing the need for swift action, Colonel L. B. Hickam, deputy commander for administration, asked Perminov to furnish any information he had on the Jennings case. Perminov obliged in a letter in which he recounted the incident. Unfortunately, when Major Dunn asked Soviet authorities the following week for permission to interview Captain Belych and his men, he found them hesitant to involve their personnel any further in the matter. The Soviets claimed that because it was dark when Jennings was picked up, the Soviet patrol did not see him in sufficient light to be able to identify him in a lineup. Frustrated in this regard, the Americans nevertheless wanted to show the Soviets that they were doing all they could to stop black market activity. Jennings faced a summary court-martial and, based on the physical evidence, was found guilty of unlawfully disposing government property, fined, and reprimanded.[36]

Closing the book on captains Smith and Hamm was not so easy. As in the Jennings case, the Soviets appeared reluctant to allow either civilians or military personnel to testify in American legal proceedings. The reasons for their reluctance are not clear, but their attitude hampered the investigation. The Soviet commander at Mirgorod, Lieutenant Colonel Mikhail Lysenko, refused to grant Major Dunn's request that another Soviet officer return to Belaya Tserkov with him to gather evidence against Smith and Hamm. Lysenko explained through an interpreter that even he did not have the authority to question Soviet civilians.[37]

Dunn recommended that either Walsh or Kessler request permission from Perminov to allow Soviet authorities to question the civilians involved in the case. Permission was not forthcoming, and the Americans were unable to go ahead with a full prosecution in the case without eyewitness testimony. Though Smith and Hamm received warnings not to engage in further black market activity, the lack of cooperation from the Soviets on this matter was not unusual. Apparently anxious to avoid involvement in Eastern Command's disciplinary problems, the Soviets had refused to allow investigating American officers to question their personnel regarding earlier allegations of harassment and would display the same attitude in the future, even when they initially reported the infraction.[38]

The foregoing cases were not the only instances of black market activity, nor would they be the last. Once Americans had access to black market rubles, their patronage of the local restaurants increased. Soviet personnel reacted negatively, perhaps believing that this newfound wealth was a result of shady economic activity. Such suspicions led to further tension between men of the two air forces and set the stage for potentially explosive confrontations. That United States personnel were conducting black market activity on Soviet soil nonetheless caused senior officers on both sides a great deal of alarm. Moscow was justifiably worried about the attitudes of its Ukrainian subjects, a concern recognized by American officials. When units of German Army Group South swept into the Ukraine in the late summer of 1941, many of the inhabitants greeted Adolf Hitler's soldiers as liberators from Russian and Soviet domination. The Nazi dictator had not come to liberate the Ukrainians, of course, and the republic subsequently suffered great deprivation and terror under German rule. The Ukraine remained a political tinderbox in Soviet eyes, a perception that was reinforced when guerrillas of the Ukrainian Insurgent Army ambushed a Soviet motor convoy in March 1944, killing Soviet General N. F. Vatutin, commander of the First Ukrainian Front. Ukrainian insurgents remained at large, fighting against Red Army units long after the Germans were gone.[39]

Given the manifestation of overt Ukrainian hostility toward Moscow, Soviet authorities were perhaps overly sensitive to anything that tended to accentuate the relative poverty of the region. McDonald reported in early August that comments made by Soviet personnel convinced him of their resentment of American material wealth. Despite a nagging shortage of rubles, the average G.I. had access to all things unavailable to the locals. Though American servicemen were instructed to avoid comparisons of American and Soviet societies, their obvious material wealth could not go unnoticed by Ukrainian civilians. This was particularly true when those G.I.s were openly selling items otherwise not in evidence in local markets and bazaars or state-run shops.[40]

Fraternization and black-marketeering were not the only problems facing Eastern Command in the summer of 1944. The relatively haphazard manner in which Eighth Air Force had selected the personnel for Eastern Command was a result of the general haste to get FRANTIC under way. Now, in July and August, with relatively little operational activity to occupy their time, the men found little sense of unit cohesion or spirit to see them through these weeks of boredom and frustration. Drawn from a number of separate units in Britain and thrown into a strange country under adverse conditions, the men lacked an attitude of willing cooperation and confident reliance on one another that was vital to the health of any military organization. Given the cynical attitudes of many of their officers, the men felt little attachment to units within Eastern Command.[41]

Though the food had improved in both quality and variety since the early days of the operation, problems persisted in the matters of sanitation and service. Bathing and living facilities also remained substandard despite persistent complaints from both permanent and transient personnel. Substandard facilities, in part, were a result of reliance on the Soviets for the provision of materials and labor necessary to effect improvements. Soviet standards for such facilities were far below those of the Americans. Thus, they placed the improvement of base facilities for Eastern Command near the bottom of their priorities. For their part, American personnel exhibited a reluctance to invest much time or energy in enhancing structures that they viewed as temporary. The persistent rumors pointing toward a termination of FRANTIC or the possible erection of prefabricated huts for the winter robbed the men of what little initiative they still possessed.[42]

Still, at no time did living conditions drop below the minimum standard for operations in the field. Indeed, morale at Mirgorod was higher than at either Poltava or Piryatin, in part because of the presence of more comfortable and permanent living quarters in the former artillery school barracks. Thus, living conditions alone could not account for the low morale prevalent at the bases because the men had tolerated worse conditions during the

Soviet women serve hot food to Eastern Command G.I.s. *Courtesy U.S. Air Force.*

preparation phase of the operation as well as the period encompassing the first two missions.

A combination of factors had led to a sudden and serious drop in the morale of the men of Eastern Command. Though they continued to seek female companionship, they did so now in an atmosphere of secrecy and harbored deep and growing resentment toward the Soviets for what they perceived to be an officially directed campaign of harassment.[43] Relatively isolated, lacking faith in their mission and their officers, and living under spartan conditions, the men of Eastern Command were simply the first victims of the impending failure of this experiment in Allied cooperation.

By late July, it was also obvious to American observers at virtually every level inside the Soviet Union that the Soviets had changed their attitude toward FRANTIC. The evidence indicated that local political authorities had a hand in stifling Soviet-American fraternization, if only because they made no apparent attempt to counter the harassment and abuse directed at Soviet women and their American escorts. At the same time, the Soviets took a dim view of American bartering activities in the surrounding area. The success of the Red Army's summer offensive contrasted sharply with the painfully slow pace of the Anglo-American advance in France. Flushed with the confidence borne of victory, the Soviets also appeared to re-evaluate the desirability of having large numbers of Americans on their soil now that the shadow of defeat loomed large over Adolf Hitler's tottering empire.

It was not long before the deteriorating situation at Eastern Command was recognized in faraway Britain. Persistently negative comments by returning crew members and staff officers regarding the efficiency of and conditions at Eastern Command aroused the interest of senior officers at USSTAF. Indeed, General McDonald's memorandum to Major General Fred Anderson, operations chief at USSTAF, pointed out many of the problems discussed above. Spaatz was sufficiently concerned to order Major General Knerr to Eastern Command to determine the probability of continued operations on the existing or perhaps a larger scale.[44]

Knerr's itinerary included stops in Moscow to see Ambassador Harriman and Major General John Deane. From the Soviet capital, he visited the three bases of Eastern Command, where he stayed from August 15 to the 21st. Issued on September 6, his report painted an extremely negative picture of conditions at the American bases. "The general appearance of the tent areas [at Poltava]," Knerr noted, "with weeds growing up to the walls of the tents, [revealed] to some degree a lack of leadership." Morale, especially at Poltava, was low. Given the attitudes of many officers with whom he spoke, Knerr also cited ineffectual leadership as a cause of the drop in esprit de corps.[45]

Highly critical of the Soviets, Knerr reported that the air defense establishment at the American bases remained so ineffective that no security existed even after the German strike of June 22. He blamed low Soviet health standards for poor messing conditions and a generally abysmal degree of sanitation at Eastern Command bases. Furthermore, he complained that Soviet enlisted men stole U.S. property with "reckless abandon," and even vehicle maintenance, previously an area in which the Americans praised their hosts, was difficult because "the Russians steal all the tools that they can get their hands on." Knerr blasted Soviet security procedures as "unacceptable."[46]

Knerr also criticized Eastern Command's senior officer, Major General Robert L. Walsh. He reported that Walsh apparently failed to support the command's inspector general, Major Dunn in resolving the myriad problems cropping up throughout the unit such as securing Soviet cooperation in investigating black market activity. Perhaps Knerr did not recognize that Soviet reluctance to cooperate in American inquiries undercut Dunn more than did a lack of support on Walsh's part. He also reported that Walsh failed to meet his command responsibilities by neglecting problems brought to his attention such as the persistence of a seven-day work week despite a dearth of operational activity. Knerr seemed to be unduly harsh toward Walsh and even appeared to contradict himself when he stated in his report that the "commanding general of Eastern Command encountered so many obstacles to freedom of action that a state of frustration exists." The only positive comments contained in Knerr's report were directed at the medical staff. The hospitals, he stated, were "the shining light of the entire Eastern Command."[47]

Knerr found little reason to continue operations in the Ukraine, much less expand them. Most of the unsatisfactory conditions he found were a result of "the failure of the Russians to provide the services expected." He perceived growing Soviet hostility to the American presence, a perception as noted, shared by many officers of Eastern Command. If any force was left in the Soviet Union, he continued, "it should be complete in itself and no dependence should [have been] placed on the Russians." The bases were now so far from the front, Knerr concluded, that they had lost their usefulness for shuttle-bombing and should either be moved westward or the operation terminated, preferably before the onset of winter.[48]

In a separate memo to Spaatz, dated August 25, Knerr was more direct in his assessment of Eastern Command than he would be in his report of September 6. While praising the Red Air Force for its spirit of cooperation, he stated that "the political control in Russia [was] neither friendly nor cooperative. [Soviet authorities were] determined that we [should] quit Russia as soon as possible." He believed that the situation in the Pacific war made bases in Siberia unnecessary and thus robbed FRANTIC of its ultimate raison d'etre. Preparing the bases for winter operations would require extensive construction to provide proper living and working facilities for the men. Based on deteriorating Soviet-American relations in the Ukraine and a hardening Soviet attitude, Knerr saw no reason to continue operations at Eastern Command. As noted earlier in this chapter, he therefore recommended terminating all American activity in the Ukraine by September 15.[49]

Operation FRANTIC and Eastern Command did not exist in a vacuum. The course of the war had already begun to undermine the entire rationale for the shuttle-bombing operation. In his reports to Spaatz, Knerr alluded to the two most important developments in this regard. In the Pacific, American forces had taken the Mariana Islands, notably Saipan, Guam, and Tinian, thus piercing Japan's inner defense barrier. As Eastern Command struggled to support a handful of sorties in July and August, American units were hurriedly preparing airfields on these newly captured islands in the Western Pacific so that heavy bombers, new B-29 "Superfortresses," could accelerate the aerial bombardment of Japan's poorly defended cities. In Knerr's opinion, therefore, the USAAF no longer required Siberian bases to bomb the Japanese mainland. Because one of FRANTIC's primary goals was to pave the way for an American presence in the Soviet Far East, it, too, was no longer necessary.[50]

Knerr also pointed out that Eastern Command was now so far from the Eastern Front that its operational value was near zero. Granted, Axis forces remained in the Balkans until September but, as was the case in the early debate over target selection, that area was within easy range of units of the Fifteenth Air Force based in Italy. In the center of the Eastern Front, Soviet forces were now ramming the Germans deep into Poland and back toward their own frontiers. As the shattered remnants of Germany's once-mighty Army Group Center streamed westward, the Red Army was taking possession of most of Eastern Command's strategic targets. Many others were so close to the front that the Soviets could now hit them with tactical air units. The Soviets also declared other targets, such as a number of oil refineries in south-central Poland, off-limits because of the proximity of advance units of the Red Army.[51]

Thus, not only was it becoming apparent to Spaatz and other air force leaders that morale at Eastern Command was deteriorating dramatically, but that much of the rationale for sustaining FRANTIC was slipping away. Now, an event that American planners could have never foreseen was about to deliver the final blow to the operation, not to mention hopes for greater Soviet-American cooperation in the postwar era.

As the Red Army's First Belorussian Front under Marshal Konstantin Rokossovskii neared the Polish capital of Warsaw in late July 1944, resistance units under the command of the Home Army (*Armija Krajowa*) rose up against their German tormentors on the afternoon of August 1, which prompted Western appeals to the Soviets to allow aerial resupply of the rebels that helped to drive the Allied coalition toward a crisis of faith in the intentions of one another. As documented in the next chapter, the ensuing crisis in Warsaw would make itself felt throughout the Eastern Command.[52]

Undaunted by an obvious Soviet coolness toward FRANTIC and the troubled state of Soviet-American relations at eastern Command, USSTAF and Spaatz persisted in attempts to expand the operation. The Americans continued to hope for a full-fledged third front in the air. In July, the Americans had put forward a proposal whereby they would deploy night-fighters and heavy antiaircraft artillery units. This plan would have expanded the American presence in the Ukraine fivefold. Reacting coolly to the American scheme, the Soviets delayed giving the Americans a firm decision regarding

their support. By the third week in July, the American air defense plan for
the bases had reached the ambassadorial level, but even Harriman was unable to secure a direct Soviet answer. Soviet diplomats informed him that
the whole question of continuing FRANTIC operations was complicated. Obviously, Moscow was in the process of reassessing the entire shuttle-bombing venture.[53]

Nevertheless, the Americans pressed forward with plans for additional
missions. The result was FRANTIC IV. Like FRANTIC III, FRANTIC IV was a
Fifteenth Air Force fighter operation. Measured against the success of the
third operation, which cost Axis forces 120 aircraft against an Allied loss
of seven P-38s, FRANTIC IV was a disappointment. Ninety P-51s and P-38s
of the veteran 52nd and 82nd Fighter Groups departed Italy on August 4
and strafed the airdromes at Focsani, Romania, in accordance with Soviet
requests. Bad weather and heavy battle damage to many of the aircraft
caused the cancellation of a mission planned from Eastern Command bases
on August 5. The next day, a much-reduced force swept the area of Ploesti
and Bucharest on the return trip to Italy. At the conclusion of FRANTIC IV,
the Americans claimed a meager six Axis aircraft destroyed, a number
equal to their own losses.[54]

While FRANTIC IV was under way, the Americans were already planning to launch the first bomber mission since the German raid of June 22,
FRANTIC V. Indeed, on August 2, Perminov requested that American units
not only strike airfields in Romania (FRANTIC IV), but also oil industry targets in the region of Cracow, Poland, and in Upper Silesia inside Germany
itself. Because of the rapid Soviet advance toward the areas in which the
targets were located, Perminov asked that FRANTIC V take place on or before
August 5. After that date, the targets would likely become part of the operational zone of combat. Content that Soviet successes against the Germans had reduced the *Luftwaffe's* threat to Eastern Command, the Americans pressed forward with the raid.[55]

As so often happened in air operations during World War II, bad weather
delayed FRANTIC V until August 6. Escorted by sixty-four P-51s of the 357th
Fighter Group, seventy-eight B-17s of the Eighth Air Force's 95th and
390th Bomb Groups struck an aircraft components factory at Rahmel, near
Gdynia in Poland. The task force was merely a portion of a vast armada of
American warplanes pounding the Reich on that day. Photo interpreters at
Eastern Command reported that the task force achieved "excellent" results
without loss to itself. The following day, fifty-seven bombers left Mirgorod
and Poltava to strike at an oil refinery at Trzebinia, Poland, and again returned without loss. The FRANTIC bombers caused an estimated drop in oil

Kessler and Perminov greet an American flyer, Captain
Frank Carney of Detroit. *Courtesy U.S. Air Force.*

refining at Trzebinia of approximately 8 percent, a loss in capacity the Germans could easily restore. Spaatz was nonetheless pleased with the strike because this refinery had long been on Eastern Command's "wish list."[56]

At this point in the war, the Soviet High Command turned its attention toward the Balkans and Hitler's unsteady allies, the Romanians, Hungarians, and Bulgarians. Prior to FRANTIC I, the Soviets refused to approve targets behind the central part of the front for fear that such strikes would telegraph their intentions to the Germans. Now, perhaps so confident in their overwhelming strength that they felt no need to rely on tactical surprise, the Soviets requested that the FRANTIC V task force strike major airfields in Romania as it flew to Italy. Thus, on August 8, thirty-seven B-17s hit the airfield at Buzau while thirty-six bombers struck the field at Zilistea.

The force returned to Italy without loss, but the damage the two relatively small bombing formations did to the Axis airfields was slight. After three days at bases of the Fifteenth, the aircraft of FRANTIC V returned to Britain on August 12, striking the airfield at Toulouse, France, on the way and destroying a large number of German aircraft on the ground.[57]

Even before FRANTIC V, many Army Air Forces officers in Britain were expressing doubts about the wisdom of continuing shuttle-bombing operations. An intelligence report from the 390th Bomb Group pointed out that there was now a "sparsity of targets within the reach of groups of this [Eastern] command when based in Russia." Nearly every possible target left under German control in eastern Europe could be reached either from Britain or Italy. Only a rapidly shrinking piece of German-occupied Poland and the Baltic states could be reached more efficiently from Eastern Command and the Soviets had shown no inclination to approve strikes against targets in that region. "Would results which might be obtained [by continuing shuttle operations]," the report's authors asked, "be commensurate with the difficulty and length of time required to transfer supplies via Persia to the Russian bases?" Apparently, still chasing dreams of Siberian bases, officers at USSTAF thought the answer to this question was affirmative.[58]

Certainly, German defenses in eastern Europe did not deter the Americans from continuing the shuttle-bombing operation. Colonel Joe Moller, operations officer of the 95th Bomb Group, later recalled an attack by a German fighter during a FRANTIC mission. "We did not run into as aggressive fighters or as well-flown fighters on the Eastern Front as on the Western Front. . . . You could see these pilots were indecisive." Moller found it easy to determine the state of his opponent's training by the way the German pilot handled his aircraft. "You could see their wings wobble and they'd be firing while their wings were wobbling, which was completely stupid." He noted that a qualitative difference existed between the German fighter units in the East and those in the West. "The fighters in eastern Germany were not like 'The Abbeville Kids' or 'The Augsburg Bluebellies.' " The Germans in the West were far more skilled and determined to fight, in Moller's opinion. "Those guys could fly. I had an 'Abbeville Kid' go between me and my wingman—and we weren't twenty yards apart—on his back! Damnedest flying I ever saw. Scared the hell out of me." Indeed, most missions, such as FRANTIC V, had been carried out at relatively low cost and apart from the damage wrought by the Germans at Poltava, missions to and from the Ukraine had not been overly costly in terms of men and machines.[59]

Moller did believe that Soviet flak posed as great a hazard to his planes as German defenses. "I always coordinated with the Russian commander who coordinated, so he said, with the Russian flak. I would hit the German-Russian lines within two to three minutes of when I said we'd be crossing them. Didn't make any difference." Moller attempted to gain better cooperation with Soviet antiaircraft batteries. "On the second shuttle we came back from bombing, I talked with the Russian commander—we were then at Poltava—and said that we'd been fired at. And he shrugged," Moller recalled, "in effect to say 'So?' They didn't hurt us or hit us, only very minimal damage but their attitude was completely different [from ours]."[60]

Virtually the entire Eastern Front was now in motion westward. Following up their smashing successes in the center, the Soviets opened yet another assault on July 14 against German Army Group North Ukraine. Hitler had weakened this formation to provide reinforcements to the hard-pressed Army Group Center on its left. Thus, by the end of the month, German units were fighting tenaciously to hold the line of the Carpathian Mountains and prevent the Soviets from breaking out onto the Hungarian Plain. Meanwhile, German Army Group North, also under Soviet pressure, was withdrawing toward the Baltic Sea in an effort to maintain contact with Army Group Center on its right. Everywhere, the German Army in the East appeared to teeter on the brink of catastrophe in the face of overwhelming Soviet might and Hitler's "stand fast" orders.[61]

By mid-August, German reinforcements, including a number of armored divisions, succeeded in shoring up the fronts of Army Groups Center and North Ukraine. Fierce German counterattacks stopped Rokossovskii's units short of Warsaw, while other units of the *Wehrmacht* managed to keep the lines of communication open to Army Group North. Still, the last great buffers of territory the Germans had acquired in the East were now virtually gone. In the meantime, disaster struck the German Army in France as units of U.S. Lieutenant General George S. Patton's newly activated Third Army finally broke out of the Normandy lodgment and began a blitzkrieg-style advance toward the German frontier. Nevertheless, the German High Command thought by August that they had gained a breathing spell in the East. They reckoned that the Soviets had exhausted themselves through their Herculean efforts of the previous weeks. As they had so often in the past, the Germans completely misread Soviet strength.[62]

Army Group South Ukraine held the part of the front shielding Romania. It, too, had been called on to give up several divisions and much of its armor to assist its beleaguered neighbors to the north because its sector had been quiet since April. The Soviet storm broke this apparent calm on the morning of August 19 when the Second and Third Ukrainian Fronts opened a massive assault against the German and Romanian armies facing them. By month's end, Romania was out of the war, Bucharest and Ploesti were in Soviet hands, and the battered remnants of yet another German army group were fighting for survival. As their troops streamed out of Romania, the Germans only narrowly averted Hungary's defection by staging a coup d'etat. Bulgaria, not at war with Moscow, nevertheless found itself invaded by the Red Army as the Soviets now declared war on her. Made untenable by the Soviet advance, the German grip on Greece, Albania, and southern Yugoslavia was broken. By the first week in October, the mauled divisions of the German Sixth and Eighth armies had just managed to form a front on the Hungarian border.[63]

Anxious to prevent any German units from escaping their grasp, the Soviets turned to USSTAF, and, on August 22, Perminov requested that FRANTIC VI get under way as soon as possible against marshalling yards in Romania. He wanted those targets hit before the 24th; Kessler doubted that could happen. Nevertheless, American planners saw an opportunity to assist the Soviets in a meaningful way and perhaps keep the door open for future FRANTIC missions. They had also hoped to succor the Polish underground in Warsaw, an idea the Soviets flatly rejected throughout August. Indeed, repeated Allied entreaties to Stalin on behalf of the Warsaw rebels did little to strengthen the Grand Alliance. While the Americans and Soviets debated the choice of bombing targets, deteriorating weather precluded heavy bomber operations over eastern Europe. FRANTIC VI, as will be noted later, failed to get off the ground in time to assist either the Poles in Warsaw or the Soviets in Romania. Once again, FRANTIC operations came to a standstill in the face of Soviet-American differences over objectives and uncooperative weather over eastern Europe.[64]

At this critical point in both the war in general and the course of FRANTIC in particular, Brigadier General McDonald issued an "appreciation" of the operation on August 21. He was far more positive in his assessment than Knerr had been. Still, it must be borne in mind that McDonald was evaluating FRANTIC from an operational and diplomatic aspect. Knerr, on the other hand, had evaluated Eastern Command itself and was concerned more so than McDonald with the means of supporting shuttle operations. In any event, McDonald assessed FRANTIC in light of the objectives that American planners had set many months ago.

McDonald based his report on a number of mission summaries as well as other documents that charted the operation's progress through July and early August. He felt that FRANTIC had succeeded in setting a precedent for American air missions from Soviet soil and in gaining valuable experience in joint operations "in the event that Russia sees fit to grant bases for use against Japan." On the other hand, McDonald believed that air attacks staged from bases in either Britain or Italy could have achieved results similar to those reached through FRANTIC. He qualified this statement by suggesting that the attacking aircraft had to pass through heavily defended areas only once because there was no return trip on the same flight. Given Moller's comments about German fighter defenses in the East, McDonald was probably correct in making this assertion.[65]

McDonald was also dubious about FRANTIC's effect on the disposition of German air defense forces. The rapid success of the Soviet summer offensives literally eliminated many of Eastern Command's potential targets. He speculated that had the Soviet advance taken longer and FRANTIC assumed larger dimensions, the Germans would have been forced to build a defensive network in the East comparable to that in the West. In fact, at the end of June, the *Luftwaffe* mustered 425 fighters on the Western Front, 370 in units based in Germany itself, while only 475 were available to cover the East. Those units that the Germans did bring eastward were thrown into the fray in ground support roles in response to Soviet attacks, not American bombers.[66]

Finally, McDonald concluded, as Knerr had, that the speed of the Soviet advance westward made FRANTIC's operational and tactical contributions to the Red Army a moot point. He also qualified this statement by pointing out, perhaps overstating things a bit, that *any* operation conducted in the East accrued some benefit to the Soviets. Overall, McDonald recognized that relations had deteriorated and hesitated to make any assessment of the health of long-term Soviet-American relations. Despite his reservations, McDonald did not call for FRANTIC's termination. He continued to hold to the hope that the Soviet government would offer the United States the use of Siberian bases for the war against Japan. Thus, he concluded, the experience in joint operations gained through FRANTIC justified the effort expended in establishing and maintaining Eastern Command.[67]

Apparently, the Soviets did not share McDonald's assessment. Through July and August 1944, they had stalled on the proposed expansion of American defenses at Eastern Command, while avoiding Allied requests that the bases be used to recover aircraft dropping supplies to Warsaw. During the last week of August, Soviet Foreign Minister Vyacheslav M. Molotov ended American hopes for an expanded FRANTIC. On the 25th, he informed Harriman and Deane that the Soviets needed the airfields of Eastern Command for their own use. This was a somewhat flimsy excuse, given the great distance between the fields and the battlefront. True, Soviet airfields farther to the west were quite crowded, but Red Air Force units were able to operate from primitive grass strips as well as recaptured airdromes. Molotov also claimed that the coming winter made an expansion of the operation impossible, and Major General Knerr agreed.[68]

Molotov assured the Americans that Moscow's decision represented only a suspension, not the abandonment, of FRANTIC. The Americans countered with a proposal to keep one of the bases under their control, albeit with a much reduced staff, through the winter of 1944–45. This base would support photo-reconnaissance missions as well as serve as a platform to resume shuttle operations in the spring of 1945. While this latter statement obviously overestimated Germany's staying power in the war, the base could be useful in repatriating American prisoners liberated in the East and in recovering crippled aircraft that landed on Soviet soil. The Soviets agreed to study the new proposal.[69]

What led to this rather abrupt Soviet decision? Soviet leaders in Moscow obviously thought FRANTIC could make no further contribution of any import to the war in the East. Their thoughts received reinforcement when the Americans were unable to respond quickly to Soviet requests for support in the Romanian sector in mid-August. Furthermore, Moscow was becoming increasingly irritated over Anglo-American requests to use Eastern Command to mount supply operations in support of the Polish uprising in Warsaw. The Soviet government under Joseph Stalin had plans for displacing the Germans as masters of Poland—plans that were in transparent conflict with the hopes and dreams of Polish rebels. Uncomfortable with an American presence on their soil, viewing the operational value of FRANTIC to have become negligible, and at odds with the Americans over the Polish uprising, the Soviets wanted Eastern Command closed down.

USAAF commanding general Henry H. Arnold was incensed by the Soviet decision. He pushed Deane and Harriman to go forward with yet another proposal for American bases in Hungary, Poland, or Romania. Though the Americans would pursue the latter scheme well into the spring of 1945, Arnold greatly exaggerated Germany's regenerative powers when he claimed the use of these bases through the winter to be absolutely essential for victory. Foul weather in western Europe, he said, would slow the bombing campaign and give the Germans a much-needed respite to rebuild their shattered industries and cities. He feared that a Soviet refusal to allow the Americans access to bases in eastern Europe would rob the USAAF, in his opinion, of the chance to deliver the "final death blow to Germany in the next few months." Subsequent events would prove Arnold's words to be a somewhat irrational assessment of the nature of the war by late 1944. Certainly it was a view that the Soviets did not share.[70]

G.I.s dine alfresco amid the tents and ruins of Poltava, summer 1944. *Courtesy U.S. Air Force.*

Against this backdrop of momentous events and decisions, Soviet-American relations at Eastern Command continued to fray. The official "line" continued to stress that Soviet and American personnel worked under conditions of cooperation and harmony. In many regards, that was true. The men of Eastern Command had made many personal and genuine friendships with Soviets. Still, the overall atmosphere by mid-August 1944 was one of tension and mutual suspicion. Given the political and diplomatic overtones of FRANTIC, therefore, incidents that might have been considered routine (if hardly welcome) in Britain or Italy, became ominous portents of the failure of the Soviet-American experiment in the Ukraine. Such an incident occurred following a shuttle mission on August 6.

On that day, First Lieutenant Phillip R. Sheridan was trying to keep his B-17 in formation in the skies of north Germany. Hit by a burst of German flak, the aircraft was losing speed. Sheridan's mates in the 390th Bomb Group watched apprehensively as his bomber began to straggle out of the protective box formation that the Flying Fortresses used to provide interlocking fields of defensive firepower. Their target, the aircraft parts factory at Rahmel, was still far to the east. Sheridan ordered the bombardier to jettison the bombs to lighten the aircraft. He managed to keep the aircraft abreast of the remainder of the FRANTIC V task force, but could not nurse the battered craft to the 390th's destination at Mirgorod. He landed the plane in a field near the Ukrainian capital, Kiev.[71]

Sheridan and his crew could not return with the rest of the task force when it departed on August 8. Salvage teams from Eastern Command retrieved his aircraft and brought it to Mirgorod. While waiting for repair crews to patch together his plane, Sheridan flight-tested other newly repaired aircraft. The young lieutenant, however, was to serve as the catalyst for one of the most explosive encounters to date at Eastern Command.[72]

On the evening of August 17, Lieutenant Sheridan and another officer went to the Soviet-operated restaurant for a few drinks. The restaurant was relatively crowded with men from both air forces. Sheridan began drinking heavily and before long was drunk and disruptive. He threw two bottles through a window. Several American officers tried to bring him under control. Sheridan turned instead on several Soviet officers and began arguing with them. Two American officers escorted Sheridan out of the restaurant, but he returned several minutes later. By now, the entire place was in an uproar. The Soviet officers present were becoming obviously nervous and upset and several American officers forced Sheridan a second time out of the restaurant.[73]

In the general confusion caused by Sheridan's behavior, a number of other potentially dangerous situations arose. Two American sergeants decided to leave the tumult in the restaurant at 9:30 P.M. As they stepped out onto the porch of the building, they saw an armed Soviet soldier. Both men later claimed they heard the soldier slide a round into the rifle's chamber, whereupon someone shouted in English that the Soviet was going to shoot an American. Several other Americans were present and corroborated the noncoms' account. The two sergeants decided to take action.[74]

One sergeant rushed the soldier and seized his rifle while the other held the man's arms. During the struggle, the soldier suffered a minor cut on the face. The American officer of the day, Warrant Officer Junior Grade James I. Carter heard someone yell "fight, fight" and rushed to the scene. Carter managed to break up the scuffle and began questioning the Americans on the scene. Another American officer reported that the Soviet soldier had been trying to escort one of his own officers, who was drunk and disorderly himself, from the restaurant. Once outside, the two Soviets began to argue and it was at this point that the two American NCOs appeared. The Soviet soldier had, in fact, loaded his weapon. The Americans at Eastern Command typically thought Soviet guards were all too often careless in discharging firearms. Fearing that this Soviet was about to shoot one of their countrymen, the two American NCOs rushed the man.[75]

Apparently agitated, Carter made the entire situation worse through his own conduct. One of the NCOs, a Sergeant O'Neal, claimed that Carter struck him on the head with a flashlight during the turmoil and shouted "What is your goddamned name?" An American officer intervened and stopped this confrontation, ordering O'Neal to the dispensary for treatment of a gash on his head caused by Carter's flashlight. Carter followed O'Neal to the medical unit, drew his pistol on the man and, in the presence of a medical orderly, said "I should have blew your damned guts out over at the club." O'Neal and several officers later claimed that Carter failed to issue any orders to stop fighting before he struck the NCO. O'Neal stated further that Carter drew his pistol both at the restaurant and the hospital for no apparent reason; Carter countered that the sergeant had attacked him.[76]

Many of the Soviet officers present were at once amused and shocked by the behavior of the Americans. While they often thought nothing of striking one of their own enlisted men, they were visibly upset that Americans had assaulted one of their guards, and that American officers were behaving in such a fashion. The Americans were embarrassed by the whole affair. Perminov sent a stern letter to Kessler reporting the incidents from the Soviet perspective and called on Eastern Command to punish the offenders. Kessler issued an apology and asked that Perminov allow American investigators to question Soviet witnesses to the evening's events. He assured the Soviet general that "every precaution will be taken to prevent a recurrence of any more incidents like the above."[77]

Though Lieutenant Sheridan had disappeared in the midst of the fracas for which he was largely responsible, he would not escape punishment. Despite a Soviet refusal to allow American officers to question their personnel, Eastern Command had sworn statements on Sheridan's behavior from nearly a dozen American officers and enlisted men. Since Sheridan was a pilot from the 390th Bomb Group and not assigned to Eastern Command, Kessler decided to forward the evidence to Spaatz's headquarters in Britain. Sheridan returned to Eighth Air Force in early September to face a court martial. Warrant Officer Carter received an administrative reprimand from Kessler for his conduct, while O'Neal and his companion escaped formal charges of assault due to an absence of testimony by the Soviets. Kessler also forbade officers and enlisted men to drink in each other's company.[78]

As the foregoing indicates, the Soviets were generally content to allow the Americans to handle their own disciplinary problems. Because the incidents involved Soviet property and personnel, however, one would expect that they would have provided witnesses and asked to be able to take some part in the proceedings. Their steadfast refusal to include their people in the investigations remains a mystery; certainly, Eastern Command officers had no explanation. Perhaps Soviet commanders did not want their soldiers to glimpse a legal process different from and possibly more equitable than their own. Whatever the reasons, this Soviet reluctance to provide material witnesses and testimony, even in cases they initiated, hobbled an American investigation and frustrated Eastern Command's officers as they attempted to substantiate charges brought against their men.

The Soviets did intervene in cases that carried political overtones. Many of the interpreters and staff officers recruited for Eastern Command were either Soviet-born or openly anti-Soviet. For example, First Lieutenant Albert M. Jaroff was Russian-born and his family had a White Russian background. Stationed at Mirgorod, Jaroff apparently exhibited what the Soviets considered hostility toward the government of Joseph Stalin and they requested his reassignment in mid-July. On the 17th, Eastern Command notified USSTAF that the Soviets wanted Jaroff out of the country. Perceiving some sort of wrongdoing on Jaroff's part, USSTAF responded on the 19th, "Return this officer to the Ninth [Air Force], the Eighth doesn't want him." When he did reach Britain, USSTAF requested a full report on Jaroff's alleged misdeeds. Eastern Command responded that his performance while at Mirgorod had been "superior." Indeed, the Soviets cited no specific incidents that prompted their displeasure with the officer. Eastern Command officers speculated that Soviet objections centered on the ties of Jaroff's family with the counter-revolutionary Whites more than two decades before.[79]

Obviously, Russian-language skills made certain officers prime candidates for Eastern Command, and many of those serving as interpreters were likely to have been Russian émigrés. Thus, it was inevitable that the Soviets would find some of these men objectionable because of their backgrounds or hostility to Soviet communism. USSTAF did try to take Soviet sentiments into account, even in the case of American-born personnel. As early as May, for example, Major General John R. Deane, as head of the Military Mission in Moscow, requested that Lieutenant Colonel Vincent Sheean not come to Eastern Command because of his previous anti-Soviet political activities and writings. Deane feared that Sheean's presence in the Ukraine would "arouse Soviet suspicion of our motives and in that way complicate an already difficult situation." USSTAF complied with Deane's request.[80]

Given Deane's sensitivity about Sheean, it is all the more surprising that such a man as First Lieutenant Hanlon E. Davies made it to Eastern Command. In mid-July, Kessler learned from Ambassador Harriman that Davies, who was serving on Kessler's staff, had been an investigator in the 1930s for the House Committee on Un-American Activities, chaired by Congressman Martin Dies of Texas. A West Point graduate, Davies earned a billet with Eastern Command because of his supposed knowledge of the USSR. On July 15, Kessler cabled USSTAF that Davies was being returned and that a replacement was not required.[81]

After his return to Britain, Davies prepared a lengthy memo at the direction of Lieutenant Colonel Aram S. Tootelian, the chief administration officer for the director of intelligence, describing his experiences during a six-week sojourn in the Soviet Union. Davies produced a highly critical document, dated July 28, 1944, which cited, albeit quite accurately, the many personnel and social problems of Eastern Command. He concluded by recommending that the United States stop "playing the political angle" through FRANTIC—that Eastern Command adopt a policy of nonfraternization and that its personnel "do the job," rather than serve as "ambassadors." Indeed, many officers agreed with Davies and shared his frustration, but nevertheless accepted the political and diplomatic importance of the operation and were therefore less vocal about their feelings.[82]

McDonald initially treated Davies' observations seriously. He pointed out to Spaatz that many of the deficiencies noted in the memo had been corrected already. He suggested that Knerr and Deane receive a copy in case they wished to conduct their own investigations based on Davies' report. Knerr agreed with many of Davies' conclusions, including the view that the Soviets wanted all foreigners out of their country once the success of their great summer offensive became evident. McDonald classified Davies' memo "Top Secret," the highest security rating, because its largely negative assessment of the Soviets could compromise Soviet-American relations. Indeed, the Soviets had been aware of Davies' past but once Deane ordered his removal, they did not appear concerned about his behavior.[83]

Davies' political views apparently prompted him to use his now classified memo to continue his prewar crusade against communism. Because of the memo's security classification and its potentially controversial contents, McDonald ordered Davies to destroy all notes he had used in preparing his report and to refrain from making any references to his experiences in the Ukraine. On August 3, Davies duly certified to McDonald that he had complied with the general's instructions and had destroyed all notes and references pertinent to his time at Eastern Command. Tootelian still suspected that, contrary to McDonald's orders, Davies was circulating copies of his memo and talking openly about his views of FRANTIC. Paradoxically, Lieutenant Jaroff, back in Britain at the Soviets' request, reported that Davies was indeed continuing to spread his views. Angered over the lieutenant's indiscretion, McDonald charged the junior intelligence officer with disobeying orders and violating security regulations. Davies was court-martialed in October, found guilty of the charges, and reprimanded. Fortunately, this potentially embarrassing incident went largely unnoticed in Moscow.[84]

One should note here that many of Eastern Command's personnel problems emerged in July 1944, at roughly the same time that the Soviets toughened their stance on fraternization and complained of American black market activity. It is quite possible that the Soviets had concluded by then that the American presence in the Ukraine was undesirable if not dangerous. Unsavory political opinions, displays of American affluence, and intimate personal relations between G.I.s and Soviet women may have combined to alarm Soviet authorities and lead them to direct that a measure of distance be put between Soviet civilians and military personnel and their Western guests.

At the same time, the Soviets were certainly justified in viewing Davies' presence as a slight to their government and he should have been weeded out as Sheean was long before he set foot on Soviet soil. On the other hand, Soviet objections to Jaroff seemed to have been based solely on his background, not on his behavior. He was simply the first of a number of American officers and NCOs who would be sent back to Britain in order to maintain good relations with the Soviets.

In the meantime, a number of incidents took place that highlighted the continuing decline of Soviet-American relations at Eastern Command. Perminov reported to Kessler on a number of incidents between American and Soviet personnel that allegedly occurred in the first weeks of September 1944. The Soviets accused two American officers of Russian descent of starting an argument with Soviet officials at the operations headquarters at Piryatin on the evening of September 7. The two Americans, Captain Michael Kowal and First Lieutenant George Fischer, also supposedly attacked a female switchboard operator who was rescued by some Soviet officers who happened on to the scene. These Soviet soldiers claimed to have reported the case to a Major Yerko, the Soviet base commander.[85]

Major Dunn, the inspector general, investigated the charges against the two officers, and found no evidence to support them. Major Yerko and his adjutant, a Captain Malioff, both claimed to know nothing of the incident. Once again, the Soviets refused to produce witnesses, and all charges against Kowal and Fischer were dropped.[86]

Perminov also reported that on September 7, several American NCOs broke into the Soviet-run restaurant at Mirgorod. When a Soviet patrol arrived, the Americans allegedly started a fight. According to Perminov's information, the Americans escaped and their names were not taken. Again, the base commander had supposedly received a briefing on the incident. When questioned, neither the American nor Soviet commanders at Mirgorod, nor the restaurant manager, knew anything about the break-in. In the absence of witnesses from the Soviet patrol and lacking names of suspects, Dunn dropped the investigation.[87]

Indeed, the Americans perceived an emerging pattern of flimsy allegations made on the part of what Eastern Command records termed unknown "political" elements. American investigators found several cases, such as minor arguments and unauthorized disposal of unserviceable equipment, to have some foundation. Several other cases brought to light in the first half of September led Dunn to suspect that individuals outside the Red Air Force were purposely mounting a campaign of petty harassment aimed at American servicemen. In particular, the inspector general believed the Soviets had singled out Soviet-born or Russian-speaking Americans, because virtually every complaint, in which they provided Eastern Command with names, involved such personnel. Neither Perminov nor any of his staff seemed to have any firsthand knowledge of these complaints. As in the earlier problems with fraternization, the Americans sensed that an unseen political force was responsible for stirring up trouble between members of the two air forces.[88]

Whatever problems existed at Eastern Command by late summer of 1944, U.S. military planners and diplomats had to face the fact that the Soviets no longer had any interest in FRANTIC. At the beginning of September, Moscow had still not responded to an American proposal for carrying out reduced operations through the winter at a single base. Ambassador Harriman tried to emphasize the supposed tactical and strategic contributions made to the Allied war effort by the shuttles to the USSR. He stressed the political and diplomatic aspects of the operations in an August 29 letter to Molotov. "The project has made the people of the United States," he wrote, "feel much closer to the Soviet people, and a great contribution has been made to their lasting friendship." Despite the clear overstatement in this regard, Harriman maintained that abandoning FRANTIC would adversely affect psychological and morale factors between the two nations.[89]

Still, the Americans persisted in their efforts to continue flying operations into the Soviet Union. Despite Molotov's stance that the bases be returned to Soviet control, Spaatz cabled Kessler on September 4 that plans for FRANTIC VI were on hold because of poor weather and that preliminary planning for FRANTIC VII was already under way. Therefore, he recommended that Eastern Command remain intact at least until September 15.[90]

Thus, as temperatures dropped at night in the Ukraine signaling the approach of autumn, the high hopes of FRANTIC's architects of the past summer were all but gone. The Americans of Eastern Command felt increasingly isolated and bitter. No longer able to fraternize freely, they believed themselves to be the targets of hostile political elements in the Soviet armed forces and government—forces that were determined to weaken good Soviet-American relations. Faced with a diminished operational tasking, many of the men of Eastern Command believed that the AAF had made a mistake in deploying them to the Soviet Union. Their attention was now focused not on their role in the great air war against Germany, but on their spartan living conditions, tiresome diet, and lack of recreation. As a result, morale plummeted, smoldering resentment led to physical violence, and boredom led to excessive drinking and black-marketeering.

For their part, the Soviets underwent a rapid change in attitude toward the Americans. Perhaps they were disturbed by the presence of less-than-friendly émigrés or shady entrepreneurs among the Americans or sensational stories in the Western press of the sexual escapades of American G.I.s and Soviet women in the Ukraine. Perhaps their own military successes led them to discount the help of their ally. Certainly, they now exhibited an uneasiness over the presence of large numbers of Americans on their soil, particularly in the politically volatile Ukraine. Whatever the reasons for this change in attitude and behavior, that change exacerbated American morale problems, which, in turn, led to further clashes and misunderstandings. An atmosphere of tension and mistrust replaced the earlier mood of enthusiasm and cooperation.

FRANTIC and Eastern Command had, by August, become largely irrelevant to the course of the war, both in the air and on the ground. The Americans persisted in maintaining an AAF presence in the Ukraine because of their stubborn faith in their ability to draw the Soviets closer to them as allies. In particular, they hoped to enlist the support of the Soviets in the Pacific War following an Allied victory in Europe. The Red Army now held nearly every significant target for Eastern Command, and the American conquest of the Mariana Islands had made AAF use of Siberian bases, the ultimate goal of FRANTIC, far less important in prosecuting the war against Japan. The Soviets had surged nearly 400 miles westward and had very nearly cleared the Balkan peninsula of the Germans. Thus, Eastern Command was now too far from the front to be of much value.

Two missions remained for FRANTIC, one routine and the other quite extraordinary. The latter of these, the last of the operation, would attempt to supply the fighters of the Polish Home Army struggling to liberate the Polish capital from the Germans before the Red Army arrived. As the war entered its sixth and final year, the Warsaw uprising was to be a watershed in Allied relations, and the controversy it generated among the Big Three powers would be felt at the isolated and lonely American airfields in the Ukraine.

MISSION TO WARSAW

September 1944

The Red Army was approaching the Polish capital. In the summer heat, a small group of Polish teenagers crouched around a radio, rotating the tuning dial. For days they had watched columns of German troops, tired and dirty, trudging through the city of Warsaw, apparently retreating westward. Now, on July 29, 1944, these young men and women, members of the Polish Home Army (*Armija Krajowa* or AK), sensed that the hour of Warsaw's liberation was near. The eager youths could hear the rumble of artillery in the East as the Red Army clawed its way forward. They strained to listen as a broadcast in Polish from Moscow crackled on the radio. "Warsaw . . . hears . . . the . . . guns. . . . Poles, the time of liberation is at hand! Poles, to arms!" One member of the group, fourteen-year-old Julian Kulski, actually felt disappointed by the announcement. He wrote in his diary that "We [had] been sitting here for almost a week, and now the Communists [were] going to beat us to the fight."[1]

The Polish uprising in Warsaw provided Eastern Command and FRANTIC with an opportunity to make a significant contribution to the course of the war in eastern Europe. Anxious to assist the Poles in their struggle against the Germans, Anglo-American leaders soon turned to the idea of employing the shuttle bases in the Ukraine so that Allied aircraft could drop supplies to the beleaguered Home Army. In this setting, the hopeful youths of Julian Kulski's small band, as well as the men of Eastern Command, would soon find themselves in the middle of one of the most controversial episodes of World War II.

Under the command of Polish Lieutenant General Tadeusz Bor-Komorowski, the Home Army served as the resistance arm of the Western-backed Polish government-in-exile in London. For months, General Bor-Komorowski and his staff quietly prepared to order the Home Army to rise up against the Germans at the earliest opportunity and thereby legitimize the London Poles' claim to a voice in governing postwar Poland. The Soviet dictator Joseph Stalin, on the other hand, had openly lent support to a rival group, hastily established on July 22 in the newly liberated Polish city of

Chelm, known as the "Polish Committee of National Liberation," or the "Lublin Poles."[2]

Polish leaders in London, including Prime Minister Stanislaw Miko-lajczyk, viewed the Soviets with great suspicion. They recalled bitterly that under the provisions of the Ribbentrop-Molotov Pact of August 1939, the Soviets had invaded Poland on September 17, 1939, to occupy the eastern part of the country while the Germans took the remainder. Polish-Soviet relations remained stormy even after Germany invaded the USSR in June 1941. In April 1943, German troops uncovered a mass grave in the Katyn Forest near Smolensk that contained the remains of several thousand Polish officers who had disappeared following the Soviet occupation of eastern Poland. Polish inquiries into possible Soviet involvement in the Katyn Massacre enraged Moscow, which interrupted relations with the London Poles. In the weeks that followed, the Soviets began organizing and equipping a Polish army division, supposedly at the request of the Moscow-based "Union of Polish Patriots." Stalin claimed that his support of this group and its new military arm was not designed to replace the Polish government in London but, in his words, to "improve its composition."[3]

As the Red Army continued its westward march in autumn of 1943, the London Poles watched apprehensively as Red Army spearheads neared the Soviet-Polish border of 1939. The Soviets had made it known to their Allies as early as 1941 that they were not content to settle for the pre-1939 frontier with Poland. Instead, Stalin put forth the Curzon Line as the postwar Soviet-Polish border. This meant that the Soviets would essentially retain most of the territory they had seized while collaborating with the Nazis in 1939. The London Poles found the Curzon Line completely unacceptable, despite pressure from the British that they compromise with Stalin. Among other Polish leaders, Bor-Komorowski was determined to preserve Polish territorial integrity.[4]

The London Poles' fear of Soviet intentions was evident in a statement released by the Polish representative in Washington on January 5, 1944. Red Army units had crossed the 1939 Polish frontier several days earlier. In response to this development, the statement declared that the Poles had been the first to "take up the German challenge" and despite terrible suffering and more than four years of Nazi occupation, had not produced "a single Quisling. . . . The Polish Nation therefore is entitled to expect full justice and redress as soon as it will be set free of enemy occupation." The message stated further that the Poles hoped to establish close ties with the Soviets as two sovereign states. They also hoped that the Soviets would not fail to respect the rights and interests of the Polish Republic and of its citizens.[5]

A three-way struggle for Poland—German, Polish nationalist, and Soviet—was rapidly taking shape. By the spring of 1944, the Polish First Army was operating under Soviet command, and communist-led partisan and underground units in Poland were clashing with units of the Home Army. Of the nearly 250,000 men and women of the Home Army, only 32,000 were armed. While Home Army leaders implored London to send supplies, Moscow kept the A.K.'s rivals relatively well-equipped. The Red Army frequently cooperated with A.K. units until an area was cleared of Germans; at that point, the Home Army fighters found themselves at the mercy of the Soviets, who often treated them harshly.[6]

In the last week of July, as the Red Army appeared literally on the horizon, representatives of the Polish exile government in London who were operating in Warsaw determined to answer the Soviet call to arms. Their goal, however, was to liberate their own capital and establish Mikolajczyk's government as a force with which Stalin would have to reckon in the future. Reports from Home Army officers reached General Bor-Komorowski on July 29 that Soviet tanks were battling the Germans across the Vistula River in Warsaw's eastern suburb of Praga. He knew the Home Army had to act if it was to escape the stigma of virtual collaboration with the Germans or being written off by Stalin as a nonentity.[7]

Bor-Komorowski knew that an uprising in Warsaw was a tremendous risk should the Germans resist and the Soviets fail (or decline) to press forward to assist the Home Army. Other members of the Polish government-in-exile, including Commander-in-Chief Kazimierz Sosnokowski, did not favor a general uprising in Warsaw at this point, believing the Germans too strong and Soviet help unlikely. Bor-Komorowski was also aware that the British had turned down a request by the Polish ambassador, Count Edward Raczynski, for direct support of an uprising by the Royal Air Force. Still, a revolt against the Germans was a gamble the Home Army commander was willing to take to save Poland from simply exchanging masters. On July 31, therefore, Bor-Komorowski ordered his units to begin the uprising at 5:00 P.M. the next day.[8]

In the meantime, at the suggestion of President Franklin D. Roosevelt, Mikolajczyk had traveled to Moscow to meet with Stalin in an attempt to reach some sort of understanding with the Soviet leader. The Polish Prime Minister arrived in the Soviet capital on the afternoon of July 30. He authorized his representatives in Warsaw to order Bor-Komorowski to begin the uprising when the situation appeared favorable. He was aware that a successful Polish revolt in Warsaw would strengthen his hand in his dealings with Stalin. Mikolajczyk's visit to the Kremlin was destined to be a disappointment. While in Moscow, the Polish leader endured a series of frustrating and humiliating meetings with Stalin, Foreign Minister Vyacheslav Molotov, and members of the Polish Committee of National Liberation. None of these gatherings gained Mikolajczyk's government any leverage or altered Soviet attitudes toward Poland.[9]

In Warsaw, Bor-Komorowski realized that the situation was changing rapidly. On the last day of July, his officers reported that some ten German divisions were now active on the Warsaw sector of the front. The streets of the city shook under the weight of the tanks of the Hermann Goering Panzer Division as they crossed the Vistula bridges to join the fighting in the eastern suburb of Praga. The front east of Warsaw, indeed, was teeming with Germans. Nevertheless, he thought the time was right to strike at the Germans. At exactly five o'clock in the afternoon of August 1, units of the Home Army attacked Poland's German tormentors in the capital city. Bor-Komorowski's uprising, Operation TEMPEST, had begun.[10]

At almost the same time that Bor-Komorowski decided to launch his attack, Marshal Konstantin Rokossovskii, commander of the First Belorussian Front, ordered Soviet units that were deployed opposite Warsaw over to the defensive. Assorted Western historians of the war on the Eastern Front have seemed to agree that the Soviet marshal had no idea that a Polish rising was about to take place in Warsaw and that Rokossovskii was simply attempting to rest and regroup his exhausted armies. In his postwar memoirs, Rokossovskii considered the Home Army's actions ill-timed and poorly coordinated. Whether the Soviets were unable to aid the Poles with artillery fire or air support and were incapable of retaking the initiative until January 1945 are questions that remain open to debate.[11]

Meanwhile, German Army Group Center, now under the command of Field Marshal Walter Model, had regained its balance. An expert in defensive tactics, Model had carefully husbanded the considerable reinforcements reaching the front, and possessed a sizeable force of armored divisions. He planned to counterattack the Soviets in the north of Poland to regain contact with German units trapped in the Baltic states of Estonia, Latvia, and Lithuania. He also saw an opportunity to lash out at the overextended Soviet units that were struggling to consolidate bridgeheads on the west bank of the Vistula to the south of Warsaw. In a brilliant counterstroke, Model hurled the Hermann Goering, 19th Panzer, and *S.S. Wiking* Panzer divisions against the Soviet Third Tank Corps to the north of Warsaw. The Germans mauled the Soviet force on July 31, convincing Rokossovskii of the wisdom of stopping the Soviet advance.[12]

Paradoxically, as the sound of combat grew louder inside Warsaw, it faded in the distance as the Red Army began falling back from its exposed forward positions along the east bank of the Vistula. Caught by surprise, and in some cases literally in the open, the Germans lost control of large areas of the city during the first few days of the uprising as units of the Home Army mounted nearly continuous assaults against their positions. For the time being, the Home Army faced a motley collection of regular *S.S.*, police, and *Luftwaffe* troops, the only regular German soldiers in Warsaw not destined for the front at the beginning of August being 960 troops of the battered Ninth Army. But the Poles quickly learned of their own limitations when detachments of the A.K. made a foolhardy attempt to halt elements of the Hermann Goering Division as it made its way eastward through the city center toward the Vistula. The Poles' light weapons were of little use against German tanks. At the same time, the Home Army found it nearly impossible to cope with the well-fortified German strongpoints scattered throughout the city.[13]

After the initial shock of the Polish attack subsided, the Germans began to prepare to retake the city and crush the Home Army. Model knew that he could not afford to lose Warsaw, which served his army group as a communications hub and supply depot. If he was to keep the Soviets at bay, he could not tie up his tanks and regular infantry in time-consuming and costly street-fighting. The German commander in Warsaw, *Luftwaffe* Lieutenant General Rainer Stahel, maintained his composure, fortified his headquarters in the Bruehl Palace in the Old City, and waited for help. The Germans managed to hold the bridges over the Vistula, the main airfields, and the Citadel, an old fortress on the banks of the river. Before long, reinforcements from Germany would be streaming toward Warsaw, including units of siege artillery and rocket launchers, flame-thrower detachments, and deadly inventions such as miniature cable-steered tanks packed with 200 pounds of explosives, the "Goliaths."[14]

Nothing German technology could produce would equal the destruction and terror wrought by the men rushed forward to crush the uprising. Anxious not to divert regular troops while the fighting continued in Praga, Hitler still saw an opportunity to destroy the troublesome Poles once and for all. Within twenty-four hours of the onset of the uprising, Hitler appointed *S.S. Obergruppenfuehrer* Erich von dem Bach-Zelewski, a specialist in antipartisan operations in Belorussia, as commander of the Warsaw operation. Bach-Zelewski would eventually have at his disposal, in addition to some regular army, police, and *Waffen S.S.* formations, several *S.S.* brigades composed largely of brutes and riff-raff for whom an operation such as this was a delight.[15]

Chief among these last formations were an *S.S.* police regiment under *S.S. Standartenfuehrer* (Colonel) Oskar Dirlewanger and *S.S. Sturmbrigade* RONA, otherwise known as the Kaminski Brigade, after its commander, Mieczyslaw Kaminski. Dirlewanger was a drunkard who had once been expelled from the *S.S.* for a moral offense! His 4,000-man unit was composed, except for the officers, of men from concentration camps and common criminals who had nothing to gain by showing any signs of human compassion. Kaminski was a Pole who claimed Russian nationality and had attempted to organize his own version of the Nazi Party. His men were Cossacks and other deserters from the Red Army who, as they drifted westward with the retreating *Wehrmacht,* resembled a sixteenth-century mercenary band, complete with camp followers. Undisciplined and haphazardly armed and uniformed, Kaminski's 6,000 renegades marauded wherever they went. Their impulse to brutality would serve the Germans well in Warsaw.[16]

As August 1944 unfolded, both Poles and Germans realized that the Red Army was not going to take Warsaw any time soon. As German units bent on revenge poured into the battered city, the citizenry of the Polish capital endured some of the most barbarous acts of the war. If the uprising was to succeed, the Home Army would need help from the outside. Because it appeared that aid was not forthcoming from the east, the Poles appealed first to London and then Washington.

With messages arriving in London from Warsaw telling of German atrocities, British Prime Minister Winston S. Churchill concluded that something had to be done to sustain the Poles. Since the German invasion of Poland in September 1939 had sparked Britain's entry into the war, Churchill believed he could not abandon the Poles now. The Royal Air Force had already judged as unrealistic Polish requests that British aircraft drop Polish parachutists in Warsaw or that British fighter aircraft land on airfields near the city—behind Soviet lines—to provide air support for the rebels. The only option remaining was to drop supplies to the beleaguered resistance. All special-duty squadrons in Britain were supporting the Normandy front and Warsaw was outside the normal operating range of Britain-based bombers unless they could land in Soviet territory, an option that would require Stalin's sanction. With no other resources available, Churchill ordered the RAF in Italy to do what it could to support the Poles.[17]

The British Prime Minister was thus determined to aid the Home Army in Warsaw. On August 4, he sent a message to Stalin informing him that the RAF was planning to fly sixty tons of supplies to the Poles, weather permitting. In his reply, Stalin expressed doubts that Churchill's information about the scope of the uprising, provided by Mikolajczyk's representatives, was accurate. Even if it were, Stalin claimed that the Poles had no chance of success against the more heavily-armed Germans. British Air Marshal Sir John Slessor, RAF commander in the Mediterranean and deputy to Mediterranean Allied Air Force commander Lieutenant General Ira C. Eaker, was hesitant to risk his aircraft on the 1,750-mile round-trip from southern Italy to Warsaw. His crews would have to cross hundreds of miles of enemy-held territory at night, and then attempt to drop supplies at tree-top level over the city, exposing themselves to murderous ground fire. Still, he had at his disposal the 1586th Polish Special Duties Flight, and if Poles were prepared to die for Poland, he believed he had no right to stand in their way.[18]

The RAF made its first flight to Warsaw on the night of August 8 when three four-engine British Halifaxes of the 1586th dropped supplies to the rebels. The following night, four other aircraft successfully completed the mission. Slessor viewed this "success" sadly; in his opinion, all that the two missions had accomplished was to raise false hopes among the Poles in London and Warsaw.[19]

Throughout August and into September, British, Polish, and Dominion crews flying American-built B-24 "Liberators" and British Halifaxes made the trip to Warsaw. Inevitably, losses mounted. On several nights, 40 percent of the relatively small formations failed to return. By September 1, for example, RAF 205 Group, assisting in the airlift, listed twelve Halifax bombers serviceable out of forty-nine assigned. On August 12, Churchill cabled Stalin that he had received distressing news from the rebels in Warsaw, who "implore machine-guns and ammunition." In an apparent reference to the difficulty that Slessor's crews were experiencing, Churchill ended the message by asking Stalin, "Can you not give them some further help, as the distance from Italy is so very great?"[20]

Stalin remained unmoved. He responded to Churchill on the 16th. The Soviet dictator's reply was ominous. He dismissed the whole affair in Warsaw as a "reckless and fearful gamble," and blamed the Poles themselves for their precarious position in Warsaw. "Soviet headquarters have decided," he concluded, "that they must dissociate themselves with the Warsaw adventure since they cannot assume either direct or indirect responsibility for it."[21]

If Churchill was failing in his efforts to enlist Stalin's active assistance on behalf of the Poles, he had some success with Roosevelt. By the middle of August, the president had become sufficiently moved by the plight of the Poles that he ordered Chief of Staff General George C. Marshall to use

FRANTIC operations to assist the Home Army. Marshall passed the president's directions to Supreme Allied Commander General Dwight D. Eisenhower, who then tasked USSTAF to begin planning a supply run to Warsaw. Unfortunately, the Americans faced the same obstacle as the British: they needed Soviet approval to use Eastern Command bases for the bombers.[22]

U.S. Ambassador to Moscow W. Averell Harriman saw little hope of Soviet cooperation. By the 15th, he had concluded that the Soviets were intending to use the faltering uprising as a means to discredit the London Poles in the eyes of their countrymen. If his conclusion correctly reflected the Soviet position, then Harriman opined that Stalin's refusal to allow landing rights for Allied aircraft was based on ruthless political considerations, not on any real operational difficulties. Moscow's formal position was that because it did not wish to be associated with the reckless adventure in Warsaw, it could not grant landing rights for American aircraft dropping supplies to the Home Army. On August 20, Churchill and Roosevelt sent a joint message to Stalin requesting that the Soviets drop supplies to the Home Army in Warsaw immediately or assist Allied planes in doing it at once. Calling those who launched the uprising "power-seeking criminals," the Soviet dictator again dismissed his Allies' appeals.[23]

Some of Roosevelt's airmen also had their doubts about the wisdom of such an operation. Several high-ranking officers feared that pressing the Soviets on the matter of Warsaw might scuttle all plans requiring Soviet cooperation, including continued shuttle operations. Major General Fred Anderson, deputy commander of operations at USSTAF, told Harry Hopkins, Roosevelt's special assistant, that the United States ran the risk of destroying its good relations with the Soviet Union over the matter of supplying the Home Army. Anderson did not believe bombers dropping supply cannisters would meet with much success because of the inaccuracy of parachute drops. He thought, moreover, that the risk to the crews involved in such an undertaking was not worth the possible benefit to the Poles. Roosevelt remained unmoved by such arguments and was committed to aiding the rebels in Warsaw. As far as the President was concerned, USSTAF and Eastern Command had only to await permission from Moscow to proceed.[24]

Meanwhile, in early August, USSTAF had already made plans for FRANTIC VI but weather had delayed its start. On both August 15 and 16, the Soviets reminded Major General John Deane that they would refuse landing rights to any aircraft involved in dropping supplies to Warsaw. On August 22, Soviet Major General Alexei Perminov passed on a request from the Red Army that FRANTIC VI hit marshalling yards in Romania as the Red Army hoped to trap as many German troops in that country as possible.

Bad weather prevented the Eighth Air Force from fulfilling the Soviet request, and on the 23rd, Spaatz notified Deane that the Fifteenth was so heavily committed to supporting the Allied drive in Italy and the landings in southern France that it would not undertake in any new shuttles before early September.[25]

By the end of August, the Soviets occupied most of the targets they had requested that the Americans strike in Romania, and FRANTIC VI was postponed once again. In the meantime, the Soviets approved a mission against Koenigsberg, capital of German East Prussia. Then, on the same day of the postponement of FRANTIC VI, the Soviets withdrew approval for Koenigsberg as well. Perhaps they feared an American trick, because a formation of B-17s heading for East Prussia could quite easily turn southward toward Warsaw. There is no indication in the records that the Americans planned anything of the kind, but the Soviets appeared to be taking no chances that a shuttle mission might reach Warsaw.[26]

At the turn of the month, the Polish situation in Warsaw was deteriorating in the face of vicious German counterattacks. On September 2, Home Army units holding the city center, or Old City, collapsed. The German troops were now backed by tanks and assault guns of the Hermann Goering Division, while an armored train used the rail lines in the city to provide overwhelming firepower on demand. German dive-bombers went unchallenged by either Soviet ground fire or fighters. A German 24-inch mortar, built on a huge tracked chassis, hurled two-ton shells into Polish-held buildings.[27]

When the Germans or their auxiliaries recaptured an area such as the Old City, they committed unspeakable atrocities. They usually shot all male captives and used women and children as shields for tanks and vehicles as they advanced on their next objective. The wounded were dispatched in a most cruel fashion. The Germans either doused them with gasoline and set them afire or burned the unfortunates with flamethrowers. That Polish resistance had not collapsed sooner could be attributed, ironically, to the savagery and incompetence of the Dirlewanger and Kaminski brigades, whose men often stopped in the middle of an operation to rape and pillage. With the Soviets still uncomfortably close to the city, the Germans remained hesitant to commit large numbers of trained regulars to fighting the insurgents.[28] The foregoing aside, time was running out for the Home Army.

Anderson's fear that the situation in Warsaw would have an adverse effect on Soviet-American relations likewise appeared to be realized. Deane noted that with the outbreak of the Polish controversy, the Soviets had begun to harass American airmen in Soviet Russia in "a very petty way."[29] In addition to Molotov's rather abrupt announcement that the Soviets wanted the bases of Eastern Command returned to them before winter, the command's deputy commander, Brigadier General Alfred Kessler, reported in August that the Soviets had begun restricting the number of reconnaissance flights to and from the American air bases.[30]

Meanwhile Ambassador Harriman questioned motives behind the Soviet actions regarding the air bases. In a message to Washington, he cited a number of issues on which the Soviet government now appeared to be stalling. In addition to the unresolved issue of FRANTIC winter operations, he pointed to Soviet delays in allowing an American damage assessment team into Romania to inspect the recently captured oil fields and facilities at Ploesti. USAAF commander General Henry H. Arnold considered such evaluations essential to the improvement of American bombing techniques. Harriman also accused Moscow of taking a "ruthless attitude toward the uprising in Warsaw" and stated that "getting the Soviet government to play a decent role in international affairs [was] . . . going to be more difficult than we had hoped." Harriman did not blame the Soviet military for the controversy surrounding Warsaw. In fact, Harriman reported that Soviet officers appeared embarrassed by the attitude expressed through the Soviet Foreign Office. Nevertheless, while the ambassador may have felt little animosity toward the Red Air Force, the men of Eastern Command had little reason to feel welcome in the Soviet Union as tension increased at Poltava, Mirgorod, and Piryatin.[31]

While the Germans closed in about the Polish Home Army in Warsaw, the Soviets manifested their displeasure with Allied appeals for Soviet cooperation in aiding the rebels through their actions at the bases of Eastern Command. The Soviets continued to nibble away at the privileges remaining to the Americans in the Ukraine. Previously, the Soviets allowed Eastern Command personnel, as well as visiting aircrews, to take photographs of whatever they fancied. On September 12, Perminov reported to Kessler that Soviet authorities had apprehended three Americans from the base at Poltava who allegedly made, in Perminov's words, a "special effort to photograph local fights, dirty gypsies and all the unpleasant scenes they could find to the great resentment of the local Soviet citizens."[32]

The Americans moved quickly to investigate charges that Eastern Command personnel were using their cameras to embarrass the Soviets. Poltava's commander, Lieutenant Colonel Charles Dahlberg, spoke with his Soviet counterpart, Lieutenant Colonel Mikhail Lysenko, who stated that after questioning them, the Soviet patrol had released the three Americans but failed to confiscate the film in their cameras. Lysenko requested that

Dahlberg retrieve the film and hand it over to him. Dahlberg agreed, and on the afternoon of the 12th he gave Lysenko two rolls of film that he had taken from the soldiers in question. Dahlberg reported that Lysenko appeared to understand that the Americans had not intended to take any special type of picture, as they had attended a lecture previous to their arrival in regard to pictures they could and could not take. The Americans could not understand the sudden twist in Soviet attitudes but, to maintain amicable relations, Walsh issued an order prohibiting the taking of photographs outside the base area itself.[33]

Perminov also forwarded a complaint against Corporal Peter Nicolaef, an American soldier of Russian descent. The Soviet general repeated an allegation made to him by sources unknown to the Americans that Nicolaef made several anti-Soviet speeches in Mirgorod, "assailing the form of government [of the Soviet Union] to the great resentment of the local Soviet population." An investigation by Eastern Command officers found no evidence or witnesses to substantiate the charge. Major Ralph Dunn, Eastern Command's inspector general, recommended that Nicolaef leave the Soviet Union, again so as to maintain "amicable relations." Nicolaef departed the Ukraine during the second week of September.[34]

Though Soviet charges against some of its personnel were baseless, Eastern Command also suffered great embarrassment from the behavior of some of its officers. On September 12, the Soviet restaurant at Poltava was again the scene of an American fracas similar to that caused by Lieutenant Phillip Sheridan the previous month. First Lieutenant Cherry C. Carpenter, a medical supply officer, and Second Lieutenant Igor C. Reverditto, a Russian-born member of Eastern Command's headquarters staff, had been drinking heavily at the eating establishment. Another American officer, First Lieutenant Michael Dubiaga, warned Reverditto about his use of foul language in the presence of enlisted men. At 10:55 P.M., Dubiaga heard a scuffle in the hallway and went to investigate. There, he found Reverditto and Carpenter, both of whom were drunk, pinning an American corporal against the wall. Reverditto was telling the enlisted man how little he cared for him when Dubiaga attempted to intervene. Carpenter told Dubiaga to mind his own business, but Dubiaga persisted and tried to lead the men down the stairs and out of the building.[35]

Carpenter and Reverditto now attacked Dubiaga. Carpenter went into a blind fury, striking Dubiaga repeatedly. As the three tumbled down the hallway, several other officers arrived and broke up the fight. First Lieutenant William Kaluta, a Russian-born interpreter, tried to calm Reverditto, who responded by starting a fight with Kaluta. When additional officers appeared, transient pilots in this case, Reverditto stopped fighting and verbally assaulted the restaurant manager. He began to speak in Russian, telling the bewildered man how little he thought of the communist government. Carpenter, in the meantime, had disappeared, but Reverditto persisted, moving back into the restaurant, insulting American enlisted men, including one man who simply had looked at him in a manner he did not like. At this point, Kaluta could take no more of Reverditto's nonsense, whereupon he challenged Reverditto to step outside to settle the matter. Sensing a riot in the making, Dubiaga immediately summoned additional help. A number of other officers arrived and were able to prevent further trouble.[36]

The Soviets had obviously disliked Reverditto for some time, for even in the opinion of other Russian-born Americans he was belligerently anticommunist. On one previous occasion, Eastern Command's commanding officer, Major General Robert L. Walsh, had warned Reverditto about his anti-Soviet behavior. As a result of Reverditto's actions on the 12th, Walsh fined him half of one month's pay and withdrew his promotion recommendation. Carpenter received similar punishment and both were shipped out to pacify the Soviets. Unfortunately, the Soviets, to Walsh's dismay, used incidents such as this one to justify additional but unsubstantiated complaints against other Russian-born or Russian-speaking Americans.[37]

On the same evening of the aforementioned brawl, an incident that contained the potential for even greater trouble occurred at the airfield. At 8:30 P.M., an intoxicated Soviet officer entered the American Air Traffic Control Section where Captain Ernest Wagner and Private First Class William Swertferger were on duty. Wagner asked the unruly officer to leave. Not only did he refuse to do so, the Soviet officer demanded transportation. Wagner denied his request. The Soviet became angry and drew his pistol, pointing it at Wagner. The American captain reacted quickly and knocked the weapon from the Soviet's hand.[38]

Wagner contacted Soviet headquarters and informed a Major Bondarenko, the Soviet duty officer, of the incident. Swertferger left in a weapons carrier to Soviet headquarters to get the Soviet major and transport him to the Air Traffic Section. He was unable to find Bondarenko at the headquarters and returned to the section. Shortly thereafter, Bondarenko, accompanied by a female interpreter named Rya, strolled into the section, took the Soviet officer's pistol and left by himself. Rya asked Wagner to wait in the office for Bondarenko to return. Shortly after 9:00 P.M., Wagner and Swertferger heard several shots. When Bondarenko came back, his coat was spattered with blood. Wagner called Bondarenko's attention to the blood on his coat but the Soviet major passed off the observation. Bondarenko departed again about 9:30 P.M., this time with Rya and the drunken officer in tow. The Soviet major told Wagner the following day that he had been forced to shoot a Soviet officer during the time he was absent from the premises of the Air Traffic Section.[39]

The Americans apparently had no desire to pursue this incident, perhaps because Dunn believed it was purely a Soviet affair. He wrote "Drop it" on the disposition sheet contained in the report's file. Nevertheless, it was one more indication of the dangerously tense, if not downright strange, state of Soviet-American relations at Eastern Command in September. In any event, there were other matters for the Americans to investigate.

On September 14, Master Sergeant Orval Moore was standing outside the "Enlisted Men and Russian Club" in Mirgorod talking to his Ukrainian girlfriend when the club manager approached them and insisted that the woman come with him. The woman refused and the two Soviets began to argue. Moore told the manager to leave the woman alone. In response, the Soviet swung at Moore but missed. The American NCO struck back, his own blow landing on the manager's chin. The Soviet ran back into the club with Moore in pursuit. Moore was stopped by friends. The Soviets accused Moore of striking the woman first and then pushing the club manager when he attempted to intervene. Moore denied the allegation and stated further that his girlfriend told him that the club manager had beaten her before. The Soviet staff could produce no witnesses and refused to provide any official statements, even from the club manager. With nothing else to go on but Moore's own testimony, Dahlberg recommended dropping the case unless the Soviets came forward with more evidence or pressed the matter further. Moore was never charged.[40]

As these accounts showed, American personnel were no longer safe from bodily harm inflicted by Soviets. In the past, Soviet personnel physically assaulted only their own women or fellow soldiers. That this was no longer the case was reinforced by yet another incident that occurred on September 24. Technician Fifth Grade Charles E. Neeck was walking down a path in the park in Poltava by himself. It was nearly dark when two Soviet soldiers approached him. As they neared Neeck, one of the soldiers drew a dagger and threatened him. The Soviets then took Neeck's wristwatch and flashlight and fled. Neeck reported the incident to the Troop Commandant, First Lieutenant Gordon L. Cunningham. The records do not contain any indication of a Soviet investigation into or resolution of the matter.[41]

Cast against the backdrop of tense Soviet-American differences over aid to the rebels in Warsaw, these incidents, with their hints of violent confrontation and harassment, were indicators of the continuing slide in Soviet-American relations at Eastern Command. Harriman was persuaded that this downturn was the result of a deliberate Soviet policy to "protect the Russian people from almost all contact with and influence of Western civilization and ideas" by forcing the exasperated Americans out of the Ukraine. This desire was reflected in Soviet behavior at Eastern Command and their decision to close down the American bases. Harriman wrote to the State Department that the "NKVD and the [Communist] Party never liked the idea of our troops coming into Russian bases. Influence was perhaps brought to bear from these sources to close them down as soon as possible." Recent events at Eastern Command certainly validated his belief.[42]

Problems notwithstanding, the Americans forged ahead with plans to maintain a foothold in the Ukraine. On September 1, Walsh returned to Poltava from a conference at Caserta, Italy, where representatives of USSTAF approved tentative plans for winter operations using one base, Poltava, manned by 200 to 300 American personnel. USSTAF forwarded this proposal to Deane, then began to plan for the winter drawdown of Eastern Command. During the next few days, messages flew back and forth between London and the Military Mission in Moscow about the disposition of the men and equipment of the three bases.[43]

Neither USSTAF's commander, Lieutenant General Carl A. Spaatz, nor Major General Deane were ready to abandon Eastern Command. Spaatz continued to hope for Soviet clearance of FRANTIC VI. For his part, Deane informed Spaatz that it would also be "politically disadvantageous if we made additional [FRANTIC] missions impossible before the battle for Warsaw [was] decided." He also did not want to give the Soviets the impression that the Americans had abandoned the insurgents in Warsaw by initiating preparations to reduce Eastern Command.[44]

The Soviets finally cleared FRANTIC VI on September 10, after many delays because of weather and their own reluctance to approve further missions that could in fact be part of a Western effort to assist the Home Army in Warsaw. The Soviets approved industrial targets in the eastern German cities of Chemnitz and Breslau. The following day, the 45th Bomb Wing's 96th and 452nd Bomb Groups returned to FRANTIC operations. Seventy-seven B-17s and sixty-four P-51s of the 67th Fighter Wing's 20th Fighter Group took off from their bases in Britain in the first FRANTIC mission to take place in more than a month. FRANTIC VI, a mission to Chemnitz, Germany, was uneventful. Two of the bombers turned back because of mechanical malfunctions and German defenses claimed one P-51. The bombers struck a machine tool factory, the crews estimating the results of the raid as "fair to poor." One B-17 and two P-51s landed in Soviet territory. The rest of the task force reached Eastern Command bases early in the evening.[45]

The raid on Chemnitz was actually the most effective FRANTIC mission flown. While the majority of the bombs missed their mark, those that hit the target destroyed not simply a machine-tool plant but the factory that, by September 1944, produced all engines for the "Panther" and "Tiger" tanks. After the war, a U.S. Strategic Bombing Survey team discovered that three-quarters of the factory was destroyed in the FRANTIC VI raid, largely by the sixty tons of incendiaries the bombers dropped. German records indicated that the raid set back tank engine production at Chemnitz for nearly six months.[46]

The FRANTIC VI task force was due to return to Britain, via Italy, the very next day. However, the Americans and Soviets could not agree on targets for the outbound mission, and FRANTIC VI to Italy was delayed twenty-four hours. The crews now had some time to spend at the bases. Their comments were remarkable given the state of Soviet-American relations at that point.[47]

Comments by crewmen reflected relatively positive attitudes toward the Soviets. For example, 22-year-old Staff Sergeant I. K. Miller of Campbellsville, Kentucky, found the run enjoyable if tiresome. A waist gunner on a B-17 with the 96th Bomb Group, he was pleased to get an opportunity to see how peoples of other nations were taking the war. Apparently impressed by what he saw, he said, "My hat's off to the Russians."[48]

The Soviets apparently continued to treat visiting aircrews well. Captain Edward Martin, a pilot with the 96th, complimented the Soviets for showing him a pleasant time. The 29-year-old North Carolinian remarked that the Soviets wanted "to be as friendly as any people I've ever seen." He also noted that "women work really hard there. . . . One woman was a guard, and the toughest I've ever seen." He probably surprised no one by concluding that winning the war was the foremost objective of the Soviets. The ball turret gunner of the B-17 "Frivolous Sal," Technical Sergeant Charles J. Turner, met a Ukrainian peasant as he stepped from the plane. "The first thing I heard when I landed was someone calling 'Hello, Americanski,' " he later recalled. "When I turned around, I saw a . . . peasant running toward us with a bottle in his hand." The peasant's warm greeting overwhelmed Turner as did the contents of the bottle, which turned out to be vodka. Turner took a drink, and before he could thank the Ukrainian, he remembered, "the sudden heat and tears caused by the vodka" were too much for him. Struggling to regain his composure, Turner managed to mutter, "Hello yourself, Russki."[49]

Crew briefing in partially destroyed warehouse. The structure was usable in good weather only as the entire roof was missing. *Courtesy U.S. Air Force.*

The crews passed September 12 by taking in as many of the sights as possible, apparently oblivious to the tension between Eastern Command and the Soviets. Though some of the aircrew members helped break up the fights caused that night by Reverditto and Carpenter at the restaurant in Poltava, none of them appeared unduly distressed or alarmed by the incident. By the morning of the 13th, the Soviets and Americans had agreed on the target for the return mission of FRANTIC VI. The bombers would strike a steel works at Diosgyor, Hungary. The crews of seventy-four B-17s and sixty-two P-51s, apparently pleased with having had a chance to visit the Soviet Union, set off for Italy. The mission was again relatively uneventful, with only one bomber returning to base and no aircraft lost to hostile action. Photo interpreters concluded that bombing results were "very good." Unfortunately, teams of the Strategic Bombing Survey never got a chance to make a postwar evaluation of the strike because of Soviet obstructionism.[50]

Quite inexplicably, by the second week in September, the Soviet government reversed its stance vis-à-vis the rebels in Warsaw in a number of ways. During the afternoon of the 10th, Soviet artillery opened an immense barrage against the Germans across the river in the suburb of Praga. Indeed,

Rokossovskii considered the fall of Praga as the point at which a Polish uprising should have taken place in Warsaw. Sensing that the long-awaited Soviet drive into the city had begun, Bor-Komorowski hardened his position in negotiations he had recently opened with the German sector commander, a Major General Rohr. He informed the German general that he would negotiate only with the commander of the German Second Army, which was holding the line north of the city. The Polish leader believed he could get better treatment for his men from a general of the German Army than from the *S.S.* He also demanded that the German radio service, *Deutschlandsender*, broadcast the surrender terms to the world, thereby increasing the likelihood that the Germans would keep their word to grant the Home Army prisoner of war status. Enraged by Bor-Komorowski's impudence, Rohr terminated the talks.[51]

In an even more startling turnaround, the Soviet government finally agreed, on September 9, to allow Allied bombers that were dropping supplies to the Home Army in Warsaw access to Soviet airfields. In a reply to a British request of September 5 asking for Soviet cooperation in air drops to the Polish rebels, Moscow issued a blistering condemnation of the Home Army's leadership for its alleged failure to coordinate the uprising with the Soviet command. The message also castigated the British, alleging that London failed to notify the Red Army of the Poles' plans in the same manner in which the British failed to give the Soviets advance warning of the Polish government-in-exile's position on Katyn. Tucked away in a few lines among all the inflammatory rhetoric and self-justification, the Soviets agreed, albeit grudgingly, to participate in aerial resupply efforts.[52]

Had Polish resistance in Warsaw collapsed by this point, FRANTIC VI would probably have been the operation's last. On September 11, however, Deane notified Spaatz that the Soviets had finally agreed to a supply drop over Warsaw. From Moscow, Deane notified Spaatz and Arnold of Soviet approval. The British notified Eisenhower who, in turn, gave Arnold the green light on September 11 to fly to Warsaw. USSTAF ordered Eastern Command to send the aircraft of FRANTIC VI to Italy to eliminate crowding at the Ukrainian bases. Spaatz planned to send a task force of bombers and fighters from Eighth Air Force to Warsaw on the 13th, but foul weather over Britain delayed the mission for twenty-four hours. FRANTIC VI, itself delayed in the Soviet Union, left for Italy on that date.[53]

Bad weather continued to stymie FRANTIC VII. The mission was postponed a second time on the 14th and rescheduled for the next day. USSTAF remained hesitant to employ the Fifteenth Air Force, possibly because that unit was still heavily committed to Allied operations in the Mediterranean.

At seven o'clock on the morning of the 15th, 110 B-17s and sixty-four P-51s took off for Warsaw and Eastern Command. Another ninety-six P-51s were aloft to escort the bombers across Germany but these aircraft would return to Britain. Unfortunately, foul weather over northwestern Germany caused the task force to return to Britain. USSTAF planned to try again on the 17th.[54]

On the night of the 13th, while FRANTIC VII was stuck in Britain, the Poles in Warsaw got a surprise from the Red Air Force. Soviet fighters now swept the hated Stuka dive-bombers from the skies, while other aircraft swooped in low to drop containers of American canned food and ammunition.[55]

Unfortunately, the Soviets dropped ammunition designed to fit Soviet weapons; most of those used by the Home Army were of German manufacture. The Red Air Force also used light aircraft which required several runs to drop a meaningful amount of supplies. The Poles had to keep the "reception points" illuminated all night, a practice that invited German shelling. The RAF, on the other hand, using Halifax and Liberator bombers, usually made only a single pass each night that lasted no longer than ten or twelve minutes, thus minimizing the risks to the Poles retrieving the delivered equipment.[56]

The Soviet technique for supply dropping operations was unusual by American or British standards. The Red Air Force dropped parcels without parachutes, allowing them to fall freely to the ground. When the Poles scampered out of their hiding places to retrieve the goods, they usually found three-quarters of them smashed and worthless. The remainder, however, was welcomed by the starving soldiers of the Home Army. Julian Kulski recalled that it was "sufficient to keep us alive and fighting. That [was] good enough for Soviet purposes and for Soviet propaganda."[57]

The Home Army's position continued to deteriorate. With Praga in Soviet hands by the 15th, the Germans now concentrated on reducing the Polish-held sectors on the Vistula, Zoliborz and Czerniakow, which could serve as Soviet bridgeheads. Bor-Komorowski dispatched a group of soldiers, including a Red Army captain named Konstantin Kalugin, to the east bank of the river on the night of the 18th. Kalugin, who had been operating with partisans behind German lines, turned up on his own in Warsaw and was reporting to Rokossovskii, via the Poles' radio link to London, on the situation in the city since the early days of the uprising. In his memoirs, Rokossovskii made no mention of Kalugin.[58]

Kalugin's group successfully reached the opposite bank, charged by Bor-Komorowski to coordinate a river crossing operation with the Red Army.

Bor-Komorowski never heard from them again. His other messages sent directly to Rokossovskii went unanswered. Two Soviet officers who parachuted into the city at the end of September did not possess the authority to pass on to the Poles the intentions and plans of the Red Army. They were merely to report back to Rokossovskii on the fighting in Warsaw. Marshal Georgy Zhukov, then in command of the First Ukrainian Front, claimed that Bor-Komorowski refused to meet the two Soviet officers and was decidedly hostile to all communications with Soviet commanders. Without the ability to coordinate their actions with the Soviets, the leaders of the Home Army did not know what to expect next from the Red Army. Indeed, the fall of Praga had heartened and emboldened the Poles; subsequent Soviet inactivity cast a pall of hopelessness across the city.[59]

Nevertheless, the British and American governments were not prepared to write off the Home Army without making at least some gesture of support. Many U.S. airmen were still reluctant to go ahead with the supply operation. They feared alienating the Soviets and now faced an entirely new situation in the West, which made undertaking FRANTIC VII at this point a severe drain on the resources of the Eighth Air Force.[60]

In mid-September, the Allies were on the eve of launching Operation MARKET GARDEN, a combined airborne and ground assault in Holland designed to seize bridges across the lower Maas, Waal, and Rhine rivers, thereby outflanking Germany's western defenses. The brainchild of British Field Marshal Bernard L. Montgomery, the operation involved three airborne divisions—two American and one British—as well as the British Second Army. If successful, MARKET GARDEN would place a large, powerful armored force on the north German plain and perhaps undermine German resistance in the West. Eisenhower approved the plan on September 10.[61]

MARKET GARDEN required extensive air support. More than a thousand troop carrier aircraft would transport the paratroops of the three Allied airborne divisions. In direct support of the operation, Eighth Air Force would commit 891 heavy bombers. Hitherto diverted to support Operation OVERLORD in Normandy, other bomb groups resumed the offensive against the German oil industry at the beginning of the month. The heavy bombers of the Eighth roamed deep into Germany once more, drawing the *Luftwaffe's* fighters eastward, away from the landing sites in Holland. Spaatz informed Eighth Air Force commander Lieutenant General James Doolittle that the airborne operation took priority over FRANTIC VII. Nevertheless, with Roosevelt himself demanding an operation to Warsaw, Spaatz knew he would have to provide the aircraft to drop supplies to the Poles as soon as the weather broke, regardless of the demands of MARKET GARDEN.[62]

The weather now cleared over northwest Germany and Holland, allowing MARKET GARDEN to begin on September 17. A weather front east of the Danish peninsula, however, delayed FRANTIC VII another twenty-four hours. The Soviets duly approved a flight plan to Warsaw for the 18th. They also agreed to attack German airfields in the vicinity of the Polish capital and send up fighters to meet the American formation over the city. Eighth Air Force operations officers briefed the crews to watch for Soviet aircraft over Warsaw. On the morning of September 18, the weather reports contained the long-awaited news: skies were clear across north Germany and Poland. FRANTIC VII was in motion at long last.[63]

Three bomb groups of the 13th Combat Wing, the 95th, 100th, and 390th, each FRANTIC veterans, took to the air, 110 B-17s in all. Each bomber carried a dozen supply cannisters in place of their usual bomb loads. Providing escort were three squadrons of the 355th Fighter Group. Seventy-three P-51s would accompany the bombers all the way to the Soviet Union, while another eighty-six returned to Britain. After takeoff, three of the bombers and nine of the long-range escorts returned early because of mechanical problems.[64]

Many of the crews heading for Warsaw had gained experience in such operations by dropping supplies to the *Maquis,* the French resistance. The trip to Warsaw would be something quite different from dropping bundles over a relatively deserted French wood or meadow. The Polish capital was heavily defended by German antiaircraft batteries and fighters. The bombers would be coming over Warsaw in daylight at altitudes of between 13,000 and 18,000 feet, far lower than that which most of the crews were accustomed to when approaching a defended target. At that height, the big silver bombers would make attractive targets for German flak gunners and their eighty-eight millimeter cannons.[65]

This mission, destined to be FRANTIC's last, was unlike any other carried out thus far in terms of objectives and the degree of German resistance. The escorts encountered enemy fighters over the Schleswig area of north Germany. The flight was relatively uneventful from that point until the aircraft were some twenty minutes west of Warsaw. Obviously aware of the formation's destination, German antiaircraft batteries opened fire on the task force. The bombers reached Warsaw shortly after noon. A misdirected message caused USSTAF planners to select an initial point (I.P.) for the run to the Warsaw drop zones that would carry the task force over the most heavily defended area of the city. German flak intensified and was very accurate. In the parlance of bomber crews, this would be no "milk run."[66]

The day was a hot one in Warsaw. Kulski and some of his comrades were resting in the sun when they heard an unfamiliar sound. Kulski looked into the sky and saw a large formation of aircraft. He later recalled seeing the bombers approach, "[f]lying in perfect military formation, the silver planes [shimmering] in the sun." The Poles realized that the planes were not German or Soviet, but American. They watched in awe as small black dots descended from the aircraft. Were they Polish paratroops from Britain? As the parachutes of the small dots opened, lowering the objects slowly earthward, Kulski could see they were supply cannisters. The Poles began shouting with joy, clapping, jumping up and down, and embracing one another. "We now knew," Kulski recalled, "that our struggle was not as lonely as it had seemed during the last six weeks—that others would help in our hour of need."[67]

The three bomb groups each had different drop zones and crossed over their objectives at slightly different times. One section of the 390th had descended to 15,500 feet when at 12:37 P.M., German fighters swooped in to attack. Major Bernie Campbell, commander of the 568th Bomb Squadron, saw red puffs of smoke amongst the bursts of flak. He knew that this was "fighter call," that the gunners on the ground were signaling German fighters lurking at the fringes of the formation that they were about to cease firing. This time, however, the flak did not stop and the German aircraft, ME-109s and FW-190s, stormed in from all sides, right through their own flak.[68]

The B-17s of the 390th were still more than ten minutes from their drop zones. First Lieutenant Francis L. Akins was attempting to hold his aircraft on course when he was struck in the face by a burst of cannon fire from a German fighter. Akins was killed instantly. His muscles tightened and his co-pilot could not pry his fingers off the control column. Tom Stotler, a twenty-three-year-old navigator assigned to another section of the group, heard Akins' panic-stricken co-pilot scream into the radio, "The damned cockpit's full of blood." Stotler would always remember that moment. He had felt excitement when he learned that the group was going on a humanitarian mission instead of a regular bomb run. Now, the young co-pilot's cries echoed in Stotler's head. Other members of the group watched as the crippled bomber began to straggle out of formation, pursued by German fighters.[69]

The German fighters continued to press their attacks after the bombers had reached their drop zones. The pilot of another B-17 lost his leg to a fighter's twenty-millimeter cannon shell. As the formation dropped its cannisters and turned off the drop run, the co-pilot of the latter aircraft contacted Campbell over the radio. The major recalled the young man saying

" 'My pilot's hit, my navigator's wounded, I've got wounded in the waist, it's hard for me to control the airplane. What can I do?' " Campbell attempted to calm the co-pilot. "We'll slow as much as we can. You can't do much. Stay with us, fella," he warned, "it's your only hope." The co-pilot and crew chief of the crippled bomber combined efforts to nurse the plane to Mirgorod. The pilot was dead, the navigator and one of the waist gunners were wounded. The entire crew had to be treated for shock.[70]

By 1:00 p.m., the task force of FRANTIC VII had dropped 1284 containers of food, light weapons, medicines, and other supplies. Below, in the streets of Warsaw, the initial exultation gave way to gloom as the Poles watched helplessly as most of the containers fell into areas now held by Germans. The bombers, though flying at slightly less than half the normal attack altitude, were still too high for the kind of pin-point accuracy required by this drop. The wind caused many of the containers to drift for some distance, some splashing into the Vistula. The heavy German flak complicated the crews' task, and the thick pall of smoke that blanketed Warsaw obscured many of the drop zones. The Home Army recovered barely a quarter of the supplies. Bor-Komorowski believed that had the mission taken place early in the uprising when large areas of the city were under Polish control, his fighters would have recovered the bulk of the supplies. The result, he thought, might have had a decisive effect on the outcome of the struggle.[71]

Still, the Poles were heartened by the American mission. Home Army commanders reported an upswing in the morale of their soldiers as a result of the supply drop. Simply seeing a formation of huge bombers overhead thrilled the weary civilians and troops struggling to survive in the ruins of Warsaw. Within a few days, the somber reality of their situation cast the spirits of the Poles down once more as famine and disease began to sweep their ranks. In the meantime, Polish observers could see Soviet troops and tanks on the eastern bank of the Vistula, barely 250 yards away.[72]

As for FRANTIC VII, it suffered relatively heavy casualties for a FRANTIC mission. One B-17 and two P-51s were lost while one B-17 was deemed irreparable and eighteen others suffered heavy battle damage. Another thirty bombers and three fighters listed minor damage in their reports. Of thirteen aircraft in the 390th's "B" group, only three were capable of immediate operations upon landing in in the Ukraine. Crew losses stood at one killed in action and two wounded while twelve were listed as missing in action: the crew of Akins' craft plus two fighter pilots.[73]

The task force droned on to Eastern Command. Badly damaged, one B-17 could limp only as far as Brest-Litovsk, but the rest of the formation reached the bases of Eastern Command. Forty-six bombers landed at Mir-

Ground personnel pose with Red Air Force guards. At the grassroots level, many American and Soviet troops formed sincere friendships and close personal relationships. *Courtesy U.S. Air Force.*

gorod, fifty-nine went to Poltava. USSTAF had planned earlier FRANTIC operations with an eye toward avoiding serious battle damage because of the relative lack of maintenance facilities in the Soviet Union. The political decision to aid the rebels in Warsaw sent FRANTIC bombers against a well-defended objective. Following the Warsaw mission, ground crews somberly assessed the servicability of the aircraft. By taking parts from the more heavily damaged bombers, the maintenance teams determined that they could have eighty-four of the 105 B-17s operational within twenty-four hours. The fighters were apparently in better shape with repair crews deeming sixty-one of sixty-two operational. Following a closer inspection of the P-51s, however, this number would drop considerably.[74]

For some of the crews, this was their first trip to the Soviet Union. Many were not quite sure what to expect. After landing at Poltava, Major Bernie Campbell wanted to see for himself the damage done to his unit's aircraft. He walked toward one of the B-17s which even at a distance exhibited signs of serious battle damage. "This one," Campbell later recalled, "had a flat tire and one engine looked like it was ready to droop—basically, it was all shot full of holes." Each plane was under the watch of a Soviet guard and these men were under orders to allow no one near their charges. As Campbell approached the bomber, the Soviet sentry raised his rifle and shouted "Stoi!" — "stop." Campbell halted in his tracks. "Da, Americanski," he replied, pointing to himself. "Da, da," the guard replied. "Airplane Americanski," Campbell continued. "Da, da," the guard nodded. Believing he made his point, the 568th commander took another step forward. The guard raised his rifle a second time and shouted "Stoi!" Campbell decided to look for help. He managed to locate an American officer who was talking with a Soviet colonel. He told the American what had just happened. As the Soviet officer chuckled softly, Campbell's American colleague said, "Oh good Lord! He said 'stoi' twice? They usually say it once and then shoot!" Following this incident, the American bomber crews decided to let the ground crews fix the planes while they stayed out of the way.[75]

Otherwise, the aircrews received the same warm welcome that the Soviets had extended to previous task force members. The official history of the 100th Bomb Group noted that its members "returned to another warm welcome at Mirgorod after Warsaw." The crews strolled about and ate and drank their fill. The 100th's history pointed out that "[q]uite a few of the Russians spoke English and conversation flourished."[76]

Many of the crew members were simply too tired after the eleven-hour flight to do much more than get something to eat, have a few drinks, and go to bed. Lieutenant Tom Stotler was not even aware that he was at an American-run base at Poltava. In the European theater for little more than a month, he already had more than half a dozen missions to his credit. He remembered just two things about the trip. He recalled a briefing prior to take-off at which crews were warned not to wander around Poltava, since unexploded butterfly bombs from the German raid in June remained in the fields near the airdrome. He also recalled seeing fifteen or twenty six-foot-long tables covered with food and alcohol after they landed. He did not speak with any of the Soviets other than the women dishing out the food. He managed to say "thank you" but could not understand what these Soviet women said in reply.[77]

The crews of more than a dozen bombers and seven fighters got the chance to spend a little more time in the Soviet Union, while ground crews patched together their aircraft. The rest of the force, ninety-three B-17s and fifty-five P-51s, left for Italy on the 19th. George Zadzora, a gunner and radio operator on one of the 568th's bombers, enjoyed a brief stay in the Ukraine. Because his plane had suffered several flak bursts, the requisite re-

Eastern Command scavenge parts from a wrecked P-51 while curious Soviet troops crawl all over the aircraft. *Courtesy U.S. Air Force.*

pairs would give Zadzora and his crew a chance to see some of the country. To pass the time, he and a friend took a truck from the Poltava motor pool into the city and gave civilians rides. Whether or not the officer-in-charge at the motor pool approved of or was even aware of their pastime was apparently not an issue with the idle aircrews. On the 24th, ten bombers and seven fighters were ready to leave, via Tehran and North Africa. A Soviet radio operator and navigator joined Zadzora's crew for the leg of the flight to Iran. The radio operator brought food for the trip: a large roast duck, a round loaf of bread, and a chunk of butter that Zadzora guessed weighed at least a pound. Lacking utensils, they simply ate their fare with their hands.[78]

While Zadzora and his mates marked time at Eastern Command, the FRANTIC VII task force flew the last of the operation's missions. The B-17s struck the marshalling yard at Szolnok, Hungary, on their way to Italy. The formation encountered "meagre" flak over the target and landed in Italy without loss. The raid appeared to have cut many of the tracks in the yard at Szolnok, possibly disrupting the movement of German troops to the threatened southern sector of the front. Following three days of inactivity at the bases of the Fifteenth Air Force, the task force proceeded across France for Britain. Several bombers and fighters turned back because of malfunctions and it was not until the end of the first week in October that the last of FRANTIC VII's aircraft returned to Britain.[79]

Meanwhile, the Poles' position in Warsaw continued to worsen. Mikolajczyk appealed to the West for continued assistance. He stated that, although the Soviets were supplying the city with food and weapons by air, they did so only in very limited quantities at irregular intervals. The Home Army had made its last regular issue of rations on September 6. Since then, the scattered Polish units and civilians survived on whatever they could find, including the wheat and barley stocks in a brewery that somehow escaped destruction.[80]

Signals from Warsaw to London painted a bleak picture as well. A British airman in Warsaw named John Ward sent a number of messages to London via the Home Army's radio set. The Germans had captured Ward in 1941 but he later managed to escape and had lived in hiding in Warsaw for some time before the uprising. Ward reported on the 25th that rumors were circulating among the population that the Germans were planning to exterminate the inmates at the concentration camps of Auschwitz-Birkenau, and Buchenwald. Ward used this news in an attempt to prod the Allies into further action, hinting darkly that after the *S.S.* slaughtered the camps' inmates, the civilians of Warsaw would be next. Bor-Komorowski also sent a personal plea for help to London on September 26. He warned that remaining food stocks would soon be exhausted. Disease was taking its toll on his ill-clad and poorly fed people. "Only regular British and American droppings of concentrated foods," he cabled, "followed by dropping of clothes, [could] bring relief."[81]

The Home Army at that point received assistance from an unexpected quarter—from units of the First Polish Army, fighting under the direction of the Red Army. Polish troops actually crossed the Vistula on the night of September 16 and 17. They established contact with the handful of Home Army troops still clinging to the riverfront district of Czerniakow as well as several smaller bridgeheads. Rokossovskii had moved these Polish troops, commanded by Brigadier General Zygmunt Berling, into the line opposite Warsaw weeks ago. His apparent motive had been to allow Polish soldiers backed by Moscow to liberate the city. Now, Berling moved without Soviet permission. Bereft of air and artillery support, his men could make no headway against German armor. They became nothing more than a strain on the meager resources of the Home Army, whose troops had to share their scanty rations with the "Berlingmen." The Polish regulars were not the vanguard of a mighty Red Army offensive; on the 24th, Rokossovskii ordered Berling's men back to the eastern bank of the river.[82]

Would the Americans mount another large-scale air drop similar to the one of the 18th? British Air Marshal Norman H. Bottomley asked Spaatz that question on the 26th. The Soviets, Bottomley stated, continued to deny the British access to Soviet airfields. Only further "shuttle missions" could make any significant improvement in the Poles' situation. On an official level, the Americans appeared willing to carry out FRANTIC VIII, provided the Soviets agreed and the weather cooperated. For the time being, Moscow left open the use of Eastern Command airfields for more supply drops to Warsaw but no one at USSTAF knew how long that approval would last. Spaatz ordered the three Eastern Command bases held at full readiness until October 5, after which a partial evacuation in preparation for winter would begin.[83]

The Americans were still not totally committed to the dropping operations over Warsaw. On September 24, USSTAF's Director of Operations, Major General Fred L. Anderson, wrote to Major General Laurence S. Kuter of the Air Staff's Plans Division that "[t]hese Warsaw supply operations should be discouraged in the very highest U.S. circles." The mission of the 18th, he wrote, simply reaffirmed their "impracticableness." He went so far as to cite Soviet claims that Red Air Force supply drops were sufficient to sustain the Poles. Anderson further pointed to the losses suffered on the mission of the 18th—two bombers and two fighters—and that several dozen aircraft were so badly damaged that they had to be left at bases along the route back to Britain. Against this effort, the Poles reported that they recovered only 130 containers thus far out of the nearly 1300 which the bombers dropped. Anderson closed by saying that continuing this operation risked delaying the timely evacuation of Eastern Command prior to winter.[84] Outwardly, Anderson expressed his negative views only among fellow American airmen. In a telephone conversation on the 29th with British Prime Minister Winston Churchill, he promised that USSTAF stood ready to send another task force as soon as the weather allowed. The next day, he made the same committment in a letter to Mikolajczyk.[85]

The American and British governments remained committed to helping the Poles in Warsaw. The British continued night air-drop operations over the Polish capital until the weather precluded further missions on September 22. By then, aircraft losses among the 1586th Polish Special Duties Flight and the other units involved in the runs to Warsaw had outstripped replacements. The RAF in Italy could make no further flights to Warsaw in the foreseeable future.[86]

Ambassador Harriman called on Stalin on the 23rd and asked his opinion of the course of the fighting in Warsaw. The Soviet dictator claimed he was displeased by events. The Vistula had proven to be a tremendous obstacle, he said. German artillery fire prevented the use of Soviet tanks in a river crossing. Without tanks, he said, the Red Army stood little chance of carrying out a successful frontal assault against German positions situated on higher ground. Harriman chose not to remind Stalin that the Soviet dictator himself had belittled similar explanations of the difficulties the Allies had faced in crossing the English Channel and landing in France.[87]

Nevertheless, USSTAF pressed forward with plans to mount FRANTIC VIII to Warsaw. On the 28th, Spaatz informed Eastern Command of his intention to move forward with the mission because of the Poles' desperate situation. On the 30th, he signaled Poltava that he had a "firm committment" from Washington that FRANTIC VIII would take place. He asked that Eastern Command obtain Soviet clearance because the mission was set to go forward the moment the weather cleared.[88]

Meanwhile, foul weather continued to blanket northern Europe. USSTAF postponed FRANTIC VIII from the 1st of October to the 2nd. Late on the 1st, Spaatz delayed the mission until the 3rd because of continuing unfavorable weather forecasts. At six o'clock on the morning of the 2nd, however, Anderson received a message from Deane that put an end to the matter once and for all. The Soviets disapproved the flight plan for the second of October. The Red Army had reports that the Poles had surrendered to the Germans. Therefore, a supply mission would only benefit the enemy. The Soviets stated further that they would refuse to approve any further Allied missions to Warsaw. The Americans knew that without Soviet approval to use the bases, any mission to the Polish capital from Britain would be impossible.[89]

The Poles were indeed surrendering. By the end of September, regular soldiers of the German Ninth Army under General Freiherr Smilo von Luttwitz had entered the battle. The pace and progress of the German attacks increased accordingly. On October 2, Bor-Komorowski, still waiting for some reply from Rokossovskii to his earlier appeals for help, decided that the time had come to stop fighting. Most of the ruined city was now in German hands. The Polish leader received a promise from *S.S. Obergruppenfuehrer* von dem Bach-Zelewski that soldiers of the Home Army would be treated as legal combatants, subject to the protection afforded all prisoners of war. Perhaps even members of the *S.S.* were thinking of their future following an Allied triumph. Still wary of the Germans, Bor-Komorowski ordered his representatives to sign the surrender agreement on the second. Civilians began moving through the German lines the next day. On the fifth, at 9:45 A.M., the battered remnants of the Home Army marched out to meet their German captors.[90]

Young Julian Kulski had already surrendered with his unit in Zoliborz on September 30. Amidst the flames and smoke of the fighting, Kulski's unit laid down its arms under the cold stares of hundreds of German soldiers. Racked by fever and illness, Kulski admitted that he "shamelessly prayed for a quick end." The teenage insurgent managed to survive both disease and captivity and greeted American troops as they liberated the camp in which he was interned in Germany in May 1945.[91]

Warsaw had held out for sixty-two days. The Home Army lost some 15,000 of the 30,000–40,000 men and women with which it began the up-rising. The Germans kept their promise of proper treatment for the combat-ants but most of the civilians were deported to labor camps or simply dumped in the countryside. Nearly 200,000 noncombatants died in the fighting. The Germans reckoned their losses at 10,000 killed, 7,000 miss-ing, and 9,000 wounded. Hitler ordered what remained of the city razed to the ground. Warsaw, in the words of the historian John Erickson, was "a gaunt, fire-blackened tomb for all its dead [which] still lay ahead of the So-viet troops." The Red Army would finally liberate Warsaw in mid-January of 1945.[92]

Thus, the Soviets were correct; the uprising had in fact collapsed by Oc-tober 2. Moscow now condemned the surrender in the same venomous fashion with which it dismissed the beginning of the uprising. The Soviets portrayed the Home Army's leaders as having abandoned their troops to the Germans, and claimed falsely that some Polish groups had chosen to fight their way through to Soviet lines instead of remaining under the London Poles' command. Bor-Komorowski and his lieutenants, according to a So-viet statement, "[prefered] to surrender them [their men] to the Germans, rather than unite with the Polish Forces in battle."[93]

As John Erickson pointed out, Stalin, by granting approval to the Americans to use Eastern Command bases in their resupply of Warsaw, had avoided a widening breach with his allies over Poland. By waiting so long before giving his consent, however, the Soviet ruler had side-stepped the em-barrassment of underwriting a *fait accompli* devised by the London Poles which would have undercut his support for the National Committee of Lib-eration. The historian Gerhard Weinberg, on the other hand, wrote that

Stalin was simply allowing the Germans to do "his dirty work for him." After all, the men of the Home Army were not "his Poles." Even an observer as sympathetic to the Soviets as Alexander Werth wrote that the leadership of the Home Army would have been eliminated "one way or another by the Russians.[94]

The Warsaw episode aggravated the already deteriorating situation at Eastern Command. Soviet dissatisfaction over the Western Allies' stance on Warsaw manifested itself at the American bases in a number of ways. Moscow's displeasure was evident in the continuing harassment of American soldiers, particularly those of Russian descent. Molotov's abrupt demand that the operation be terminated and the bases returned to Soviet control was a stark reminder that the Americans could only proceed with FRANTIC, as well as their future plans involving Soviet territory in the Far East, if the Soviets saw it to be in their interests. With the war in eastern Europe obviously now decided in their favor, the Soviets no longer wished to tolerate an American presence on their soil, especially if that meant foreign meddling in what Moscow regarded as its own affairs. Though transient United States aircrews may have continued to think highly of their Soviet hosts, the personnel assigned to Eastern Command thought otherwise. Apparent since early July, the decline in the status of Soviet-American relations accelerated at Eastern Command as a result of the pervasive tension at all levels between the two allies.

Some American airmen, such as Major General Anderson, feared that pushing the Soviets on the issue of supply runs to Warsaw would jeopardize future FRANTIC operations, as well as cast the Army Air Forces' hopes for Siberian bases into the fires of power politics. That FRANTIC and other joint Soviet-American operations would have flourished in the absence of the controversy surrounding the Home Army's rebellion is problematic, at best. The tension generated between Moscow and Washington over the Warsaw uprising certainly did nothing to bring Soviets and Americans closer. Moreover, relations between members of the two nations' air forces at Eastern Command had already begun to deteriorate long before the Warsaw rising.

The Warsaw experience should have awakened Americans to the cold, hard facts about the Soviet government. Stalin acted on what he perceived to be his own best interests. Simply fighting the Germans was not his only goal in autumn of 1944. The Soviets betrayed their true assessment of the value of the shuttle operation by denying the use of the bases to supply the Polish capital until a time Moscow deemed appropriate. George Kennan, an American diplomat in the Soviet Union, later wrote that the Warsaw Uprising was the moment when, "if ever, there should have been a full-fledged and realistic political showdown with the Soviet leaders."[95] Instead, the Americans persisted in their efforts to win Soviet cooperation in Siberia and on other projects by keeping Eastern Command alive through the winter and maintain an American presence on Soviet soil.

On October 4, Eastern Command received a message from Spaatz stating that the operational portion of FRANTIC was over. He ordered Walsh to proceed with the evacuation of personnel and equipment in preparation for winter. As the next chapter will document in detail, the Soviets agreed on September 29 and reconfirmed their assent in early October to the AAF scheme put forward at the beginning of September to allow 200 Americans to remain at Poltava as a caretaker winter detachment, pending the resumption of shuttle operations in the spring of 1945. For many of the men of Eastern Command, tired of life in the Ukraine, weary of the constant bickering with the Soviets, and anxious to find more meaningful assignments, the news of the impending evacuation could not have come sooner. The first train for the evacuation of American personnel was due to leave Mirgorod on October 7. Like the armies of an earlier era, Eastern Command prepared to move into winter quarters and await the better campaigning weather of spring.

SIX

WINTER QUARTERS

October 1944–February 1945

With the collapse of Polish resistance in Warsaw, the immediate need for American bases in the Ukraine disappeared. Soviet Foreign Minister Vyacheslav Molotov's announcement on August 25, 1944, that FRANTIC would be suspended had already prompted USSTAF to set in motion a flurry of planning aimed at keeping at least one of the three bases in American hands through the winter of 1944–45. Undeterred by the obvious break-down in Soviet-American relations at Eastern Command or the Kremlin's cynical attitude toward the Poles, Army Air Forces leaders were determined to persist in the moribund FRANTIC project. Their objective remained the maintenance of direct Soviet-American cooperation in Europe and American use of air bases in Siberia.

During September, Eastern Command personnel prepared to leave the Soviet Union. Still, the crisis in Warsaw delayed any significant movement toward deactivation of the bases so that American aircraft could use the bases for shuttle-type supply drops to the Polish Home Army in the event Moscow gave its assent. While Warsaw burned, rumors circulated through-out the command that USSTAF wanted to keep one base open as a winter detachment that could serve as a recovery and repair center for disabled American aircraft that landed in Soviet-controlled territory.

Meanwhile, on September 1, Major General Robert L. Walsh, com-manding general at Eastern Command, returned to Poltava from a high-level conference at Caserta, Italy, with the American plan for winter opera-tions in the Ukraine. That afternoon, he called a meeting to discuss the Caserta plan with the Soviet area commander, Major General Alexei Permi-nov. Walsh proposed that the Americans retain Poltava through the winter. The base would be manned by between 200 and 300 American personnel. He explained that USSTAF wanted this reorganization to be completed by November 1. Perminov agreed on the proposed site but, as in all negotia-tions with the Soviets, the final decisions had to come from Moscow.[1]

On two separate occasions, August 29 and September 28, U.S. Ambas-sador W. Averell Harriman forwarded American proposals for a winter detachment at one base but the Kremlin withheld a decision on the proposal for several weeks. The head of the U.S. Military Mission in Moscow, Major General John R. Deane, grew impatient as the weeks trickled away without a decision from the Soviets. He assumed that the Soviets would approve the plan because Red Army troops, by the first week in October, were assisting the Americans in winterizing the base at Poltava. Molotov finally swept away all speculation when he notified Harriman on October 7 that the Soviet government agreed to the conditions for a winter detachment at Poltava contained in the American proposal.[2]

With the last of the FRANTIC missions completed, the Americans moved quickly to evacuate Eastern Command. Because of the strained relations with their Soviet hosts, boredom, and isolation, many of the command's personnel wanted out of the Soviet Union as soon as possible. USSTAF commander Lieutenant General Carl A. Spaatz ordered that all personnel assigned to Eastern Command who had come from Mediterranean Allied Air Force (MAAF) units were to be sent to the Fifteenth Air Force in Italy. Those personnel from the Eighth Air Force, a majority of the command's strength, would be returned to Britain, where they would be processed for future assignments through the casual pool of the 70th Replacement Depot. General officers, Walsh and his deputy, Brigadier General Alfred A. Kessler, and all full colonels were to report to Headquarters, USSTAF, to await permanent reassignment.[3]

In April and May 1944, the largest contingent of Eastern Command personnel, the Fourth Echelon, had traveled from Britain to the Ukraine by an exhaustive water, rail, and road route via North Africa, Palestine, Transjordan, Iraq, and Iran. Some 800 evacuees would now have to retrace that route. The first Soviet troop train that was to evacuate Americans arrived at Mirgorod on October 7; two additional trains arrived at Poltava on the 11th. Following the overland portion of their journey, the men would embark from Port Said, Egypt, for the final leg of the journey to Britain.[4]

Of the remaining personnel, 185 would fly out of the Soviet Union. Two officers and twenty-nine enlisted men were destined for Italy, while fifty-seven officers and ninety-seven men flew to Britain via the Air Transport Command route across North Africa. This contingent contained the highest-ranking officers as well as enlisted communications experts to whom Spaatz assigned top priority for reassignment, because their skills were apparently needed by the Eighth Air Force. By October 5, only one day after Spaatz ordered the evacuation to proceed in earnest, eighty-eight officers and men had already departed by air, including the entire contingent bound for Italy.[5]

An F-5 reconnaissance version of the P-38 undergoes minor repairs at Eastern Command. *Courtesy U.S. Air Force.*

The Winter Detachment's medical staff was drawn from the doctors, nurses, and medical technicians running Eastern Command's three field hospitals. Lieutenant Colonel William Jackson, the command's able chief surgeon, turned his duties over to Captain Earl H. Koepke. By October 12, Koepke would have under his direction two other surgeons, four female nurses, and sixteen enlisted technicians and staff. Koepke was proud of his detachment, writing that "all personnel have had special training or have shown special aptitude for their assignments, assuring a high quality of medical care."[6]

The Winter Detachment was simply a much-reduced version of Eastern Command. Many of the personnel for the Winter Detachment were volunteers who, for one reason or another, wished to remain in the Soviet Union. Poltava retained American maintenance and supply sections, a headquarters squadron, and an operations staff, including weather and intelligence offices. Though Spaatz wanted communications specialists kept to a minimum, Eastern Command retained four officers and forty-two enlisted men in its signals sections to enable the base to communicate with American aircraft, the Military Mission, and other AAF units. Poltava also retained its own engineers, ordnance troops, finance section, and chaplain. The total strength of the Winter Detachment stood at twenty-nine officers and 126 enlisted men.[7]

The Americans had to dispose of a great deal of material. As early as August 30, Deane notified USAAF commander General Henry H. Arnold that supplies destined for Eastern Command should be returned to Britain or the Persian Gulf Command. American supply officers were already en route to northern Soviet ports to help determine which items should be returned, sent on to Eastern Command, or turned over to the Soviets under Lend-Lease. Deane also dispatched five officers from Moscow to Poltava to oversee the transfer to the Soviets of equipment that could not be used during the winter or economically shipped out. Less than a week later, while the struggle for Warsaw continued, Arnold notified Deane and Walsh that he had canceled all requisitions for the FRANTIC project. Spaatz ordered cancellation of shipments of recreational supplies, even winter sports equipment. He did leave Poltava the option of resubmitting a request if the equipment was still desired.[8]

Air Force leaders were not in agreement on the disposition of Eastern Command's stockpiles. Spaatz wanted all Air Force supplies not required by the Winter Detachment returned to the United Kingdom or American depots in the Persian Gulf region. Arnold, on the other hand, wanted to use the steel matting employed in constructing runways as bargaining chips for other proposals, particularly for bases in the Soviet Maritime Provinces. Arnold apparently overestimated the impact FRANTIC had made on the Soviets when he wrote that "at this time we can afford to be as tough with the Soviets as they have been previously with us." Deane, however, notified Arnold and Eastern Command that on instructions from Washington, all pierced steel matting at the three bases was to be turned over to the Soviets. Deane saw this as a gesture of goodwill toward the Red Air Force. Shipping several tons of steel matting to northern Russian ports and thence to Britain would require a great deal of effort for little return; neither the British nor the American air forces needed additional matting.[9]

In evacuating their stocks and supplies, the Americans were fortunate that they had brought into the Ukraine only what the Soviets could not provide them. The Soviets had agreed to provide both the bombs and machine gun ammunition for the American warplanes. Anticipating 800 sorties a month, Eastern Command had accumulated significant stocks of ordnance. When FRANTIC did not achieve the scope for which USSTAF had planned, the explosives literally piled up. By the first of October, Eastern Command still had on hand several thousand 250- and 500-kilogram bombs and millions of rounds of .50-caliber (Soviet 12.7-mm) machine gun ammunition.

Eastern Command transferred much of this material back to the Soviets who could put it to good use at the front.[10]

The Americans had transported millions of gallons of high octane aviation fuel to the Ukraine through the Persian Gulf Command. USSTAF discontinued further allocations of gasoline on September 1. At the end of the month, Eastern Command still had more than 2 million gallons of fuel on hand. Poltava would require only a portion of that fuel for its activities. The Soviets took possession of part of the stockpile, under Lend-Lease, while Eastern Command retained the remainder pending the resumption of shuttle operations in the spring of 1945.[11]

Poltava also retained a considerable stock of motor vehicles and other equipment. According to the Americans, and indeed even Molotov, the Winter Detachment was a manifestation of the suspension of FRANTIC, not its abandonment. Thus, Eastern Command stored equipment so that when the warm spring weather arrived to mark the resumption of operations, there would be little delay at the Ukrainian end of the shuttle route.

On October 15, Colonel Thomas K. Hampton assumed control of Eastern Command when Walsh and Kessler departed for USSTAF. Recently promoted, Hampton had served as deputy commander for operations at Poltava. Major General Edmund W. Hill took the post as chief of the Air Division at the Military Mission in Moscow following Walsh's departure. Hampton's counterpart at Poltava was Soviet Lieutenant General S. K. Kovalev, who replaced Perminov in October. On the 15th, USSTAF officially activated the Winter Detachment.[12]

Eastern Command's new mission reflected the state of the war by autumn of 1944. The Soviet front was now deep in Poland, Slovakia, Hungary, and Yugoslavia. American aircraft that were crippled in operations over the eastern portion of Hitler's crumbling empire could more easily reach Soviet-occupied territory than if they attempted a return flight to the West. Poltava would serve as a recovery and repair depot for both aircraft and crews. In addition, the base remained the eastern terminus for photo reconnaissance flights, as the Allies wanted to monitor any German attempts at the further dispersal of their hard-hit war industries. The Americans also did not completely rule out the possibility of further shuttle flights during the coming winter, provided the weather cooperated. Finally, the Army Air Forces wanted to keep the base active, anticipating a full-scale resumption of FRANTIC in the spring of 1945.[13]

General Arnold was not at all pleased with the Soviet position on American airfields in Eastern Europe, despite the agreement to keep Poltava open. Within a week of Moscow's decision to suspend FRANTIC, Arnold wanted additional bases farther west in Romania. During the first week in September, he bombarded Deane with messages exhorting the head of the Military Mission to press Moscow for bases in eastern Europe, including Poland. He was convinced that the Germans would recover strength during a breathing spell granted them by foul winter weather over both northwestern Europe and the Alps that would preclude sustained bomber operations from the Eighth and Fifteenth Air Forces, respectively. Arnold saw the acquisition of bases in Soviet-held areas of eastern Europe as essential to the Allied war effort.[14]

The Army Air Forces' chief was partially correct in his assessment of German recuperative powers. Hitler's minister of armaments, Albert Speer, had wrought miracles in his efforts to mobilize German industry, and had overseen a dramatic increase in production throughout 1943 and 1944, despite the Allies' best efforts to destroy German industry from the air. Arnold betrayed his faith in the power of strategic bombing when he declared that the Allied air forces were capable of inflicting "the final death blow to Germany in the next few months." The Soviets, because of their obstinacy or xenophobia, had no right, he said, "to deny the combined allied effort this assurance of an early victory."[15]

By November 1944, the Americans had once again entered the planning stage for the establishment of additional American air bases on Soviet or Soviet-occupied soil. Officials at the State Department realized that it would be politically unwise to ask the Soviets for bases in Poland, but bases in Romania would be, in their opinion, acceptable to Moscow. Then, with elements of the Red Army deployed on the outskirts of Budapest, Army Air Forces leaders switched their focus from Romania to Hungary. Indeed, Mediterranean Allied Air Force commander Lieutenant General Ira C. Eaker recommended moving the entire Fifteenth Air Force to bases near the Hungarian capital. He reasoned that the move would place the Fifteenth 300 miles nearer its targets. Eaker recognized the difficulties involved in planning the original FRANTIC operation and wrote that he would accept two bases in the area of Budapest as an interim solution until such time as arrangements could be made to move the Fifteenth from southern Italy to Hungary.[16]

Spaatz also expressed approval in November of what was now termed "FRANTIC II," a reborn shuttle-bombing project, not to be confused with the FRANTIC mission of June 21, 1944. He saw the scheme to relocate bases in the region of Budapest as a way to intensify the multifront aerial onslaught against Germany without waiting for spring. Spaatz informed Arnold that bases on Germany's southeastern flank were essential to meet

the growing threat of the German fighter force and, of course, to better retrieve damaged aircraft.[17] To be sure, the *Luftwaffe* was showing signs of
renewed vigor toward the end of the year, including the limited deployment
of jet fighters. But Spaatz may have been overstating the case to make his
point on the supposed need for bases in Hungary. In May 1940, when the
Germans attacked France, they had mustered some 1,369 fighters. In
autumn of 1944, facing enemies on three fronts as well as the skies over
Germany itself, the *Luftwaffe* could call on only 1,561 fighters.[18]

Nevertheless, Spaatz was not altogether incorrect when he warned of a
resurgent enemy fighter force. Despite American claims that the *Luftwaffe*
was a spent force following the aerial onslaught during Operation ARGU-
MENT the previous spring, the Germans showed that they were still capable
of sending large formations of fighters against the American bomber
streams. In late November, for example, some 400 German fighters challenged American bombers over Leipzig. The Americans were spared heavy
casualties only because the Germans had been slow in assembling their
forces, giving the escorts time to react. On November 26, 550 German
fighters tore into an American force of nearly a thousand B-17s and B-24s,
shooting down twenty-five of the heavies over Hannover. In the face of this
apparent German resurgence in the air, Spaatz and Arnold were anxious to
keep the pressure on the *Luftwaffe* by any means necessary, including the
implementation of FRANTIC II.[19]

Eaker, Spaatz, and Arnold continued to pursue FRANTIC II. In late September, Eaker claimed that Fifteenth Air Force bases near Foggia in southern Italy were, like Poltava, now too far from remaining targets. Photo reconnaissance showed the presence of numerous existing airdromes on the
Hungarian plain having concrete runways, which could be converted for use
by American heavy bombers with relatively little effort.[20]

The logistical requirements for FRANTIC II, however, dwarfed those of
the original operation. Had Eaker's plan to relocate the Fifteenth Air Force
to Hungary come to fruition, the Americans would have been compelled
to ship 100,000 tons of steel matting for the construction of additional
airfields, nearly ten times the quantity required for Eastern Command. The
size of the force involved would have also required the construction of a
1,200-mile pipeline from ports in northern Italy to supply gasoline.[21]

The Germans held grimly to Budapest and northern Italy, and on November 15, Arnold quashed the plan to move the Fifteenth Air Force. He
decided to settle for two bases for shuttle operations only in the spring of
1945. The personnel of the Winter Detachment at Poltava would become
part of this new American ground organization. Recalling that negotiations

over the original FRANTIC project had required several months, Spaatz persuaded Arnold to complete detailed plans for Deane to present to the Soviets. Thus, even as Eastern Command went into hibernation and the number of significant targets in German hands dwindled, the Army Air Forces continued to plan for further combat air operations from Soviet or Soviet-held soil.[22]

Deane, however, did not share the Air Force generals' enthusiasm for another FRANTIC project. He opined to Arnold that from a political point of view, such a project was no longer as important as it had been a year ago. Political advantages incident to FRANTIC, he wrote, had already been attained. What those advantages might have been in November 1944 were apparently not evident to Arnold and the other airmen (or to Eastern Command, for that matter). They still had no firm commitment from Moscow on bases in Siberia.[23]

If Arnold was looking for bargaining chips to gain political advantages from the Soviets, Deane believed he had to look no further than the runways of his heavy bomber bases. At the same meeting in February 1944 at which he had given his approval for shuttle-bombing operations using Soviet bases, Soviet dictator Joseph Stalin gave a nod to the operation of American bombers from Siberia once the USSR went to war with Japan. Shortly thereafter, the Soviets floated a request for several hundred B-17s and B-24s as part of the Fourth Protocol of Lend-Lease. Early in 1944, the United States did not have the aircraft to spare for such a venture, given the demands of the European and Pacific theaters as well as the appalling losses suffered by the Eighth Air Force during 1943 and early 1944. It was, therefore, a bargaining chip of dubious value in early 1944.[24]

Nevertheless, Deane recommended to the Joint Chiefs of Staff in April 1944 that if the Soviets would agree to the immediate preparation of plans for the operation of both Soviet and American strategic air forces against Japan, providing them with bombers would be a wise move. He believed that a Soviet strategic force was too late in coming to be of much value in the European war but would be an important addition in the air campaign against Japan. By providing the Soviets with four-engine aircraft, the Americans could avoid arousing Japanese suspicion when they shipped the necessary supplies and equipment to Siberia, and, in Deane's opinion, the bombers would guarantee an American foothold on Siberian territory for future operations. As U.S. aircraft production increased as well, the planes would become available by the middle of the present year.[25]

Arnold almost gave away the store in August, two weeks before Molotov announced FRANTIC's suspension. In a meeting with Soviet Lieutenant General Leonid G. Rudenko, head of the Soviet Purchasing Commission, Arnold inexplicably promised the Soviets the delivery of 200 B-24 "Liberators" at the rate of fifty a month. He agreed to provide American instructors for both ground and aircrews. The aircraft would be delivered via the Persian Gulf route. Aghast, Deane moved quickly to squelch this unauthorized and untimely deal. He persuaded Arnold to go back to Rudenko with the news that the aircraft would be forthcoming only after negotiations for Siberian bases were successfully completed. Deane also stipulated that the aircraft had to come via the Alaska-Siberia route so as to force the development of installations along that route capable of handling heavy bombers.[26]

Despite several additional months of negotiating and planning, this plan floundered when the Soviets balked at the introduction of more American servicemen for the purpose of training Red Air Force personnel. The Soviets, in Deane's opinion, chose to forego a strategic air force rather than make any further commitments to the Americans before they were absolutely ready to do so. Soviet air doctrine paid little attention to strategic operations of the type executed by the Americans and British. The Red Air Force planned to support any Soviet military moves against the Japanese in the same fashion—largely tactical air support—that they had on the Eastern Front in Europe. Moscow thus dropped the project when it appeared to be more trouble to them than it was worth. The Soviets remained committed only in principle to projected American operations based in Siberia.[27]

If the ultimate American objective of attempts at air cooperation was to gain access to Siberian air bases, then Deane's plan appeared to be more sound than FRANTIC. But even he overestimated Soviet interest in strategic bombing operations by attempting to gain concessions from the Kremlin with a promise of delivery of four-engine bombers. The Americans would obviously deliver the bombers only as part of a package including additional U.S. personnel and the use of Siberian bases by the AAF. Moscow, therefore, apparently did not believe that accepting the American proposals would accrue benefits to the Red Air Force commensurate with the necessity of acquiescing to more American demands. Unlike Deane, Arnold and Spaatz were concerned as much with the prosecution of the air war against Germany as with future operations from Siberia. In the view of the Air Force generals, the establishment of bases in Hungary while simultaneously drawing down operations in the Ukraine made good sense operationally, for the result would be to increase the pressure on Germany from all directions.

Meanwhile, as American airmen pondered moving an entire numbered air force hundreds of miles, the personnel at Poltava concerned themselves with preparing the base for winter. Already in October, the unheated tents in which most of the permanent staff had lived during the summer proved to be of little protection against the nighttime cold. Eating in open-air field kitchens and working in war-damaged buildings provided the men with little comfort as well. At Poltava, central plumbing was unavailable. As Major General Hugh J. Knerr, USSTAF's director of logistics, predicted during his inspection trip in August, all the foregoing and more would have to be rectified to make the camp habitable, by American standards, through the winter. By the first week in October, accordingly, sixty-five railcars containing building materials for the new winter camp facilities were on their way to Poltava, even as other trains evacuated personnel.[28]

The new camp was very compact, its buildings placed close together to allow access to newly installed water and sewage lines. The hospital was located at a crossroads, approximately midway between the headquarters building and the airfield, and across the street from the main portion of the winter camp site. The hospital would utilize prefabricated huts similar to those used at bases in Britain and Italy. Doctors, nurses, and medical staff helped to construct the new facility. "Much hidden talent for carpentering, painting, and plumbing was found among the medical personnel," Koepke reported, though personnel from all duty sections assisted in erecting the hospital.[29]

In just a few weeks, the hospital buildings, four in all, were nearly complete. By mid-November, work crews had installed the electrical wiring, plumbing, cabinets, and other furniture. Kerosene stoves provided heat. Koepke proudly reported that the new hospital, complete with "American flush latrines," was comparable to "any installation of the Zone of the Interior [continental United States] of like size." By nightfall on November 1, the handful of patients were moved from the old hospital into the new wards. One week later, the last piece of equipment was removed from the old site. The new hospital retained a small kitchen for the special dietary needs of some patients, but the new base mess, itself in a prefabricated building, was less than 50 yards from the hospital. Koepke was so proud of his new facilities that he sent a packet of photographs and a diagram of the hospital to USSTAF's chief surgeon in Britain.[30]

General living conditions at the three bases had long been a source of complaints by the men. Except at Mirgorod, where the permanent staff had been quartered in the barracks of an old artillery school, most Eastern Command personnel at Piryatin and Poltava lived in unheated tents. With the onset of colder weather, Poltava's outdoor portable shower units installed at a nearby stream, as well as the unheated ablution tents, would be

Winter quarters under construction at Poltava, October 1944. The winter camp, built to house the remaining 200 Eastern Command personnel after the end of FRANTIC operations, was much more substantial than previous facilities at the American bases in the Ukraine. *Courtesy U.S. Air Force.*

completely useless. Thus, the sense of urgency with which USSTAF evacuated Eastern Command was a result in part of the knowledge that existing structures were unsuitable for long-term occupancy during the Ukrainian winter.

Beginning in mid-October, the troops of Eastern Command worked to winterize their camp. This activity, in turn, had a salutary effect on their morale, giving them a sense of pride and unit identification that had been missing throughout the summer. By December, Poltava had been transformed into a base comparable to any in Britain. Eastern Command was no longer operating largely under field conditions. Not only did the men now live in standard prefabricated huts, they enjoyed comforts that some had not known since departing Britain the previous spring. One apparently satisfied member of the command described the new facilities as possessing "inside latrines, American toilet bowls, showers, hot water, no mess kits needed, electric lights, three stoves, a phone and radio in each barracks, an excellent club."[31]

The Soviets did not display the same enthusiasm during construction of the winter camp as they had during the initial setup in April and May. Soviet headquarters sent idle aircraft mechanics to help with the manual labor, which included digging ditches for water lines. The Americans complained that the mechanics dug crooked ditches, loafed more than American G.I.s, and were generally uncooperative and irresponsible. The Soviets came and went as they pleased, and talked back to the American officers supervising their work. Apparently, they thought that the Americans could not discipline them. Eastern Command kept track of its problems with Soviet laborers, however, and the Soviet Headquarters Section was quick to punish shirkers and "goldbricks" by assigning them to guard duty.[32]

Despite the improvements at Poltava, Eastern Command still faced serious threats to the health of its men. For example, on December 3, the Soviets warned Koepke, who had just been promoted to the rank of major, that they were treating thirty cases of typhus in Poltava. The medical staff gave lectures to the men on the disease and what they could do to protect themselves against it. Surgeons conducted weekly inspections of the barracks as well as the men themselves, and they distributed insecticide powder liberally. Given the close quarters in which the men now lived, an outbreak of typhus would quickly spread and cripple Eastern Command, perhaps permanently.[33]

While the men constructed the winter camp, Poltava saw little operational activity. Recently promoted, Major Michael Kowal, as the Winter Detachment's Operations Officer, retained control over American flights, while airdrome operations—flight clearances and the like—were the responsibility of a Soviet lieutenant colonel. Eastern Command had only two C-47 cargo planes, and, because of Soviet restrictions on foreign flights within its territory, these could be flown only by Soviet crews with an American engineer onboard. The Soviets permitted flights by C-47s to a restricted number of destinations: Poland, Moscow, certain forward areas, and other local airfields deemed necessary by the American base commander. From October 1, 1944, to April 1, 1945, the Soviet pilots flew the C-47 aircraft on forty-nine separate missions, including twenty-five to Poland. In an exception to the rules regarding crew composition, Colonel Hampton and Major Kowal occasionally piloted the C-47s. These missions were usually in support of the Military Mission in Moscow or other American activity in the Soviet Union. Hampton made two round-trips to the airfield at Saki in the Crimea during the Yalta Conference in February 1945, providing transportation for, among others, British Air Chief Marshal Arthur Tedder, chief of the Allied Expeditionary Air Forces in Europe. On each of these flights a Soviet navigator and radio operator accompanied the

American crews. In March, three additional C-47s arrived from France to provide transportation for U.S. aircrews forced down on Soviet soil. An American pilot commanded these aircraft, though each carried a mixed crew.[34]

For the first time since Eastern Command's inception, American servicemen had to rely extensively on the flying skills of Soviet pilots. The results of this close cooperation were often mixed. In general, the Americans admired the flying abilities of the Soviets but a number of negative incidents soured their attitudes. A C-47 returning from Lwów, Poland, on October 23, for example, provided the Americans with a glimpse of the manner in which the Soviets flew their aircraft. The Soviet pilot, a Captain Kvochkin, became lost because of the heavy overcast. He finally managed to locate Poltava, which had all its navigational aids operational and the landing field illuminated, and he still could not find a break in the clouds. He flew off to Mirgorod, made an unsuccessful attempt to land, and then returned to Poltava. Kvochkin spotted signal flares from the field and decided to land. He brought the C-47 down *perpendicular* to the landing strip, causing many of his American passengers to fear for their lives.[35]

Captain Joseph Johnson, the American maintenance officer, was astonished at the condition of the aircraft. The gas tanks were nearly empty, the results of Kvochkin's meandering search for a break in the clouds. The passengers also reported that when he attempted to land at Mirgorod, Kvochkin bounced the aircraft off the ground twice and missed the landing strip entirely. Johnson found wheat and leaves in the oil coolers, twigs lodged in the control surfaces, and ears of corn in the wheel wells. Kvochkin removed the left side of the windshield, perhaps hoping he could see better, and flew in that fashion for nearly an hour and a half.[36]

Unhappy with all-Soviet crews, Hampton instituted a policy of utilizing mixed crews. Unfortunately, this policy generated more problems than it resolved. Questions now arose as to who would fly in the left seat as the first pilot in charge of the aircraft. The Soviets insisted that the first pilot had to be one of their own when flying within the borders of the Soviet Union. On January 17, 1945, Hampton saw firsthand the trouble his new policy was creating.[37]

Hampton clashed with a Soviet Lieutenant Rocklikov regarding which of them was to be in charge of the C-47 they were flying in support of the Yalta Conference. Because the crew was Soviet, the flight orders stated that the Soviet pilot was in command of the aircraft but Hampton was the first pilot. Rocklikov refused to relinquish control. In the ensuing argument, one of the plane's passengers, Air Chief Marshal Arthur Tedder, intervened on

Hampton's behalf. After persuading a Soviet marshal who was aboard that the American colonel should fly the aircraft, Tedder took the controls as co-pilot. Irritated by his behavior, Hampton wanted Rocklikov banned from flying Eastern Command aircraft. He charged that Rocklikov was irresponsible in his flying and could not get along with Americans. General Kovalev agreed to reassign him.[38]

By March, however, Rocklikov was still at Poltava. On the 29th, Hampton sent another complaint to Kovalev, accusing the Soviet lieutenant of "buzzing" villages and towns in a recently repaired aircraft, losing control of the plane, landing improperly, and causing damage to the aircraft by taxiing through an ice-covered section of the airfield. Hampton forbade Rocklikov to fly any American aircraft but the Soviets, praising their pilot's skill and initiative, continued to delay transferring the lieutenant. As for Hampton's original complaint regarding the command of mixed-crew aircraft, Hill managed by March of 1945 to get the Soviets to accept Americans as first pilots.[39]

Hampton had caused quite a stir among the Soviets by his own behavior in January 1945, and may have contributed to Kovalev's hardening attitude toward cooperating with the American colonel on the matter of Lieutenant Rocklikov. On January 29, 1945, Hampton flew a C-47 from Saki back to Poltava to ferry men and equipment from Eastern Command to help prepare for the arrival of large numbers of Americans, including President Franklin Roosevelt, prior to the "Big Three" meeting at Yalta. As Hampton neared the field, Major Kowal notified him from the control tower that Kovalev would not clear him for a return flight to Saki once he landed. The reason Kovalev gave was that "Moscow" had refused clearance for all Eastern Command aircraft that day. Hampton decided to land anyway, believing that the hour he had to spend on the ground would be more than adequate to clear up what he believed was an obvious misunderstanding.[40]

After landing, Hampton persuaded Kovalev to call Moscow and obtain the necessary clearance. Twenty minutes had passed when Kovalev called Hampton and told him that Colonel General A. V. Nikitin, deputy commander of the Red Air Force, had canceled all American flights for the day. He gave no reason. Hampton replied that he had to return several American officers to Saki and that the return trip had already been cleared by the commander of the Black Sea Naval Air Force. Kovalev promised to call Moscow again.[41]

Hampton grew impatient when he did not hear from Kovalev after half an hour. He decided to take off without Soviet permission. Kowal warned him via the radio that he still lacked clearance. Hampton believed he was acting properly, given the importance of his mission. When he landed at Saki, Hampton reported Moscow's apparent lack of cooperation to the Black Sea Fleet headquarters, only to hear that the commander of the Soviet naval air forces was furious as a result of the American colonel's actions. For his part, Kovalev remarked in the presence of the American operations staff at Poltava that he expected such behavior from a young fighter pilot but not from the American commander. Hampton accepted full responsibility and was admonished by Hill that he was to adhere strictly to Soviet guidelines in the future. Hampton reacted bitterly to the entire incident. This, together with the Rocklikov incident, led to an increasingly truculent attitude toward the Soviets by the American colonel.[42]

Despite the camaraderie generated by the construction work, the men of Eastern Command still felt as though they were no longer participating in the war in a meaningful fashion. By late autumn, they began to refer to themselves as "the forgotten bastards of the Ukraine." As they had in the past, the Soviets delayed visas for the entry of additional Americans, among them members of a USO troupe. That delay, and the fact that popular radio programs never ended with a salutation to the Americans at Poltava, made the men feel isolated and neglected. In February 1945, the Military Mission in Moscow attempted to address the sense of uselessness at Eastern Command by sending the first unit patches issued by an American outfit deployed in the USSR. Triangular in shape, the patch depicted an eagle on a red and white background with the word "America" written in Cyrillic. This relatively minor action helped relieve some of the self-pity in which the men indulged by giving them a tangible unit symbol with which they could identify.[43]

The Americans did have access to relatively good facilities for recreation and relaxation. The Soviets provided the labor and the Americans the lumber and other materials for a camp theater. By Soviet standards, it was quite fancy, including dressing rooms, orchestra pit, large stage, cloak rooms, and a lobby. The Americans and Soviets agreed to share the theater for plays, movies, and other ceremonies. Soviet troops attended en masse to watch American musicals or comedies while the G.I.s seemed to enjoy the stage shows put on by the Soviets.[44]

Soviet authorities opened their observance of national holidays to American servicemen. For example, Hampton gave Eastern Command personnel the day off on November 8, 1944, in honor of the anniversary of the Bolshevik Revolution. After conferring with Kovalev, Hampton decided to march his men into Poltava for the ceremonies. They stood in the square for nearly two and a half hours listening to political speeches that few of them understood. The G.I.s also disliked the Soviet habit of standing at attention as the Soviet national anthem was played at the mere mention of Stalin's name. Hampton decided further to restrict American personnel to base during the evening to avoid the possibility of trouble because the Soviets were celebrating with large quantities of vodka. The enlisted men in particular were irritated by Hampton's plan for the day. The official history of Eastern Command noted that "they were given a day off, then forced to attend a celebration at which they understood nothing of what was said and then finally restricted to the airdrome."[45]

Captain Paul Doran, the Winter Detachment's Special Service officer, did all that he could to provide the command with entertainment and recreational opportunities. He consolidated all recreational materials in a Special Service hut where the men could sign items out for their own use. He managed to acquire portable phonographs, snow skis and snow shoes, and a large number of books for the base library. Doran organized Russian-language classes, bingo games, and scheduled movies for the post theater on nights when no other entertainment was available.[46]

Doran was frustrated in his attempts to organize dances, as the Soviets continued to display the same hostility toward fraternization that they had during the previous summer. The Soviets declined to provide women for a dance on January 30 but suggested that the Americans would not be stopped from inviting the women themselves. To attend, the Russian women would need passes granted through Soviet headquarters. These documents required the applicant's full name, home address, and time of visit and had to be submitted forty-eight hours in advance. A Soviet officer, Lieutenant Colonel Mikhail Bondarenko, stated frankly that the information would be used to "weed out undesirables." Many of the women reported to their American friends that the NKVD, the Soviet secret police, did not want women who had lived under German occupation to mingle with the Americans. This restriction might have stemmed from existing Soviet mistrust of these women or Moscow's hesitance to allow its citizens to see too much of yet another Western culture. The Americans cancelled plans for the dance.[47]

Many G.I.s persisted in their attempts to fraternize with local women but because of prevailing Soviet attitudes they were forced to maintain secretive liaisons. Some women, particularly those who worked on the base and had never lived under German occupation, were permitted by Bondarenko to attend dances and parties. First Lieutenant William Kaluta, an engineering officer, fluent in Russian, learned to his dismay that several women had been apparently assigned to gather information from their American dates. Hampton made no attempt to curtail contact between American servicemen and Soviet women other than to place the base off-limits to non-Eastern Command personnel. Given Soviet restrictions on issuing passes, the restriction appeared superfluous.[48]

The Winter Detachment did not see the same types of open confrontations between U.S. and Soviet personnel over women that had taken place during the previous summer. The primary reasons for a decline in confrontation were the much-reduced number of Americans together with the cold weather, which literally forced couples off the streets. Armed with their own passes, which guaranteed free movement in the local area, G.I.s still visited women in their homes. The Soviet headquarters appeared aware of such visitation and monitored it closely.

The Soviets did not restrict their interference with fraternization to Eastern Command. Lieutenant Kaluta went to the Crimea on 1 February 1945 on temporary duty to serve as an interpreter for the American operations officer at the Saki airdrome. The Soviets organized a dance on the fifth night of Kaluta's stay. Three pilots went into town and brought back women they had met during the past few days. An hour after the dance started, the Americans noticed that their dates were gone. Kaluta asked a Soviet officer why the women had left. The Soviet answered that one had become ill, one had to go home, and the other had to go to work. Having watched the women leave after a Soviet officer had spoken to them, Kaluta did not believe him.[49] As he finished his discussion with the Soviet officer, Kaluta noticed that the people who had been talking with the Americans suddenly departed en masse. Then, several minutes later, all the Soviets walked out of the dance hall. The Soviets kept the Americans in the building for another five minutes, then allowed them to leave. Perplexed and angry, the Americans walked back to their barracks and went to bed.[50]

The Americans also made increased use of the facilities on or near the base as a result of problems with fraternization and the difficulties associated with moving about the area under winter conditions. The restaurant at Poltava, scene of so many ugly incidents during the summer months, became Eastern Command's social center. Staffed by a competent group of women sent from Moscow, the restaurant served cold cuts, soups, meat, and a complete line of liquors, wines, vodka, cognac, and champagne. It was open to all Americans as well as to Soviet officers. Soviet enlisted men could enter only if invited by their superiors. The restaurant offered the men a welcome change from the fare at the mess hall, and its business soared on days when the base kitchen served "C" rations. The men stayed on their best behavior, as they were well aware that this establishment would be placed off-limits if another brawl took place.[51]

Indeed, few disciplinary problems arose at Eastern Command throughout the winter of 1944–45 and into the following spring. Among the most serious infractions involved the missing of bed-check by G.I.s. Bed-checks had been introduced in response to an outbreak of venereal disease in December 1944.[52]

Eastern Command spent a quiet Christmas in the Ukraine. Chaplain Clarence Strippy, recently promoted to major, worked side-by-side with American and Soviet enlisted men as they built the base chapel in early December. Highly regarded by the Soviets for his pleasant demeanor and efforts to master Russian, Strippy welcomed them to his services and gave them nearly 300 rosaries. On Christmas Eve, Strippy held a candlelight service that drew most of the command, as well as quite a few Soviets. When he was transferred to Ahwaz, Iran, for medical treatment on January 15, Soviet and American soldiers alike were saddened by his departure. Eastern Command went without another chaplain until Captain H. T. Murphy, a Catholic priest arrived for a four-day visit in late February. A Protestant chaplain, Captain Nathaniel H. Tracy, arrived on March 30 for what was to be a short stay as well; he wound up staying longer than planned when the Soviets grounded all American aircraft at the end of the month. By then, he could not even use the chapel because it was serving as a barracks for nearly 200 aircrew members who had been evacuated from crash sites in the forward areas.[53]

The four female nurses of Eastern Command also helped to brighten the Christmas season at Poltava. Chief Nurse Captain Sophie Tripodi supervised the making and placing of wreaths for nearly every building on the post. She and her nurses put up and decorated a Christmas tree in the main hospital ward that, in the opinion of Lieutenant Kaluta, "looked almost American." All four nurses, together with Colonel Hampton and one of the surgeons, Major Robert H. Wiseheart, made a trip in an ambulance to a small American cemetery to place wreaths on the graves of the five Americans who were buried there, casualties from previous FRANTIC operations.[54]

While Eastern Command spent the holiday season in the Ukraine, their comrades-in-arms were having anything but a peaceful Christmas. Hundreds of miles away, in the Ardennes forest of Belgium and Luxembourg, on December 16, two dozen German divisions representing Adolf Hitler's last strategic reserve smashed into the U.S. VIII Corps. Hoping to retake Antwerp and trap the British and Canadian forces in Holland, Hitler was desperately gambling for time. The Nazi dictator believed that this operation, if successful, would shake the determination of the Western Allies to continue the war. An armistice in the West would allow the Germans, so Hitler thought, to focus their efforts on holding the Red Army in the East. The American line buckled and bent, but never completely broke. The unexpectedly fierce resistance of American units, including the 101st Airborne Division that was trapped at Bastogne, Belgium, slowed and finally halted the German drive short of the Meuse River.[55]

In the East, Soviet units remained immobile to the north of the Carpathian Mountains, along the line they had reached the previous autumn. Two German armies, the remnants of Army Group North, lay cut off on the Courland Peninsula in Latvia, a monument to Hitler's blurred strategic vision. The Red Army was moving forward only in the area of Budapest, against fierce German opposition. Szolnok, Hungary, FRANTIC VII's last target, fell to the Second Ukrainian Front on October 30. Soviet and German tanks had been dueling in the suburbs of the Hungarian capital since the first week in November. By December 26, the Soviet trap snapped shut around the city. German and Hungarian units would hold out until February 14 in one of the most ferocious city-battles of the entire war.[56] With events such as these altering the shape of the war, it was little wonder that the men of Eastern Command, virtually bereft of an operational mission, considered themselves the "forgotten bastards of the Ukraine."

The command had other problems in its day-to-day dealings with the Soviets. In January, the civilian women and girls who worked in the mess hall began complaining for the first time about working conditions. They apparently thought their duty hours were excessive, and were upset that Americans came in to get something to eat after posted serving times. At the end of the month, Doran established a system whereby only those men holding special passes could eat earlier or later than the normal hours.[57]

American actions did not appear to satisfy either the women or the Soviet authorities. On February 1, Soviet officers complained to Eastern Command's executive officer, Lieutenant Colonel M. L. Alexander, that the women worked too many hours, that they worked too hard, and that most of them did not have the fancy clothes the Americans expected them to wear while on duty. Doran and Alexander met with Soviet officials the following day and worked out a compromise solution. The Americans asked for, and received, seven additional women so that they could establish two shifts of ten workers each. Doran agreed to have uniforms made or ordered for the kitchen help. He also allowed a Soviet officer access to the mess every Wednesday in order for him to conduct his own inspection. Apart from one woman who was dismissed for allegedly stealing soap and other supplies, the workers seemed happy with the new arrangements.[58]

The two sides worked amicably to solve the labor dispute in the mess. Still, the dispute was another indicator that the Soviets were tiring of their guests. In the past, the women working in the mess hall were among the most enthusiastic and satisfied of the Soviet workforce at Eastern Command. That even they were no longer willing to work for the Americans regardless of conditions illustrated perhaps that most Soviets knew the Americans would be leaving soon and that it was time to extract from them as many concessions as possible.

One of the greatest problems faced by Eastern Command following the activation of the Winter Detachment was theft. Both aircrews and permanently assigned personnel had complained of pilfering during the summer months. The hurried evacuation conducted during September and October, however, left a great deal of equipment insufficiently guarded. By November, thieves were breaking into American aircraft, vehicles, and storerooms. On November 29, representatives of Eastern Command and the Red Air Force met to discuss a solution to the rising tide of thefts. The Soviets agreed to strengthen the roving guard, responsible for the security of an entire area, and the stationary guard, which stood watch over a specific building or piece of equipment. Soviet headquarters would retain full control over the issuance of passes and the stationing and relieving of guard detachments. Perhaps betraying a degree of skepticism regarding the efficiency of Red Air Force security measures, the Americans declared their two storage depots off-limits to the Soviets unless they were accompanied by a member of Eastern Command.[59]

Despite such precautions and agreements, the theft rate at Eastern Command soared during December, January, and February. American maintenance crews continued to find aircraft broken into and tools missing from their work kits. Eastern Command personnel caught Soviet soldiers stealing tires, siphoning gasoline from vehicles and aircraft, as well as carrying off personal items from the barracks. Stealing was not limited to the Soviets. Hampton understood clearly that the thriving black market in Poltava was fueled by merchandise provided by American soldiers, a point the Soviets were quick to make. American personnel routinely drove off in unlocked vehicles and helped themselves to the tires of parked vehicles when they lacked a spare to replace a flat.[60]

Eastern Command officers placed much of the blame for the high rate of theft on the Soviet guards themselves. The soldiers were required to stand watch in five-hour shifts. The Americans realized that considering the cold weather, the sentries would inevitably seek shelter. Unfortunately, on numerous occasions, American duty officers found the guards asleep in the piles of clothing in the laundry or that they had simply wandered off. One American officer reported discovering a theft in progress while the Soviet guard stood by watching. The motor pool also claimed that it was nearly impossible to maintain its fleet, because Soviet guards used the vehicles' service records to roll cigarettes. Eastern Command knew of only two instances in the period December through February in which a guard successfully halted a break-in.[61]

The Soviets were stung by accusations of theft and insisted that Americans were as guilty as Soviets. The Soviet executive officer, Lieutenant Colonel Bondarenko, pointed to the abundance of American-made goods in the local bazaar as evidence that Eastern Command personnel stole commodities to sell on the black market. Hampton was aware that the Soviets were keeping detailed records of every incident and that he did not have the manpower to do the same. In January, he requested that USSTAF send an officer with legal training to investigate all American claims of theft so as to provide his headquarters the ammunition to challenge Soviet accusations. Spaatz replied that USSTAF did not have an officer available with the desired qualifications; Hampton would have to work the problem out himself.[62]

The Americans and Soviets had no choice but to act together to curb the stealing. Eastern Command's duty officers increased their patrols, and all personnel were repeatedly admonished to secure their equipment. Workers installed new locks on all doors and windows of its buildings. The Soviets, in turn, meted out punishment, usually in the form of guard duty, to those caught stealing. The Americans were not altogether happy with this form of punishment, because the Soviets routinely assigned men who had been apprehended to stand guard over the very things they had been caught pilfering! Nevertheless, the number of thefts declined dramatically in March and April.[63]

Sleeping on duty and standing by while other Soviets stole were not the only complaints the Americans lodged against Soviet guards. The Americans were thoroughly enraged by some of the activities in which Soviet sentries engaged to pass the time. Several G.I.s had adopted stray dogs as pets and, with the permission of the American headquarters, kept them in the camp area. On the morning of March 26, a Soviet sentry shot and killed a dog belonging to one of Eastern Command's enlisted men. This was not the first such occurrence. On two previous occasions, guards shot or bayoneted pet dogs belonging to Americans. Hampton was incensed. In a strongly worded letter to Kovalev, he pointed out how deeply attached his men were to the animals. He warned the Soviet general that "if my men ever catch a Russian guard in the act of injuring or shooting at a dog in our area, I refuse to take any responsibility for what might happen to the Russian guard." Hampton's warning apparently had no effect; Soviet guards continued to shoot pet dogs. The G.I.s restrained their anger and wisely refrained from confronting the armed sentries.[64]

Despite their own problems in maintaining physical security at Poltava, the Soviets were certainly on the mark when they linked black market activity to American thieves. U.S. military clothing was so much in evidence among the local population a Soviet officer groused that "you [could not] tell an American soldier from a civilian." A bit of an overstatement, perhaps, but the officer made two points. Soviet citizens wore G.I. clothing with rank insignia and patches still attached, while American personnel, even when on duty, wore civilian caps and jackets. Hampton instituted routine inspections of work areas to ensure that his men were wearing the proper uniform and that American soldiers going off-base on pass were checked by the officer of the day to check that they were not carrying what was ostensibly an extra change of clothes—clothes that they intended to sell on the black market.[65]

Black market activity plummeted following the evacuation in October 1944, but recovered somewhat after the arrival in March 1945, of large numbers of downed aircrews evacuated from the forward areas who were awaiting transportation out of the country. Despite their best efforts, the Soviet and American commands could not stem illicit buying and selling of American goods or currency. Personnel arriving from Poland reported that Polish citizens were trading 100 to 250 rubles for every dollar, nearly fifty times the official exchange rate. Each crew member carried forty-eight dollars in his escape kit, while Eastern Command personnel used dollars for purchases at the post exchange, camp clubs, and post office. U.S. currency was thus readily available for trade. Despite the importance which they attached to this issue, the Soviet headquarters continued to refuse to allow American officers to question Red Air Force personnel or local civilians, and several G.I.s suspected of black market activity were released due to a lack of evidence.[66]

Thus, Eastern Command struggled with the same problems that had plagued it during the summer. While living conditions had improved immeasurably during autumn, Soviet restrictions and American camp regulations isolated the men from the surrounding community even more than before. The Soviets continued to prevent Americans from fraternizing freely with civilians while G.I.s felt neglected and forgotten by their own army. As in the Warsaw episode, events elsewhere in eastern Europe would soon place Eastern Command at the center of controversy between the United States and the Soviet Union.

SEVEN

SPRING EVACUATION

February–June 1945

The war had entered its last year. By mid-January 1945, Adolf Hitler's Ardennes offensive had clearly failed. As the Western Allies struggled to regain their balance and resume the advance to the Rhine, the Red Army completed a massive buildup opposite the German front in Poland. In the meantime, the Soviet advance in Hungary had bogged down to the northwest of Budapest in the face of strong counterattacks by German armor.

The Germans had largely recovered from the disasters that befell them in the summer of 1944. Despite round-the-clock aerial bombardment, German industry turned out record numbers of tanks and aircraft. Nevertheless, Hitler had squandered his last reserves in the futile thrust into Belgium and his pointless insistence on continuing offensive operations in Hungary. In central Poland, an enormous Soviet host had gathered on that part of the front most essential to a successful defense of the Third Reich. At their chosen points of attack, the Soviets now outnumbered the Germans 9:1 in men and 10:1 in armor and artillery. In the Magnuszew bridgehead south of Warsaw alone, the Soviets had as many men and more equipment than the Germans could muster on the entire front from East Prussia to Hungary.[1]

When the Red Army opened its offensive in Poland on January 12, 1945, the results were a foregone conclusion. Three weeks later, Soviet troops were on the Oder River, less than 50 miles from Berlin. East Prussia was virtually cut off and the Soviets held much of the industrial region of Upper Silesia. The Germans now faced the avenging hordes of the Red Army on their own soil for the first time in the war. Many German civilians expected the Soviets to seize Berlin before the month was out. The pace of the Soviet advance, however, produced grave logistic difficulties for the Red Army, and the presence of large numbers of German units on their overextended flanks persuaded Soviet marshals at the front of the need to pause and regroup.[2]

The Soviet advance changed the entire complexion of the war. Soviet dictator Joseph Stalin could face Franklin D. Roosevelt and Winston S. Churchill at the Yalta Conference with troublesome Poland in his pocket.

The Western Allies had only recently regained the line they had held nearly two months before at the outset of the Ardennes Offensive. Berlin appeared ripe for Soviet conquest. Might not the Western Allies meet the Soviets on the Rhine instead of the Elbe?

In their push to the Oder, the Soviets also directly affected the mission of Eastern Command. USSTAF kept the base at Poltava open for the stated purpose of using it as a recovery and repair depot for crippled American aircraft. With the Soviet front now so far to the west, significant numbers of crippled bombers and long-range fighters could land on Soviet or Soviet-held territory with far greater ease than returning to their bases in Britain and France.

Since November, Eastern Command had faced the difficult task of locating and recovering downed aircraft and crews. With only two C-47s at their disposal, unfortunately, and dependent on the Soviets for flight clearances, the Americans could do little to carry out that task on their own. The American headquarters at Poltava lacked direct communications to the forward areas and would have to rely on the Soviets for information provided on downed aircraft. The Red Army's reporting system was cumbersome and slow. Advanced units reported aircraft locations to Red Air Force headquarters in Moscow, which, in turn, transmitted the information to Kovalev's headquarters at Poltava, whence it was passed to Eastern Command. The Americans tried to augment data provided by the Soviets with information gained during trips to crash sites. Officers accompanying aircraft recovery teams sought out local Soviet and Polish headquarters, queried the locals, and interrogated stranded aircrews or released prisoners of war to see if they had any knowledge of other disabled aircraft. These information-gathering methods were not effective either, and led the Americans down many a blind alley as they attempted to investigate every report of a downed plane.[3]

American units in Britain and Italy also tried to help in the search. Both Eighth and Fifteenth Air Forces reported the number of missing bombers from raids carried out in central Europe. Eastern Command passed such information to the Soviets, who would then conduct their own search and report their findings back to Poltava.[4]

American aircrews who bailed out over Soviet or Soviet-held territory were not necessarily assured of a warm reception. Early in the planning for FRANTIC, American and Soviet officers agreed on the procedures crews should follow if they found themselves behind the Red Army's front. Crews were instructed to raise their hands in the air if approached by Soviet troops and refrain from suspicious activity such as attempting to flee or hide or

Seemingly cheerful Ukrainian civilians clear snow at Poltava with large wooden paddles, January 1945. *Courtesy U.S. Air Force.*

speaking German. To assist downed airmen, escape kits issued to FRANTIC crews contained language cards on which were printed key phrases in Russian. Each flyer was also issued an identification card with "United States Army Air Forces. Pilot (name)" printed in Russian. After successfully identifying himself, the downed crew member was to seek out the nearest Red Army headquarters and attempt to establish contact with an American unit or representative. Despite the fact that they had landed on supposedly friendly soil, the crews were still to follow the standard procedures of destroying maps, orders, and other sensitive materials.[5]

Downed Americans often endured a few fearful moments while Soviet troops attempted to identify them as friend or foe. On February 3, 1945, Major Robert Rosenthal of the 100th Bomb Group was leading the Third Bombardment Division in a raid on Berlin. His plane was hit by flak, which started a fire in the bomb bay and knocked out one engine. Rosenthal stayed on course and managed to drop some of his bombs short of the city before heading eastward toward Soviet lines. The plane's electrical system was apparently damaged, as the crew could not release the remaining bombs, which now hung dangerously in the smoke-filled bomb bay. After ordering the rest of the crew to bail out, Rosenthal jumped from the burning plane at 2,000 feet. The plane exploded in the air shortly thereafter, about a half mile from where Rosenthal landed.[6]

Upon landing, Rosenthal fractured his right arm and was in great pain. He was surrounded by Soviet soldiers, one of whom swung at Rosenthal with his rifle but missed and hit instead one of his own soldiers. Rosenthal shouted "Amerikanski," whereupon the soldiers looked over his uniform and noticed the Eighth Air Force patch on his shoulder. When Rosenthal produced his identity card, the Red Army troops relaxed. Satisfied now that he was an American, the Soviets took him to their headquarters, where he spent the night as a guest of two Red Army generals. Soviet medics set his arm and gave him the best treatment available. After moving from one location to another during the next three weeks, Rosenthal arrived in Moscow on February 24 and at Poltava four days later. Unfortunately, of the eleven crew members in Rosenthal's aircraft, seven were still missing. The other three crewmen were provided the same kind of care the Soviets gave the major.[7]

In fact, most American airmen were treated well by Soviet soldiers after they had established their identities. On March 19, 1945, Second Lieutenant W. I. Knox and his crew from the 452nd Bomb Group had just opened their bomb doors and were preparing to drop their bombs on an oil refinery at Ruhland, Germany, when a group of German jet fighters, probably twin-engine ME-262s, attacked the formation. One jet made a pass at Knox's aircraft, scoring a hit with 30-mm cannon fire on the number two engine. When flames spread to another engine, the plane slowed and began to fall out of formation. Knox continued eastward, jettisoned his deadly cargo, and made a successful crash landing 30 miles east of Posen, Poland.[8]

A group of Polish civilians kept a respectful distance from the aircraft and twenty minutes passed before three Soviet officers arrived. They did not question the crews' identity and took the Americans to a nearby Red Air Force airdrome. Before departing the crash scene, the Soviets posted a sentry at the aircraft. At the airfield, Soviet officers took away the crews' sidearms. They did so, the officers explained, because they were going to break out the vodka and "a gun was a dangerous thing to have when under the influence." A Soviet captain and female sergeant acted as interpreters, and that evening the Americans were treated to a concert put on specifically for their entertainment.[9]

On March 21, the Soviets gave the crew new sets of winter flying clothes, returned their firearms, and put them on a truck bound for the small town of Opole, southwest of Lublin. When the truck became mired in mud en route to this new destination, the Soviets would not allow the

Americans to help and instead rounded up local women and some oxen to do the job of freeing the vehicle. In Opole, the Soviets staged another concert and showed a movie for the Americans. The Soviet garrison commander, a colonel, put a truck at the crews' disposal, and even commandeered a Polish barber shop, ordering the two barbers there to serve the Americans before any Poles. When he realized that the crew would still have to wait, the colonel sent his men out in search of more haircutters; the soldiers returned with six additional barbers. After enjoying several days of such kind treatment, the Americans left for Poltava aboard an Eastern Command C-47 sent to pick them up.[10]

Certainly not every downed American flyer received good or even considerate treatment. Some were robbed of personal effects or left to their own devices for days, living off the local civilians before they were able to reach an American representative or a Soviet unit that would care for them. But in general, Soviet soldiers and their officers greeted the airmen in an open and friendly manner, and did whatever they could to take care of the crew members' needs.

Soviet treatment of released American and British prisoners of war, on the other hand, infuriated the Americans at every level. Among the many issues addressed by the Allied leaders at Yalta in February was a plan regarding the treatment and repatriation of prisoners of war freed by their advancing armies. Deane had negotiated an outline accord with representatives of the Soviet High Command in late January. As ratified at Yalta, this pact committed each side—the Western Allies and the Soviets—to segregate liberated Allied citizens from enemy prisoners of war and to safeguard these newly freed individuals from combat or injury. Representatives of the Allied nations were granted the right of immediate access to holding camps, and these collection points could not be relocated without the consent of the government of the affected citizens. The liberating force was also obligated to provide food, quarters, clothing, and medical care equal to that given their own soldiers and free of charge to the prisoners. Each nation agreed to make every effort to relocate their charges to rear areas as quickly as possible and to bring about the repatriation of liberated citizens without delay.[11]

From Moscow, Major General Edmund Hill notified Eastern Command on February 14 that Poltava was to serve as an administrative and processing center for those American prisoners who were released by recent Soviet advances. Supreme Headquarters, Allied Expeditionary Force (SHAEF), Hill wrote, was dispatching ten officers and ten enlisted men who would serve as POW contact teams to carry out the repatriation of ex-prisoners, as outlined in the Yalta agreement. Though the Military Mission in Moscow estimated that nearly a thousand Americans were at large in Poland, because of limited space and facilities at Eastern Command, Hill tasked Poltava with processing liberated prisoners in batches of a hundred. He predicted, wrongly as it turned out, that as many as 15,000 Americans would be freed in the coming months and that Eastern Command was to begin preparing its facilities so that 300 men could pass through the base at one time. Thirty tons of supplies for the ex-prisoners—food, clothing, and medicine—were awaiting shipment to Poltava from Tehran while another fifty tons was due to arrive from Murmansk and Archangel in the north.[12]

Unfortunately, Hill's plans would never come into play. From the beginning, the Soviets failed to live up to the clauses of the agreement to which they were party. To the Red Army, prisoners of war were traitors who had to be punished for falling into enemy hands. The Germans had captured enormous numbers of Soviet soldiers, taking more than 3.3 million in 1941 alone. By 1945, the *Wehrmacht* had taken 5.7 million Soviet troops captive. Many Soviet captives had worked as forced laborers in German factories, while an estimated 800,000 served in some capacity with the German armed forces. As the Allies closed in on Germany in 1945, barely 1 million Soviet prisoners were still alive. Many of them now wondered how their comrades would treat them upon liberation.[13]

The Soviets' harsh attitude toward their captured troops contrasted sharply with that of the Americans. Deane, as the senior American officer in the USSR, wrote that he saw it as his personal responsibility to see that liberated U.S. personnel "received the sympathetic treatment and [the] warm reception which they [had] earned by their valor and suffering." Apparently unaware of the Soviet view of prisoners of war, Deane also viewed the Yalta agreement on repatriation as a vehicle to bring the Allied nations closer together by "the solicitude we displayed for each other's liberated prisoners." The chief of the Military Mission was in for a great disappointment.[14]

The first significant numbers of American prisoners encountered by the Soviets were several hundred inmates of the German camp *OFLAG 64,* located near Szubin, Poland. On January 21, the Germans ordered the prisoners to march westward. Three American officers hid in the camp and avoided the march, then met a Soviet armored column the next day. During the next three days, the Soviets rounded up some 150 Americans from the area and together with eighty-three sick prisoners whom the Germans had left behind, moved them to the town of Rembertow, southeast of Warsaw. The three officers, Lieutenants William R. Cory, Hill Murphy, and Peter

Gaich, together with other physically able prisoners, were allowed to proceed eastward; 128 sick Americans remained at Rembertow.[15]

The lieutenants set off on their own, hitchhiking or waiting at Soviet traffic control stations for places on eastbound trucks. On February 9, they reached Lublin, where they received excellent treatment from the local Polish civilians. After they arrived in Lwów, however, the men were interrogated at length by officers of the NKVD. Following a full day of questioning, they were taken to a hotel. There, they met Majors Donald Nicholson and Robert Wiseheart of Eastern Command. Nicholson was an intelligence officer and Wiseheart was assistant surgeon at Poltava. The two officers had come to Lwów to assist in the evacuation of a downed aircrew. While there, the two field grade officers located approximately a hundred hospitalized American ex-prisoners. Many of the reports Wiseheart received from the Poles and other Americans indicated that sick and wounded Americans were living under deplorably crowded and filthy conditions. Under the Yalta agreement, Wiseheart believed he was empowered to evacuate these men to Poltava to care for them. The Soviets disagreed.[16]

Wiseheart thereupon informed the Soviets that Cory, Murphy, and Gaich were coming with him on the plane back to Poltava. Because the three men were ex-prisoners, the Soviets refused. By this point, the Red Army was putting a plan into motion whereby all liberated Americans were to go not to Poltava but to Odessa, a port on the Ukraine's Black Sea Coast. From there, they would be evacuated by ship. Wiseheart reported later that he had stood his ground, informing the Soviets that "no one was leaving unless the three men [the lieutenants] came along." After some discussion, the Soviets agreed.[17]

Deane considered the use of Odessa as a transient camp as undermining the Yalta agreement on repatriation. By transporting ex-prisoners directly to the port city, the Soviets would delay the work of U.S. contact teams. He opined that sending ex-prisoners directly to Odessa would interfere with American attempts to account for their repatriates and violated the clauses of the accord that guaranteed U.S. representatives free access to both the freed soldiers and the facilities in which they were kept.[18]

After returning to Poltava, Wiseheart expressed his anger and resentment toward the Soviets for the poor treatment he believed they were according liberated Americans. Major Earl Koepke, Eastern Command's surgeon, reported to USSTAF that his unit was "prepared to evacuate all sick and injured [Americans] by plane to our hospital here" and wrote that he could not understand Soviet intransigence on the matter or their insistence on using Odessa as a processing center.[19]

On January 31, the Red Army liberated *Stalag 3C* near Kustrin, Germany, on the Oder River. Seemingly unaware that the camp contained prisoners, the Soviets had shelled it during their approach. As the Germans marched the prisoners westward, Soviet tanks opened fire on the columns of men, mistaking them for Hungarian soldiers fighting alongside the German Army. Several Americans were killed and wounded by the gunfire. After a few minutes, the firing stopped when the Soviets realized who the men were. The Soviets told the ex-prisoners to stay put at the camp, then moved those who remained to the rear several days later.[20]

Not all the newly freed Americans were willing to follow Soviet instructions. Two enlisted men, Sergeant Maurice J. Fifield of the 101st Airborne Division and Sergeant Joseph Newmann of the 9th Infantry Division, posed as wounded officer aircrew members in order to receive better treatment from the Soviets and perhaps succeed in getting evacuated to Poltava instead of Odessa. The ruse worked. On March 25, a contingent from Eastern Command located the two men, together with Captain John L. Ernest of the 100th Bomb Group in a Soviet hospital in Lodz, Poland. Fifield and Newmann had suffered multiple lacerations and bone fractures as a result of being hit with shell fragments when the Red Army tanks fired on their column. The Eastern Command personnel succeeded in evacuating all three to Poltava, together with nine stranded aircrew members. Koepke noted bitterly in a report of April 6 that because of Soviet refusals to allow his doctors to treat and evacuate wounded American prisoners, Eastern Command had resorted to a "practice of human smuggling."[21]

Most liberated American prisoners were not quite as fortunate as Fifield and Newmann. Those who were left in Poland or eastern Germany awaiting transportation to Odessa, particularly the sick and wounded among them, endured conditions that were not much better than those under which they suffered as prisoners of the Germans. At Rembertow, for example, the Soviets held several thousand evacuees, both civilian and military, in a single large building. Already weakened by months or even years of captivity, many otherwise healthy American servicemen fell victim to dysentery, tuberculosis, and other diseases. Bathing and toilet facilities were nonexistent.[22]

The Soviets initially quartered some freed Americans at the former Nazi death camp known as Maidanek. On February 24, they moved the men to a building in the city of Lublin. Conditions there were appalling. All the structure's toilets were stopped up and had overflowed; no outside latrines were available. The building lacked hot water and bathing facilities. The men had received no new clothing, toilet articles, or medicines. Eighty-one men were infested with lice. Most slept on piles of straw on the floor, and the Soviets had given each man a single blanket. They received black bread and a thin, watery gruel twice daily, though at irregular intervals.[23]

The Soviets simply directed ex-prisoners to transit centers in south-central Poland at Lodz, Wreznia, Rembertow, Lublin, and Cienchocinek. Despite the clause in the Yalta agreement requiring the liberating nation to provide transportation, the Americans reached these points by hitchhiking, jumping on trains, or waiting for vacant spots in trucks headed for the rear. In the view of American representatives visiting the area, the Soviets were completely negligent in caring for recently liberated prisoners.[24]

American ex-prisoners at large behind Soviet lines were by no means safe. American repatriates reported that their treatment was better at the front where discipline was stricter among Red Army units. As the evacuees passed through second and third echelons, Soviet treatment of them was indifferent at best and abusive at worst. Red Army soldiers dragooned one group of Americans who were waiting for transportation into their column, which was en route to the front. A Polish-speaking American NCO found, in his words, a sober Soviet officer who agreed to set them free. The liberated prisoners had to beg food from the local populace before they decided to return to their former prison camp where they hoped to find an American representative. The Soviets eventually sent them to Odessa.[25]

Many repatriated Americans reported being left to "wander about" for up to two weeks without a secure source of food or shelter. The Soviets waited nearly three weeks before reporting to the Military Mission in Moscow on February 12 that they had liberated American prisoners. Despite their stated plan to evacuate these men through Odessa, the Soviets did not start sending them there, in boxcars, until February 22.[26]

It was not until March 1 that the Red Army officially announced collection points for prisoners. There were only four of these in Poland, one each at Cracow, Lodz, Rembertow, and Lublin. On the 13th, without consulting the Americans, the Soviets simply declared the transit center at Lublin closed. The Soviet plan from that date was to send ex-prisoners directly to Odessa from points at the front. The remaining three sites would serve only to collect any stray prisoners left in Poland or those liberated at a later date who had not been processed in forward areas. By the last week in February, 2,422 Americans had arrived at Odessa. Most had yet to speak to a representative of the U.S. military or government.[27]

Though Eastern Command had been alerted by Hill's directive of February 14 to prepare to receive hundreds of Americans, the only noncombat crew members passing through Poltava did so only as the result of subterfuge. Watching helplessly from the sidelines, the Americans at Eastern Command resented the Soviets' apparent refusal to allow them to participate in the rapid evacuation of their countrymen.[28]

Soviet obstruction of the movements of the prisoner of war contact officers sent from SHAEF via Moscow also deepened American resentment toward their Allies. On February 16, one of two prisoner contact teams arrived at Poltava from Moscow. Headed by Lieutenant Colonel James D. Wilmeth, the team received instructions from the American embassy to fly into the forward areas and investigate the increasing number of reports regarding liberated prisoners of war. He was assisted by Lieutenant Colonel Curtis B. Kingsbury, a Medical Corps surgeon, and Corporal Paul Kisil, an interpreter. On February 17, a C-47 left Poltava for Poland. Kovalev refused to allow any of the contact team members to board the aircraft. The Soviet general informed both Poltava's commander, Colonel Thomas K. Hampton, and Wilmeth that reports reaching the Americans about ex-prisoners running loose in the forward areas were false. If any Americans were there, Kovalev assured them, these men would be "in capable Soviet hands and well cared for." Wilmeth protested, to no avail, that Kovalev was violating an agreement made at the highest levels of the Allied coalition. The Soviet general claimed he was simply following the latest guidance from Moscow. Wilmeth believed that the Soviets were purposely stalling until they could present a model demonstration of the handling of the prisoners of war.[29]

While Wilmeth marked time at Poltava, Deane tried to get a clear picture from the Soviets as to what they planned to do with American prisoners. He informed Eastern Command for the first time on February 18 that the Soviets were contemplating the use of Odessa, not Poltava, as a processing center. Wilmeth inspected the American base and decided that if Moscow did agree to use it as a transit center, Poltava possessed the facilities and supplies for only short-term stays by the evacuees. Though he preferred using the American air base rather than Soviet facilities at Odessa, the contact team chief realized that Eastern Command's limited housing and hospital space made it unsuitable for anything other than the rapid processing of ex-prisoners. From Poltava, he recommended sending them to the Persian Gulf Command whose greater resources made it the logical staging camp for refitting, questioning, treatment and other rehabilitation functions.[30]

On the 20th, Deane notified Wilmeth that the Soviets were now definitely planning to use Odessa and that Soviet Lieutenant General K. D. Golubev, head of Moscow's Prisoner Repatriation Commission, had granted Wilmeth permission to travel to Lublin aboard Soviet aircraft. From there,

Deane initially wanted Wilmeth to travel to Odessa so as to be there when the first Americans arrived at the end of February. But in a second message sent on that day, he notified Wilmeth that a second contact team was going to that Black Sea port.[31]

Deane's messages could still not get Wilmeth moving from Poltava. The Soviets now argued with the Americans over which nation's aircraft should transport the contact team to Lublin. Wilmeth was angered further when Kovalev informed him that once in Poland, he would be restricted to the local area and denied the use of American aircraft to move to other locations. Such restrictions violated the repatriation agreement's clauses on the free movement of prisoner contact teams. In the meantime, the members of the second contact team arrived in Poltava. After suffering a number of frustrating delays and wasting days bickering with the Soviets, both teams finally left for their respective destinations on February 26.[32]

Arriving in Poland on February 27, Wilmeth's contact team faced immediate resistance and hostility by the Soviets. That afternoon, he and his small team met with four members of the Soviet Repatriation Commission and the city's commandant, a Colonel Bogdanov. The Soviets informed Wilmeth that they were adequately handling the situation and that the Americans were not needed. Besides, they continued, the headquarters of the Soviet repatriation group in Poland had moved to Praga just the day before.[33]

Undeterred by this cold reception, Wilmeth requested permission to see American ex-prisoners being held at Lublin. The Soviets responded that he had no permit to show that he had a right to be in Lublin. Exasperated, Wilmeth asserted that the fact that he arrived via a Soviet aircraft should constitute permission to be there. The Soviet chief of the Lublin collection site, a Major Sigulya, stated that Wilmeth needed written permission that would now have to come from Praga. Only after Wilmeth requested to send a message to Deane in Moscow did the Soviets relent and allow him access to the ex-prisoners.[34]

Wilmeth and Kingsbury, accompanied by six Soviet officers, then visited the ex-prisoners' barracks. There were ninety-one Americans and 129 Britons. Some of the Americans were from *OFLAG 64*, a camp overrun by the Red Army on January 21. The ex-prisoners were living under filthy conditions and were improperly fed. Needless to say, Wilmeth was not at all happy with what he found.[35]

The chief of the Soviet repatriation group arrived from Praga the next day, on the 28th, and met with Wilmeth to discuss evacuation plans. The Soviet team chief reported that apart from the Americans at Lublin, there were only forty-five Allied prisoners still at Praga. He explained that 280 had left Lodz for Odessa on the 26th. Wilmeth requested that he be permitted to move his team to Praga, open direct communication to Moscow, and visit all collection points, including Odessa. When his Soviet counterpart refused, Wilmeth attempted to give him a copy of the Yalta agreement that granted such rights to the prisoner contact teams. The Soviet refused to accept a copy of this agreement as well.[36]

While at Lublin, Wilmeth did his best to improve the prisoners' conditions. He lodged an official protest with the Soviets on March 5, demanding that they improve conditions at Lublin. When his demands met no response, Wilmeth spent his own money on purchasing soap, toothbrushes, light bulbs, scrub brushes, and brooms. He also bought shovels and picks from local merchants so the men could construct latrines.[37]

The Soviets, of course, were uncomfortable with Wilmeth's presence in Poland, and on the 12th, they informed him that the "permit" allowing him to be in Lublin had expired on the 11th, hence the American contact team had no right to remain in the city. Wilmeth then calmly informed the Soviets that he was under orders from Major General Deane to remain in Lublin as the chief of the Military Mission was planning to visit the area to see the plight of the Americans for himself. Three days later, a C-47 arrived from Poltava with a letter to Wilmeth from Deane confirming his intention to visit Lublin. Still, the Soviets on the crew told Wilmeth he had to return with them to Eastern Command the next day. Wilmeth ignored the Soviet demand, saying that he would await further orders from Deane. The American team chief did compromise, however, telling the Soviets that if Deane failed to arrive by the 22nd, he would gladly leave.[38]

In the meantime, the Soviets informed Deane that he could go to Poland if he requested permission for the trip from the Polish National Government (the Lublin Poles), a process that could take several days. Sensing Soviet delaying tactics, Ambassador Harriman sent a message to President Roosevelt asking that he intercede with Stalin on Deane's behalf. In a cable to Stalin on the 18th, Roosevelt pointed out that previous Soviet claims that all prisoners had been removed from a certain area had turned out to be false. He gently chided the Soviets for their failure to allow the American contact teams freedom of movement, thereby violating the Yalta agreement.[39]

Stalin issued a terse reply to Roosevelt's message on the 22nd. He denied that large numbers of Americans remained in Poland and that he could not meddle in the affairs of the repatriating authorities. Such matters were under the jurisdiction, he claimed, of the Soviet commanders at the front. Accusing the United States of mistreating Soviet ex-prisoners, he ended his message by claiming that Russian personnel had suffered beatings and unlawful persecutions at the hands of the Americans. The American ex-prisoners, Stalin claimed, had received far better care than their Soviet counterparts.[40]

The Americans vehemently denied the dictator's charge of mistreatment. In Italy, for example, American authorities immediately notified the Soviet Military Mission upon the liberation of Red Army prisoners. Soviet ex-prisoners were left unguarded and were permitted to establish their own camp administration. After an initial screening, all Soviet ex-prisoners were moved to a camp near Florence where they received new clothing, PX supplies such as cigarettes and candy, and other amenities in the same quantities as those received by American soldiers. They were then flown to Bari on the southeastern coast of Italy to await shipment to the Soviet Union. Representatives of the Soviet Military Mission in Italy were pleased, reporting to Moscow that American treatment of their freed prisoners was "too good."[41]

Nevertheless, Stalin's message ended both Deane's chances of getting to Lublin and Wilmeth's activities as well. On March 17, Major Sigulya gave Wilmeth a written order from the deputy chief of the Soviet Repatriation Commission in Moscow, a Major General Revyakin, directing the American team to return to Poltava aboard the next aircraft. Deane sent Wilmeth a message of his own on the 23rd ordering him to return to Moscow. No aircraft were scheduled to arrive for several days, and on the 27th the Soviets ordered Wilmeth out by train. Sigulya threatened him with a "big scandal" if he did not leave. A C-47 arrived unexpectedly from Poltava that afternoon. On the 28th, Wilmeth and his party climbed aboard and left Lublin, angry with the Soviets for their seemingly incomprehensible attitude toward ex-prisoners.[42]

The contact team sent to Odessa produced happier results for the Americans. Headed by Major Paul S. Hall, the second team reported that, while shortages of clothing existed and facilities and food were considered below American standards, the Soviets had provided the best they could. The Americans' main complaint regarding Odessa was the mode of transportation the Soviets used to transport ex-prisoners to the Black Sea port. Regardless of their physical condition, the men were loaded on boxcars that often spent many days on rail sidings or at stations during the journey to the port city.[43]

The U.S. Military Mission in Romania also experienced difficulties in evacuating downed airmen from that nation. In April 1945, the Soviets attempted to send eighty-eight downed airmen to Odessa as if they were repatriated prisoners. Soviet authorities appeared confused and unaware of any agreements regarding the repatriation of foreign nationals. More than two dozen of the airmen were too ill to travel to Odessa and American officers managed to retain them in Bucharest for medical care while the remaining airmen were sent on to the Black Sea port city. The issue required the intervention of the U.S. Embassy in Moscow before the Soviets relented and allowed the ill Americans to remain in the Romanian capital. Still, the Soviets persisted in using Odessa as a repatriation camp despite American requests that downed airmen be evacuated to Italy directly from Bucharest.[44]

While the Americans agonized over the fate of their prisoners of war, Eastern Command attempted to fulfill its primary mission, that of recovering downed aircraft and crews. In this endeavor, they were more successful in fulfilling their tasks than were the prisoner of war contact teams. Eastern Command held responsibility for aircraft salvage north of the Carpathians, while an American mission in Romania oversaw similar operations to the south of that mountain range. The American recovery teams were usually composed of a handful of mechanics, an officer to debrief the crew, and a medic or doctor. Whether dispatched aboard Soviet or American aircraft, these teams were always under the watchful eye of Soviet liaison officers. The Americans were not allowed to travel to any site in Poland without Soviet escorts, leading the Americans to refer to them derisively as "bird dogs."[45]

The Eastern Command elements sent to Poland on recovery missions accused the Soviet liaison officers of hampering them in the fulfillment of their tasks. Many crash sites were in remote or rural areas. Team members often had to sleep aboard their aircraft, despite the cold weather, because the Soviets refused to allow them to stay in the homes of Polish civilians. Escorting officers routinely refused to clear flights because of bad weather, even though the weather at the destination was good.[46]

Despite Soviet interference, the salvage teams sent from Poltava managed to recover a fair number of men and planes. Between October 1944 and March 1945, nearly 550 Americans were processed through Poltava. As noted, not all were downed combat crew members. Eastern Command's maintenance detachment maintained the C-46s flying the route from Tehran and five permanently assigned C-47s. At Poltava, the detachment repaired nine B-24s, two B-17s, and one P-51. They also repaired Ambassador Harriman's C-47, nicknamed "Becky," on three different occasions. This was quite a feat for a maintenance section with an effective strength of fewer than two dozen men. Not until the end of February did MAAF send nearly forty additional mechanics trained to work on B-24s. In addition to its normal work at the base, the Poltava maintenance unit recovered and repaired at various locations six B-24s, five B-17s, and two P-51s while salvaging parts from three B-24s, one B-17, and one C-46.[47]

Eastern Command continued to have difficulty locating downed aircraft, and in March still had no independent source of information. The Soviets were often slow to notify Poltava of the landing of a crippled aircraft. On several occasions, recovery personnel arrived at a reported crash site only to find that the Soviets had sent the crew on to Odessa or that they had completely dismantled the aircraft.[48]

Major General Hill was alarmed over the increasing number of reports indicating that the Soviets were dismantling American aircraft or unnecessarily delaying their repair. He recommended that Hampton establish a forward operating location at an airfield in Poland, which the Eastern Command mechanics could use as central point for repair and recovery of aircraft and crews. Hampton followed Hill's suggestion and by the third week in March an American detachment arrived at Lodz, Poland. Several disabled American aircraft were already in Lodz and, in marked contrast to their attitudes toward the prisoner contact teams, the Soviets apparently had no objection to a small group of Americans working in that area. Like so much else at this stage of the war, Soviet attitudes regarding this American presence in Poland would soon change.[49]

On March 19, three C-47s arrived at Lodz with equipment for the new detachment. The Soviet colonel in charge at the base informed Major Koepke, who had arrived on one of the C-47s, that on March 15 two Americans were killed when their parachutes failed to open as they bailed out of a crippled B-24. Other members of the crew were quartered nearby. Three of the crew attended a funeral service held by the Poles for their dead comrades. The bodies were placed in wooden caskets and displayed in a private home for viewing by the local populace. Polish policemen, in full uniform, acted as pallbearers during the funeral procession through town. A priest celebrated a High Mass that was attended by several hundred Poles and the local Soviet commander. Polish soldiers fired a three-gun salute, and the caskets, covered with homemade American flags, each bearing only twenty-four stars, were lowered into the earth. Moved by this account, Koepke took several photos of the graves, which were marked with black crosses and a metal plate bearing each man's name, serial number, date of death, and "US Army Air Forces." When the Eastern Command surgeon visited the cemetery, the graves were still covered with wreaths and flowers brought by civilians.[50]

The only negative report generated by this visit was the now standard Soviet refusal to allow Eastern Command personnel to evacuate ex-prisoners. On the morning of the 21st, as an Eastern Command crew prepared to leave Lodz, First Lieutenant Louis Sokol, Poltava's weather officer, ordered four ex-prisoners whom he had located the day before in Lodz to report to the airfield. Three were in hospital at the time, but the fourth, Staff Sergeant Joseph Francis, managed to get the men to the hotel where the American crew was billeted. The Soviet liaison officer, a Captain Cheridov, demanded to know who the men were. Sokol lied that they were members of a downed B-17's crew. Cheridov did not believe the story and said they could not go with the crew. Sokol ignored him, but as the crew ate breakfast in the Soviet mess at the airfield, a Soviet colonel demanded to see the "downed airmen's" papers. When Sokol could not produce them, the colonel indignantly announced that all ex-prisoners were to go through Odessa. The crew reluctantly left the four behind and returned to Poltava.[51]

The new extension of the American presence in eastern Europe at Lodz contained a three-man communications team whose job it was to establish a direct radio link with Poltava and thus bypass the Soviets. The Americans viewed this setup as a decided improvement over the clumsy system in place whereby every message was routed through Moscow. The rest of the detachment was made up of a weather NCO, a medic, an interpreter, eight mechanics, and an aircraft maintenance officer in charge of the group, Captain Jack Pogue. Pogue was not permanently assigned to Eastern Command but had arrived at Poltava from Italy on February 24 together with the other personnel sent from MAAF to assist the command's maintenance section.[52]

The men of the Lodz detachment were treated well by the Soviets. The Americans were invited into the base mess where the Soviets toasted them with massive quantities of vodka. The Soviets billeted the Americans at the Grand Hotel in Lodz, the best any of them had seen since leaving western Europe. Considering that earlier recovery teams had slept in dugouts or their own aircraft, these were plush accommodations. The men enjoyed modern rooms and relatively fine dining. Even those men who stayed at the Lodz airdrome, so that they could be nearer the field, commented that they had been well treated by the Soviets. At this point in the war, the good treatment accorded Pogue's detachment by the Red Army and Air Force was increasingly rare in Soviet-American relations.[53]

Indeed, Moscow was tightening its grip all across eastern Europe even as Germany continued to hold out. At the end of February, Molotov's deputy, Andrei Vishinsky, handed Romania's King Michael a two-hour ultimatum demanding that the king dismiss his prime minister. Just four days after that, without consulting the Allied Control Commission in Bucharest, Vishinsky gave the king a second ultimatum. This time, the Soviets called for the installation of Petru Groza as Prime Minister. Groza was leader of the Romanian Communist Party. In Hungary, the newly formed Provisional Government accepted an armistice with the Allies, but Molotov later summed up Moscow's attitude toward the entire region. "It was not necessary for the Soviet Union to conclude an armistice with Hungary," he said, "since the Red Army was practically the master of that country. It could do what it wished."[54]

Wherever Soviet units stood in control, Moscow began to impose its will directly or through indigenous supporters. Its backing of the communist-dominated Fatherland Front in Bulgaria, for example, was coupled with Soviet dominance of the Allied Control Commission in that country. The Soviets had agreed to the Declaration on Liberated Europe at Yalta. The Western Allies had no other option than to accept Stalin's word that he would allow free and independent elections in those countries under occupation by the Red Army.[55]

Pogue, Wilmeth, and indeed all the Americans in the Ukraine and eastern Europe were allowed to operate, more or less freely, only as long as the Soviets did not perceive a threat from a Western presence in areas they now believed theirs by right of liberation or conquest. Poland, of course, had long been a flashpoint in Allied relations. Stalin presented his partners with a fait accompli on January 5 by unilaterally recognizing the "Provisional Government of Liberated Democratic Poland," the Lublin Committee, as the legitimate government of Poland. Meanwhile, Stanislaw Mikolajczyk resigned as prime minister in disgust over the Western Allies' apparent acceptance of Stalin's claim of the Curzon Line as the Soviet Union's western frontier. Stalin forged ahead with plans to re-establish Poland's western frontier with Germany without the approval of Britain or the United States.[56]

Not surprisingly, American military men moving about Poland, mingling with the populace and gaining a firsthand look of the country under Soviet occupation began to provoke in Moscow a paranoiac fear of a vast American intelligence network functioning in collusion with the Polish underground. This paranoia manifested itself in Soviet flight restrictions, assignment of liaison officers to aircraft recovery teams, and the Red Army's interference with American prisoner of war contact teams. Before long, even Pogue and his little outpost would fall victim to Soviet suspicions.

Unfortunately, a number of incidents for which the Americans were responsible came to light in March 1945 that seemed to confirm Soviet fears and anxieties. On February 3, a B-17 of the 401st Bomb Group flown by First Lieutenant Myron L. King ran into intense flak over Berlin. A shell burst destroyed the oil cooler on the number two engine and tore a hole in the right nose gun window. The newly installed number four engine inexplicably began streaming oil as well. With two engines shut down, King had no choice but to head eastward for Soviet-held territory. The aircraft limped to Warsaw where the crew fired recognition flares and King rocked the wings to show the Soviets that the plane was friendly. Unable to land at Warsaw because of heavy damage to the runway, King nursed the plane to a landing field southeast of the city. The Soviets were able to repair the B-17's engines and on February 5, King and his crew followed a Soviet C-47 to the airfield at Szczuczyn where they could get 100-octane gasoline. The Soviets did not appear to know anything about the base at Poltava. After landing, the crew went looking for fuel and food.[57]

Far from being grateful allies, King and his men actively deceived the Soviets. When they left for Szczuczyn, the crew took a Pole aboard. King later claimed that he thought the Polish national was a Red Air Force interpreter who had simply missed the Soviet C-47 that had taken off before them. Once aloft, the Pole said he wanted to return to England, not the Soviet Union. King noticed that he was wearing a British uniform under a Soviet jacket. After landing at Szczuczyn, King failed to notify the Soviets of the presence of the Pole. The Americans gave him a flight suit and an alias, "Jack Smith."[58]

When the Soviets requested a crew roster, they saw Jack Smith listed as interpreter and waist gunner and became suspicious. They quickly realized who "Smith" was when he could not be accounted for on the Soviet C-47 that landed at Szczuczyn with the American B-17. Outraged, a Soviet major shouted at King that in the Red Army "they had *discipline*." Thoroughly frightened, King was not sure what was going to happen next.[59]

The Soviets now undertook their own investigation and required King to make a written statement. He claimed that he had intended to turn Jack Smith over to the first British or American unit he contacted and that he was simply trying to avoid causing trouble for the Soviets. His statement was read aloud to the local commander who simply nodded in silence. Still angry, the major who had shouted at King earlier threatened to shoot him in the back if he got the chance. He then altered his mood and began admiring King's wristwatch. The American lieutenant took the hint, slipped the watch off his wrist and gave it to the Soviet. Brusquely dismissed from the Soviets' presence, King returned to his aircraft, only to find five large concrete rollers in front of it.[60]

When the Soviet unit at Szczuczyn received orders to move to a new base, the Red Air Force commander told King that he and his plane would accompany them. The Soviets led the Americans to understand that they were not to try to leave formation once aloft. After another two weeks in Soviet custody, King managed to secure clearance to fly to Kiev on March 18th. The weather was clear and once in the air, King decided to fly straight to Poltava, arriving there early that evening.[61]

The Military Mission immediately wanted to know why King had been missing for so long. King did not initially relate the full story of Jack Smith to the debriefers at Poltava, claiming later that the Soviet commander at Szczuczyn had told him not to tell anyone and that the case was closed. He told the operations staff at Eastern Command that the Soviet commander in Poland would not let him leave for fear something might happen to him.[62]

When American officers at Poltava questioned some of what King reported, he finally told the truth. Realizing the possible diplomatic ramifications of King's actions, Hampton forwarded the lieutenant's story to Deane on the 29th. Outraged, the chief of the Military Mission notified Eastern Command to hold King at Poltava. He decided to bring charges against the irresponsible lieutenant. He appointed Wilmeth, just back from Lublin, as the investigating officer.[63]

On March 30, Deane received a formal letter from the chief of the Red Army General Staff, General Alexei Antonov. The Soviet general laid out the Soviet version of the King incident, referring to "Jack Smith" as a "terrorist-saboteur brought into Poland from London." Apart from this accusation, Antonov's account did not differ significantly from King's. In the next paragraph, Antonov raised yet another incident. On March 22, a B-24 flown by Captain Donald Bridge had landed, out of fuel, at the airfield at Mielec, Poland. The Soviets refueled the aircraft and housed and fed the crew for the evening. The Soviet commander at the field ordered Bridge not to attempt to take off without Soviet clearance. The following day, Bridge and his crew asked for permission to go to the aircraft and retrieve some personal belongings. The Soviets agreed but when the crew got to the airplane they climbed aboard, taxied out, and took off. Antonov claimed that the responsible Soviet officer, Engineer-Captain Melamedov, was so outraged over the Americans' behavior that he shot himself! Antonov stated that "the facts listed are a rude violation of the elementary rights of our friendly mutual relationship." Deane responded on March 31, apologizing for the behavior of King and Bridge and attempting to explain Wilmeth's predicament. He informed Antonov that he had already preferred charges against King and would do everything he could to prevent similar incidents from occurring in the future.[64]

In a message to Marshall and Arnold on the 31st, Deane expressed his satisfaction and relief that Antonov "came out in the open" with these incidents. Ordinarily, he reported, the Soviets would not "say anything but simply [react] by placing more restrictions on our freedom of movement." Unfortunately, Deane misjudged the extent of the Kremlin's anger over these incidents. On the same day on which Deane wrote to Antonov and notified Marshall of the incidents, Kovalev informed Hampton that, on orders from Moscow, all American aircraft inside the Soviet Union were grounded indefinitely.[65]

The Soviet action caught Eastern Command in an awkward position. The hospital's nurses were all in Moscow on a three-day pass and would have to seek rail transportation to return to Poltava. Six seriously wounded patients awaiting transfer to Tehran were stranded. Five C-47s, two C-46s from the Persian Gulf Command and two newly repaired bombers sat on the airfield. One hundred and eighty-three rescued combat crew members were also at Poltava, staying in the base chapel.[66]

Pogue's detachment at Lodz felt the effects of Moscow's decision as well. On April 2, the Soviet garrison commander at Lodz informed Pogue that Americans were to cease all work and seal their aircraft. He offered no explanation for this sudden change and ordered the men of the Eastern Command detachment to move to Opole, thirty-five kilometers away. The Soviets refused to provide transportation and Pogue was forced to leave a great deal of valuable equipment behind. The Americans had a single jeep into which the mechanics piled as many tools and supplies as they could. In Opole, the Soviets took even the jeep and restricted the Americans to their billets. On April 13th, the Soviets informed the Americans that they were going to return to Poltava via rail. A Red Air Force officer informed Pogue that from that date forward all downed American aircraft were war trophies of the Soviet Union. Bewildered and apprehensive about this sudden turn of events, Pogue and his men climbed aboard boxcars. Their jeep was nowhere to be found. They reached Kiev a week later, finally arriving at Poltava on April 21. Pogue learned of the Soviet order grounding all American aircraft only after he returned to Poltava.[67]

Deane received another letter on March 31, this time from Lieutenant General N. V. Slavin of the Red Army General Staff. Slavin accused the crew of an American B-24 that had made a forced landing in Hungary on March 8 of smuggling Soviet Engineer-Captain M. I. Shendarov to Italy two weeks later. He indignantly pointed out that the Soviets had cared for the crew and repaired and refueled the aircraft. The Americans had repaid this Soviet cooperation, Slavin charged, by violating their trust. He demanded that Shendarov be returned and that the crew receive severe punishment.[68]

General Deane had to act quickly to calm the Soviets' anger aroused over the string of incidents noted above. He turned first to Eastern Command. Since the beginning of the year, the Military Mission had received a number of unfavorable reports regarding Colonel Hampton's relations with the Soviets. Not only did Kovalev and his staff view the American commander as increasingly hostile, some of his own staff officers worried that his truculent attitude would scuttle what remained of Soviet-American friendship at Poltava. On April 12, Deane accordingly relieved Hampton of command. His replacement, the openly anticommunist Major Michael Kowal, was even less acceptable to the Soviets, and they raised such strong objections that by the end of the same day he too had been dismissed. Lieutenant Colonel Alexander, Hampton's executive officer, was also relieved.[69]

Into Hampton's place stepped Captain Robert J. Trimble. Trimble had only recently been assigned to Poltava on temporary duty. He had no idea, other than that prompted by Hampton's side of the story, as to why he now found himself in command at Poltava. In an unenviable position, influenced by Hampton, Kowal, and Alexander, Trimble also adopted a hostile attitude toward the Soviets. Deane simply expected him to hold things together at Eastern Command until the current crop of problems had been resolved. Hampton and the other two officers arrived at USSTAF Headquarters on April 22.[70]

The Military Mission also had to deal with specific incidents that apparently had brought about the harsh Soviet moves. On orders from Deane, Wilmeth conducted an investigation of the King case. He convened a General Court Martial on April 25 in Moscow. King was charged with violating the 96th Article of War by "willfully concealing from Soviet authorities" the presence of a stowaway and thereby discrediting the U.S. armed forces. On the 26th, the court found him guilty of the charge. King received an official reprimand and was fined 100 dollars a month for six months. On the 27th, King flew out of Poltava for Tehran.[71]

On April 6, Deane notified Slavin that Shendarov was being held in Italy pending a full investigation. The American general explained that the crew had been unaware that the Soviet officer was aboard until after they were aloft. Shendarov apparently tried to tell the crewmen that he held American citizenship in an effort to gain their sympathy. Nevertheless, by the 9th, the

Americans had selected a crew and aircraft to return the hapless officer to Moscow via Poltava.[72]

On April 12, the Americans at Eastern Command watched as a B-17 touched down unannounced on the runway. Armed Soviet officers and men surrounded the aircraft and prevented all but a refueling crew from approaching the aircraft. Soviet personnel brought the crew food from the mess hall but the weather officer was denied permission to brief the crew. Shortly after refueling, the bomber took off. Rumors circulated at Poltava that a "political prisoner" whom the Americans were returning to the Soviets was on board. Shendarov's fate remained unknown. The scuttlebutt at Eastern Command was that the unfortunate officer had been shot as he stepped off the plane in Moscow.[73]

Deane moved to close the books on the two remaining cases. Because Bridge had flown back to his base in Italy, Deane could only forward the Soviet complaint against him to USSTAF. Apparently, Bridge received a reprimand for making an unauthorized takeoff; fortunately, no foreign nationals were tucked away in his aircraft. Deane also stood by Wilmeth, accepting full responsibility for his actions in Poland and blaming poor communications for the contact team's delayed departure from Lublin.[74]

The Soviets were only partially satisfied. They saw the foregoing succession of incidents as proof that an organized American effort to undermine Soviet control in eastern Europe was under way. On the 15th of April, Stalin informed Harriman that American aircraft were flying into Poland for the purpose of dropping supplies to the remnants of the London-backed Home Army, which the Kremlin now viewed as an illegitimate group of bandits and criminals. When the ambassador denied these allegations, Stalin made reference to the King case as evidence of American collusion with the London Poles. He called the recent spate of incidents outrageous and stated that the Americans lacked discipline. Harriman assured the Soviet leader that the United States would do all it could to prevent further occurrences of this nature. He did not attempt to defend what had happened. Such abuses, Harriman admitted, "were the acts of stupid soldiers, brave men perhaps but somewhat stupid."[75]

The following day, Antonov repeated Stalin's charges in a meeting with Rear Admiral Clarence Olsen, head of the Navy Division of the Military Mission. While the Soviet general was pleased with guarantees that the Americans were taking action against the offending officers, Antonov insisted that such incidents indicated clearly a widespread sympathy among the American armed forces for elements hostile to the Soviet Union.[76]

Still, the Soviets' grip on Eastern Command slowly loosened. On April 9, the nurses arrived by train. Alarmed over the delay in transferring six severely wounded men to Iran, Major Koepke managed to persuade Kovalev to arrange a special medical flight. To the great relief of the hospital staff, the wounded men left on the 15th. They arrived safely at the 113th General Hospital in Ahwaz, Iran, on the 20th. Also on the 15th, the Soviets allowed the evacuation of stranded combat crew members, though Moscow restricted the flights to one C-46 per day. On April 27th, Trimble notified Deane that the Soviets had lifted flight restrictions and reported that they were once again "quite cooperative."[77]

In the wake of this near-total collapse in Soviet-American cooperation, the United States decided to terminate all joint projects still pending with the Soviets. At Yalta, the Red Air Force had given its assent to the establishment of the American bases in the Budapest area for a reborn shuttle-bombing operation, FRANTIC II. Lieutenant General Eaker and a team of American officers surveyed possible sites in March. The Soviets showed no inclination to move forward on the project. Lieutenant General A. V. Nikitin summed up the Soviet attitude toward the continuance of shuttle-bombing at this late stage in the war: it had "lost reason."[78]

At the end of the month, Spaatz expressed doubt about the operational desirability of the bases, considering the rate at which Hitler's empire was shrinking. On April 3, Hill complained to Spaatz that the Soviets were purposely delaying the Budapest project. The USSTAF commander notified Arnold on the following day that unless he had other reasons to press the matter, the Americans should inform the Soviets that the project was canceled. Though Spaatz wavered, clinging to the idea of bases near Budapest as late as the 13th, FRANTIC II was dead. U.S. Chief of Staff General George C. Marshall notified Arnold and Spaatz on the 19th of the Joint Chiefs' decision to formally terminate the plan to use bases in Hungary or Austria.[79]

Eastern Command's days were also numbered. On April 13, Spaatz notified Arnold of his desire to close Poltava "ASAP" because of "operational difficulties," a possible reference to Moscow's grounding of all American aircraft. On the 19th, Marshall transmitted the Joint Chiefs' approval of that recommendation. He directed Spaatz and Arnold to request that the Soviets repair any remaining American aircraft stranded in eastern Europe and evacuate the crews to a central point in the Balkans (probably Bucharest where another American Military Mission was in operation). The Joint Chiefs also directed Spaatz to "express our gratitude for the hospitality that they have extended to us in connection with the FRANTIC bases."[80]

What of the coveted air base complex in Siberia? Stalin had dangled this prize before the Americans for quite some time. He had agreed at Yalta to allow the establishment of U.S. air bases in Siberia. As with FRANTIC II, the spirit of Yalta did not translate into decisive action. The project never got beyond staff discussions, and the Soviets refused permission for American survey teams to enter Siberia. By the end of March 1945, the American planning group realized that, barring an immediate reversal of Soviet behavior, American strategic operations based in Siberia in 1945 were out of the question. In any event, considering the rapid advance of American forces in the Pacific, the Joint Chiefs questioned the wisdom of undertaking such a massive logistic effort this late in the war. Though they still desired Soviet involvement in the Pacific war, America's military leaders, in April, wrote off the Siberian project. Deane expressed relief that the United States no longer had to fear Soviet retribution involving the proposed Siberian bases for every slight, real or imagined, to the Kremlin.[81]

Eastern Command now prepared to close down for good. The men began an inventory to decide which equipment would be returned to American depots and which would be left behind for the Soviets as part of Lend-Lease. Flight clearance difficulties reappeared in May when C-46s, carrying Eastern Command cargo to the Persian Gulf Command, strayed too close to restricted airspace over Sevastopol in the Crimea. Otherwise, Eastern Command's evacuation was delayed only by the length of time it took the Americans to sort and count supplies.

The final weeks of the American presence at Poltava were marked by a handful of notable incidents. On April 12, in the midst of Eastern Command's internment, President Roosevelt died unexpectedly at Warm Springs, Georgia. On the 13th, Kovalev, in a show of respect, marched his men onto the American base and presented the condolences of the Red Air Force. All Soviet flags were lowered to half-staff. The next day, the G.I.s held a memorial service for the late president. For the first time, an American flag flew at the head of a procession, as the men marched in formation to the base theater where the chaplain conducted a thirty-minute service. Many Soviets reportedly asked anxious questions about "this man [Harry S.] Truman" who had succeeded to the American presidency. The Americans believed that the Soviets felt Roosevelt's loss almost as much as they.[82]

On April 17, Eastern Command witnessed its first wedding. First Lieutenant William Kaluta married Second Lieutenant Clotilde Govoni, one of the nurses at the hospital, in the only marriage recorded at the Poltava air base. The ceremony was a simple one, held in the nurses' quarters. Deane's policy of the previous spring prohibited both members of a newly married couple to remain in the Soviet Union. Following the couple's honeymoon in Cairo, which was delayed by the Soviets' flight restrictions, Kaluta returned to Poltava and Govoni sailed to Britain.[83]

On May 7, the British Broadcasting Corporation announced Germany's surrender. Eastern Command personnel celebrated on that day but the general rejoicing found the Soviets unaware of the news. The Soviets refused to believe the Americans until Moscow Radio broadcast the surrender on May 9. The celebrating temporarily eased the tension hanging over Soviet-American relations. Members of the two air forces held a joint parade through Poltava, an American flag once again leading the Eastern Command contingent.[84]

On May 9, Spaatz cabled Deane and Hill to shutdown Poltava immediately. He wanted all remaining supplies, other than such critical equipment as precision tools and medical supplies, turned over to the Soviets under Lend-Lease. Throughout the remainder of May and early June, Air Transport Command C-46s flew regular missions between Poltava and the Persian Gulf Command and Cairo, bringing out personnel and equipment. By June, Poltava was virtually closed down. Unfortunately, Eastern Command had two more embarrassing incidents to address before the last Americans could leave.

On April 19, Sergeant George Atkinson was driving a weapons carrier and towing a disabled vehicle through Poltava to the main depot at the air base. Second Lieutenant Martin Schlau was in the vehicle under tow. Both were stranded aircrew members who had volunteered to help with some of the work around the base. Atkinson turned a corner but failed to signal his intention to do so to Schlau who was unable to turn his vehicle sharply enough to avoid hitting an unattended Soviet truck that was protruding into the road. Schlau struck the Soviet vehicle, which apparently had no parking brake. It rolled forward some 40 feet, striking 36-year-old Lukeria Tverdochleb. She died an hour later of massive internal injuries.[85]

While Eastern Command officers investigated this accident, word reached Trimble of another mishap on May 28. Corporal Connie L. Steele was driving a three-quarter-ton truck through Poltava. The horn on the vehicle was inoperative, because the motor pool had been unable to get the necessary parts to fix it. He and his passenger, Corporal Robert D. Chambers, noticed some children playing in the road ahead. Steele was driving at approximately 20 miles an hour, well below the posted speed limit. Seeing them move off the road, the two Americans assumed that the children saw the approaching truck. As the vehicle reached the point at which the children were standing, a little girl, Zina Osipovna Grigorenko, inexplicably turned about and ran into the side of the vehicle. She died at the scene within minutes from the shock of the collision.[86]

The Soviets brought charges against the Americans in both cases. They charged Atkinson with exceeding the speed limit and using a tow chain that was too short. Eastern Command's investigation exonerated Atkinson on the ground that he was not a driver but a trained aerial gunner and was unaware of local Soviet traffic laws. The investigating officer, Major Herbert Hoffheimer, Jr., argued that Soviet soldiers routinely violated the speed limit and other rules of the road.[87]

In Steele's case, both Soviet witnesses and the testimony of his companion pointed to the fact that the little girl hit the truck, not the other way around. The Soviets charged Steele with driving with an inoperable horn and leaving the scene of an accident. Steele had left the road to summon an American surgeon from Poltava to help the little girl and the truck had been without a horn for several months. Hoffheimer concluded that Steele was not at all responsible but that the U.S. government should make some sort of settlement because of an inoperative horn on an American military vehicle.[88]

The Americans moved to reach a settlement with the Soviets over the two fatal accidents. Eastern Command awarded surviving family members monetary settlements to compensate for the deaths caused by these unfortunate accidents. These were the last notable acts to take place at Eastern Command and were somber notes on which to conclude the American presence in the Ukraine.

EIGHT

CONCLUSION

The Americans had persisted in maintaining Poltava through the winter of 1944–45 hoping that shuttle missions might resume in the spring. They also hoped to keep direct Soviet-American cooperation alive so as to ease the move to a Siberian air base complex for strategic bombing operations against Japan. The base at Poltava served well during that time as a recovery and repair center for downed or damaged American aircraft and their aircrews. Its role in the repatriation of ex-prisoners of war, however, proved to be bitter and frustrating. Meanwhile, the Soviets became increasingly uncomfortable with the U.S. military presence in eastern Europe. By March 1945, incidents committed by Americans over whom Eastern Command had little or no control placed the base in the position of hostage to Moscow's anger or whims. The Kremlin, of course, could manipulate operations at Poltava with an eye toward altering the behavior of the United States.

By April 1945, one year after Brigadier General Alfred A. Kessler and his men began preparing the bases at Poltava, Mirgorod, and Piryatin for Operation FRANTIC, Soviet restrictions had grounded all American aircraft in the country. After months of steadily deteriorating relations at all levels between Moscow and Washington, the Army Air Forces as well as the top military leadership of the United States decided to cut their losses in the matter of joint operations with the Soviets, hence terminated planning for any future activity on Soviet soil.

By June 23, 1945, all equipment and supplies, save those that the Americans were leaving behind for the Soviets, had been transported out of Poltava. The remaining members of Eastern Command escorted officials from the Military Mission in Moscow, which was itself entering its last days, on a final inspection of the base. One year and one day after the devastating German raid of June 22, 1944, Poltava ceased to function as a U.S. military installation. The great experiment in direct Soviet-American cooperation in combat was over.[1]

Whatever else it was, the American experience at Eastern Command represented the longest sustained contact between members of the United

States' and Soviet military establishments during World War II. In light of the many negative events that had transpired at the American bases in the Ukraine, from the German strike on Poltava in June 1944 to the grounding of all American aircraft by the Soviets in April 1945, many AAF officers could only wonder whether the FRANTIC project had been worth the expense and effort. For the purposes of evaluating FRANTIC's contribution to the war, the objectives of the operation, though varied, can be divided generally into two categories: purely military goals and those having diplomatic and political overtones.

As outlined in Chapter One, the military or operational objectives of FRANTIC included the following: strategic bombing on the Eastern Front; shuttle-bombing on a cross-continental scale; tactical air support for Soviet operations; and improvement of Soviet-American communications. Those goals having more than just military considerations included development of Soviet-American relationships in general and the stimulation of Russian support for American operations in the Far East.

While the operation was still under way, high-ranking American officers were already expressing doubt about FRANTIC's effectiveness. In August 1944, Major General Hugh J. Knerr, USSTAF's deputy commander for administration, considered the logistic demands of continuing the operation beyond the summer months of 1944 to be too great, given the Soviets' increasingly negative attitude toward the American presence in the Ukraine and the shortage of targets caused by the swift advance of Soviet ground forces into eastern Europe. Conceding that the targets bombed in conjunction with Eastern Command could have been hit with equal if not greater efficiency from bases in Italy and Britain, Brigadier General George C. McDonald, director of intelligence for USSTAF, remained hopeful in August that FRANTIC might still yield benefits in the Far East.[2]

The AAF intended shuttle-bombing to threaten Germany from the East and cause the *Luftwaffe* to redistribute its fighters away from the West prior to D-day. Starting on June 2, 1944, four days before OVERLORD, Operation FRANTIC began too late to be of much good to units taking part in the Normandy invasion. No evidence existed during the operation or has come to light since the end of the war that the Germans transferred fighters or additional flak batteries to the Eastern Front in response solely to FRANTIC. The *Luftwaffe* High Command had actually withdrawn many of its fighter units from the east and sent them west in the early months of 1944 to deal with the resumption of American deep penetration raids staged as part of Operation ARGUMENT. Moreover, most of the fighters assigned to the eastern air fleets were flying ground support missions for the hard-pressed German Army.[3]

The Germans did not completely ignore FRANTIC, and the fact that the *Luftwaffe* risked its carefully husbanded force of bombers against Poltava was not simple opportunism, but demonstrated German anxieties over another strategic air threat forming in the East. Adolf Galland, commander of the German fighter arm in 1944 and thereby responsible for the defense of Germany, later claimed that the second shuttle raid against the Ruhland oil refinery on June 21 caused a stir in the *Luftwaffe* High Command. Surprisingly, other German airmen considered the fighter missions of FRANTIC—the sweeps flown by Fifteenth Air Force P-38s and P-51s in July and August—to be more alarming than strategic strikes against German industrial targets. Fighter missions did not inflict serious lasting damage; that some Germans feared them suggests that the other FRANTIC missions were possibly less effective than even the operation's most skeptical observers believed.[4]

Events conspired to prevent FRANTIC from assuming the scope of strategic bombing on the Eastern Front envisioned by American planners. USSTAF originally hoped for 800 bomber sorties a month. The fear of additional German strikes prompted the AAF to suspend all bomber operations in July 1944 while the Americans and Soviets wrangled over night-fighters and improved air base defenses at Eastern Command. In June, August, and September, FRANTIC produced little more than half the planned sortie rate, and of those, more than 100 were involved in the supply run to Warsaw. The failure of the AAF to live up to its promised level of activity in the East, and the Red Army's successes at the front led, in part, to Soviet Foreign Minister Vyacheslav Molotov's abrupt demand for the return of the shuttle bases to Soviet control in late August 1944.

Even those targets that FRANTIC bombers did strike were all within range of bases in Italy or Britain. McDonald recognized this in August, and the official Army Air Forces history of the war went so far as to state that "some of the attacks would probably not have been regarded as worth making but for the desire to use those [Eastern Command] bases." Only the supply run to Warsaw from bases in Britain required the use of Soviet airfields.[5]

The AAF at first blamed the Soviets for refusing to clear the targets it wanted to hit. It was USSTAF, however, that provided the list of potential objectives, and if American aircraft struck targets designated by the Soviets while the aircraft operated from the Ukrainian bases, this was part of the original agreement. Admittedly, the Soviets denied permission to strike at installations in northern Poland or the Baltic states, areas actually outside the range of aircraft flying from British or Italian bases. USSTAF could have suspended operations as a show of its dissatisfaction with the Soviets if the main goal was simply to hit targets otherwise out of range of existing bases.

By the end of the war, FRANTIC's targets were all in Soviet hands, with the exception of the tank engine factory at Chemnitz. The Soviets refused to honor a promise made at Yalta to allow U.S. Strategic Bombing Survey (USSBS) teams access to most POINTBLANK objectives behind their lines.[6] The USSBS provided detailed information to the AAF on the actual results of most of its strategic campaign against the Axis. Of course, contemporary evaluations made by combat crews and photo interpreters were invariably positive and led AAF leaders to view the results of FRANTIC with some satisfaction.

As AAF leaders realized both during and after the war, however, most targets had to be hit repeatedly if lasting damage was to result. The high priority targets of POINTBLANK included oil refineries and aircraft industries. FRANTIC missions hit the aircraft plant at Rahmel, near Danzig, Poland, and the oil refineries at Ruhland, Germany, and Drohobycz and Trzebinia in Poland. The remainder of the targets were airdromes, marshalling yards, the tank engine factory at Chemnitz, and a few minor industrial plants. Except for the Focsani and Galatz airdromes in Romania, none of the targets were hit by FRANTIC aircraft more than once before they fell into Soviet hands.[7]

The Soviets recognized that airdromes and marshalling yards were relatively easy to repair unless attacked repeatedly and only requested strikes against them from the Americans when the Red Army was in "hot pursuit" of Axis forces in the target area. Red Air Force officers favored these types of raids in keeping with the tactical outlook of their air doctrine. Indeed, that the Soviets asked for missions against Romanian airdromes and Hungarian marshalling yards was a sign that the two air forces could indeed cooperate, a point often overlooked in evaluations of FRANTIC.

USSTAF did claim that by using shuttle bases, FRANTIC missions lost fewer aircraft than if the bombers had been forced to return to Britain or Italy across more heavily defended areas of Nazi-held Europe. While this may be true, the destruction of nearly fifty B-17s at Poltava on June 22 represented one of the AAF's most costly days of the entire war. USSTAF consoled itself with the knowledge that at least the crews of the destroyed aircraft had not been sacrificed.[8]

The only clear-cut success for FRANTIC was the undeniable progress made in air and signals communication between the Soviet Union and the United States. Poltava was essentially an American air terminal within the USAAF's Air Transport Command network. Eastern Command's unofficial history commented favorably on the extensive exchange of weather data between the two air forces and the installation and extensive use of radio communications among Poltava, Caserta, Italy, London, Tehran, and Washington.[9]

What FRANTIC could have accomplished if the Soviet summer offensive had not been so successful is a matter that is open to conjecture. Military operations must be evaluated not in terms of "might-have-been" theories, only in terms of concrete results. Clearly, FRANTIC failed to live up to either American or Soviet expectations. It was also obvious that by midsummer 1944, the AAF persisted in the operation, despite reports such as McDonald's or Knerr's, simply to maintain an American presence in the Ukraine so as to achieve what had become FRANTIC's overriding objectives—improved American relations with the Soviets and eventual Soviet cooperation in the Far East. In its military role, then, FRANTIC was largely a failure.

Surprisingly, Major General John R. Deane and U.S. Ambassador W. Averell Harriman considered FRANTIC a military success that struck targets that Deane wrongly believed were outside the range of other bases. Both men also believed that the presence of American air forces operating from the Soviet Union must have had a devastating impact on German morale. On the contrary, the German leadership looked at FRANTIC largely as a publicity stunt. Perhaps the deep personal involvement of both men in helping to make FRANTIC possible colored their views of military success because neither Deane nor Harriman seemed to think that the operation had much of a positive effect on Stalin or his government.[10]

The Soviets viewed FRANTIC as a mere footnote to the Great Patriotic War. During and after the war, official Soviet histories continued to stress the central—even premier—role played by the Soviet Union in the defeat of Nazi Germany. Typical of Soviet attitudes toward the strategic bombing campaign was an article in the July 1975 issue of *Soviet Military Review*. The article's authors, both Soviet military officers, correctly pointed out that POINTBLANK failed in bringing about a German collapse as a result of aerial bombardment alone. They went on to denigrate Anglo-American efforts in general, raising the issue of the delayed opening of a second front and claiming that the Red Air Force almost single-handedly defeated the *Luftwaffe*. The Soviets remained wholly unimpressed by the Anglo-American strategic bombing effort in World War II.[11]

Official Soviet accounts of the war in the air also gave FRANTIC scant, if any, attention. The Soviet Ministry of Defense's history of the Soviet Air Force in the Second World War failed to give any mention to the American shuttle-bombing campaign. A member of the Red Air Force's wartime general staff, M. N. Kozhevnikov, wrote of FRANTIC in his book, *The Command and Staff of the Soviet Army Air Force in the Great Patriotic War, 1941–1945*, published in 1975. Kozhevnikov wrote glowingly of Soviet preparations for the shuttle operations. He blamed the Americans, however, for failing to heed advice allegedly given by Soviet Major General Alexei Perminov on the evening of June 21, 1944, that the AAF task force disperse their aircraft around the field at Poltava. Kozhevnikov credited Soviet defenses with saving the base from total destruction though he believed that nothing the Soviets did could compensate for American nonchalance that resulted in the heavy losses of aircraft. After summarizing FRANTIC operations, Kozhevnikov, without mentioning the Warsaw run, concluded that American shuttle raids had no direct effect on events on the Soviet-German front.[12]

Not all Soviet references to FRANTIC have been negative. Deputy VVS commander Colonel General A. V. Nikitin was the only Soviet officer closely associated with FRANTIC to comment extensively on the operation. Two years after his death in 1973, an article he had written was published in the Soviet military press. He recounted Soviet efforts in preparing and maintaining Eastern Command's bases. Nikitin took a positive approach to the shuttle missions, referring to them as an excellent example of Soviet-American cooperation. He commented warmly on the spirit of cooperation at the bases and wrote that the Soviets fulfilled all their obligations to the Americans during FRANTIC. Nikitin's recollections differed from Kozhevnikov's account of the German strike of June 22, 1944, in that he believed that the Americans had dispersed their aircraft as much as possible around the Poltava airdrome. General Perminov, on the other hand, seems to have left no written account of his dealings with Eastern Command. Sadly, historian John F. Kreis has speculated that Perminov's close relations with the Americans at Eastern Command led to his disappearance after the war.[13]

Since the dramatic break-up of the Soviet Union in 1991, interest in FRANTIC in Ukraine has resurfaced. A January 1992 issue of the newspaper *News from Ukraine* contained a summary of the shuttle operations. The authors suggested that Ukrainian veterans of the operation meet again in reunions similar to those of other military units. The article focused on the spirit of cooperation that permeated the early days of Eastern Command. Apart from a reference to the alleged American refusal to disperse their bombers at Poltava, the authors avoided the standard derogatory remarks about the Combined Bomber Offensive or the second front. The article concluded by paying tribute to the more than 1,000 American soldiers and airmen who served in the Ukraine during FRANTIC, stating that "their [the Americans'] self-sacrifice and courage contributed greatly to victory." Perhaps more accounts of this nature will appear in the post-Soviet era.[14]

In 1944, however, the Soviet view of FRANTIC certainly did not reflect that contained in the later-day article in *News from Ukraine* or Nikitin's recollections. Moscow obviously saw little value in FRANTIC by late August 1944 when Molotov demanded return of the bases to Soviet control. The rift that formed between the Western Allies and the Kremlin over Poland and the Warsaw uprising did little to foster greater trust and warmer relations. The Allies' insistence on using the shuttle bases to supply the Polish rebels further alienated the Soviets, even though Stalin eventually relented and allowed their use for this purpose in mid-September.

It should come as no surprise, then, that FRANTIC failed to achieve its other major goals—American use of Siberian air bases in the war against Japan and closer U.S.-USSR relations. By mid-1944, the American seizure of the Mariana Islands obviated the need for bomber bases in Siberia. Still, the Americans pursued the idea of bases in Siberia well into 1945. Some AAF officers recognized that Poltava was retained through the winter of 1944–45 to make the Soviets more agreeable to the future transfer of *existing* bases on Soviet soil rather than start a completely new project in Siberia. The Winter Detachment at Poltava could have sent some of its men to the Maritime Provinces as easily as to the Budapest area where USSTAF proposed that other shuttle bases be located in the winter of 1944–45.[15]

The authors of Eastern Command's unofficial wartime history clung to the hope of U.S.-USSR cooperation in Siberia but conceded that there were no indications that FRANTIC had stimulated Soviet interest in allowing American aircraft to fly from bases in the Far East. Sensing the AAF's intense interest in Siberia, Stalin continued to string the American diplomatic and military communities along by making positive but meaningless statements about USAAF aircraft in the Maritime Provinces. Otherwise, the relatively modest accomplishments of Eastern Command in aircraft recovery operations through the winter months only barely justified keeping Poltava open long after its operational use had passed. The American base in the Ukraine was merely symbolic of the futile and naive attempts by the United States to win Soviet approval for Siberian bases. When the Soviets entered the Pacific War in the summer of 1945, it would be on the Kremlin's terms. As in eastern Europe, the Soviets would have had little use for an

American military presence in the Red Army's theater of operations in the Far East.

The forging of closer Soviet-American ties was a mixed success. On a personal level, the recollections of most American participants as well as the documentary evidence attest to the formation of strong personal friendships between Soviet citizens and American soldiers and airmen. Soviet civilians opened their homes to American G.I.s, and FRANTIC veterans commented repeatedly on the warm reception they received from the locals. Ground and aircrews found that they could work together and the heroism displayed by many Soviet troops on the night of the German raid remained a vivid image in the memories of many Americans who were there.

The Americans also realized that throughout FRANTIC, the Soviets did their best to provide for the comfort and well-being of their guests. Cultural exchanges in the form of concerts and stage shows helped bring the two groups closer together. Officers at all levels worked diligently to iron out problems and misunderstandings. Eastern Command records spoke favorably of Perminov and Nikitin. The Soviets grew to admire Eastern Command's deputy commander Brigadier General Alfred A. "Uncle Ugly" Kessler and other American officers such as Chaplain (Major) Clarence Strippy, who opened his religious services to all who wished to attend, regardless of nationality. The Americans eventually adjusted to the primitive conditions with which they were faced in the Ukraine. Their Soviet hosts must have considered the American G.I.s more as spoiled children than soldiers as Eastern Command personnel and transient aircrews complained incessantly about their living conditions, even though the messing, sleeping, and bathing facilities at the three American bases were far superior to anything the average Red Air Force "Ivan" enjoyed.

On a broader level, FRANTIC failed to bring the two nations closer together. Constantly reminded of their roles as "ambassadors" of the United States, the ground and aircrews of Operation FRANTIC still behaved in the fashion typical of most G.I.s. The Americans often did not realize the resentment their relative affluence caused among the war-weary Soviets. Many Soviets could not help but suspect, correctly in many cases, that U.S. personnel were corrupting their young women, buying their affection with consumer goods not available to the average citizen in the USSR. With memories of the German occupation still fresh, Soviet soldiers and civilians tended to view other foreigners, even allies, with caution and suspicion as well. To the end, Eastern Command personnel sensed a purposeful plan on the part of Soviet officials to thwart fraternization by Americans, particularly with women.

The Americans had been naive in their approach to the Soviet Union and its culture. Eastern Command personnel may have been impressed by the obvious bravery and reckless disregard for danger on the part of Soviet troops. Still, the G.I.s and their officers were appalled by the Red Air Force's apparent disdain for human life. Veterans of FRANTIC recalled many decades later the fatalism with which General Perminov and his men viewed the destruction caused by the German strike on Poltava. Americans watched in amazement as Soviet soldiers used their bare hands to dispose of deadly antipersonnel bombs. By summer's end, that amazement had turned to disgust.[16]

The different outlooks on the value of human life were indicative of the cultural and social chasm that separated the two countries. Just as the AAF assumed that simply exposing the Soviets to strategic bombing operations would win them over to such tactics, the Americans also believed that by sending 1,200 G.I.s to the Ukraine, they could break down long-standing barriers to greater mutual respect and understanding. By October, most Eastern Command personnel realized that "we" were not like "them" in terms of values and social mores.

Soviet behavior puzzled most Americans. A Soviet guard who gladly accepted a cigarette from a G.I. one day might shoot that American's pet dog for sport the next. Red Army troops treated downed aircrew members like heroes but viewed liberated prisoners of war as if they were soldiers of a hostile power. Soviet civilians and military personnel shared what they had with their American guests – and stole from them when their backs were turned. Certainly, the U.S. armed forces faced many of the same problems anywhere its men and women were sent. Given the political nature of FRANTIC, however, these seemingly mundane incidents reinforced enmities and suspicion.

Many American activities, such as black-marketeering or deviation from flight plans, irked Soviet officialdom. Representatives of the Communist Party, the secret police, and the bureaucracy viewed these activities as violations of Soviet security and sovereignty. Moscow's harsh reaction to the succession of incidents that occurred in March 1945 was evidence of the mistrust that had survived months of direct cooperation. The open and often tactless manner in which Americans gave vent to their political views, particularly on the part of Soviet and Russian émigrés wearing the American uniform, offended Soviet officers at all levels.

The Soviets received little in return for their efforts in FRANTIC. Admittedly, the AAF flew several missions at the behest of the Red Army. Allowing the Americans into the Ukraine did not result in the inclusion of heavy bombers in Lend-Lease assistance to the USSR or speed up the *Wehrmacht*'s collapse in the East. Stalin may have viewed his assent to FRANTIC in December 1943 as a quid pro quo for Lend-Lease aid or as means to encourage the Allies to remain faithful to their plans for a second front in France. If so, he probably came to regret that assent.

Paradoxically, instead of providing the AAF with leverage over the Soviets, FRANTIC gave Moscow a valuable bargaining chip. The Soviets could use Eastern Command to register their displeasure with the Western Allies. For example, during the Warsaw controversy, Moscow refused all AAF requests for reconnaissance flights using Eastern Command bases. As the Warsaw episode and the subsequent prisoner of war repatriation issue demonstrated, Americans on Soviet or Soviet-occupied soil were at the mercy of the Kremlin. Stalin realized that as long as his Allies believed they needed his assistance in the Far East or feared his plans for the postwar period in Europe, the Americans would mute their protests over restrictions placed on Eastern Command.

The Americans inexplicably refused to learn from earlier dealings with the Soviet Union and its leadership. Stalin's government created all efforts at cooperation and joint operations cautiously. The Kremlin's twists and turns in the VELVET and BAZAAR projects were clear indicators to American military and political leaders that Moscow moved at its own pace and in accordance with its own agenda. Stalin's cynical and callous attitude toward the ill-fated Polish uprising in Warsaw should have awakened leaders in Washington and at the Pentagon to the true nature of Soviet war aims and postwar plans. Establishing shuttle-bombing bases in the Ukraine would not alter the reality of the Soviet dictator's xenophobia or his imperial designs in eastern Europe.

Thus, FRANTIC did succeed in one sense. The operation's disappointments and difficulties finally persuaded the AAF and the Military Mission that plans for future joint operations with the Soviets in the early spring of 1945 were simply no longer worth the frustration of dealing with Moscow and its military and civil bureaucracies. This dubious accomplishment was of little comfort to the men of Eastern Command who endured isolation, theft, and harassment at the hands of the Soviets as the G.I.s attempted to fulfill their mission as soldiers and informal ambassadors.

The FRANTIC project began in an outpouring of eagerness and goodwill on both sides. Its failure was symbolic of the inability of the wartime Allied coalition to come to grips with the diverse objectives of each of its members and lay the foundations of a true and enduring peace. Even in the face of such a formidable threat as that presented by Hitler's Germany, the Allies had difficulty in laying aside their differences. A handful of shuttle missions and the presence of a few hundred G.I.s on Soviet soil could not overcome the fundamental differences, political and cultural, that separated the United States and the Soviet Union.

SUMMARY OF FRANTIC OPERATIONS

FRANTIC I
15AF, 5th Bomb Wing
    2nd Bomb Group
    97th Bomb Group
    99th Bomb Group
    483rd Bomb Group
    325 Fighter Group

Operations
    2 June 1944: Italy to USSR, Debrecen, Hungary
    6 June 1944: USSR to USSR, Galatz, Romania
    11 June 1944: USSR to Italy, Focsani, Romania

FRANTIC II
8AF, 13th Bomb Wing
    95th Bomb Group
    100th Bomb Group
    390th Bomb Group
45th Bomb Wing
    96th Bomb Group
    388th Bomb Group
    452nd Bomb Group
65th Fighter Wing
    4th Fighter Group

Operations
    21 June 1944: U.K. to USSR, Ruhland, Germany
    26 June 1944: USSR to Italy, Drohobycz, Poland
    Three additional missions flown from Italian bases, including one against
        Arad, Romania, on July 3

Sources: "Summary of Bomber Operations" and "Summary of Fighter Operations," in Papers of Robert L. Walsh, USAF Academy Library Special Collections, USAF Academy, CO, MS-12; "Information on Shuttle Misions: World War II," Special Project File, Air Force Historical Research Agency, Maxwell AFB, Ala., AFHRA K 110.7007-4, September 1959.

FRANTIC III
15th AF, 306th Fighter Wing
   14th Fighter Group
   31st Fighter Group
   82nd Fighter Group

Operations
   22 July 1944: Italy to USSR, Zilistea and Buzau, Romania
   25 July 1944: USSR to USSR, Mielec, Poland
   26 July 1944: USSR to Italy, Bucharest-Ploesti area

FRANTIC IV
15th AF, 306th Fighter Wing
   52nd Fighter Group
   82nd Fighter Group

Operations
   4 August 1944: Italy to USSR: Focsani, Romania
   6 August 1944: USSR to Italy, Bucharest-Ploesti area

FRANTIC V
8AF, 13th Bomb Wing
   95th Bomb Group
   390th Bomb Group
66th Fighter Wing
   357th Fighter Group

Operations
   6 August 1944: U.K. to USSR, Rahmel, Poland
   7 August 1944: USSR to USSR, Trzebinia, Poland
   8 August 1944: USSR to Italy, Zilistea and Buzau, Romania
   One mission also flown en route to U.K. from Italian bases

FRANTIC VI
8AF, 45th Bomb Wing
   96th Bomb Group
   452nd Bomb Group
67th Fighter Wing
   20th Fighter Group

Operations
   11 September 1944: U.K. to USSR, Chemnitz, Germany
   13 September 1944: USSR to Italy, Diosgyor, Hungary

FRANTIC VII
8AF, 13th Bomb Wing
   95th Bomb Group
   100th Bomb Group
   390th Bomb Group

65th Fighter Wing
   355th Fighter Group

Operations
   18 September 1944: U.K. to USSR, Warsaw, Poland
   19 September 1944: USSR to Italy, Szolnok, Hungary
   Last aircraft of the FRANTIC VII Task Force returned to U.K. on 8 October
     1944 because of heavy battle damage suffered over Warsaw

From 2 June to 19 September 1944, 117 photo reconnaissance missions were flown by F-5s from or to Soviet bases. These missions included thirty-three from Italy, twenty-nine to Italy, six from the U.K., and forty-nine to and from Soviet bases.

NOTES

The Genesis of FRANTIC

1. Earl F. Ziemke, *Stalingrad to Berlin: The German Defeat in the East* (Washington, D.C.: Center of Military History, 1968), pp. 311–312.

2. See Aleksandr Yuryev, "The Second Front: Plans and Reality," *Soviet Military Review* 5 (May 1989): 50–52.

3. Chester Wilmot, *Struggle for Europe* (New York: Carroll and Graf, 1986), chaps VI and VII.

4. Robert F. Futrell, *Ideas, Concepts, Doctrine: Basic Thinking in the United States Air Force, 1907–1960*, 2 vols (Maxwell AFB, Ala.: Air University Press, 1989), vol 1, pp. 78–83; Wesley F. Craven and James L. Cate, *The Army Air Forces in World War II*, 7 vols (Chicago: University of Chicago Press, 1951), vol 1, *Plans and Early Operations: January 1939 to August 1942*, pp. 48–54; Barry D. Watts, Lt Col, USAF, *The Foundations of U.S. Air Doctrine: The Problem of Friction in War* (Maxwell AFB, Ala.: Air University Press, 1984), pp. 6–9; Max Hastings, OVERLORD: *D-Day, June 6, 1944* (New York: Simon and Schuster, 1984), p. 39.

5. Michael S. Sherry, *The Rise of American Air Power: The Creation of Armageddon* (New Haven: Yale University Press, 1987), pp. 50–52.

6. Watts, p. 18; R. J. Overy, *The Air War, 1939–1945* (New York: Stein and Day, 1980), pp. 12–14. Based on a bombing survey conducted in post-World War I Germany, officers of the U.S. Air Service began formulating an industrial web theory years before Mitchell articulated such a view. See Edgar S. Gorrell, "Strategical Bombardment," in Maurer Maurer, ed., *The U.S. Air Service in World War I*, 5 vols (Washington, D.C.: Office of Air Force History, 1978), vol II, pp. 141–151; Futrell, p. 80.

7. Enzo Angelucci, *The Rand McNally Encyclopedia of Military Aircraft, 1914–1980* (New York: Military Press, 1983), pp. 265, 288; Bill Gunston, *The Encyclopedia of the World's Combat Aircraft: A Technical Directory of Major Warplanes from World War I to the Present Day* (New York: Chartwell Books, 1976), p. 24. For a brief account of the development of the heavy bomber, see Craven and Cate, vol I, pp. 54–71.

8. Watts, p. 62.

9. Ed Crowder, Colonel USAF, "POINTBLANK: A Study in Strategic and National Security Decision Making," *Airpower Journal* 1 (Spring 1992): 55–65.

10. Haywood S. Hansell, *The Air Plan That Defeated Hitler* (Atlanta: Higgins-McArthur/Longino and Porter, 1972), pp. 84–85; Crowder, p. 58. Hansell played a key role in formulating AWPD-1 as well as subsequent plans. See Headquarters, U.S. Army Air Forces, Office of the Chief of Staff, "AWPD-1," 12 August 1941, Tab 5(a), p. 5.

11. Overy, p. 13. See also John Ellis, *Brute Force: Allied Strategy and Tactics in the Second World War* (New York: Viking Penguin, 1990), p. 165; Sir Charles Webster and Noble Frankland, *The Strategic Air Offensive Against Germany, 1939–1945*, 4 vols (London: HMSO, 1961), vol I, *Preparation,* part 1, cited hereafter as Webster and Frankland.

12. For the full story behind "Bomber" Harris and the RAF Bomber Command, see Max Hastings, *Bomber Command* (London: Michael Joseph, 1979). See also Marshal of the RAF Sir Arthur Harris, *Bomber Offensive* (London: Collins, 1947); Dudley Saward, *Bomber Harris* (London: Cassell, 1984); Martin Middlebrook and Chris Everitt, *The Bomber Command War Diaries* (London: Viking Press, 1985); and Webster and Frankland, vol II, *Endeavor,* part IV.

13. Crowder, pp. 60–61; Ellis, p.173; Maurice Matloff, *Strategic Planning for Coalition Warfare, 1943–1944* (Washington, D.C.: Office of the Chief of Military History, 1959), pp. 27–28.

14. Overy, pp. 108–110; Ellis, pp. 173–174.

15. Matloff, p. 28.

16. "General Eaker's Presentation of the Combined Bomber Offensive Plan to the Joint Chiefs of Staff," 29 April 1943, contained verbatim in Watts, pp. 135–136.

17. Crowder, p. 61; Hansell, p. 168; Overy, p. 117; Ellis, p. 184; Hastings, pp. 41–42.

18. Roger Beaumont, "The Bomber Offensive as a Second Front," *Journal of Contemporary History* 22 (1987): 3–19. The RAF first struck inside Germany in early May 1940 and raided Berlin in August. Area bombing began in earnest in July 1941.

19. Message No. 3, Stalin to Churchill, 18 July 1941; Message No. 12, Stalin to Churchill, 12 September 1941; Message No. 14, Churchill to His Excellency Monsieur Joseph Stalin, 21 September 1941, in Ministry of Foreign Affairs of the USSR, *Stalin's Correspondence with Churchill, Attlee, Roosevelt, and Truman, 1941–45* (New York: E. P. Dutton, 1958), pp. 12–13, 24–25, 26–28.

20. Herbert Feis, *Churchill, Roosevelt, Stalin: The War They Waged and the Peace They Sought* (Princeton, N.J.: Princeton University Press, 1957), pp. 47–57; Wilmot, pp. 128–130.

21. Beaumont, pp. 5–6.

22. See, for example, Messages 101 and 102, p. 85, Message 118, p. 98, and Message 122, p. 99 in *Stalin's Correspondence.*

23. For postwar Soviet attitudes on Allied operations in the Mediterranean, see Yuryev, pp. 50–52; for Soviet perceptions of the CBO, see A. Orlov and N. Komarov, " 'Flying Fortresses' Over the Third Reich," *Soviet Military Review* 7 (July 1975): 51–52. See also U.S. Department of State, *Foreign Relations of the United States, Diplomatic Papers, 1943,* vol III, *The British Commonwealth, Eastern Europe, The Far East* (Washington, D.C: U.S. Government Printing Office [USGPO], 1963), p. 578, cited hereafter as *FRUS.*

24. Adam B. Ulam, *The Rivals: America and Russia Since World War II* (New York: Penguin Books, 1984), pp. 11–12.

25. See Communication, "The Minister in Switzerland (Harrison) to the Secretary of State," 21 January 1943, pp. 621–622; Communication, "The Charge in

Finland (McClintock) to the Secretary of State," 10 August 1943, p. 682; Communication, "The Minister in Sweden (Johnson) to the Secretary of State," 10 August 1943, p. 683, all in *FRUS,* vol III.

26. Communication, "The Ambassador in the Soviet Union (Standley) to the Secretary of State," 7 September 1943, in *FRUS,* vol III, pp. 576–577.

27. Watts, p. 138.

28. Williamson Murray, *Strategy for Defeat: The Luftwaffe, 1933–1945* (Maxwell AFB, Ala.: Air University Press, 1983), pp. 218–220. For a detailed study of Harris' "Battle of Berlin," including numerous eyewitness accounts, see Martin Middlebrook, *The Berlin Raids: R.A.F. Bomber Command, Winter 1943–44* (London: Penguin Books, 1990).

29. Murray, pp. 222–223; General Arnold wrote after the war that he was not at all certain in autumn of 1943 that the AAF could have sustained the punishment it was receiving during deep penetration daylight raids. See Henry H. Arnold, General of the Air Force, *Global Mission* (New York: Harper, 1949), p. 495; W. H. Tantum and E. J. Hoffschmidt, eds., *The Rise and Fall of the German Air Force (1933–1945)* (Old Greenwich, Conn.: WE, Inc., 1969), pp. 287–293, cited hereafter as Tantum and Hoffschmidt.

30. See Ellis, chap 4; and Stephen L. McFarland and Wesley Phillips Newton, *To Command the Sky: The Battle for Air Superiority Over Germany, 1942–44* (Washington, D.C: Smithsonian Institution Press, 1991). For the effects on the Germans of the appearance of American long-range fighters, see Tantum and Hoffschmidt, pp. 293–297.

31. Craven and Cate, vol III, *Europe: From* ARGUMENT *to V-E Day, January 1944 to May 1945,* pp. 308–309; cited hereafter as Craven and Cate; Headquarters, Mediterranean Allied Air Forces, "Preliminary Study of Coordinated Attacks by United States Strategic Air Forces in Europe, January–August 1944," April 1945, p. 1.

32. Message, JCS to Deane, 26 October 1943 in Headquarters, MAAF, James Parton, Major, *History of* FRANTIC: *American Shuttle Bombing to and from Russian Bases, 26 October 1943–15 June 1944,* 12 July 1944, Air Force Historical Research Agency (AFHRA), Maxwell AFB, Ala., AFHRA 622.430-6, Folder 1; Craven and Cate, vol III, p. 309; Phillip S. Meilinger, *Hoyt S. Vandenberg: The Life of a General* (Bloomington, Ind.: Indiana University Press, 1989), p. 37.

33. John R. Deane, *The Strange Alliance: The Story of Our Efforts at Wartime Cooperation with Russia* (New York: Viking Press, 1947), pp. 11, 27; Communication, "The Acting Secretary of State to the Charge in the Soviet Union (Hamilton)," 1 October 1943, *FRUS,* pp. 704–705.

34. Craven and Cate, vol III, pp. 5–8. For the coming of long-range fighters, see Stephen L. McFarland, "The Evolution of the American Strategic Fighter in Europe, 1942–44," *Journal of Strategic Studies* 10 (June 1987): 189–208.

35. AWPD-1, Tab 5(a), p. 5.

36. Richard C. Lukas, *Eagles East: The Army Air Forces and the Soviet Union, 1941–1945* (Tallahassee, Fla.: Florida State University Press, 1970), p. 139.

37. Denis Richards and Hilary St. George Saunders, *Royal Air Force, 1939–1945,* 3 vols (London: HMSO, 1954), vol II, *The Fight Avails,* pp. 77–78. For a full account of this operation, see chap V.

38. Ibid., pp. 85–86.

39. Lukas, pp. 140–141; Albert Lepawsky, *History of Eastern Command, U.S. STAF, 1941–45,* AFHRA 522.01-1, chap 1, p. 29.

40. Lukas, p. 141.

41. Ibid., p. 144.

42. Ibid., pp. 145–150.

43. Message No. 77, Churchill to Stalin, 9 October 1942, in *Stalin's Correspondence,* pp. 71–72.

44. Message No. 81, Stalin to Churchill, 8 November 1942, in *Stalin's Correspondence,* p. 74; "Notes on Anglo-American Conversation with Russian High Command, November 1942, First Meeting; Second Meeting," n.d. in AFHRA 168.605; Lukas, pp. 154–156; Feis, p. 97.

45. Message No. 59, Roosevelt to Stalin, 16 December 1942; Message No. 60, Stalin to Roosevelt, 18 December 1942, both in *Stalin's Correspondence,* pp. 44–45.

46. Churchill, quoted in Lukas, p. 163.

47. U.S. Department of Defense, *Entry of the Soviet Union into the War Against Japan: Military Plans, 1941–1945* (Washington, D.C.: no publisher named, 1955), USAF Academy Library, p. 6; Matloff, p. 100.

48. Message No. 23, Roosevelt to Stalin, 17 June 1942; Message No. 24, Roosevelt to Stalin, 23 June 1942, both in *Stalin's Correspondence,* pp. 25–27; Matloff, p. 100.

49. R. L. Maxwell, Maj Gen, U.S.A, "Notes on Moscow Conference, August 17, 1942," in Papers of Follett Bradley, MS-1, USAF Academy Library Special Collections. Bradley's team drew up rather extensive plans for the requirements of each base. Each airfield would house a single bombardment squadron with 68 officers, 334 enlisted men, and 12 four-engine aircraft. These plans were contained in "Outline for Discussion re: Siberian Air Base [*sic*]," MS-1.

50. Lukas, pp. 130–132, 135; Matloff, p. 100.

51. Ibid., pp. 136–138; Message No. 64, Roosevelt to Stalin, 30 December 1942; Message No. 66, Stalin to Roosevelt, 5 January 1943, both in *Stalin's Correspondence,* pp. 47–48.

52. *Entry of the Soviet Union into the War Against Japan,* pp. 30–36.

53. Ronald Spector, *Eagle Against the Sun: The American War with Japan* (New York: Vintage Books, 1985), pp. 324–325; Matloff, p. 15.

54. For accounts of the AVG, see Ron Heiferman, *Flying Tigers: Chennault in China* (New York: Ballantine Books, 1971); and Craven and Cate, vol I, pp. 485–492.

55. Ibid., pp. 505–507; Heiferman, p. 4–6. For Stilwell's activities in China, see Barbara W. Tuchman, *Stilwell and the American Experience in China, 1911–45* (New York: Macmillan, 1971).

56. Headquarters, U.S. Army Air Forces, "The Fourteenth Air Force to 1 October 1943," AAF Historical Office, July 1945, pp. 6–7, 160–161; Headquarters, USAAF and Eighth U.S. Army (Rear), Air Operations in the China Area, July 1937–August 1945, Japanese Monograph No. 76, distributed by the Office of the Chief of Military History, Dept of the Army, 1956, pp. 117–118.

57. Ibid., p. 446.

58. For a full account of the Japanese offensive code-named *Ichi-go,* see Spector,

chap 17. For the Japanese view of B-29 operations and their subsequent offensive, see Air Operations in the China Area, chap 8.

59. For Chennault's "side" of the story, see Claire Lee Chennault, Maj Gen, *Way of a Fighter* (New York: Putnam, 1949). For an extensive examination of American-Chinese relations, see Herbert Feis, *The China Tangle* (New York: Atheneum, 1965).

60. Headquarters, Eastern Command, USSTAF, Albert Lepawsky, "The AAF on the Russian Front, Summaries and Conclusions," Drafts and Notes, AFHRA 522.057-1, chap 12, p. 1.

61. Ibid.

62. Ibid., p. 2.

63. Ibid.

64. Ibid., p. 3.

65. Ibid., p. 4.

66. Ibid., p. 5.

67. Headquarters, USSTAF in Europe, Office of the Director of Intelligence, Brig Gen George C. McDonald, FRANTIC, to Deputy Commander, Operations, USSTAF in Europe, 21 August 1944, in Appreciation of FRANTIC, AFHRA 522.609-1, pp. 1-2.

68. "The AAF on the Russian Front," chapter 12, p. 2.

69. Ibid.

70. Lukas, pp. 42-46.

71. Matloff, p. 498.

72. To facilitate American bombing operations, the AAF would initially have to rely on Soviet target information until regular photo-reconnaissance flights from Italy could take place. See "Minutes of Meeting at Aviation General Staff Headquarters, 11 March 1944," p. 3; Daily Diary of Major Albert Lepawsky, entry of 6 April 1944, p. 7, both in Progress of FRANTIC Project, February–April 1944, AFHRA 522.117.

73. Angelucci, pp. 263, 285-286; Overy, p. 21.

74. Earl F. Ziemke, "The Soviet Armed Forces in the Interwar Period," in Allan R. Millett and Williamson Murray, eds., *Military Effectiveness, Volume II: The Interwar Period* (Boston: Unwin Hyman, 1988), pp. 16-17; Ministry of Defense, USSR, *The Soviet Air Force in World War II*, translated by Leland Fetzer, edited by Ray Wagner (Garden City, N.Y.: Doubleday, 1973), p. 20.

75. David M. Glantz and Jonathan M. House, *When Titans Clashed: How the Red Army Stopped Hitler* (Lawrence, Kans.: University Press of Kansas, 1995), pp. 23-27, 33, 37; see also Von Hardesty, *Red Phoenix: The Rise of Soviet Air Power, 1941-1945* (Washington, D.C: Smithsonian Institute Press, 1982), p. 17.

76. Ibid., p. 15; Glantz and House, p. 66. For a German perspective on the air war in the East, see Generalleutnant Hermann Plocher, *The German Air Force Versus Russia, 1941* (New York: Arno Press, 1968). For a Soviet account of the command structure of the Red Air Force in World War II, see M. N. Kozhevnikov, *The Command and Staff of the Soviet Army Air Force in the Great Patriotic War, 1941-1945* (Washington, D.C.: USGPO, 1977), published in English under the auspices of the U.S. Air Force.

77. Generalleutnant a.D. Walter Schwabedissen, *The Russian Air Force in the Eyes of German Commanders* (Maxwell AFB, Ala.: USAF Historical Division, Air University, 1960), pp. 348-349; Hardesty, p. 26.

78. Von Hardesty, "Roles and Missions: Soviet Tactical Air Power in the Second Period of the Great Patriotic War," in *Transformation in Russian and Soviet Military History: Proceedings of the Twelfth Military History Symposium, United States Air Force Academy, 1-3 October, 1986,* edited by Col Carl W. Reddel, USAF (Washington, D.C.: Office of Air Force History, 1990), pp. 151-171.

79. Ibid., pp. 158-159.

80. Hardesty, *Red Phoenix,* pp. 86, 250-251.

81. Plocher, *German Air Force Versus Russia, 1943,* p. 229; Murray, pp. 248-249; Tantum and Hoffschmidt, chap 16.

82. Schwabedissen, pp. 348-349; Overy, p. 58; Generalleutnant a.D. Klaus Uebe, *Russian Reactions to German Airpower* [sic] *in World War II* (Maxwell AFB, Ala.: USAF Historical Division, Air University, 1964), pp. 29-30. Schwabedissen and Overy also pointed out that the Soviets pragmatically refrained from building a strategic air force because the Allies had promised the Kremlin that their air forces would ravage Germany from the air.

83. Meilinger, p. 37; Deane, pp. 3-5.

84. Ibid., p. 14.

85. W. Averell Harriman and Elie Abel, *Special Envoy to Churchill and Stalin, 1941-1946* (New York: Random House, 1975), p. 239; Deane, pp. 19-20; Meilinger, p. 38.

86. Ibid.

87. Deane, p. 20; Harriman, p. 239.

88. Meilinger, p. 38; Deane, pp. 20-21.

89. Meilinger, pp. 38-39.

90. For succinct accounts of the Tehran Conference, see, for example, Feis, *Churchill, Roosevelt, Stalin,* Period Six and Period Seven; Matloff, chap XVI; communications relevant to the conference are contained in U.S. Department of State, *Foreign Relations of the United States, 1943, Diplomatic Papers: The Conferences at Cairo and Teheran* (Washington, D.C.: USGPO, 1961).

91. Harriman, pp. 269-270.

92. Deane, pp. 44-45.

93. Message, Harriman to Roosevelt, 26 December 1943, in HQ MAAF, *History of* FRANTIC.

America Comes to the Ukraine

1. Headquarters, Mediterranean Allied Air Forces (MAAF), "Negotiations for FRANTIC Bases and Operations," Tab A, p. 1, in *History of* FRANTIC: *American Shuttle Bombing to and from Russian Bases, 26 October 1943-15 June 1944,* Air Force Historical Research Agency, Maxwell AFB, Ala., AFHRA 622.430-6, Folder 1, 26 October 1943-15 June 1944.

2. Minutes of meeting with Marshal Stalin, subject: Russian Bases for American Shuttle Bombers and Photo Reconnaissance Planes, 2 February 1944, U.S. Military Mission to Moscow, Operation FRANTIC, National Archives, Washington, D.C., NA/RG 334, Box 63, "Beginning, 26 October 1943-31 March 1944."

3. "Chronological Record of FRANTIC Project," in Data Taken by General Spaatz to MAAF, Tab D, Status of FRANTIC, AFHRA 519.1612-1, April 1944.

4. Memorandum, "Suggestions for Project BASEBALL," 14 February 1944, AFHRA 522.161, General Correspondence, January–February 1944.

5. Message, Marshall to Spaatz and Deane, 19 February 1944, FRANTIC I Cables, 22 October 1943–16 May 1945, AFHRA 522.1621-1.

6. "Personnel For FRANTIC," General Correspondence, April 1944, AFHRA 522.161; "Diary of Brigadier General Alfred A. Kessler, 5 February–7 May, 1944," AFHRA 522.0591-3; Chronological Record of FRANTIC Project, AFHRA 519.1612-1; Glenn B. Infield, *The Poltava Affair: A Russian Warning, An American Tragedy* (New York: Macmillan, 1973), pp. 24–25.

7. "Minutes of Meeting, 28 February 1944," Progress of FRANTIC Project, February–April 1944, Exhibit A, AFHRA 522.117.

8. Ibid.

9. Ibid.

10. Progress of FRANTIC Project, p. 1.

11. Memorandum for General Deane, "Inspection of Russian Airdromes at Kharkov and Poltava, 10 March 1944," in Progress of FRANTIC Project.

12. Memorandum for General Deane, "Requirements for Sites for Shuttle Bombing Project, 10 March 1944," in Progress of FRANTIC Project.

13. Message, Deane to Spaatz, Progress of FRANTIC Project, Exhibit E.

14. Ibid.

15. Kessler Diary. For excellent accounts of the Red Army's drive to clear the Ukraine, see David M. Glantz and Jonathan M. House, *When Titans Clashed: How the Red Army Stopped Hitler* (Lawrence, Kans.: University Press of Kansas, 1995), chap 11, "Kursk to the Dnepr"; Albert Seaton, *The Russo-German War, 1941–45* (New York: Praeger, 1971), chap 23, "Soviet 1943 Autumn Offensives," and chap 25, "Defeat at Leningrad and in the Ukraine"; Earl Ziemke, *Stalingrad to Berlin: The German Defeat in the East* (Washington, D.C.: Center of Military History, 1966), chap XI, "Offensives on Both Flanks–The South Flank."

16. Kessler Diary; Progress of FRANTIC Project, para. 18 (b).

17. Message, Griffith to Spaatz, 2 April 1944 in General Correspondence, April 1–April 30, 1944, AFHRA 522.161.

18. "Minutes of Meeting at Red Army Air Force Building, Khalzunova Street No. 16, 28 March 1944," in Progress of FRANTIC Project, Exhibit I.

19. Message, Deane to Spaatz, 22 March 1944, in Eastern Command General Correspondence, 1 March–31 March 1944, AFHRA 522.161; Message, Deane to Spaatz, 18 March 1944, in Progress of FRANTIC Project; Minutes of Meeting at Red Army Air Force Building, 28 March 1944.

20. Memorandum for Colonel Bitting, "Supplement to Report Regarding Personnel Selected for FRANTIC," 9 May 1944 in EASCOM [Eastern Command] Miscellaneous File, April–May 1944, AFHRA 522.2823; FRANTIC History, "Negotiations and Planning," September 1943–May 1944, AFHRA 522.04-1.

21. "Narrative Report of Inspection of Colonel Griffith's Project, 18 March 1944, to CG, USSTAF," in EASCOM Miscellaneous File; Memorandum for Colonel Bitting, "Information Regarding Personnel Selected for FRANTIC, 24 April 1944," in EASCOM Miscellaneous File.

22. Ibid.; Memorandum for Colonel W. P. Young, Inspection of Enlisted Men's Classification Cards, Form #20, Station 113, 25 March 1944 in EASCOM Miscellaneous File.

23. Message, Deane to Spaatz, 9 March 1944, in EASCOM General Correspondence, 1 March–31 March 1944.

24. Message, Deane to Spaatz, 22 March 1944; Kessler Diary, 29 March 1944.

25. Ibid.; Diary of Major Albert Lepawsky, p. 2, in Progress of FRANTIC Project.

26. Kessler Diary.

27. Ibid.

28. *History of* FRANTIC, p. 10.

29. Kessler Diary; *History of* FRANTIC.

30. Headquarters, U.S. Army Air Forces, *History of the Eastern Command, USSTAF,* chap VI, "Organization," p. 109, AFHRA 522.01-2, 1941–1944.

31. John F. Kreis, *Air Warfare and Air Base Air Defense* (Washington, D.C.: Office of Air Force History, 1988), pp. 205–206; "Report on Conference with Red Army Regarding Intelligence and Reconnaissance Matters, 17 March 1944," in Progress of FRANTIC Project; M. N. Kozhevnikov, *The Command and Staff of the Soviet Army Air Force in the Great Patriotic War, 1941–1945,* translated and published under the auspices of the U.S. Air Force (Washington, D.C.: USGPO, 1977), pp. 189–190; A. V. Nikitin, " 'Chelnochnye' operatsiy," *Voenno-Istoricheskiy Zhurnal* 11 (1975): 42. On the subject of captured Allied aircraft in German service, see, for example, the first-person account of P. W. Stahl, *KG 200: The True Story* (London: Jane's, 1979); and Hans-Heiri Stapfer, *Strangers in a Strange Land* (Carrollton, Tex.: Squadron Signal, 1988).

32. Kessler Diary, entry of 31 March 1944.

33. Ibid.

34. Ibid., entry of 4 May 1944.

35. Memorandum to the Surgeon, Headquarters, Provisional Eastern Command, "Initial Sanitary Report of the Headquarters Area of Detachment 5, ASC, USSTAF, at Poltava, 28 April 1944," in Miscellaneous Documents Concerning Shuttle Missions to Russia, February–May 1944, AFHRA 622.430-6, Folder 3.

36. Kessler Diary, entry of 17 April 1944.

37. Ibid., entry 20 April 1944.

38. Headquarters, Eastern Command, USSTAF, Office of the Surgeon, "Sanitary Survey of AAF Station 560 (Piryatin)," 7 June 1944 in Miscellaneous Documents Concerning Shuttle Missions to Russia.

39. Kessler Diary, entry of 21 April 1944.

40. Headquarters, Eastern Command, USSTAF, Office of the Surgeon, "Survey of AAF Station 561 (Mirgorod)," 18 May 1944 in Miscellaneous Documents Concerning Shuttle Missions to Russia.

41. American Embassy, U.S. Military Mission to Moscow, "Observations on Requested Subjects," 30 March 1944 in Miscellaneous Documents.

42. Minutes of Meeting at Red Air Force Building, 30 March 1944 in Miscellaneous Documents: Minutes of General Conference, 29 March 1944 in Progress of FRANTIC Project.

43. Headquarters, Eastern Command, USSTAF, Office of the Surgeon, Memoran-

dum, "Special Medical Report of Eastern Command, USSTAF," 8 June 1944 in Miscellaneous Documents.

44. Message, Deane to Spaatz, repeated to Arnold, 29 April 1944, in EASCOM General Correspondence, 1 April–30 April 1944, AFHRA 522.161.

45. Minutes of Meeting at Red Army Air Force Building, 28 March 1944.

46. *History of FRANTIC*, p. 7.

47. Ibid., p. 8. The bombs initially provided by the Soviets were in welded casings instead of the solid-cast type the Americans were accustomed to using. The AAF airmen expressed doubts about the accuracy of this type of bomb. Several bombing tests proved that, with adjustments to the ballistics tables and the proper altitude, the Soviet munitions were acceptable to the "precision-minded" Americans.

48. "Minutes of Meeting at Red Air Force Headquarters, 5 April 1944"; Message, Deane to Spaatz, 29 April 1944; Kessler Diary, entry of 1 May; *History of FRANTIC*, p. 7; Seaton, pp. 435–436.

49. Kessler Diary, entry of 1 May 1944.

50. *History of FRANTIC*, pp. 7–8.

51. Kessler Diary, entries of 1 and 2 May 1944; *History of FRANTIC*, p. 12.

52. "Report on Conference with Red Army Regarding Intelligence and Reconnaissance Matters," n.d., in Progress of FRANTIC Project, Exhibit F.

53. Progress of FRANTIC Project, p. 8; *History of FRANTIC*, p. 14.

54. John R. Deane, *The Strange Alliance: The Story of Our Efforts at Wartime Cooperation with Russia* (New York: Viking Press, 1947), pp. 113–114.

55. Ibid., p. 114; *History of FRANTIC*, pp. 13–14.

56. Progress of FRANTIC Project, pp. 10–12; *History of FRANTIC*, p. 14.

57. "Conferences with Russian Officials, Poltava, April and May, 1944," in *History of FRANTIC*, Tab E, p. 3.

58. Kessler Diary, entry of 5 May 1944.

59. Ibid.

60. "Conferences with Russian Officials, Poltava, April and May, 1944." See also Daily Diary of Major Albert Lewpawsky in Progress of FRANTIC Project.

61. *History of FRANTIC*, p. 16; Infield, pp. 39–40; Kessler Diary, entry of 27 April 1944.

62. Ibid., entry of 28 April 1944.

63. Message, Deane to Spaatz, 29 April 1944 in EASCOM Cables, April–May 1944; Kessler Diary; "Report on Enemy Land-Mining Operation," to CG, USSTAF, 28 April 1944 in *History of Eastern Command*, vol 2, part 2, Appendix, AFHRA 522.01-1.

64. *History of FRANTIC*, p. 6.

65. Lepawsky Diary, entry of 21 March 1944; Chronological Record of FRANTIC Project; Message, Deane to Spaatz and Arnold, 22 April 1944 in EASCOM General Correspondence, 1 April–30 April 1944.

66. Kessler Diary, entry of 27 April.

67. Ibid.; Message, Deane to Spaatz and Arnold, 22 April 1944.

68. Captain Charles M. Manning, "Daily Diary, 4th Echelon of 'FRANTIC' during Trip from England to Russia," 19 March–16 May 1944, in *History of FRANTIC*.

69. Ibid., p. 5.

70. Ibid., pp. 7–8.

71. Ibid.; Message, Spaatz to Connolly (CG, PGC), 9 May 1944 in "Personnel— frantic," *History of* FRANTIC.

72. Interview with Mr. Lou Wampler, 1st Lt, 390th Bomb Group, by author, Colorado Springs, Colo., 12 October 1989. Wampler was a supply officer and would spend the next several months in the Ukraine.

73. "Daily Diary, Fourth Echelon," p. 9; Interview with Colonel Lewis Mundell, [acting chief of staff, EASCOM] by Major James Parton, HQ MAAF Historian, Poltava, 10 June 1944; Wampler interview.

74. *History of* FRANTIC, pp. 16–17.

75. Wesley F. Craven and James L. Cate, *The Army Air Forces in World War II,* 7 vols (Chicago: University of Chicago Press, 1951), vol III, *Europe:* ARGUMENT *to V-E Day, January 1944 to May 1945,* p. 311.

76. Message, Deane to Spaatz, 10 May 1944 in Papers of Brigadier General George C. McDonald, USAF Academy Library Special Collections, MS-16, Box 4, Folder 1; Message, Spaatz to Kessler, 26 May 1944; Message, Spaatz to Arnold, info Deane, 26 May 1944, in FRANTIC Cables, May–October 1944, Book 1, AFHRA 519.476-1.

77. "Report of Visit to Russia by Mission of USSTAF Officers," to Lieutenant General Carl A. Spaatz, Commanding General, USSTAF, 21 May 1944, p. 2, in *History of* FRANTIC.

78. Message, Deane to Spaatz, 30 May 1944 in FRANTIC Cables, Book 1.

79. Message, Eaker to Spaatz, 31 May 1944 in FRANTIC Cables, Book 1.

80. Message, Deane to Spaatz, 31 May 1944; Message, Spaatz to Deane, info Arnold, Eaker, Kessler, 31 May 1944 in FRANTIC Cables, Book 1; Brig Gen George C. McDonald, Memorandum to Deputy Commander, Operations, U.S. Strategic Air Forces in Europe, "FRANTIC," 21 August 1944, Appreciation of FRANTIC, AFHRA 522.609-1.

81. Headquarters, Fifteenth Air Force, "Units and Personnel Participating in FRANTIC Operation, 2 June 1944," n.d., in FRANTIC I Operations, AFHRA 670.476-2.

Summer Frenzy

1. Williamson Murray, *Strategy for Defeat: The Luftwaffe, 1933–1945* (Maxwell AFB, Ala.: Air University Press, 1983), pp. 222–226.

2. Ibid., pp. 225–226.

3. R. J. Overy, *The Air War, 1939–1945* (New York: Stein and Day, 1981), p. 75; Murray, p. 277.

4. Chester Wilmot, *Struggle for Europe* (New York: Carroll and Graf, 1952), p. 211; Overy, p. 77.

5. Headquarters, Mediterranean Allied Air Forces, "Plan for Operation 'FRANTIC,' " 22 May 1944, in *History of* FRANTIC, Air Force Historical Research Agency, AFHRA 622.430-6, Folder 1, 26 October 1943–15 June 1944.

6. Headquarters, Fifteenth Air Force, "Fifteenth Air Force Plan for Operation FRANTIC JOE," 28 May 1944, p. 1, in *History of* FRANTIC.

7. Ibid., p. 2.

8. Ibid., p. 11.

9. Ibid., p. 12.

10. Message, U.S. STAF to HQ, Fifteenth Air Force, 2 June 1944 in "FRANTIC Cables, May–October 1944, Book 1," AFHRA 519.476-1; *History of FRANTIC*, p. 21. See also Wesley F. Craven and James L. Cate, *The Army Air Forces in World War II,* 7 vols (Chicago: University of Chicago Press, 1951), vol III, *Europe: ARGUMENT to V-E Day, January 1944–May 1945,* p. 312.

11. HQ, 2nd Bombardment Group, Office of the Intelligence Officer, *War Diary,* "Shuttle Mission to Russia," AFHRA GP-2-SU-RE-D (Bomb), February 1943–December 1944; Maurer Mauer, ed., *Air Force Combat Units of World War II* (Washington, D.C.: USGPO, 1960), pp. 25–28, pp. 166–168.

12. "History of the 99th Bomb Group (H), AAF, for the month of June 1944," AFHRA GP-99-HI, June 1944; "Group History, 483rd Bombardment Group (Heavy)," 1 June 1944 to 30 June 1944, AFHRA GP-483-HI, 1 June 1944; Maurer, pp. 165–166, 170–171, 354–355; Glenn B. Infield, *The Poltava Affair: A Russian Warning, An American Tragedy* (New York: Macmillan, 1973), pp. 60–61

13. "325th Fighter Group History and War Diary, June 1944," AFHRA GP-325-HI, June 1944; Infield, pp. 60–62.

14. Message, Eaker to Spaatz, 2 June 1944 in "FRANTIC Cables, Book 1"; Daniel P. Bolger, "Reluctant Allies: The United States Army Air Force [*sic*] and the Soviet *Voenno Vozdushnie Sily,* 1941–1945," unpublished Ph.D. Dissertation, University of Chicago, 1986, p. 255.

15. John R. Deane, *The Strange Alliance: The Story of Our Efforts at Wartime Cooperation with Russia* (New York: Viking Press, 1947), pp. 119–120.

16. Ibid.; Message, Spaatz to Arnold, 2 June 1944 in "FRANTIC Cables, Book 1"; *History of FRANTIC,* p. 22.

17. Deane, p. 120; Message, Deane to Spaatz, 2 June 1944 in "FRANTIC Cables, Book 1"; *History of FRANTIC,* pp. 22–23; Interview with Colonel C. A. Young, assistant chief of staff, a-2, Fifteenth Air Force, 26 June 1944, Poltava, USSR, by Lt W. W. Taylor, Historical Section.

18. Deane, pp. 120–121; *History of FRANTIC,* p. 23. Eaker was unsuccessful in obtaining Soviet permission for standard air corridors across the front. The Soviets continued to express fears that the Germans would discover and exploit these corridors and that the vigilance of Soviet antiaircraft and fighter units in those sectors would also suffer. Eaker agreed to a system whereby Perminov could arrange clearance within eight hours of an American request. Message, Spaatz to Eaker, Kessler, and Doolittle, quoting Kessler, 13 June 1944 in *History of FRANTIC.*

19. "Translation—Articles in the Soviet Press, June 3rd and 4th, 1944," in *History of FRANTIC.*

20. Message, Joint Chiefs of Staff to Deane, 2 June 1944 in "FRANTIC I Cables, 22 October 1943–16 May 1945," AFHRA 522.1621-1. In this case, FRANTIC I refers to the original operation, not simply the first mission. Plans for a FRANTIC II, commencing in the spring of 1945 from bases in Hungary or Romania, never got off the ground.

21. Department of State, "Communication, The Ambassador in the Soviet Union to President Roosevelt," 11 June 1944 in *Foreign Relations of the United States, 1944,* 7 vols (Washington, D.C.: USGPO, 1966), vol IV, *Europe,* pp. 965–967.

22. Message, Harriman to Arnold, 12 June 1944, in "FRANTIC I Cables."

23. Kessler Diary, entry of April 26, 1944.

24. Office of the Historian, USSTAF, interview with Brigadier General Alfred A. Kessler, C. G. [*sic*], EASCOM, with Dr. Bruce C. Hopper, 5 July 1944, "Eastern Command Term Report," in *The History of Eastern Command, 1941–1944*, AFHRA 522.01-1, vol 2, part I; Headquarters, Eastern Command, "History of AAF Station 560 (Piryatin), April–June 1944," in *History of Eastern Command*, vol 2, part II, Appendix.

25. *History of Eastern Command*, chap 4, "Intelligence," p. 62; Kessler interview.

26. Headquarters, Eastern Command, Office of the Surgeon, "Survey of AAF Station 561 (Mirgorod)," 18 May 1944; "Sanitary Survey of AAF Station 560 (Piryatin)," 7 June 1944 in Miscellaneous Documents Concerning Shuttle Missions to Russia, February–May, 1944, AFHRA 622.430-6, Folder 3.

27. Headquarters, Eastern Command, USSTAF, Office of the Surgeon, "Sanitary Survey of AAF Station 559 (Poltava)," 5 June 1944, in Miscellaneous Documents.

28. Headquarters, Eastern Command, USSTAF, Special Service Office, "Report of Organization of a Special Service Program for the Eastern Command, 15 August 1944," in Eastern Command Term Report.

29. Ibid.

30. Headquarters, Eastern Command, William R. Kaluta, 1st Lt, *History of Eastern Command, 1 October 1944–1 April 1945* in U.S. Military Mission to Moscow, Operation FRANTIC, National Archives, Washington, D.C., NA/RG 344, Box 67, chap 2, p. 20. Cited hereafter as Kaluta I.

31. Headquarters, U.S. Strategic Air Forces in Europe, Deputy Commanding General for Administration, Office of the Surgeon, "Medical Survey of Eastern Command: Report of Sanitary Survey of AAF Station 561," 28 August 1944, in Medical and Morale Reports, Eastern Command, July 1944–June 1945, AFHRA 522.741-2.

32. Headquarters, Eastern Command, USSTAF, Office of the Surgeon, "Supplement to Initial Sanitary Report of Headquarters, EBC, located at AAF Station 559, dated 28 April 1944," 18 May 1944, in Miscellaneous Documents: Brigadier General William C. Crist, Memo to General Deane, n.d., in U.S. Military Mission to Moscow, NA/RG 334, Box 66, "Intelligence"; Headquarters, Eastern Command, Office of the Surgeon, "Report of Tour of American and Soviet Installations Location [*sic*] Near Poltava," 15 June 1944, in Eastern Command Term Report; "Sanitary Survey of AAF Station 560 (Piryatin)," 7 June 1944, in Miscellaneous Documents.

33. American Embassy, U.S. Military Mission to Moscow, Office of the Surgeon, John F. Waldron, Major, Memorandum, "Observations on Requested Subjects: Ration System in Effect in 1944," 30 March 1944, in Miscellaneous Documents Concerning Shuttle Missions.

34. Headquarters, Eastern Command, USSTAF, Office of the Surgeon, William M. Jackson, Lt. Col., "Special Medical Report of Eastern Command, USSTAF," 8 June 1944, p. 3; "Survey of AAF Station 561 (Mirgorod)," 18 May 1944 in Miscellaneous Documents Concerning Shuttle Missions, p. 2.

35. Headquarters, Provisional Eastern Command, USSTAF, Office of the Surgeon, Robert H. Newell, Captain, "Initial Sanitary Report of the Headquarters Area

of Detachment 5, ASC, USSTAF at Poltava," 28 April 1944 in Miscellaneous Documents Concerning Shuttle Missions.

36. "Supplement to Initial Sanitary Report of the Headquarters, EBC," 18 May 1944, pp. 1–2.

37. Ibid., p. 2.

38. Ibid., p. 3.

39. Crist, Memo to Deane; Headquarters, Eastern Command, U.S. Strategic Air Forces in Europe, Office of the Sanitary Engineer, John W. Finney, Major, "Report of Sanitary Survey of AAF Station 559," 23 August 1944, in Medical and Morale Reports, July 1944–June 1945.

40. History of AAF Station 560, pp. 1–2.

41. Ibid.; "Sanitary Survey of AAF Station 560 (Piryatin)," 7 June 1944, p. 2.

42. Ibid.; "Special Medical Report of Eastern Command, USSTAF," 8 June 1944, Exhibit A, "Meeting at Red Air Force Building, 30 March 1944."

43. Headquarters, Fifteenth Air Force, "Narrative Account of Shuttle Mission to Russia (FRANTIC 3)," n.d., in Fifteenth Air Force, Operation FRANTIC II, 22–26 July, and Operation FRANTIC III, 4–6 August 1944, AFHRA 670.476-3. In this instance, Fifteenth Air Force records number FRANTIC missions flown only by units of that numbered air force.

44. "Survey of AAF Station 561 (Mirgorod)," 18 May 1944, p. 2.

45. Headquarters, Eastern Command, U.S. Strategic Air Forces in Europe, Office of the Sanitary Engineer, John W. Finney, Major, "Report of Sanitary Survey of Dispersal Fields," 24 August 1944, in Medical and Morale Reports, July 1944–June 1945, p. 1; Headquarters, 13th Combat Wing, "Report on Operations in Russia," 7 July 1944, section IV, in 13th Combat Wing Report, Eastern Command Mission, June 21 to July 5, 1944, AFHRA 527.476, June–July 1944.

46. Crist, Memo to Deane; "Report of Tour," p. 1.

47. *History of FRANTIC*, pp. 15–16.

48. "Initial Sanitary Report of the Headquarters Area of Detachment 5, ASC, USSTAF, at Poltava," 28 April, p. 1; "Report of Sanitary Survey of AAF Station 559," 23 August 1944.

49. Moller interview; "Report on Operations in Russia," 13th Combat Wing Report, section IV.

50. *History of Eastern Command*, vol 2, part 3, Appendix, Hospital Station 560 (Piryatin), July 1944; Headquarters, Eighth Air Force, "Shuttle Bombing Operations," 15 June 1944, p. 3.

51. Kessler interview; History of AAF Station 560, p. 1; Kaluta I, p. 15; 1st Lt Hanlon E. Davies, Memorandum to Director of Intelligence, USSTAF, Major General Fred L. Anderson, 28 July 1944, in Papers of George C. McDonald, Brig Gen, USAF Academy Library Special Collections, USAF Academy, Colo., MS-16, Series 2, Box 3, Folder 9.

52. Interview with Lou Wampler by author, Colorado Springs, Colo., 13 October 1989; Kaluta I, p. 8.

53. Kessler interview. See also Headquarters, Eighth Air Force, Memorandum for Colonel Kenneth H. Bitting, "Supplement to Report Regarding Personnel Selected for FRANTIC," 9 May 1944 in EASCOM Miscellaneous.

54. Mr. Miller contributed his impressions of Mirgorod to the 390th Bomb

Group's anthology. See Richard H. Perry, Wilbert H. Richarz, William J. Robinson, eds., *The 390th Bomb Group Anthology,* vol 2 (Tucson, Ariz.: 390th Memorial Museum Foundation, 1985), pp. 272–275; Raymond E. Strate, "7000 Mile Shuttle Mission to Russia," in *390th Anthology,* p. 118.

55. McDonald, Memo to Anderson, "Eastern Command, USSTAF," 7 August, 1944.

56. Moller interview.

57. Interview with Leo S. Haynes by author, Colorado Springs, Colo., 13 October 1989; Interview with Major General John S. Warner, USAF, Ret., by author, Colorado Springs, Colo., 13 October 1989.

58. Interview with James Webb by author, Colorado Springs, Colo., 13 October 1989.

59. Alexander Werth, *Russia at War, 1941–45* (London: Barrie and Ruchliff, 1964), p. xviii.

60. Fifteenth Air Force, Operation FRANTIC II, Operation FRANTIC III, "Narrative Account of Shuttle Mission to Russia."

61. 13th Combat Wing Report, Eastern Command Mission, 7 July 1944.

62. Ibid.; Moller interview. Early in March, Arnold approved giving the Soviets an example of the Norden bombsight though the H2X system—over-the-cloud-bombing—was guarded from the Red Air Force.

63. *History of FRANTIC,* pp. 23–24.

64. "Summary of Bomber Operations, Part I," n.d., in Papers of Robert L. Walsh, Maj Gen, MS-12, Folder III, "Poltava Mission," USAF Academy Library Special Collections; Larry C. Lester, Major, USAF, "Project FRANTIC: The Interaction of the Politico-Military Process in American-Soviet Collaboration During World War II," Air Command and Staff College Resident Study, Maxwell AFB, Ala., 1977, Appendix B, p. 104; *History of FRANTIC.*

65. Interview with Colonel Young, 26 June 1944.

66. *History of FRANTIC,* p. 24.

67. Ibid.; Werth, pp. 852–853; "Summary of Bomber Operations, Part I"; *History of FRANTIC.*

68. Lester, p. 105; "Summary of Bomber Operations, Part I"; *History of FRANTIC,* p. 26. One of the escorting P-51s ditched in the Adriatic because of a mechanical failure but a B-17 dropped a dinghy to the pilot, and units from the Air-Sea Rescue Command retrieved him shortly thereafter.

69. Headquarters, Eastern Command, USSTAF, "Russian Attitude and Reaction," 16 June 1944, in *The History of Eastern Command, 1941-1944,* vol II, part 3, Appendix, Annex 5; Message, Eaker to Twining, quoted in *History of FRANTIC,* p. 26.

70. Headquarters, Eighth Air Force, Office of the Commanding General, "Shuttle Bombing Operations Utilizing Bases in Russia, Operation 'FRANTIC,' " 15 June 1944 in Mission to Russia, 21 June–5 July 1944, AFHRA 527.476.

71. Harry H. Crosby, *A Wing and a Prayer: The "Bloody 100th" Bomb Group of the U.S. Eighth Air Force in Action over Europe in World War II* (New York: Harper Collins, 1993), p. 104.

72. Maurer, pp. 163–165; 277–278.

73. Ibid., pp. 165–166; 275–276; 326–328; Infield, p. 129.

74. Ibid., pp. 129–130; Maurer, pp. 35–36; 231–233.

75. U.S. Air Force Oral History Program, "Interview of Lt Gen Archie J. Old, Jr.," by Hugh N. Ahmann, 26 October–2 November 1982, Riverside, Calif., AFHRA K239.0512-1357, p. v.

76. Lester, p. 107; Headquarters, 45th Combat Bombardment Wing, Archie J. Old, Jr., Colonel, task force commander, "Report on Shuttle Mission to Russia," 6 July 1944, in 45th Combat Wing Report, 6 July 1944, AFHRA WG-45-SU-OP; Message, Spaatz to Deane, 22 June 1944.

77. "Report on Shuttle Mission to Russia," p. 3.

78. Ibid.; Crist, Memo to Deane; Headquarters, Ninety-Fifth Bombardment Group (H), Office of the Operations Officer, "FRANTIC Missions of the 21, 26 June 1944 [*sic*] and 3, 5 July 1944," 6 July 1944 in 13th Combat Wing Report, Eastern Command Mission.

79. "Report on Shuttle Mission to Russia," p. 3.

80. Moller interview; John F. Kreis, *Air Warfare and Air Base Air Defense* (Washington, D.C: Office of Air Force History, 1988), p. 207.

81. Ibid., p. 207; Crist, Memo to Deane; "Report on Shuttle Mission to Russia," p. 3; Headquarters, Eastern Command, USSTAF, "Report of Proceedings of Board of Officers," 2 August 1944, p. 2, in *History of Eastern Command,* Appendix.

82. "Report of Proceedings of the Board of Officers," p. 2; "Report on Shuttle Mission to Russia," p. 4.

83. Ibid.; *History of FRANTIC,* p. 25; "Report on Shuttle Mission to Russia," p. 3; "Report of Proceedings of Board of Officers," p. 2.

84. Headquarters, Eastern Command, USSTAF, "Observation of Medical Service during Air Attack," 25 June 1944, p. 2, Exhibit "A," in 381 Project #1, Medical Reports, February–June 1944, AFHRA 522.741-1.

85. Ibid., Exhibit "B."

86. Ibid., p. 4.

87. "Report of Proceedings of Board of Officers," p. 3; "Report on Shuttle Mission to Russia," p. 3; Headquarters, Army Air Forces, Mediterranean Theater of Operations, P/W Intelligence, "A Lesson in Security," 6 August 1945, in Mediterranean Theater of Operations, Intelligence Reports, February–September 1945, AFHRA 632.619-4. See also Cajus Bekker, *The Luftwaffe War Diaries,* translated and edited by Frank Ziegler (Garden City, N.J.: Doubleday, 1968), p. 529. See also Adolf Galland, *The First and the Last: The Rise and Fall of the German Fighter Forces, 1938–1945,* translated by Mervyn Savill (New York: Holt, 1954), pp. 286–287.

88. Kreis, p. 208; "Report on Shuttle Mission to Russia," p. 4; "Report of Proceedings of Board of Officers," p. 3.

89. Headquarters, Eastern Command, USSTAF, Office of the Surgeon, "Report of Activity of Two Russian Soldiers During Emergency of 22 June 1944," to commanding General, Eastern Command, 24 June 1944, p. 1, 381 Project #1.

90. Ibid., pp. 1–2.

91. "Report of Shuttle Mission to Russia," p. 3; Haynes interview.

92. Moller interview.

93. "Observation of Medical Service during Air Attack," pp. 2–3.

94. Von Hardesty, *Red Phoenix: The Rise of Soviet Air Power* (Washington, D.C.:

Smithsonian Institution Press, 1982), p. 201; "Report of Proceedings of Board of Officers," p. 4.

95. Kreis, pp. 208–211; "Report on Shuttle Mission to Russia," p. 4; Headquarters, 13th Combat Wing, "13th CBW Summary, FRANTIC Mission," in "Report on Operations in Russia," 7 July 1944; Crist, Memo for Deane.

96. Deane, p. 122; Message, Deane to Arnold, 25 June 1944 in FRANTIC I Cables; Message, Deane to Spaatz, 23 June 1944 in NA/RG 334, Box 5, "Communiques."

97. Kreis, pp. 209–211. Hardesty, *Red Phoenix,* also provides a very detailed examination of the development of Soviet air doctrine, organization, and equipment.

98. Message, Deane to Arnold, 24 June 1944 in FRANTIC I Cables. See also, for example, M. N. Kozhevnikov, *The Command and Staff of the Soviet Army Air Force in the Great Patriotic War, 1941–1945,* translated and published under the auspices of the U.S. Air Force (Washington, D.C.: USGPO, 1977), pp. 190–191; A. V. Nikitin, " 'Chelnochnye' operatsiy," *Voenno-Istoricheskiy Zhurnal* 11 (1975): 41–46.

99. Crist, Memo for Deane; Headquarters, Eastern Command, USSTAF, Memorandum, "GAF Threat to USAAF Airfields in Russia," 16 June 1944 in McDonald Papers, Box 4. Refer to "Meeting at Aviation General Staff Headquarters," 11 March 1944 in Progress of FRANTIC Project, Exhibit "D."

100. See Richard Muller, *The German Air War in Russia* (Baltimore: Nautical and Aviation, 1992), particularly chaps 4 and 5.

101. Headquarters, Eastern Command, U.S. Strategic Air Forces in Europe, "Report on Status of Morale in the Eastern Command," 5 October 1944 in Special Events of Eastern Command, Gen. Kessler, 15 August–10 October 1944, AFHRA 522.0591-2.

102. Brigadier General George C. McDonald, Memorandum to Major General Fred Anderson, "Eastern Command, USSTAF," 7 August 1944 in McDonald Papers, Box 6, Folder 7; Moller interview; Jospeh A. Moller, letter to the author, May 14, 1991.

103. Seaton, p. 436; John Erickson, *The Road to Berlin: Continuing the History of Stalin's War with Germany* (Boulder, Colo.: Westview Press, 1983), p. 214; Earl F. Ziemke, *Stalingrad to Berlin: The German Defeat in the East* (Washington, D.C.: Center of Military History, U.S. Army, 1968), p. 315. See also David M. Glantz and Jonathan M. House, *When Titans Clashed: How the Red Army Stopped Hitler* (Lawrence, Kans.: University Press of Kansas, 1995), chap 13. For more detailed analyses of this pivotal campaign, see Gerd Niepold, *Battle for White Russia: The Destruction of Army Group Centre, June 1944,* translated by Richard Simpkin (London: Brassey's Defence, 1987); and Paul Adair, *Hitler's Greatest Defeat: The Collapse of Army Group Centre, June 1944* (London: Arms and Armour Press, 1994).

104. Letter, Deane to Slavin, 10 July 1944 in NA/RG 334, Box 63, "Airdrome Defense."

105. Minutes of Meeting, 27 June 1944 in NA/RG 334, Box 63, "Airdrome Defense."

106. 13th Combat Wing Report, Eastern Command Mission, 7 July 1944; "Summary of Bomber Operations, Part I."

107. Lester, Appendix "D," pp. 111–112; 15th Air Force Operation FRANTIC II, 22–26 July 1944, Operation FRANTIC III, 4–6 August 1944, p. 1.

Summer Breakdown

1. Headquarters, Eastern Command, USSTAF, Office of the Inspector General, Ralph P. Dunn, Major, IGD, "Special Investigation into Russian-American Relations in and about Poltava, Russia," 14 July 1944, "Statement of Sergeant Doc B. Blalock," in Soviet-American Relations, File I, part I, July–September 1944, Air Force Historical Research Agency, Maxwell AFB, Ala., AFHRA 522.2941.

2. "Statement of 1st Lt Edward A. Coutts, 13 July 1944," in Soviet-American Relations.

3. "Statement of T/4 Judson J. Sorrell, 12 July 1944," in Soviet-American Relations.

4. Office of Headquarters Commandant, Eastern Command, USSTAF, Albert Lepawsky, Major, "Reported Incidents Involving American Soldiers and Russian Personnel," 10 July 1944, in Headquarters, Eastern Command, Albert Lepawsky, *History of Eastern Command, USSTAF,* November 1944, Appendix; "Statement of T/Sgt Ralph N. Mowery, 12 July 1944," in Soviet-American Relations.

5. "Statement of Cpl Peter M. Nicolaef, 13 July 1944," in Soviet-American Relations.

6. Ibid.; See also Frederick C. Barghoorn, *The Soviet Image of the United States: A Study in Distortion* (New York: Harcourt, Brace, 1950), pp. 44–46.

7. "Reported Incidents Involving American Soldiers."

8. "Special Investigation into Russian-American Relations."

9. Headquarters, U.S. Strategic Air Forces in Europe, Office of the Director of Intelligence, George C. McDonald, Brigadier General, "FRANTIC," 21 August 1944 in Appreciation of FRANTIC, 21 August 1944, AFHRA 522.609–1; Headquarters, U.S. Strategic Air Forces in Europe, Office of the Director of Intelligence, George C. McDonald, Brigadier General, Memorandum, "Eastern Command, USSTAF," to Major General Fred L. Anderson, Director of Operations, USSTAF, 7 August 1944, in McDonald Papers, MS-16, Box 6, Folder 7, USAF Academy Library, Special Collections.

10. Headquarters, Eastern Command, Office, Deputy Commander for Operations, P. T. Cullen, Colonel, to Commanding General, Eastern Command, USSTAF, 17 July 1944 in Soviet-American Relations.

11. Ibid.

12. Headquarters, Eastern Command, USSTAF, Office of the Intelligence Officer, Daniel S. Feidt, Captain, "Report of Sgt George Witenko on Incident in [Poltava] on the Evening of 11 July 1944," 12 July 1944 in Soviet-American relations; U.S. Military Mission to Moscow, Office of the Surgeon, "Conversations on Requested Subjects," 30 March 1944; Headquarters, Eastern Command, USSTAF, Office of the Surgeon, "Special Medical Report of Eastern Command, USSTAF," 8 June 1944, both in Miscellaneous Documents Concerning Shuttle Missions to Russia, AFHRA 622.430–6; *History of Eastern Command,* vol 2, part 3, Appendix, pp. 5–6.

13. McDonald, Memo to Anderson, 7 August 1944.

14. Ibid.; Headquarters, Fifteenth Air Force, "Narrative Account of Shuttle Mission to Russia (FRANTIC III)," n.d., in Fifteenth Air Force Operation FRANTIC II, 22–26 July 1944; Operation FRANTIC III, 4–6 August 1944, AFHRA 670.476-3.

15. John Erickson, *The Road to Berlin: Continuing the History of Stalin's War with Germany* (Boulder, Colo.: Westview Press, 1983), p. 234; Department of State, "Telegram, The Ambassador in the Soviet Union to the Secretary of State," 15 July 1944, in *Foreign Relations of the United States, 1944,* 7 vols (Washington, D.C.: USGPO, 1966), vol IV, p. 893.

16. Hanlon E. Davies, 1st Lt, Memorandum to Director of Intelligence, USSTAF, 28 July 1944, in McDonald Papers, Series 2, Box 3, Folder 9; Hugh J. Knerr, Major General, Memorandum to Commanding General, USSTAF, " 'FRANTIC' Logistic Situation," 24 August 1944 in Eastern Command, Miscellaneous Correspondence, Memos, and Messages, June–September 1944, AFHRA 522.161.

17. *History of the Eastern Command, USSTAF,* chap 4, Intelligence, pp. 54–55; Message, Surles to Deane, n.d., in U.S. Military Mission to Moscow; Operation FRANTIC, Washington, D.C., National Archives, NA/RG 334, Box 5, Communiques.

18. Lepawsky, p. 55.

19. John Gunther, "Why We Can and Must Beat Germany This Year, "*The Reader's Digest,* August 1944, pp. 5–8; Lepawsky, p. 56.

20. Headquarters, U.S. Strategic Air Forces in Europe, Office of the Commanding General, Memorandum to All Unit Commanders, "Interviews Regarding Russia," 2 August 1944 in FRANTIC, June–July 1944, AFHRA 527.476; Headquarters, Eastern Command, USSTAF, Memorandum, Major General Walsh to Personnel Leaving Eastern Command, "Security, Eastern Command, U.S. Strategic Air Forces in Europe," 15 September 1944 in *History of Eastern Command,* Appendix.

21. Unofficial Memo, to Maj Gen Hugh J. Knerr from Steven J. Zand, Civilian Air Technician, 11 October 1944, p. 2 in *History of Eastern Command, USSTAF,* Appendix, vol 2, part 3.

22. McDonald, Memo to Anderson, 7 August 1944, p. 4; William R. Kaluta, 1st Lt, *History of Eastern Command, 15 October 1944–15 April 1945,* chap 2, "Dates (NKVD)," NA/RG 334, Box 67, Kaluta, History, pp. 26–32.

23. Headquarters, Eastern Command, U.S. Strategic Air Forces in Europe, Special Service Office, Charles M. Heintzelman, Captain, "Report of Organization of a Special Service Program for the Eastern Command," 15 August 1944 in Eastern Command Term Report, *History of Eastern Command,* vol 2, part 1, 1941–44, 522.01-1.

24. Headquarters, Eastern Command, U.S. Strategic Air Forces in Europe, "Report on Status of Morale in the Eastern Command," to Commanding General, Eastern Command, 5 October 1944, p. 2, in Special Events of EASCOM, General Kessler, 15 August–10 October 1944, AFHRA 522.0591-2.

25. Ibid.

26. Headquarters, Eastern Command, "History of AAF Station 560 (Piryatin)," July 1944, in *History of Eastern Command,* Appendix.

27. "Report on Status of Morale," p. 5; McDonald, Memo to Anderson, p. 4.

28. Ibid.

29. "Report on Status of Morale," p. 5; "History of AAF Station 560," p. 1.
30. "Report on Status of Morale," p. 4.
31. Davies, Memo to Director of Intelligence, p. 2.
32. Ralph P. Dunn, Memorandum to Brigadier General Kessler, 2 August 1944, p. 1; Office of the Liaison Officer, AAF Station 561, Eastern Command, Elias Bacha, 1st Lt, "Sales of American Goods to Soviet Civilians," 27 July 1944 to Commanding Officer, AAF Station 561, both of which are in Soviet-American Relations. V-mail was mail transmitted overseas during World War II on microfilm, and enlarged at the point of reception. This procedure helped eliminate bulky shipments of personal mail between soldiers, sailors, and airmen and their families and friends.
33. Dunn, Memo to Kessler, p. 1.
34. "Sales of American Goods"; Headquarters, AAF Station 561, Eastern Command, Elias Bacha, 1st Lt, Memorandum, "Driving Vehicles on the Poltava-Mirgorod Road," 27 July 1944 in Soviet-American Relations File.
35. Letter, Perminov to Colonel L. B. Hickam, Deputy Commander for Administration, Eastern Command, n.d., in Soviet-American Relations File.
36. Letter, Hickam to Perminov, 22 July 1944; Ralph Dunn, Major and George Grant, 1st Lt, Memorandum, 29 July 1944; Memorandum for File, reference Court Martial Record, Case #1, Headquarters, Eastern Command, USSTAF.
37. Ralph P. Dunn, Major, Inspector General, Memorandum for File, n.d. in Soviet-American Relations File.
38. Dunn, Memo to Kessler.
39. Gordon Wright, *Ordeal of Total War, 1939–1945* (New York: Harper and Row, 1968), p. 137. For a detailed analysis of German policies, in the Soviet Union, see Alexander Dallin, *German Rule in Russia, 1941–1945: A Study of Occupation Policies* (Boulder, Colo.: Westview Press, 1981); Erickson, p. 182.
40. McDonald, Memo to Anderson, p. 6.
41. "Report on Status of Morale," p. 2.
42. Ibid., pp. 2–3.
43. Ibid., p. 4.
44. Knerr, Memorandum to Commanding General, USSTAF, 24 August 1944, p. 1.
45. Headquarters, Mediterranean Allied Air Forces, Hugh J. Knerr, Major General, Memorandum to Commanding General, ASC, U.S. Strategic Air Forces in Europe, "Report of Visit to the Eastern Command," 6 September 1944, pp. 1–2, in Papers of Hugh J. Knerr, MS-8, Box 7, USAF Academy Library Special Collections.
46. Ibid., pp. 3–4.
47. Knerr, Memorandum to Commanding General, USSTAF, 6 September 1944, p. 4.
48. Ibid., p. 5.
49. Knerr, Memorandum to Commanding General, USSTAF, 24 August 1944, p. 2
50. Ronald H. Spector, *Eagle Against the Sun: The American War with Japan* (New York: Vintage Books, 1985), pp. 301–320.
51. Message, Eaker to Spaatz, 1 August 1944, in McDonald Papers, Box 4, Folder 1.
52. Erickson, pp. 272–273.
53. U.S. Embassy in Moscow, Minutes of Conversation, American ambassador, Mr. Harriman with A. Y. Vyshinski, Assistant People's Commissar for Foreign Af-

fairs, 21 July 1944 in U.S. Military Mission in Moscow, Operation FRANTIC, NA/RG 334, Box 63, Air Defense. Earlier in the month, Harriman communicated directly with Soviet Foreign Minister V. Molotov about the issue of expanding the American air defense role at Eastern Command.

54. Summary of Fighter Operations, part I, in Papers of Robert L. Walsh, MS-12, Folder III, "Poltava Mission," USAF Academy Library Special Collections.

55. Message, Walsh to Spaatz, 2 August 1944 in FRANTIC, May–October 1944, Book 2, AFHRA 519.476-1.

56. Summary of Bomber Operations, in Walsh Papers; Headquarters, Eighth Air Force, "Report of Shuttle Bombing Mission, 6–12 August, 1944," to Commanding General, Army Air Forces, Washington, D.C., 19 May 1945, pp. 1–2 in Eighth Air Force Tactical Mission Report, Operation #523, Report of Shuttle Bombing Mission, 6–12 August 1944, AFHRA 520.331.

57. "Report of Shuttle Bombing Mission, 6–12 August 1944," pp. 4–6.

58. Headquarters, 390th Bombardment Group, Office of the Intelligence Officer, Waldo E. Hardell, Major, Letter to Colonel Carl Norcross, A-2, Third Bombardment Division, 11 July 1944, Addendum, in FRANTIC, June–July 1944, AFHRA 527.476.

59. Interview with Joseph A. Moller, 13 October 1989, Colorado Springs, Colo.

60. Ibid. See Letter from Colonel Kovalev to Colonel Cullen, 4 August 1944 in Eastern Command Term report in *History of Eastern Command*.

61. Earl F. Ziemke, *Stalingrad to Berlin: The German Defeat in the East* (Washington, D.C.: Center for Military History, 1966), pp. 329–331.

62. Ibid., pp. 340–345.

63. Ibid., 346–358; Erickson, pp. 356–369.

64. Message, Deane to Spaatz, 15 August 1944; Message, Kessler to Spaatz, 16 August 1944 both in FRANTIC I Cables, 22 October 1943–16 May 1945, AFHRA 522.1621-1; *History of Eastern Command,* chap 5, Intelligence; Message, Kessler to Spaatz, 22 August 1944; Minutes of Meeting, Brigadier General Kessler and Major General Perminov, translated by Lt Grant, 22 August 1944, in FRANTIC VII, AFHRA 522.312-1.

65. McDonald to Deputy Commander for Operations, USSTAF, pp. 1–2.

66. Ibid., p. 2; Williamson Murray, *Strategy for Defeat: The Luftwaffe, 1933–1945* (Maxwell AFB, Ala.: Air University Press, 1983), p. 285.

67. McDonald, p. 7.

68. Message, Deane to Arnold, 25 August 1944; Message, Deane to Arnold, 28 August 1944 both in FRANTIC I Cables, AFHRA 522.1621-1.

69. American Embassy, Moscow, Letter, Harriman to Molotov, 29 August 1944 in NA/RG 334, Box 63, Airdrome Defense; Message, Deane to Walsh, 31 August 1944 in EASCOM Messages, July 24, 1944 to August 25, 1944, AFHRA 522.162-6.

70. Message, Arnold to Deane, 5 September 1944 in McDonald Papers, Box 4, Folder 2.

71. Operations Narrative, Mission 172, 390th Bomb Group, 16 August 1944.

72. Ibid., p. 2.

73. Headquarters, Eastern Command, U.S. Strategic Air Forces in Europe, Office of the Inspector General, Ralph P. Dunn, Major, "Investigation of Incident at Russian Restaurant, AAF Station 561, on 17 August 1944," 1 September 1944 to Commanding General, Eastern Command, pp. 2–3, in Soviet-American Relations File.

74. Ibid., p. 2.

75. Ibid., p. 3.

76. Ibid., pp. 3–4.

77. Letter, Perminov to Kessler, 21 August 1944; Letter, Kessler to Perminov, 2 September 1944, both in Soviet-American Relations File.

78. "Investigation of Incident," p. 5; Headquarters, Eastern Command, U.S. Strategic Air Forces in Europe, "Transmittal of Statements," to Commanding General, U.S. Strategic Air Forces in Europe, 2 September 1944 in Soviet-American Relations File; Headquarters, Eastern Command, U.S. Strategic Air Forces in Europe, "Administrative Reprimand, Carter, James I.," 2 September 1944; "Investigation of Incident," both in Soviet-American Relations File.

79. William R. Kaluta, 1st Lt, *History of Eastern Command, October 1944–March 1945*, chapter 8, "Politics," pp. 120–121.

80. Message, Deane to Spaatz, 9 May 1944 in McDonald Papers, Box 4, Folder 1.

81. Memorandum, McDonald to Spaatz, 29 July 1944 in McDonald Papers, Box 3, Folder 9; Kaluta, p. 122.

82. Statement of Lt Col Aram S. Tootelian, 31 August 1944; Memorandum, Hanlon E. Davies, 1st Lt, to Director of Intelligence, USSTAF, 28 July 1944; both in McDonald Papers, Box 3, Folder 9.

83. Memorandum, McDonald to Spaatz, 29 July 1944 in McDonald Papers, Box 3, Folder 9.

84. Memorandum, Davies to McDonald, 3 August 1944; Letter, McDonald to Colonel J. S. Allard, Chief of Staff, Headquarters, Eighth Air Force, 7 August 1944; Memo, McDonald to Headquarters, 1st Bombardment Division, 19 October 1944.

85. Eastern Command, U.S. Strategic Air Forces in Europe, Office of the Inspector General, "Special Investigation under AR 20–30, dated 23 May 1942," to Commanding General Eastern Command, 16 September 1944, p. 1 in Soviet-American Relations file.

86. "Special Investigation," 16 September 1944, p. 2.

87. Eastern Command, U.S. Strategic Air Forces in Europe, Office of the Inspector General, "Special Investigation under AR 20–30, dated 23 May, 1942," to commanding general, Eastern Command, 18 September 1944, pp. 1–2, in Soviet-American Relations File.

88. Unsigned Memorandum for Record, 20 September, attached to Report of Conference with General Perminov, 14 September 1944 in Soviet-American Relations File.

89. Letter, Harriman to Molotov, 29 August 1944 in NA/RG 334, Box 63, Airdrome Defense.

90. Daily Summary, 4 September 1944 in General Kessler, Special Events of Eastern Command.

Mission to Warsaw

1. Julian Eugeniusz Kulski, *Dying, We Live: The Personal Chronicle of a Young Freedom Fighter in Warsaw, 1939–1945* (New York: Holt, Rinehart, and Winston, 1979), p. 197.

2. Earl F. Ziemke, *Stalingrad to Berlin: The German Defeat in the East* (Wash-

ington, D.C.: Center for Military History, 1968), p. 341; Message 301, "Secret and Personal from Premier J. V. Stalin to the Prime Minister, Mr. W. Churchill, July 23, 1944," in *Stalin's Correspondence with Churchill, Attlee, Roosevelt and Truman, 1941–45* (New York: E. P. Dutton, 1958), pp. 241–242, hereafter referred to as *Stalin's Correspondence.* For a full account of the organization and structure of the Polish underground, see Stefan Korbonski, *The Polish Underground State: A Guide to the Underground, 1939–1945* (New York: Columbia University Press, 1978).

3. Message No. 150, Stalin to Churchill, April 21, 1943; Message No. 156, Stalin to Churchill, May 4, 1943 in *Stalin's Correspondence.* See also Stanislaw Mikolajczyk, *The Rape of Poland: A Pattern of Soviet Aggression* (New York: McGraw-Hill, 1948), chap 4.

4. Neil Orpen, *Airlift to Warsaw: The Rising of 1944* (Norman, Okla.: University of Oklahoma Press, 1984), p. 8. See also Herbert Feis, *Churchill, Roosevelt, Stalin: The War They Waged, The Peace They Sought* (Princeton, N.J.: Princeton University Press, 1957), pp. 376–377; Mikolajczyk, pp. 53–54; Tadeusz Bor-Komorowski, *The Secret Army* (Nashville: Battery Press, 1984), pp. 184–85, 193.

5. Department of State, *Foreign Relations of the United States: Diplomatic Papers, 1944*, 7 vols (Washington, D.C.: USGPO, 1965), vol III, *The British Commonwealth and Europe*, pp. 1216–1217, "Telegram, Text of Statement, from Charge to the Polish Government in Exile (Shoenfeld) to the Secretary of State," 5 January 1944, hereafter referred to as *FRUS.*

6. John Erickson, *The Road to Berlin: Continuing the History of Stalin's War with Germany* (Boulder, Colo.: Westview Press, 1983), pp. 259–265.

7. Ibid., pp. 270–271.

8. Kulski, p. 198; Bor-Komorowski, pp. 201–205, 213–215.

9. Feis, pp. 376–377; Mikolajczyk, p. 61.

10. Orpen, pp. 25–27.

11. In this regard, historians John Erickson, Earl Ziemke, Alan Clark, David Glantz, and Jonathan House agree that Rokossovskii's men were at the end of their tethers and suffering from vicious German counterattacks. At the same time, mustering the necessary force to break through the line opposite Warsaw would have required a major shifting of Soviet forces along the front. For his own account of events outside Warsaw, see Konstantin Rokossovskii, *A Soldier's Duty* (Moscow: Progress, 1985), pp. 254–263.

12. Ziemke, pp. 340–341; David M. Glantz and Jonathan M. House, *When Titans Clashed: How the Red Army Stopped Hitler* (Lawrence, Kans.: University Press of Kansas, 1995), pp. 212–214. See also G. K. Zhukov, *The Memoirs of Marshal Zhukov* (New York: Delacorte Press, 1971), pp. 551–552.

13. Orpen, p. 58; Erickson, p. 272.

14. Ibid.

15. Ibid. See also Bruce Quarrie, *Hitler's Samurai: The Waffen S.S. in Action* (Wellingborough, U.K.: Patrick Stephens, 1986), p. 14.

16. Orpen, p. 59; Ziemke, p. 344. In an interesting twist, the Germans soon tired of Kaminski and his refusal to obey orders. Even Bach-Zelewski was appalled by his ferocity. German S.S. troops killed Kaminski some four weeks into the operation, making his murder appear to be a Polish ambush, complete with bullet-ridden car and a liberal application of animal blood. See Erickson, p. 400.

17. Orpen, p. 55.

18. Message No. 311, Churchill to Stalin, 4 August 1944; Message No. 313, Stalin to Churchill, 5 August 1944, in *Stalin's Correspondence*, pp. 248–249; Orpen, p. 64.

19. Ibid.

20. Message No. 317, Churchill to Stalin, 12 August 1944 in *Stalin's Correspondence*, p. 252. See Richard C. Lukas, "The RAF and the Warsaw Uprising," *Aerospace Historian* (December 1975): 188–194; Thomas A. Julian, "The Role of the United States Army Air Forces in the Warsaw Uprising, Aug–Sep 1944," *Airpower History* 42 (Summer 1995): 22–35.

21. Message No. 321, Stalin to Churchill, August 16, 1944 in *Stalin's Correspondence*, p. 254. For his version of the meeting in Moscow, see Mikolajczyk, pp. 72–78.

22. Orpen, p. 125.

23. Harriman, quoted in Feis, p. 386; Message No. 322, Roosevelt and Churchill to Stalin, 20 August 1944; Message No. 323, Stalin to Roosevelt and Churchill, 22 August 1944 in *Stalin's Correspondence*, pp. 254–255.

24. "Minutes of Conference with Mr. Harry Hopkins at 11:00 A. M. at the White House, 7 September 1944" in Warsaw Dropping Operations, 13 August–5 October 1944, Air Force Historical Research Agency, Maxwell AFB, Ala., AFHRA 519.476-2.

25. Daily Summaries, 15 August and 16 August 1944 in General Kessler, Special Events of Eastern Command, 15 August–10 October 1944, AFHRA 522.0591-2, p. 1; Message, Deane to Spaatz, 15 August 1944; Message, Kessler to Spaatz, 16 August 1944 both in FRANTIC 1 Cables, 22 October 1943–16 May 1945, AFHRA 522.1621-1; Daily Summary, 23 August 1944 in Special Events, p. 3.

26. Message, Deane to Spaatz, 22 August 1944 in "FRANTIC 7-Operation #1, Cables Pertaining to this Operation," in FRANTIC, May–October 1944, Book 3, AFHRA 519.476-1.

27. Kulski, p. 244; Ziemke, p. 344; Rokossovskii, p. 260.

28. Kulski; Ziemke; Erickson, p. 274. See also Alan Clark, *Barbarossa; The Russian-German Conflict, 1941–45* (New York: Morrow, 1965), p. 392.

29. John R. Deane, *The Strange Alliance: The Story of Our Efforts at Wartime Cooperation with Russia* (New York: Viking Press, 1947), p. 123.

30. See Daily Summaries through late August in Special Events of Eastern Command.

31. Department of State, *Foreign Relations of the United States, 1944*, vol IV, *Europe*, "The Ambassador in the Soviet Union (Harriman) to Mr. Harry L. Hopkins, Special Assistant to President Roosevelt, 10 September 1944," pp. 988–990.

32. Memo for File, Minutes of Meeting, 14 September 1944, in Soviet-American Relations, File I, part I, July–September 1944, AFHRA 522.2941.

33. Headquarters, Eastern Command, U.S. Strategic Air Forces in Europe, AAF Station 561, Letter, Lt Col Charles Dahlberg to Commanding General, Eastern Command, "Report of Incident of Unauthorized Photographs," 20 September 1944; Memorandum for File, 20 September 1944, both in Soviet-American Relations File.

34. Minutes of Meeting, 14 September 1944; Memorandum for File, 20 September 1944, both in Soviet-American Relations File.

35. Statement of Michael Dubiaga, 1st Lt, n.d., in Soviet-American Relations File.

36. Ibid.

37. Memorandum for File, 20 September 1944; Headquarters, Eastern Command, "Notice of Intention to Impose Punishment under the 104th Article of War," to 1st Lt Cherry C. Carpenter, 13 September 1944; "Notice of Intention to Impose Punishment under the 104th Article of War," to 2nd Lt Igor C. Reverditto, 13 September 1944, in Soviet-American Relations File.

38. Headquarters, Eastern Command, U.S. Strategic Air Forces in Europe, Air Traffic Section, "Report of Incident between American and Russian Personnel," to Commanding General, Eastern Command, USSTAF, 26 September 1944 in Soviet-American Relations File.

39. Ibid.

40. Statement of Master Sergeant Orval O. Moore, 21 September 1944 in Soviet-American Relations File; Headquarters, Eastern Command, U.S. Strategic Air Forces in Europe, AAF Station 561, "Investigation," to Commanding Officer, Detachment #3, Headquarters, Eastern Command, U.S. Strategic Air Forces in Europe, AAF Station 561, 21 September 1944; Headquarters, Eastern Command, U.S. Strategic Air Forces in Europe, AAF Station 561, "Altercation at Mirgorod Restaurant," to Commanding Officer, Headquarters, Eastern Command, from Charles W. Dahlberg, Lt Col, 22 September 1944, in Soviet-American Relations File.

41. Headquarters, Eastern Command, U.S. Strategic Air Forces in Europe, "Official Report," to Commanding General, Headquarters, EC, USSTAF, 25 September 1944 in Soviet-American Relations File.

42. *FRUS,* vol IV, Telegram, "The Ambassador in the Soviet Union (Harriman) to the Secretary of State," 20 September 1944, pp. 992–998.

43. Daily Summaries, Special Events of Eastern Command, pp. 6–8.

44. Ibid.; Message, Deane to Spaatz, info Walsh, 15 September 1944 in Papers of Brigadier General George C. McDonald, MS-16, Box 4, Folder 1, USAF Academy Library Special Collections.

45. Headquarters, Third Bombardment Division, "Tactical Report of Mission, FRANTIC VI-Chemnitz, 11 September 1944," n.d. in FRANTIC, 18–19 September 1944, AFHRA 527.476B; "Information on Shuttle Missions: World War II," September 1959, AFHRA K110.7007-4, Special Project File; "Tactical Report of Mission, FRANTIC VI,"; "Summary of Bomber Operations," Papers of Robert L. Walsh, MS-12, Folder III, "Poltava Mission," USAF Academy Library Special Collections, USAF Academy, Colorado.

46. "Summary of Bomber Operations," Walsh Papers, Folder III, "Poltava Mission"; U.S. Strategic Bombing Survey, *Auto Union AG, Chemnitz and Zwickau,* Book 84 (Washington, D.C.: USGPO, 1947), p. 15.

47. Message, Spaatz to Walsh, info Eaker, 11 September 1944 in FRANTIC, May–October 1944, Book 3, AFHRA 519.476-1; Daily Summary, 12 September 1944, Special Events of Eastern command, p. 10.

48. Crew Comment Extract in "Tactical Report of Mission FRANTIC VI."

49. Ibid.

50. Headquarters, 3rd Bombardment Division, "Tactical Report of Mission,

FRANTIC VI-Dyosgyor, Hungary," n.d., in FRANTIC, 18–19 September 1944, AFHRA 527.476B

51. Bor-Komorowski, pp. 337–338; Ziemke, pp. 344–345; Rokossovskii, p. 260.

52. "Message of the Soviet Government in Reply to Message of the British Government of 5th [*sic*] September 1944," Moscow, 9 September 1944 in Records of the U.S. Military Mission to Moscow, NA/RG 334, Box 22, Poland, National Archives, Washington, D.C.

53. Message, Curtis to Spaatz, 11 September 1944 in FRANTIC, Book 3; Message, Deane to Spaatz, info Arnold, 11 September 1944; Message, Arnold to Spaatz, 11 September 1944 in FRANTIC, May–October 1944, Book 3; Message, Eisenhower to Joint Chiefs of Staff, 12 September 1944 in McDonald Papers, Box 4, Folder 1; Message, Spaatz to Walsh, 12 September 1944 in FRANTIC, Book 3.

54. Message, Curtis to Spaatz, 15 September 1944; Message, Spaatz to Walsh, 16 September 1944 in FRANTIC, Book 3.

55. Bor-Komorowski, p. 342.

56. Ibid., p.343.

57. Kulski, p. 250.

58. Bor-Komorowski, pp. 344–347.

59. Ibid.; Zhukov, p. 550.

60. Marvin W. McFarland, "Air Power and the Warsaw Uprising, August–September 1944," *Air Power Historian* 3 (January 1956): 186–194.

61. Chester Wilmot, *Struggle for Europe* (New York: Carroll and Graf, 1952), pp. 484–485.

62. Ibid., pp. 501–502; Message, Spaatz to Doolittle, 16 September 1944 in FRANTIC, Book 3.

63. Message, Walsh to Spaatz, 13 September 1944 in McDonald Papers, Box 4, Folder 1; Message, Curtis to Spaatz, 18 September 1944 in FRANTIC, Book 3. See Wilmot, chaps XXVI and XXVII; and Cornelius Ryan, *A Bridge Too Far* (New York: Simon and Schuster, 1974).

64. Summary of Bomber Operations, part I; Summary of Fighter Operations, part I, both in Papers of Robert L. Walsh, MS-12, Folder III, "Poltava Mission," USAF Academy Library Special Collections; Message, Curtis to Spaatz, 18 September 1944 in FRANTIC, Book 3.

65. Interview with Bernie J. Campbell, commander of the 568th Bomb Squadron, 390th Bomb Group, Colorado Springs, Colo., October 13, 1989; Headquarters, Third Bombardment Division, "Tactical Report of Mission, FRANTIC VII-WARSAW, 18 September 1944," n.d., in FRANTIC, 18–19 September, 1944.

66. Larry C. Lester, Major, USAF, "Project FRANTIC: The Interaction of the Politico-Military Process in American-Soviet Collaboration During World War II," Air Command and Staff College Resident Study, AFHRA K239.043-18, p. 122; Julian, p. 31; Campbell interview; "Tactical Report of Mission, FRANTIC VII."

67. Kulski, p. 253; Rokossovskii, pp. 257–262.

68. Campbell interview.

69. Interview with Tom Stotler, Colorado Springs, Colo., October 13, 1989; Operations Narrative, 24 September 1944, 390th Bomb Group Mission File 191, Special Collections, SMS 575, Box 2, USAF Academy Library.

70. Campbell interview; Operations Narrative, Mission File 191.

71. Bor-Komorowski, p. 350; Orpen, p. 159; Message, Walsh to Spaatz, 18 September 1944 in FRANTIC, Book 3.

72. Letter, Lt Col Utnik, Polish General Staff to Col A. R. Maxwell, director of operations, Eighth Air Force, 21 September 1944; Special Force Headquarters, Block 2, Montagu Mansions, Montagu Street, London, "Report on "FRANTIC 7," 28 September 1944, to Commanding General, USSTAF; Letter, Prime Minister of the Republic of Poland (Mikolajczyk) to John G. Winant, U.S. Ambassador to Great Britain, 25 September 1944, all in Warsaw Dropping Operations, Maj Gen F. L. Anderson, 13 August–5 October 1944, AFHRA 519.476-2; Kulski, p. 253.

73. Summary of Bomber Operations, part I; Summary of Fighter Operations, part I in Walsh Papers; Lester, p. 122; Campbell interview.

74. Message, Walsh to Deane, 18 September 1944 in FRANTIC VII, AFHRA 522.312-1; Message, Kessler to Deane, 18 September 1944 in FRANTIC VII.

75. Campbell interview.

76. 100th Bombardment Group, *Contrails—My War Record* (New York: John F. Callahan, 1947), p. 86.

77. Stotler interview.

78. George Zadora, "Warsaw Shuttle Mission," in *The 390th Bomb Group Anthology,* Wilbert H. Richarz, Richard H. Perry, William J. Robinson, eds. (Tucson, Ariz.: 390th Memorial Museum Foundation, 1983), vol I, pp. 126-132.

79. Lester, p. 123; Message, Kessler to Spaatz, 18 September 1944 in FRANTIC VII; Summary of Bomber Operations, part I.

80. Mikolajczyk to Winant, 25 September 1944; Bor-Komorowski, p. 357.

81. Ibid., p. 351; Message, J. Ward, from Warsaw, dated 25 September 1944, received [in London], 26 September 1944 in Warsaw Dropping Operations; Message, Bor-Komorowski to the [Polish] Prime Minister, 26 September 1944 in Warsaw Dropping Operations.

82. Erickson, p. 288; Bor-Komorowski, p. 353; Rokossovskii, pp. 260-261.

83. Message, Bottomley to Spaatz, 26 September 1944 in McDonald Papers, Box 4, Folder 1; Letter, Anderson to Mikolajczyk, 30 September 1944 in Warsaw Dropping Operations.

84. Letter, Anderson to Kuter, 24 September 1944 in Warsaw Dropping Operations; Richard G. Davis, "Operation 'Thunderclap': The U.S. Army Air Forces and the Bombing of Berlin," *Journal of Strategic Studies* 14 (March 1991): 91-111.

85. Text of Telephone Conversation between Major General F. L. Anderson and the Right Honorable Winston S. Churchill, Prime Minister, 29 September 1944; Letter, Anderson to Mikolajczyk, 30 September 1944, both in Warsaw Dropping Operations.

86. Orpen, pp. 160-161.

87. Feis, p. 389.

88. Daily Summaries, 29 and 30 September 1944 in Special Events of Eastern Command.

89. Ibid., 1 and 2 October 1944; Letter, Anderson to Churchill, 2 October 1944 in Warsaw Dropping Operations.

90. Orpen, p. 161; Bor-Komorowski, pp. 363-376; Erickson, p. 289. See also Jan Novak, *Courier From Warsaw* (Detroit: Wayne State University Press, 1982).

91. Kulski, pp. 265–266, 291.

92. Erickson, pp. 289–290.

93. Text of Soviet Message, Deane and Walsh to Spaatz, 3 October 1944 in Warsaw Dropping Operations.

94. Erickson, p. 289; Gerhard L. Weinberg, *World in the Balance: Behind the Scenes of World War II* (London: University Press of New England, 1981), p. 47; Alexander Werth, *Russia at War, 1941–45* (London: Barrie and Ruchliffe, 1964).

95. George F. Kennan, *Memoirs: 1925–1950* (Boston: Little, Brown, 1967), vol 1, p. 211.

Winter Quarters

1. Daily Summary, 1 September 1944, in General Kessler, Special Events of Eastern Command, 15 August–10 October 1944, Air Force Historical Research Agency, Maxwell AFB, Ala., AFHRA 522.0591-2.

2. Letter, Molotov to Harriman, 7 October 1944 in U.S. Military Mission to Moscow, National Archives, Washington, D.C., NA/RG 334, Box 63, Airdrome Defense.

3. Message, Spaatz to Walsh, 6 September 1944; Message, Spaatz to Walsh, 25 September 1944, both in FRANTIC 1 Cables, 22 October 1944–16 May 1945, AFHRA 522.1621-1.

4. "Personnel Shipment Status," 5 October 1944 in Papers of Robert L. Walsh, USAF Academy Library Special Collections, USAF Academy, Colorado, MS-12, Folder III, Poltava Mission; Daily Summaries, 16 September and 3 October 1944 in Special Events of Eastern Command, p. 12.

5. "Personnel Shipment Status"; Message, Spaatz to Walsh, 10 September 1944 in FRANTIC Cables.

6. Headquarters, Eastern Command, U.S. Strategic Air Forces in Europe, Office of the Surgeon, "Informal Report of Progress and Problems," to Surgeon, Headquarters, USSTAF, 12 November 1944 in 381 Project 2, Medical Reports, July 1944–June 1945, AFHRA 522.741-2, pp. 1–2.

7. "Personnel Shipment Status," "Organization Chart, Winter Detachment, Eastern Command, USSTAF," both in Walsh Papers, Folder III.

8. Message, Deane to Arnold, 30 August 1944 in FRANTIC Cables; Message, Arnold to Deane and Spaatz, 5 September 1944 in FRANTIC Cables; Message, Spaatz to Walsh, 10 September 1944 in FRANTIC Cables.

9. Message, Arnold to Deane and Harriman, 7 September 1944 in FRANTIC Cables; Daily Summary, 20 September 1944 in Special Events of Eastern Command; Message, Deane to Arnold and Spaatz, 20 September 1944 in FRANTIC Cables.

10. Headquarters, Eastern Command, "Daily Operational and Supply Status," 1 October 1944, in Walsh Papers.

11. Statistical Control, Eastern Command, "Aviation Gasoline, Monthly Requirements," 25 September 1944, in Walsh Papers.

12. Headquarters, United States Strategic Air Forces in Europe, "Orders, CG, AAF Units, Installations, and Activities in Russia," 13 November 1944 in Walsh Papers, Folder 1.

13. Letter, Harriman to Molotov, 29 August 1944 in NA/RG 334, Box 63, Airdrome Defense.

14. Message, Arnold to Deane, 1 September 1944, in Papers of George C. McDonald, USAF Academy Library Special Collections, MS-16, Box 4, Folder 2; Message, Arnold to Deane, 5 September 1944 in FRANTIC Cables.

15. Message, Arnold to Deane, info Spaatz, 5 September 1944 in FRANTIC Cables.

16. Message, Deane to Arnold, 3 September 1944 in FRANTIC I Cables; Message, Deane to Arnold, 18 November 1944 in FRANTIC II, Vienna-Budapest Area, 20 November 1944–9 May 1945, AFHRA 522.1621-3.

17. Letter, Spaatz to Arnold, 27 November 1944, in FRANTIC II. Spaatz actually framed the idea of a new operation called FRANTIC II. The reader should not confuse this new operation with the second mission of FRANTIC that took place on 21 June 1944.

18. Williamson Murray, *Strategy for Defeat: The Luftwaffe, 1933–1945* (Maxwell AFB, Ala: Air University Press, 1983), p. 303.

19. Wesley F. Craven and James L. Cate, *The Army Air Forces in World War II* (Chicago: University of Chicago Press, 1951), vol III, *Europe: ARGUMENT to V-E Day, January 1944 to May 1945*, p. 664. For accounts of the *Luftwaffe's* last big throw, Operation *Bodenplatte*, see two books by Danny S. Parker, *Battle of the Bulge: Hitler's Ardennes Offensive, 1944–1945* (Philadelphia: Combined Books, 1991), p. 232, and *To Win the Winter Sky: Air War over the Ardennes, 1944–1945* (Philadelphia: Combined Books, 1994); see also Air Ministry, W. H. Tantum IV and E. H. Hoffschmidt, eds., *The Rise and Fall of the German Air Force (1933–1945)* (Old Greenwich, Conn: WE, Inc., 1969), pp. 374–381.

20. Message, Eaker to Spaatz, 27 September 1944 in FRANTIC II.

21. Headquarters, Mediterranean Allied Air Force, James H. Parton, Lt Col, *The History of the Mediterranean Allied Air Force,* April 1945, chap XVII, "Relations with Russia," p. 371, AFHRA 622.01-1.

22. Message, Spaatz to Arnold, 27 November 1944 in FRANTIC II.

23. Message, Deane to Arnold, 18 November 1944 in FRANTIC II; H. H. Arnold, General of the Air Force, *Global Mission* (New York: Harper, 1949), p. 470.

24. John R. Deane, *The Strange Alliance: The Story of Our Efforts at Wartime Co-operation with Russia* (New York: Viking Press, 1947), p. 229.

25. Ibid., pp. 230–231.

26. Ibid., p. 233.

27. Ibid., p. 235.

28. Headquarters, Mediterranean Allied Air Forces, Hugh J. Knerr, Maj Gen, Memorandum, "FRANTIC Logistic Situation," for Commanding General, USSTAF, 25 August 1944, p. 2, in Eastern Command, Miscellaneous Correspondence, Memoranda, and Messages, June–September 1944, AFHRA 522.161; Message, Deane to Kessler, 1 October 1944 in FRANTIC I Cables.

29. "Informal Report of Progress and Problems," 12 November 1944, p. 1.

30. Ibid., p. 2.

31. Kaluta, chap 3, p. 13.

32. Ibid., pp. 8–10.

33. Headquarters, Eastern Command, U.S. Strategic Air Forces in Europe, Office

of the Surgeon, "Informal Report of Progress and Problems," 11 December 1944, in 381 Project 2, July 1944–June 1945, Medical reports, AFHRA 522.741-2.

34. Kaluta, chap 2, p. 11.

35. Ibid., p. 15.

36. Ibid.

37. Ibid., p. 18.

38. Letter, Kovalev to Hampton, 23 December 1944 in Incidents (U.S. and Soviet), NA/RG 334, Box 10.

39. Letter, Hampton to Kovalev, 29 March 1945 in Incidents (U.S. and Soviet); Kaluta, chap 2, p. 16; Message, Hill to Hampton, 8 March 1945, in FRANTIC I Cables.

40. Memorandum Colonel Thomas K. Hampton to Commanding General, U.S. Army Air Forces in USSR (Hill), n.d., in FRANTIC, General, NA/RG 334, Box 66, p. 1.

41. Ibid., p. 2.

42. Ibid., pp. 2–3; Kaluta, chap 2, p. 23; Message, Hill to Hampton, 28 February 1945 in FRANTIC I Cables.

43. Kaluta, chap 3, p. 22.

44. Headquarters, Eastern Command, Paul F. Doran, 1st Lt, "Report of Special Service Officer," n.d. in FRANTIC, Reports, NA/RG 334, Box 68.

45. Kaluta, chap 3, p. 18.

46. Headquarters, Eastern Command, Paul F. Doran, 1st Lt, "Report for 16 January to 31 January, 1945," n.d.; and "Report for 1 February to 15 February, 1945," n.d. in FRANTIC, Reports.

47. "Report for 16 January to 31 January, 1945"; Kaluta, chap 3, pp. 28–30.

48. Ibid.

49. Headquarters, Eastern Command, U.S. Strategic Air Forces in Europe, William R. Kaluta, 1st Lt, "Report on Trip to Sarabuz, Crimea — 1 February 1945," 22 March 1945 in EASCOM Reports, 21 March–2 April 1945, AFHRA 522.152-1, p. 4.

50. Ibid.

51. Kaluta I, pp. 25–26.

52. Ibid.

53. Ibid., p. 20.

54. Headquarters, Eastern Command, U.S. Strategic Air Forces in Europe, Office of the Surgeon, "Informal Report of Progress and Problems," 18 January 1945, in 381 Project 2, Medical Reports.

55. Chester Wilmot, *Struggle for Europe* (New York: Carroll and Graf, 1952), chap XXX.

56. Earl F. Ziemke, *Stalingrad to Berlin: The German Defeat in the East* (Washington, D.C.: Center of Military History, 1968), pp. 378–386.

57. Special Service, "Report for 16 January to 31 January, 1945," p. 3.

58. Special Service, "Report for 1 February to 15 February, 1945," pp. 2–3.

59. Headquarters, Eastern Command, Office of the Adjutant, "Minutes of Meeting Between VVS Officials and Headquarters, Eastern Command," 29 November 1944 in FRANTIC, General, NA/RG 334, Box 66.

60. Kaluta, chap 3, pp. 6–10.

61. Ibid., 4–6.

62. Message, Hampton to Spaatz, 14 January 1945 in EASCOM [Eastern Command] Cables, January 1945, AFHRA 522.1621.

63. Headquarters, Eastern Command, 1st Lt William R. Kaluta, *History of Eastern Command, April–June 1945,* FRANTIC, History, Kaluta, NA/RG 334, Box 66, pp. 11–15, hereafter referred to as Kaluta II.

64. Letter, Hampton to Kovalev, 26 March 1945 in FRANTIC, General.

65. Kaluta I, p. 15.

66. Memorandum, Brigadier General George C. McDonald to Lieutenant Colonel John H. Starr, War Department, "Operations of Eastern Base Command," 1 July 1944 in Papers of George C. McDonald, USAF Academy Library Special Collections, USAF Academy, Colo., MS-16, Box 3, Folder 9; Kaluta I, chap 3, pp. 15–16; Kaluta II, pp. 12–13.

Spring Evacuation

1. Earl F. Ziemke, *Stalingrad to Berlin: The German Defeat in the East* (Washington, D.C.: Center of Military History, 1968), pp. 416–417. See also Chester Wilmot, *Struggle for Europe* (New York: Carroll and Graf, 1986), p. 621.

2. Ziemke, pp. 438–440. This phase of the war in the East is covered in great detail in Christopher Duffy, *Red Storm on the Reich: The Soviet March on Germany, 1945* (New York: Atheneum, 1991). See also David M. Glantz and Jonathan M. House, *When Titans Clashed: How the Red Army Stopped Hitler* (Lawrence, Kans.: University Press of Kansas, 1995), chaps 15 and 16. John Erickson devotes an entire chapter to the Vistula-Oder campaign as well. See *The Road to Berlin: Continuing the History of Stalin's War with Germany* (Boulder, Colo.: Westview Press, 1983), chap 7.

3. William R. Kaluta, *The History of Eastern Command, USSTAF 1 October 1944–1 April 1945,* National Archives, Washington, D.C., NA/RG 334, Box 66, History, Kaluta, chap 2, p. 27, cited hereafter as Kaluta I.

4. Ibid.

5. Headquarters, Fifteenth Air Force, "Procedures for Crews Landing on Soviet Territory or on Territory Occupied by Germans," n.d., in Fifteenth Air Force, FRANTIC 1 Operations, June 1944, Air Force Historical Research Agency, Maxwell AFB, Ala., AFHRA 670.476-2, p. 1.

6. Interrogation Form, 401st Bomb Group, 28 February 1945, Eastern Command, Statement of Major Robert Rosenthal, o-792349, in U.S. Military Mission to Moscow, Operation FRANTIC, NA/RG 334, Box 67, Interrogation Reports, p. 1.

7. Ibid., pp. 2–4.

8. Interrogation Form, 452 Bomb Group, 26 March 1945, Eastern Command, Narrative of Major Donald S. Nicholson, interrogator, in Interrogation Reports.

9. Ibid.

10. Ibid., p. 2.

11. Message, Deane to Marshall, Smith, and McNarney, 21 January 1945 in U.S. Military Mission to Moscow, NA/RG 334, Box 23, Prisoners of War.

12. Letter, Hill to Commanding Officer, Eastern Command, subject, "United

States Prisoners of War Escaping from German Prison Camps," 14 February 1945 in Prisoners of War.

13. Alexander Dallin, *German Rule in Russia, 1941–1945: A Study of Occupation Policies* (Boulder, Colo.: Westview Press, 1981), p. 426.

14. Deane, p. 182.

15. "Statement of Escaped Prisoners," n.d. in Interrogation Reports, p. 1.

16. Ibid.; Headquarters, Eastern Command, U.S. Strategic Air Forces in Europe, Office of the Surgeon, "Informal Report of Progress and Problems," 22 February 1945 in 381 Project 2, Medical Reports, AFHRA 522.741-2, July 1944–June 1945, p. 2.

17. "Statement of Escaped Prisoners," p. 2.

18. Deane, p. 195.

19. "Informal Report on Progress," 22 February 1945, p. 2.

20. Headquarters, Eastern Command, U.S. Strategic Air Forces in Europe, "Report of Trip to Rzeszow and Lodz, Poland, 25 March 1945," in EASCOM Reports, 21 March–2 April 1945, AFHRA 522.152-1.

21. Headquarters, Eastern Command, U.S. Strategic Air Forces in Europe, Office of the Surgeon, "Informal Report of Progress and Problems," 6 April 1945, in 381 Project 2, Medical Reports, p. 2.

22. Staff Study for the Relief and Recovery of U.S. PWs from the Soviet Zone (including Outline Plan), Tab E, Annex 1, Extracts from Secret War Department Documents Entitled Statement of Evacuees from German Prisoner of War Camps Regarding Experiences in Russia, 23 April 1945, "Statement of Major John W. Dobson," AFHRA 519.973-6 [1945], p. 7, hereafter referred to as Relief and Recovery of U.S. PWs.

23. Headquarters, Eastern Command, U.S. Strategic Air Forces in Europe, trip to Lublin, Poland, 27 February–28 March 1945, made by Lt Col James D. Wilmeth and party for the purpose of Repatriating American ex-Prisoners of War, in U.S. Military Mission to Moscow, Prisoners of War, p. 3, hereafter referred to as Wilmeth Report.

24. Ibid., p. 13.

25. U.S. War Department, Memorandum for assistant chief of staff, G-1, WDGS, "Questionnaires received from United States Prisoners of War recovered from Germany," 19 April 1945, in Military Mission to Moscow, Prisoners of War, p. 2.

26. Wilmeth Report, pp. 13–14.

27. Ibid.

28. "Informal Report of Progress and Problems," 6 April 1945, pp. 3–4.

29. Wilmeth Report, p. 1; Message, Wilmeth to Deane, 17 February 1945 in EASCOM Cables, February 1945, AFHRA 522.1621.

30. Message, Wilmeth to Deane, 19 February 1945 in EASCOM Cables, AFHRA 522.1621, February 1945.

31. Message 1, Deane to Wilmeth, 20 February 1945; Message 2, Deane to Wilmeth, 20 February 1945, both in EASCOM Cables, February 1945.

32. Kaluta I, chap 3, p. 74.

33. Wilmeth Report, p. 1.

34. Ibid., p. 2.

35. Ibid., p. 3.

36. Ibid., p. 5.

37. Ibid., p. 6.

38. Ibid., p. 8.

39. Message No. 278, Roosevelt to Stalin, 18 March 1945, in Ministry of Foreign Affairs of the USSR, *Stalin's Correspondence with Churchill, Attlee, Roosevelt, and Truman, 1941-45* (New York: E. P. Dutton, 1958), pp. 195-196, cited hereafter as *Stalin's Correspondence*; Deane, p. 198.

40. Message No. 279, Stalin to Roosevelt, 22 March 1945 in *Stalin's Correspondence*, pp. 196-197.

41. James Parton, Lt Col, Headquarters, Mediterranean Allied Air Forces, *The History of the Mediterranean Allied Air Forces,* April 1945, AFHRA 622.01-1. See also Harriman and Abel, pp. 416-417. For an example of a German military unit made up of Soviet citizens being turned over to the Red Army, see James Lucas, *Last Days of the Third Reich: The Collapse of Nazi Germany, May 1945* (New York: William Morrow, 1986), pp. 74-75.

42. Wilmeth Report, pp. 10-11; Headquarters, Eastern Command, U.S. Strategic Air Forces in Europe, "Trip to Lublin, Poland, 27 March 1945," 29 March 1945 in EASCOM Reports, 21 March-2 April 1945; Telegram, 15th AF to U.S. Embassy, Moscow, 6 April 1945; in NA/RG 334, Box 65, Downed Aircraft.

43. American POW Contact Team, Odessa, USSR, "Interim Report on Transit Camp," 5 March 1945 in U.S. Military Mission to Moscow, Prisoners of War.

44. Telegram, 15th AF to U.S. Embassy, Moscow, 6 April 1945 in NA/RG 334, Box 65, Downed Aircraft.

45. Richard C. Lukas, *Eagles East: The Army Air Forces and the Soviet Union, 1941-1945* (Tallahassee, Fla.: Florida State University Press, 1970), pp. 211-212; Kaluta I, p. 16.

46. Ibid., chap 3, p. 32.

47. Lukas, p. 212.

48. Kaluta I, chap 3, pp. 34-35.

49. Ibid., p. 35.

50. Headquarters, Eastern Command, U.S. Strategic Air Forces in Europe, "Report of Flight to Lodz, Poland, 19 March 1945," 22 March 1945, p. 3, in EASCOM Reports, 21 March-2 April 1945.

51. Headquarters, Eastern Command, "Report on Trip to Poland," 22 March 1945, p. 4, in EASCOM Reports, 21 March-2 April 1945.

52. Message, Trimble to Deane, "Summary of Report of Capt J. Pogue," 22 April 1945 in U.S. Military Mission to Moscow, Operation FRANTIC, NA/RG 334, Box 65, Downed Aircraft.

53. Headquarters, Eastern Command, U.S. Strategic Air Forces in Europe, "Report of Flight to Lodz, Poland, 19 March 1945," 22 March 1945, pp. 1-2 in EASCOM Reports, 21 March-2 April 1945, AFHRA 522.152-1.

54. Wilmot, p. 659; Herbert Feis, *Churchill, Roosevelt, Stalin: The War They Waged and the Peace They Sought* (Princeton: Princeton University Press, 1957), pp. 548, 566-568.

55. W. Averell Harriman and Elie Abel, *Special Envoy to Churchill and Stalin, 1941-1946* (New York: Random House, 1975), pp. 413-414.

56. Ibid., p. 373; Wilmot, p. 631; Lukas, p. 213.

57. Interrogation Form, 401st Bomb Group, 19 March 1945, Eastern Command, Narrative Statement in NA/RG 334, Box 67, Interrogations; Message, Hampton to Deane, 21 March 1945 in Cables in the Case of 1st Lt Myron L. King, NA/RG 334, Box 10, Incidents (U.S. and Soviet).

58. Statement of First Lieutenant Myron L. King at Poltava, 27 March 1945 in Incidents (U.S. and Soviet).

59. Ibid.

60. Ibid.

61. Ibid.

62. Interrogation form, 19 March 1945.

63. Message, Deane to Hampton, 29 March 1945 in NA/RG 334, Incidents.

64. Letter, Antonov to Deane, 30 March 1945; Message, Deane to Marshall, info Arnold, 31 March 1945; Letter, Deane to Antonov, 31 March 1945 in NA/RG 334, Box 65, Downed Aircraft.

65. Message, Deane to Spaatz and Cannon, 31 March 1945 in Downed Aircraft; Headquarters, Eastern Command, U.S. Strategic Air Forces in Europe, Office of the Surgeon, "Informal Report of Progress and Problems," 6 April 1945, in 381 Project 2, Medical Reports, p. 3.

66. William R. Kaluta, *The History of Eastern Command, USSTAF, 1 April–23 June 1945,* NA/RG 334, Box 66, Kaluta, History, chap 1, p. 1, cited hereafter as Kaluta II; "Informal Report of Progress and Problems," 6 April 1945, p. 3.

67. Message, Deane to Trimble, 22 April 1945 in NA/RG 334, Box 65, Downed Aircraft.

68. Message, Deane to Marshall and Arnold, 5 April 1945 in Downed Aircraft.

69. Headquarters, Eastern Command, Albert Lepawsky, Major, *History of Eastern Command, USSTAF, 1941–1945,* AFHRA 522.01-2, chap 8, pp. 110–111.

70. Ibid.

71. Message, Deane to USSTAF and AGWAR, "General Court Martial Trial," 12 May 1945, in NA/RG 334, Incidents; Message, Olsen to Trimble, 26 April 1945 in EASCOM Cables, April–May 1945, AFHRA 522.1621.

72. Letter, Deane to Slavin, 6 April 1945; Letter, Deane to Slavin, 9 April 1945 both in NA/RG 334, Downed Aircraft.

73. Kaluta II, chap 1, pp. 3–4.

74. Letter, Deane to Slavin, 9 April 1945.

75. Embassy of the United States of America, Moscow, Minutes of Meeting, "Recovery of American Aircraft," 15 April 1945 in NA/RG 334, Downed Aircraft.

76. Meeting at Red Army General Staff Headquarters, 16 April 1945, "Operation of United States Aircraft in Soviet-Occupied Areas," in NA/RG 334, Incidents.

77. "Informal Report of Progress and Problems," 2 May 1945; Kaluta II, chap 2, pp. 3–4.

78. A. V. Nikitin, " 'Chelnochnye' operatsiy," *Voenno-Istoricheskiy Zhurnal* 11 (1975): 41–46.

79. Message, Spaatz to Eaker, info Arnold and Deane, 30 March 1945; Message, Hill to Spaatz, 3 April 1945; Message, Spaatz to Arnold, 13 April 1945, all in FRANTIC II—Vienna-Budapest area, AFHRA 522.1621-3, 20 November–9 May 1945, cited hereafter as FRANTIC II; Message, Marshall to Olsen, Eisenhower, Spaatz, and McNarney, 19 April 1945 in NA/RG 334, Downed Aircraft.

80. Ibid. See Deane, p. 141.

81. Lukas, p. 226; Deane, pp. 264–266.

82. Message, Trimble to USSTAF and French and British *Stars and Stripes,* 14 April 1945 in NA/RG 334, Box 5, Communiques.

83. "Informal Report of Progress and Problems," 2 May 1945, p. 3.

84. Kaluta II, chap 2, p. 2.

85. Headquarters, Eastern Command, U.S. Strategic Air Forces in Europe, Accident File, Exhibit M, "Narrative Statement and Nature of Accident," 12 May 1945; "Report of Autopsy," both in NA/RG 334, Box 63, Accident File.

86. Headquarters, Eastern Command, U.S. Strategic air Forces in Europe, "Statement of Reasons for Recommendation in the Case of Zina Osipovna Grigorenko," 9 June 1945 in Accident File.

87. "Narrative Statement and Nature of Accident."

88. "Statement of Reasons"; "Investigating Officer's Report," p. 3, n.d. in Accident File.

Conclusion

1. See Headquarters, Eastern Command, William R. Kaluta, Lt, History of Eastern Command, USSTAF, 1 April–23 June 1945, chap 3, "Deactivation," in FRANTIC, History, Kaluta, National Archives, Washington, D.C., NA/RG 334, Box 6; Richard C. Lukas, *Eagles East: The Army Air Forces and the Soviet Union, 1941–1945* (Tallahassee, Fla.: Florida State University Press, 1970), p. 214.

2. Headquarters, Mediterranean Allied Air Forces, Maj Gen Hugh J. Knerr, Memorandum for CG, USSTAF, " 'FRANTIC' Logistic Situation," 25 August 1944 in Eastern Command, Miscellaneous Correspondence, Memoranda, and Messages, June–September 1944, Air Force Historical Research Agency, Maxwell AFB, Ala., AFHRA 522.161; Headquarters, U.S. Strategic Air Forces in Europe, Office of the Director of Intelligence, Brig Gen George C. McDonald, Memorandum to Deputy Commander, Operations, U.S. Strategic Air Forces in Europe, "FRANTIC," 21 August 1944 in Appreciation of FRANTIC, 522.609–1.

3. Alfred Price, *The Last Year of the Luftwaffe, May 1944 to May 1945* (Osceola, Wis.: Motorbooks International, 1991), pp. 73–74; Williamson Murray, *Strategy for Defeat: The Luftwaffe, 1933–1945* (Maxwell AFB, Ala.: Air University Press, 1983), p. 284; McDonald, "FRANTIC," p. 4.

4. Adolf Galland, *The First and the Last: The Rise and Fall of the German Fighter Forces, 1938–1945,* translated by Mervyn Savill (New York: Henry Holt, 1954), pp. 284–285; Generalleutnant a. D. Walter Schwabedissen, *The Russian Air Force in the Eyes of German Commanders* (Maxwell AFB, Ala.: U.S. AF Historical Division, 1960), p. 384.

5. Wesley F. Craven and James L. Cate, *The Army Air Forces in World War II,* 7 vols (Chicago: University of Chicago Press, 1951), vol 3, *Europe: ARGUMENT to V-E Day, January 1944 to May 1945,* p. 318.

6. Ibid., p. 791.

7. Larry C. Lester, Major, USAF, "Project FRANTIC: The Interaction of the Politico-Military Process in American-Soviet Collaboration During World War II,"

Maxwell AFB, Ala.: Air Command and Staff College Resident Study, 1977, AFHRA K239.043-18, pp. 103–123. See also Price, p. 95.

8. The worst day of the war for the AAF was October 17, 1943, when sixty B-17s were destroyed during the Schweinfurt-Regensburg raid.

9. Albert Lepawsky, Major, "The AAF on the Russian Front, Summaries and Conclusions," in Drafts and Notes, 1941–44, AFHRA 522.057-1.

10. John R. Deane, *The Strange Alliance: The Story of Our Efforts at Wartime Cooperation with Russia* (New York: Viking Press, 1947), p. 124; W. Averell Harriman and Elie Abel, *Special Envoy to Churchill and Stalin, 1941–1946* (New York: Random House, 1975), pp. 312–313.

11. See A. Orlov and N. Komarov, " 'Flying Fortresses' Over the Third Reich," *Soviet Military Review* (July 1975): 51–52. See also Nikolai Kobrin, Colonel, "The Last Summer of the War," *Soviet Military Review* (June 1989): 45–47; and Nikolai Kurov, Colonel, "The Breakthrough to Berlin and the Battle in the Ardennes," *Soviet Military Review* (December 1989): 45–47.

12. M. N. Kozhevnikov, *The Command and Staff of the Soviet Army Air Force in the Great Patriotic War, 1941–1945,* translated by and published under the auspices of the U.S. Air Force (Washington, D.C.: USGPO, 1977), pp. 165–168.

13. A. V. Nikitin, " 'Chelochnye' operatsiy," *Voenno-Istoricheskiy Zhurnal* 11 (1975): 41–46. See also John F. Kreis, *Air Warfare and Air Base Air Defense* (Washington, D.C.: USGPO, 1988), p. 210.

14. Leonid Lyubymsky and Mykola Mykhailenko, "The Year 1944: Operation 'FRANTIC'," *News from Ukraine* 3 (January 1992): 2.

15. Headquarters, U.S. Strategic Air Forces in Europe, R. W. Bonneville, Colonel, Memorandum for the Advisory Council, "Proposed New FRANTIC Operation," n.d. in FRANTIC II: Vienna-Budapest area, 20 November 1944–9 May 1945, AFHRA 522.1621-3.

16. For a critical assessment of Soviet and Allied strategy and tactics, see John Ellis, *Brute Force: Allied Strategy and Tactics in the Second World War* (New York: Viking Press, 1990).

BIBLIOGRAPHY

Discussions of FRANTIC have appeared in various monographs and memoirs. The head of the U.S. Military Mission to Moscow from 1943 to 1945, Major General John R. Deane, described in his memoirs his involvement with the Soviets in establishing FRANTIC's Ukrainian bases. Von Hardesty's study of the Soviet air force in World War II, *Red Phoenix*, devoted a handful of pages to FRANTIC as well. Wesley F. Craven and James L. Cate's official account *The Army Air Forces in World War II* also provides a brief overview of the operation. Richard C. Lukas devoted an entire chapter to FRANTIC in his excellent book *Eagles East: The Army Air Forces and the Soviet Union, 1941–1945*. Usually, however, authors refer to FRANTIC in the context of the successful German strike at the main American base at Poltava in the Ukraine on the night of 21/22 June 1944.

Perhaps the best known book-length treatment of FRANTIC is Glenn B. Infield's 1973 monograph *The Poltava Affair: A Russian Warning, An American Tragedy*. Infield's work, however, is less an operational study of FRANTIC than an indictment of the Soviets for failing to properly defend Poltava from German bombers. As the title suggests, Infield implies Soviet duplicity and even complicity in the German raid on Poltava and likens that attack to Pearl Harbor. Unfortunately, the book does not contain footnotes or other citations. Nevertheless, *The Poltava Affair* is a valuable source of information on early FRANTIC operations and provides a glimpse of the German units involved in the 22 June 1944 strike on Poltava.

Two as yet unpublished doctoral dissertations also exist that describe FRANTIC in great detail. Thomas Julian's 1967 "Operation FRANTIC and the Search for American-Soviet Military Collaboration, 1941–1944," deals, as the title suggests, with the diplomatic, political, and military wrangling that took place between the United States and the Soviet Union as the administration of Franklin D. Roosevelt sought ways to improve Soviet-American military cooperation. More recently, Daniel P. Bolger presented a detailed operational analysis of FRANTIC missions in the context of the air war in his 1986 dissertation "Reluctant Allies: The United States Army Air Forces and the Soviet Air Force, 1941–1945."

Primary Sources

UNPUBLISHED OFFICIAL RECORDS

U.S. Army Air Forces, 390th Bombardment Group. Mission Files. USAF Academy Library Special Collections, USAF Academy, Colorado. Materials cited from this collection are preceded by SMS.
U.S. War Department. Official Papers. National Archives, Washington, D.C. Mate-

rials cited from this collection in this study, including the records of the U.S. Military Mission to Moscow, are preceded by NA/RG.

U.S. War Department. Official Papers. U.S. Air Force Historical Research Agency, Maxwell Air Force Base, Alabama. Materials cited from this collection in this study are preceded by AFHRA.

PERSONAL PAPERS AND MANUSCRIPT COLLECTIONS

The papers of the following general officers are held in the Special Collections Branch of the USAF Academy Library, USAF Academy, Colorado:

Major General Follett Bradley
Major General Hugh J. Knerr
General Laurence S. Kuter
Brigadier General George C. McDonald
Major General Robert L. Walsh

UNPUBLISHED OFFICIAL STUDIES

Kaluta, William R. *History of Eastern Command, U.S. Strategic Air Forces in Europe: 1 October 1944 to 1 April 1945.* Headquarters, Eastern Command, 1945.

——. *History of Eastern Command, U.S. Strategic Air Forces in Europe: 1 April to 23 June 1945.* Headquarters, Eastern Command, 1945.

Lepawsky, Albert. *History of Eastern Command, U.S. Strategic Air Forces in Europe, 1941-1944.* Headquarters, USSTAF, 1944.

Mediterranean Allied Air Forces. *The History of* FRANTIC, *American Shuttle-Bombing to and from Russian Bases, 26 October 1943-15 June 1944.* Headquarters, MAAF, 1944.

INTERVIEWS AND CORRESPONDENCE

All interviews were conducted by the author in Colorado Springs, Colo., from 11-13 October 1989. The following men listed were all assigned to the 390th Bombardment Group based at Framlingham, England, during the time of FRANTIC, with the exception of Joseph A. Moller, who served as the operations officer for the 95th Bomb Group prior to assuming command of the 390th in mid-September 1944.

Campbell, Bernie S.
Haynes, Leo S.
Jackson, Moody S.
Moller, Joseph A.
Perry, Richard H.
Stotler, Thomas
Waltz, Robert W., Brigadier General, USAF, Retired
Wampler, Louis
Warner, John S., Major General, USAF, Retired
Webb, James S.
Letter, Joseph A. Moller, to the author, 14 May 1991
Letter, John S. Warner, Major General, USAF, Retired, to the author, 19 June 1991

MEMOIRS AND FIRST-PERSON ACCOUNTS

Arnold, Henry H. *Global Mission*. New York: Harper and Brothers, 1949.
Barghoorn, Frederick C. *The Soviet Image of the United States: A Study in Distortion*. New York: Harcourt, Brace, 1950.
Bor-Komorowski, Tadeusz. *The Secret Army*. Nashville: The Battery Press, 1984.
Chennault, Major General Claire Lee. *Way of a Fighter*. New York: Putnam, 1949.
Deane, John R. *The Strange Alliance: The Story of Our Efforts at Wartime Co-operation with Russia*. New York: Viking Press, 1947.
Galland, Adolf. *The First and the Last: The Rise and Fall of the German Fighter Forces, 1938-1945*. Translated by Mervyn Savill. New York: Henry Holt, 1954.
Hansell, Haywood S. *The Air Plan That Defeated Hitler*. Atlanta: Higgins-McArthur/Longino and Porter, 1972.
Harriman, W. Averell and Abel, Elie. *Special Envoy to Churchill and Stalin, 1941-1946*. New York: Random House, 1975.
Harris, Marshal of the RAF Sir Arthur. *Bomber Offensive*. London: Collins, 1947.
Hawkins, Ian, ed. *Courage, Honor, Victory: A First Person History of the 95th Bomb Group*. Bellevue, WA: 95th Bomb Group Association, 1987.
Kennan, George F. *Memoirs: 1925-1950*. Boston: Little, Brown, 1967.
Kulski, Julian Eugeniusz. *Dying, We Live: The Personal Chronicle of a Young Freedom Fighter in Warsaw, (1939-1945)*. New York: Holt, Rinehart, and Winston, 1979.
Kuter, Laurence S. *Airman at Yalta*. New York: Duell, Sloan, and Pearce, 1955.
Mikolajczyk, Stanislaw. *The Rape of Poland: Pattern of Soviet Aggression*. New York: McGraw-Hill, 1948.
Nikitin, A. V. " 'Chelnochnye' operatsiy." *Voenno-Istoricheskiy Zhurnal* 11 (July 1975): 41-46.
Nowak, Jan *Courier from Warsaw*. Detroit: Wayne State University Press, 1982.
Richarz, Wilbert H., Richard H. Perry, and William J. Robinson. *The 390th Bomb Group Anthology*, 2 vols. Tucson, Ariz.: 390th Memorial Museum Foundation, 1983.
Rokossovskii, Konstantin K., Marshal of the Soviet Union, ed. Robert Daglish. *A Soldier's Duty*. Moscow: Progress Publishers, 1985.
Stevens, Edmund. *Russia Is No Riddle*. New York: Greenberg, 1945.
White, William L. *Report on the Russians*. New York: Harcourt, Brace, 1945.
Zhukov, Georgy K., Marshal of the Soviet Union, trans. APN. *The Memoirs of Marshal Zhukov*. New York: Delacorte Press, 1971.

OFFICIAL PUBLICATIONS

Tantum, W. H. and E. J. Hoffschmidt, Air Ministry of the U.K., eds. *The Rise and Fall of the German Air Force (1933-1945)*. Old Greenwich, Conn.: WE, Inc., 1969.
Craven, Wesley F. and James L. Cate. *The Army Air Forces in World War II*. 7 vols. Chicago: University of Chicago Press, 1951. Vol I, *Plans and Early Operations, January 1939 to August 1942*.
———. *The Army Air Forces in World War II*. Chicago: University of Chicago Press, 1951. Vol III, *Europe: ARGUMENT to V-E Day, January 1944 to May 1945*.

Deichmann, Paul, General der Flieger a. D. *German Air Force Operations in Support of the Army,* USAF Historical Studies: No. 163. Maxwell AFB, Ala.: USAF Historical Division, 1962.

Futrell, Robert F. *Ideas, Concepts, Doctrine: Basic Thinking in the United States Air Force, 1907–1960.* 2 vols., Maxwell AFB, Ala.: Air University Press, 1989.

Kozhevnikov, M. N. *The Command and Staff of the Soviet Army Air Force in the Great Patriotic War, 1941–1945.* Translated and published under the auspices of the U.S. Air Force. Washington, D.C.: U.S. Government Printing Office [USGPO], n.d., c. 1985.

Matloff, Maurice. *Strategic Planning for Coalition Warfare, 1943–1944.* Washington, D.C.: Office of the Chief of Military History, 1959.

Ministry of Defense of the USSR. *The Soviet Air Force in World War II.* Translated by Leland Fetzer. Edited by Ray Wagner. Garden City, N.Y.: Doubleday, 1973.

Ministry of Foreign Affairs of thé USSR. *Stalin's Correspondence with Churchill, Attlee, Roosevelt, and Truman, 1941–45.* English Edition. New York: Dutton, 1958.

Plocher, Generalleutnant Hermann. *The German Air Force Versus Russia, 1943.* USAF Historical Studies: No. 155. Edited by Harry R. Fletcher. New York: Arno Press, 1967.

Reddel, Carl W., ed. *Transformation in Russian and Soviet Military History: Proceedings of the Twelfth Military History Symposium, USAF Academy, 1986.* Washington, D.C.: Office of Air Force History, 1990.

Richards, Denis and Hilary St. George Saunders. *Royal Air Force, 1939–1945,* 3 vols. Vol II: *The Fight Avails.* London: HMSO, 1954.

Schwabedissen, Walter, Generalleutnant a. D. *The Russian Air Force in the Eyes of German Commanders.* USAF Historical Studies: No. 175. Maxwell AFB, Ala.: USAF Historical Division, 1960.

Suchenwirth, Richard. *Historical Turning Points in the German Air Force War Effort.* USAF Historical Studies: No. 189. Maxwell AFB, Ala.: USAF Historical Division, 1959.

Uebe, Klaus, Generalleutnant a. D. *Russian Reactions to German Airpower in World War II.* USAF Historical Studies: No. 176. Maxwell AFB, Ala.: USAF Historical Division, 1964.

U.S. Department of State. *Foreign Relations of the United States, Diplomatic Papers, 1943,* 6 vols. Vol. III, *The British Commonwealth, Eastern Europe, and the Far East.* Washington, D.C.: USGPO, 1963.

U.S. Department of State. *Foreign Relations of the United States, Diplomatic Papers, 1944,* 7 vols. Vol IV, *Europe.* Washington, D.C.: USGPO, 1966.

U.S. Strategic Bombing Survey. *European War: Overall Report.* Book 2. Washington, D.C.: USGPO, 1945.

———. *Auto Union AG, Chemnitz and Zwickau.* Book 84. Washington, D.C.: USGPO, 1947.

Watts, Barry D. *The Foundations of US Air Doctrine: The Problem of Friction in War.* Maxwell AFB, Ala.: Air University Press, 1984.

Webster, Sir Charles and Noble Frankland. *The Strategic Air Offensive Against Germany,* 4 vols. London: HMSO, 1961.

Secondary Sources

BOOKS

Adair, Paul. *Hitler's Greatest Defeat: The Collapse of Army Group Centre, June 1944.* London: Arms and Armour Press, 1994.

Angelucci, Enzo. *The Rand McNally Encyclopedia of Military Aircraft, 1914–1980.* Translated by S. M. Harris. New York: Military Press, 1983.

Bekker, Cajus. *The Luftwaffe War Diaries.* Translated by Frank Ziegler. Garden City, N.Y.: Doubleday, 1968.

Clark, Alan. *Barbarossa: The Russian-German Conflict, 1941–45.* New York: Morrow, 1965.

Dallin, Alexander. *German Rule in Russia, 1941–1945: A Study of Occupation Policies,* 2nd ed. Boulder, Colo.: Westview Press, 1981.

Duffy, Christopher. *Red Storm on the Reich: The Soviet March on Germany, 1945.* New York: Atheneum, 1991.

Ellis, John. *Brute Force: Allied Strategy and Tactics in the Second World War.* New York: Viking Penguin, 1990.

Erickson, John. *The Road to Berlin: Continuing the War with Germany.* Boulder, Colo.: Westview Press, 1983.

Ethell, Jeffrey L. and Alfred Price. *Target Berlin: Mission 250; 6 March 1944.* London: Arms and Armour Press, 1981.

Feis, Herbert. *Churchill, Roosevelt, Stalin: The War They Waged and the Peace They Sought.* Princeton, N.J.: Princeton University Press, 1957.

———. *The China Tangle.* Princeton, N.J.: Princeton University Press, 1953; New York: Atheneum, 1965.

Glantz, David M. and Jonathan M. House. *When Titans Clashed: How the Red Army Stopped Hitler.* Lawrence, Kans.: University Press of Kansas, 1995.

Gunston, Bill. *The Encyclopedia of the World's Combat Aircraft: A Technical Directory of Major Warplanes from World War I to the Present Day.* New York: Chartwell Books, 1976.

Hardesty, Von. *Red Phoenix: The Rise of Soviet Air Power.* Washington, D.C.: Smithsonian Institution Press, 1982.

Hastings, Max. OVERLORD: *D-Day and the Battle for Normandy.* New York: Simon and Schuster, 1984.

Heiferman, Ron. *Flying Tigers: Chennault in China.* New York: Ballantine Books, 1971.

Herring, George C., Jr. *Aid to Russia, 1941–1946: Strategy, Diplomacy, The Origins of the Cold War.* London: Columbia University Press, 1973.

Infield, Glenn B. *The Poltava Affair: A Russian Warning, An American Tragedy.* New York: Macmillan, 1973.

Kennan, George F. *Russia and the West Under Lenin and Stalin.* Boston: Little, Brown, 1960.

Korbonski, Stefan. *The Polish Underground State: A Guide to the Underground, 1939–1945.* Translated by Marta Erdman. New York: Columbia University Press, 1978.

Kreis, John F. *Air Warfare and Air Base Air Defense.* Washington, D.C.: Office of Air Force History, 1988.

Lucas, James. *Last Days of the Third Reich: The Collapse of Nazi Germany, May 1945.* New York: William Morrow, 1986.

Lukas, Richard C. *Eagles East: The Army Air Forces and the Soviet Union, 1941–1945.* Tallahassee, Fla.: Florida State University Press, 1970.

Maurer, Maurer, ed. *The U.S. Air Service in World War I,* 5 vols. Washington, D.C.: Office of Air Force History, 1978.

——. *Air Force Combat Units of World War II.* Washington, D.C.: USGPO, 1960.

McFarland, Stephen L. and Wesley Phillips Newton. *To Command the Sky: The Battle for Air Superiority Over Germany, 1942–1944.* Washington, D.C.: Smithsonian Institution Press, 1991.

Meilinger, Phillip S. *Hoyt S. Vandenberg: The Life of A General.* Bloomington, Ind.: Indiana University Press, 1989.

Middlebrook, Martin. *The Berlin Raids: R.A.F. Bomber Command, Winter 1943–44.* London: Viking Press, 1988.

Middlebrook, Martin and Everitt, Chris, *The Bomber Command War Diaries.* London: Viking Press, 1985.

Muller, Richard. *The German Air War in Russia.* Baltimore: Nautical and Aviation Publishing Co. of America, 1992.

Murray, Williamson. *Strategy for Defeat: The Luftwaffe, 1933–1945.* Maxwell AFB, Ala.: Air University Press, 1983.

Niepold, Gerd. *Battle for White Russia: The Destruction of Army Group Centre, June 1944.* Translated by Richard Simpkin. London: Brassey's Defence, 1987.

Orpen, Neil. *Airlift to Warsaw: The Rising of 1944.* Norman, Okla.: University of Oklahoma Press, 1984.

Overy, R. J. *The Air War, 1939–1945.* New York: Stein and Day, 1981.

Parker, Danny S. *Battle of the Bulge: Hitler's Ardennes Offensive, 1944–1945.* Conshohocken, Pa.: Combined Books, 1991.

——. *To Win the Winter Sky: Air War over the Ardennes, 1944–1945.* Conshohocken, Pa.: Combined Books, 1994.

Price, Alfred. *The Last Year of the Luftwaffe, May 1944 to May 1945.* Osceola, Wis.; Motorbooks International, 1991.

Quarrie, Bruce. *Hitler's Samurai: The Waffen S.S. in Action.* Wellingborough, U.K.: Patrick Stephens, 1986.

Ryan, Cornelius. *A Bridge Too Far.* New York: Simon and Schuster, 1974.

——. *The Last Battle.* London: Collins, 1966.

Saward, Dudley. *Bomber Harris.* London: Cassell, 1984.

Seaton, Albert. *The Russo-German War, 1941–45.* New York: Praeger, 1970.

Sherry, Michael S. *The Rise of American Air Power: The Creation of Armageddon.* New Haven, Conn.: Yale University Press, 1987.

Spector, Ronald H. *Eagle Against the Sun: The American War with Japan.* New York: Free Press, 1984; New York: Vintage Books, 1985.

Stahl, P. W. *KG 200: The True Story.* Translated by Alex Vanags-Baginskis. London: Jane's, 1981.

Stapfer, Hans-Heiri. *Strangers in a Strange Land.* Carrollton, Tex.: Squadron/Signal Publications, 1988.

Tuchman, Barbara. *Stilwell and the American Experience in China, 1911–45.* New York: Macmillan, 1971.

Tys-Krokhmaliuk, Yuriy. *UPA Warfare in Ukraine: Strategical, Tactical, and Organizational Problems of Ukrainian Resistance in World War II.* Translated by Walter Dushnyck. New York: Vantage Press, 1972.

Ulam, Adam B. *The Rivals: America and Russia Since World War II.* New York: Viking Press, 1971; New York: Penguin Books, 1984.

Weinberg, Gerhard L. *World in the Balance: Behind the Scenes of World War II.* London: University Press of New England, 1981.

Werth, Alexander. *Russia at War, 1941–45.* London: Barrie and Ruchliff, 1964.

Whiting, Kenneth R. "The Soviet Air Force Against Germany and Japan." In *Case Studies in the Achievement of Air Superiority.* Edited by Benjamin Franklin Cooling, 179–221. Washington, D.C.: USGPO, 1994.

Wilmot, Chester. *Struggle for Europe.* New York: Carroll and Graf, 1986.

Wright, Gordon. *The Ordeal of Total War, 1939–1945.* New York: Harper and Row, 1968.

Ziemke, Earl F. *Stalingrad to Berlin: The German Defeat in the East.* Washington, D.C.: Center of Military History, 1968.

———. "The Soviet Armed Forces in the Interwar Period." In *Military Effectiveness: Volume II, The Interwar Period.* Edited by Allan R. Millett and Williamson Murray, 1–38. Boston: Unwin Hyman, 1988.

ARTICLES

Beaumont, Roger. "The Bomber Offensive as a Second Front." *Journal of Contemporary History* 22 (1987): 3–19.

Crowder, Ed. "POINTBLANK: A Study in Strategic and National Security Decision Making." *Airpower Journal* 1 (Spring 1992): 55–65.

Davis, Richard C. "Operation 'Thunderclap': The US Army Air Forces and the Bombing of Berlin." *The Journal of Strategic Studies* 14 (March 1991): 90–111.

Gunther, John. "Why We Can and Must Beat Germany This Year." *Reader's Digest* 45 (August 1944): 5–8.

Hicks, Dr. Edmund. "Soviet Sojourn." *The Air Power Historian* 1 (January 1964): 1–5.

Julian, Thomas A. "The Role of the United States Army Air Forces in the Warsaw Uprising, Aug–Sep 1944." *Air Power History* 2 (Summer 1995): 22–35.

Kobrin, Nikolai. "The Last Summer of the War." *Soviet Military Review* 6 (June 1989): 45–47.

Kurov, Nikolai. "The Breakthrough to Berlin and Battle in the Ardennes." *Soviet Military Review* 12 (December 1989): 45–47.

Lukas, Richard C. "The RAF and the Warsaw Uprising." *Aerospace Historian* 4 (Winter, 1975): 188–194.

Lyubymsky, Leonid and Mykola Myhailenko. "The Year 1944: Operation 'FRANTIC.' " *News from Ukraine* 3 (January 1992): 2.

McFarland, Marvin W. "Air Power and the Warsaw Uprising." *Air Power Historian* 1 (January 1956): 186–194.

McFarland, Stephen L. "The Evolution of the American Strategic Fighter in Europe, 1942–44." *Journal of Strategic Studies* 10 (June 1987): 189–208.

Orlov, A. and N. Komarov. " 'Flying Fortresses' Over the Third Reich." *Soviet Military Review* 7 (July 1975): 51–52.

Sytin, Volodymyr. "What WWII Veterans Think and Remember." *News from Ukraine* 3 (January 1992): 2.

White, William L. "Report on the Russians, Part I." *Reader's Digest* 45 (December 1944): 101–122.

———. "Report on the Russians, Part II." *Reader's Digest* 46 (January 1945): 106–128.

Yuryev, Aleksandr. "The Second Front: Plans and Reality." *Soviet Military Review* 5 (May 1989): 50–52.

Unpublished Sources

Bolger, Daniel P. "Reluctant Allies: The United States Army Air Forces and the Soviet Air Force, 1941–1945." Unpublished Ph.D. dissertation, University of Chicago, 1986.

Headquarters, Mediterranean Allied Air Forces. "Preliminary Study of Coordinated Attacks by United States Strategic Air Forces in Europe, January–August 1944." April 1945.

Headquarters, U.S. Army. "Peculiarities of Russian Warfare." Historical Division, Special Staff, September 1948.

Headquarters, U.S. Army Air Forces. "AWPD-1." Office of the Chief of the Air Staff. 12 August 1941.

Headquarters, U.S. Army Air Forces. "The Fourteenth Air Force to 1 October 1943." AAF Historical Office, July 1945.

Headquarters, USAFFE and Eighth U.S. Army (Rear). "Air Operations in the China Area, July 1937–August 1945." Japanese Monographs, No. 75, Office of the Chief of Military History, 1956.

Julian, Thomas A. "Operation FRANTIC and the Search for American-Soviet Military Collaboration, 1941–1944." Unpublished Ph.D. dissertation, Syracuse University, 1967.

U.S. Department of Defense. "The Entry of the Soviet Union into the War Against Japan: Military Plans, 1941–1945." Washington, D.C., 1955.

INDEX